The Immigrant World of Ybor City

LIBRARY PRESS@UF

AN IMPRINT OF UF PRESS AND
GEORGE A. SMATHERS LIBRARIES

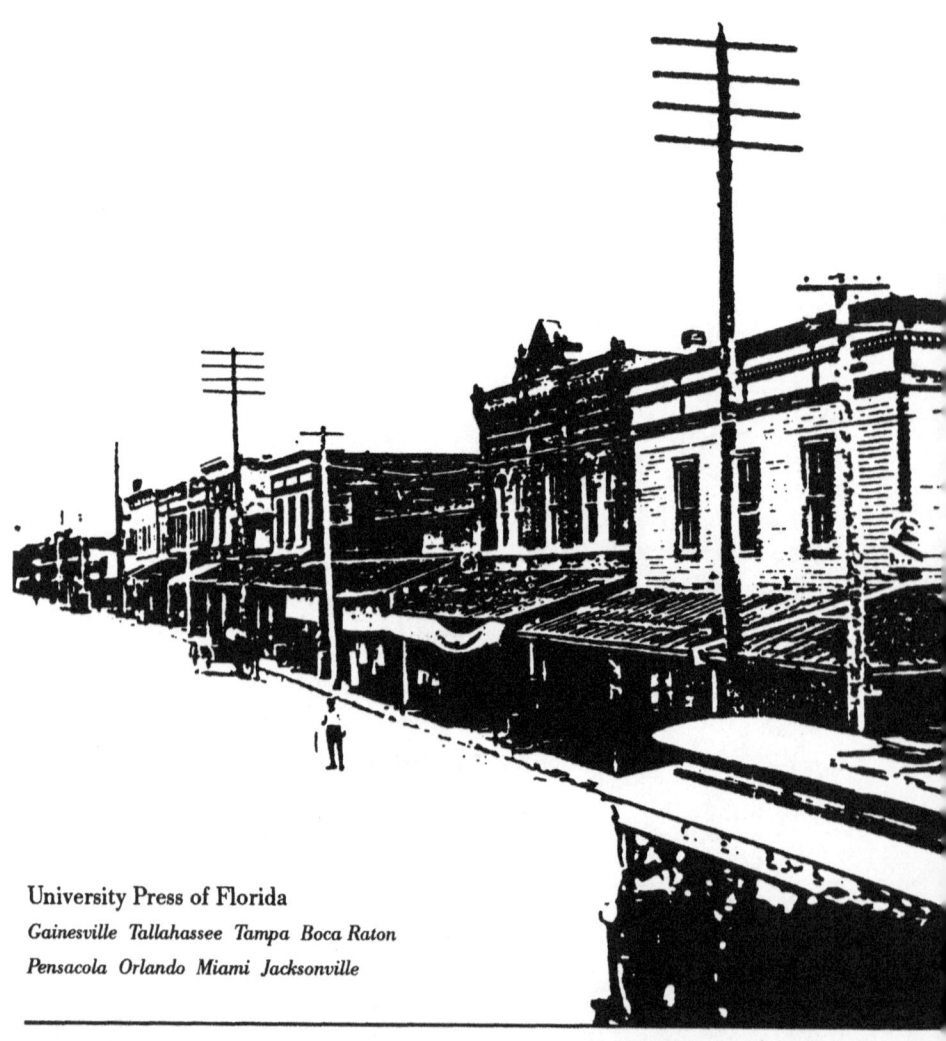

University Press of Florida
Gainesville Tallahassee Tampa Boca Raton
Pensacola Orlando Miami Jacksonville

The Immigrant World of Ybor City

Italians and Their Latin Neighbors in Tampa, 1885–1985

GARY R. MORMINO AND GEORGE E. POZZETTA

LibraryPress@UF
GAINESVILLE, FLORIDA

Cover: Map of the West Indies, published in Philadelphia, 1806. From the Caribbean Maps collection in the University of Florida Digital Collections at the George A. Smathers Libraries.

Reissued 2017 by LibraryPress@UF on behalf of the University of Florida
This work is licensed under a Creative Commons Attribution-Noncommercial-No Derivative Works 4.0 Unported License. To view a copy of this license, visit https://creativecommons.org/licenses/by-nc-nd/4.0/. You are free to electronically copy, distribute, and transmit this work if you attribute authorship. Please contact the University Press of Florida (http://upress.ufl.edu) to purchase print editions of the work. You must attribute the work in the manner specified by the author or licensor (but not in any way that suggests that they endorse you or your use of the work). For any reuse or distribution, you must make clear to others the license terms of this work. Any of the above conditions can be waived if you receive permission from the University Press of Florida. Nothing in this license impairs or restricts the author's moral rights.

ISBN 978-1-947372-64-1 (pbk.)
ISBN 978-1-947372-65-8 (ePub)

LibraryPress@UF is an imprint of the University of Florida Press.

| LIBRARY PRESS@UF |

AN IMPRINT OF UF PRESS AND
GEORGE A. SMATHERS LIBRARIES

University of Florida Press
15 Northwest 15th Street
Gainesville, FL 32611-2079
http://upress.ufl.edu

The Florida and the Caribbean Open Books Series

In 2016, the University Press of Florida, in collaboration with the George A. Smathers Libraries of the University of Florida, received a grant from the National Endowment for the Humanities and the Andrew W. Mellon Foundation, under the Humanities Open Books program, to republish books related to Florida and the Caribbean and to make them freely available through an open access platform. The resulting list of books is the Florida and the Caribbean Open Books Series published by the LibraryPress@UF in collaboration with the University of Florida Press, an imprint of the University Press of Florida. A panel of distinguished scholars has selected the series titles from the UPF list, identified as essential reading for scholars and students.

The series is composed of titles that showcase a long, distinguished history of publishing works of Latin American and Caribbean scholarship that connect through generations and places. The breadth and depth of the list demonstrates Florida's commitment to transnational history and regional studies. Selected reprints include Daniel Brinton's *A Guide-Book of Florida and the South* (1869), Cornelis Goslinga's *The Dutch in the Caribbean and on the Wild Coast, 1580–1680* (1971), and Nelson Blake's *Land into Water—Water into Land* (1980). Also of note are titles from the Bicentennial Floridiana Facsimile Series. The series, published in 1976 in commemoration of America's bicentenary, comprises twenty-five books regarded as "classics," out-of-print works that needed to be in more libraries and readers' bookcases, including Sidney Lanier's *Florida: Its Scenery, Climate, and History* (1876) and Silvia Sunshine's *Petals Plucked from Sunny Climes* (1880).

Today's readers will benefit from having free and open access to these works, as they provide unique perspectives on the historical scholarship on Florida and the Caribbean and serve as a foundation upon which today's researchers can build.

Visit LibraryPress@UF and the Florida and the Caribbean Open Books Series at http://ufdc.ufl.edu/librarypress.

Florida and the Caribbean Open Books Series Project Members

LIBRARYPRESS@UF

Judith C. Russell
Laurie N. Taylor
Brian W. Keith
Chelsea Dinsmore
Haven Hawley

EDITORIAL ADVISORY BOARD

Gary R. Mormino
David R. Colburn
Patrick J. Reakes

UNIVERSITY OF FLORIDA PRESS

Meredith M. Babb
Linda Bathgate
Michele Fiyak-Burkley
Romi Gutierrez
Larry Leshan
Anja Jimenez
Marisol Amador
Valerie Melina
Jane Pollack
Danny Duffy
Nichole Manosh
Erika Stevens

This book is reissued as part of the Humanities Open Books program, funded by a grant from the National Endowment for the Humanities and the Andrew W. Mellon Foundation.

To our wives and children
Lynne, Amy, and Becky
Sandy, Jimmy, and Adrienne

Contents

Preface to the 1998 Edition   ix

Acknowledgments   xiii

Introduction   3

1. *"We Live in Order Not to Die"*
   The Origins of Tampa's Italian Community   16

2. *Tampa's Evolution as an Urban Center*   43

3. *Ybor City and the Beginning of a Latin Community, 1886–1900*   63

4. *Italians and the Culture of Labor in a Latin Community*   97

5. *Italians and the Radical Culture*
   From Contadini to Compañeros   143

6. *The Cradle of Mutual Aid*
   Italians and Their Latin Neighbors   175

7. *The Religious Encounter*   210

8. *Social Relations in a Latin Community*   233

9.	*Economic Adjustments*	260
10.	*World War II and Beyond*	297
	Conclusion: Class, Culture, and Community	317
	Bibliography	325
	Index	357

Preface to the 1998 Edition

Twenty years ago, George Pozzetta and I discussed the possibilities of writing a history of Ybor City. In May of 1978 we met at the decaying but still august L'Unione Italiana, eager to investigate the community about which we had heard so much but knew so little. From that first magical moment, Ybor City enthralled and captivated us.

Describing what Ybor City was *not* seemed an easier task than understanding what it was. Expecting to find tightly defined ethnic boundaries organized around Italian, Cuban, and Spanish identities, we encountered instead an integrated "Latin" community. Expecting to find elderly immigrants defending ethnic turf, we discovered Italians playing dominoes at the Centro Asturiano and Cubans playing *scoppa* at the Italian Club. We located an extraordinarily fluid and tolerant enclave where Afro-Cubans had lived and worked alongside "white" Italians, Cubans, and Spaniards. Fortune had blessed two young historians with a remarkable subject. We soon realized that we would have to question the conventional study of individual ethnic groups and go beyond the black-white model of southern studies.

Each generation must come to terms with its Ybor City. We tried to understand a community in constant turmoil and change. Most of all, our book was an attempt to clarify relationships and the meaning of community in a multiethnic immigrant enclave. Whatever Ybor City represented, it was never static. In spasms of prosperity and bust, immigration and Americanization, Ybor City fluctuated wildly from the years of revolution and labor unrest in the 1890s to the decade of war and suburbanization of the 1940s.

Not everyone agreed with the conclusions or content of *The Immigrant World of Ybor City*. Shortly after the book's publication, I received a phone call from an agitated reader. He asked probing questions about my involvement in the writing of the book, and he then asked me to turn to page 148.

He proceeded to read the sentence beginning "Other anarchists such as Pietro Scaglione, Salvatore Lodato, and Luigi Lodato ordered leftist papers . . . and made them available in various club libraries." The anonymous individual then identified himself as Salvatore Lodato's son. "My father was *not* an anarchist," he bellowed, adding that he was on his way to the university, where, he announced, he was going to kick my ass! Mercifully, Lodato did not pummel the defenseless historian; instead, he began to describe his father, an immigrant stonemason, musician, and agitator, concluding, "My father wasn't an anarchist, but I tell you, he wouldn't take any abuse from the Catholic Church or greedy owners." To my delight, Lodato introduced me to his brothers, one of whom subsequently wrote a biography of their father and donated it to the university's library. "As youngsters," wrote Vincent Lodato, "we listened to [Father's] expounding the cause of real freedom through education." The brothers informed me that they preferred the term "recalcitrant Sicilian" to "anarchist."

The meaning and memory of Salvatore Lodato and of Ybor City endure; not so clear is the fate of Ybor City. In 1998, the community awaits the millennium with a nervous optimism. Since the early 1990s, venture capitalists and city/state governments have invested staggering sums to revive Seventh Avenue and the surrounding neighborhood. Part honky-tonk French Quarter, part preservation chic, and part authentic restoration, a revitalized Ybor City has become a popular lunch setting for lawyers and city workers and an evening magnet for tourists and bohemians. Forlorn pawn shops, Cuban sandwich parlors, and mom-and-pop grocery stores have yielded to Irish pubs, tattoo parlors, and upscale fusion cuisine. In a less forgiving era, serving black beans with yellow rice was considered heretical; today, black bean salsa accompanies sushi, while beignets and decaf latte compete with Cuban bread dunked in *café con leche*. The world has rediscovered Ybor City, drawn to the quarter's elegant architecture and exotic features. A new generation promenades along the old-world coffee bars and new-age bandstands.

In 1998, Ybor City stands on the threshold of even greater change. The Yaromir Steiner Associates, designers of Cocowalk in Coconut Grove, will soon begin a $50 million redevelopment. The project includes a 200,000-square-foot plaza, highlighted by the restoration of the majestic Centro Español. Hundreds of apartment units—the first new private residential units erected since the 1920s—will soon welcome upscale homesteaders. The mutual aid societies, once doomed, have benefited from millions of dollars of state preservation funds. The City of Tampa, which once assisted in the neighborhood's "urban renewal," has agreed to erect an $11 million parking garage. The city council recently voted to bring back a trolley line serving Ybor City.

Alas, the surging crowds returning to Ybor City include few of the men and women who rolled the cigars and built the community that made Tampa famous. In 1978, when we were researching this book, Ybor City was tattered and poor, but it still retained a glorious remnant of its pioneers. Victoriano Manteiga, hunchbacked and craggy, seemed like a character from the Victor Hugo novels he read as a *lector* in 1915. José Vega Díaz, Joe Maniscalco, and Emmanuel La Rosa simply sparkled when they discussed the days of cigars and roses. They are all gone now.

During the last decade, I have mourned from back pews and funeral parlors the passing of Tony Pizzo, Paul Longo, and so many others who helped make this study special. Such occasions resonated with bittersweet reminiscences: bitter because death intones a finality; sweet because those pioneers lived lives of full trajectory, having lived and loved in fullest measures. The deaths, while sad, were understandable.

The death of George E. Pozzetta in May 1994 defied understanding and cut short a life and career filled with joy and talent. He died at the peak of his life, but we should remember and love him for what he was, not what he would have been. Every once in a great while, we meet a person who makes everyone around him better, who represents the very best in our private and professional lives. Such a man, husband, father, son, and colleague was George E. Pozzetta. His life was so humane, so passionate in its friendships and associations, that as we all came to know him better, a camaraderie grew between us, and after a time it seemed he was a very part and fiber of our own lives.

George Pozzetta would be delighted with the reissue of *The Immigrant World of Ybor City*. He loved Ybor City and would hope along with me that this book inspires and challenges a new generation to study the community.

Gary R. Mormino
Tampa, May 1998

Acknowledgments

An Italian proverb warns, "Never return an empty dish." In researching and writing this book we have borrowed heavily from the cupboards of innumerable friends and institutions. It is our hope that *The Immigrant World of Ybor City* helps fill the dishes.

We gratefully acknowledge the P. K. Yonge Library of Florida History, University of Florida, and in particular Ms. Elizabeth Alexander and Dr. Steven Kerber, for generous help in locating documents and sources. Numerous colleagues in Gainesville read portions of this study and offered constructive suggestions, especially David Colburn, who read the entire manuscript in one form or another and in special ways has lived with it from the beginning. We owe him much for his steadfast support and encouragement. Patrick Geary, David Chalmers, and Eldon Turner, also of the University of Florida, read portions or all of this material and made improvements along the way. Kermit Hall read an early draft and assisted greatly in providing focus and direction. James Amelang's understanding of the difficult junctures between class and culture proved immensely helpful, as did his sure sense of style. Bertram Wyatt-Brown generously read the entire manuscript in a late-draft stage and made numerous helpful suggestions. Cheryll Cody and Tom Gallant gave from their fund of quantitative skills to improve the tables. Conversations with Darrett Rutman helped clarify our conceptions of community. Seminar students at both our institutions, in particular Helen Smith, Earl Hendry, and Caroline Coleman, assisted by providing a forum for criticism and analysis; they also produced seminar papers of substantial merit.

In their visits to Ybor City and Gainesville, and in later communications, Professors Robert Harney and Rudolph Vecoli offered encouragement, friendship, and insight into our study. They also provided valuable suggestions for improving early versions of this material. Professors

Donna Gabaccia and Randall Miller read drafts of much of this volume and saved us from a number of embarrassing errors. Along the way Professors Blaine Brownell, Numan Bartley, and Silvano Tomasi, examined certain portions of the manuscript with care and patience. Theresa Sears, our copy editor, through meticulous care and scouring detail, assisted this book through the rite of passage. Dick Wentworth, editor and director, exhibited a professionalism characteristic of the University of Illinois Press.

Colleagues at the University of South Florida supported the idea of this study from the beginning. Ray Arsenault, John Belohlavek, David Carr, Jim Swanson, and Roy Van Neste unselfishly shared their ideals and ideas; without their encouragement this book would not have been completed. The manuscript benefited from cogent readings by Susan Greenbaum, Leland Hawes, Richard Long, and L. Glenn Westfall. Donna Parrino and Nancy Hewitt kept the authors alert with their penetrating questions and thoughtful conversations. Our respective deans, Wallace Russell and Charles Sidman, supported this venture with university resources and, more important, with the confidence that such endeavors add something to the university community. J. B. Dobkin and Paul Camp of the Special Collections Department at the University of South Florida Library played an instrumental role in this work, building and maintaining a first-rate archive. President John Lott Brown and Provost Gregory O'Brien demonstrated a consistent faith that this project exemplified the mission of the University of South Florida.

Fr. Gianfausto Rosoli, director of the Centro Studi Emigrazione (Rome), and Professor Pietro Russo, of the Istituto di Studi Americani at the University of Florence, generously made the holdings of their respective institutions available to us. They also contributed with their own suggestions and viewpoints. Professor Calogero Messina, of the University of Palermo, provided us with contacts in the Sicilian villages of origin, as well as with the fruits of his own extensive research into Sicilian history. Since none of these friends has seen the volume in its present form, we alone are responsible for errors of fact or perversities of interpretation.

Sam Proctor generously assisted in the provision of tapes, transcriptions, and storage for many of our oral history materials. The University of Florida Oral History Program stands as part of his legacy to Florida history. Cheryl Combs, Adrienne Turner, Nancy Dilley, Mern Johnston-Loehner, and especially Tina Slick proved to be masters of the word processor, cheerfully and expertly guiding the manuscript through its many revisions. Financial support, that necessary handmaiden of primary research, was supplied by the American Philosophical Society, the Fulbright-Hays Commission, the Florida Endowment for the Humanities, and the Immigration History Research Center (University of Minnesota), and is gratefully acknowledged.

Portions of the following essays appear in various chapters of this book and are reprinted by permission: Mormino, "Tampa and the New Urban South," *Florida Historical Quarterly* 60 (Jan. 1982): 337–56; "We Worked Hard and Took Care of Our Own," *Labor History* 23 (Summer 1982): 395–416; Mormino and Pozzetta, "The Cradle of Mutual Aid," *Tampa Bay History* 7 (Fall/Winter 1985): 36–58; "Immigrant Women in Tampa," *Florida Historical Quarterly* 61 (Jan. 1983): 296–312; "Spanish Anarchists in Tampa, Florida, 1886–1921," in *Struggle a Hard Battle*, ed. Dirk Hoerder (DeKalb: Northern Illinois University Press, 1985), 171–99; Pozzetta, "Concord and Discord," in *Italian Americans*, ed. Lydio F. Tomasi (New York: Center for Migration Studies, 1985), 341–57.

The authors must express special appreciation to Tampans Tony Pizzo and Fortune Bosco for their extraordinary help. Tony Pizzo labored as a pioneer—and a lone one for many years—in this field, and his generosity and sharing will long be remembered. Fortune Bosco's classical wit, inimitable personality, and unerring skill with the Italian language made both the authors' lives and the study richer. Dr. Ferdie Pacheco's painting graces the dust jacket of this book. The authors deeply appreciate his sharing his passion for life.

To Nelson Palermo, Paul Longo, Joe Maniscalco, and so many others who endured our intrusions into their lives and shared with us countless hours of tape-recorded memories, the authors express their enormous gratitude. The intimate thoughts and reflections of these people provided a human dimension to the immigrant experience. Also, the lessons of humble courage and simple dignity so evident in their lives made the labor of producing this book much more easy to accept.

"*Casa senza donna, barca senza timoni*" (A house without a woman is like a boat without a rudder), an Italian folk wisdom assures us. It is true. This volume would be incomplete and uncompleted without the love our families provided. Force-marched across Italy and frustrated by marathon writing sessions, our wives and children sacrificed much but gave generously. It is to them that we dedicate this book.

Abbreviations

AFL	American Federation of Labor
CMIU	Cigar Makers International Union
CMS	Center for Migration Studies, New York
FWP	Federal Writers' Project
HCC	Hillsborough County Courthouse
HCMS	Hillsborough County Medical Society
ICF	Investigative Case Files, Department of Justice
IHRC	Immigration History Research Center, University of Minnesota
IWW	Industrial Workers of the World
OHP	Oral History Program, University of Florida, Gainesville
PKY	P. K. Yonge Library of Florida History, University of Florida, Gainesville
THS	Tampa Historical Society
TWIU	Tobacco Workers International Union
UFG	University of Florida, Gainesville
USF	University of South Florida, Tampa

*The Immigrant World
of Ybor City*

Introduction

> For years the old Italians have been dying
> all over America.
> For years the old Italians in faded felt hats
> have been sunning themselves and dying . . .
> The old anarchists reading *L'Umanità Nuova*
> The ones who loved Sacco & Vanzetti
> They are almost all gone now . . .
> In Little Italies all over America
> The old dead dagos
> hauled out in the morning sun
> That does not mourn for anyone . . .
>
> Lawrence Ferlinghetti, "The Old Italians Dying"

Ybor City resembles America's older walking cities. To understand its contours one must explore the alleys and avenues of this aging Florida community. Although it has long since been incorporated into Tampa, Ybor City still breathes an air of romance. One continues to be drawn to its musty, abandoned cigar factories, where thousands of artisans once rolled Flor de Ybors and Tampa Royals. Its ubiquitous wrought iron balconies are now rusted and forlorn, but in times past friends leaned over them to pass along the gossip of the street. Under urban renewal much of the housing was razed, and in the early 1970s practically all of the Spanish, Cuban, and Italian residents of the community were displaced. Yet Ybor City still whispers of its former glory.

When the authors first strolled through Ybor City in late May 1978, it was one of those last spring days prior to the summer rains, just before the blanket of humidity descends upon all of Florida. We passed Naviera Mill, where for three generations the antiquated coffee roasters have filled the air with an intoxicating smell of *café cubano*. From the street one could see workers methodically tending the antique machinery, turning out thousands of Café Norma packages daily.

Not far away eighty-year-old Julio Cuevas was selling coffee from his own store; in reality his aromatic shop serves as a gathering place for social discourse. In three languages the elderly Spanish immigrant lectured patrons on the glories of a *zarzuela* (musical comedy), the gaiety of former Spanish *verbenas* (picnics), and the godliness of a perfect cup of *café con leche* (coffee with scalded milk). A block away a stoop-backed Victoriano Manteiga was putting the finishing touches to his life's passion, the trilingual weekly newspaper *La Gaceta*. As a *lector* (reader) in the cigar factories, a crusader for social justice, and editor, publisher, and owner of *La Gaceta*, Manteiga had witnessed the labor wars, the red scares, and the horrors of urban renewal. Cuevas and Manteiga are anachronisms—the last vestiges of the old Ybor City. The young people no longer drink coffee brewed from the *colador* or get their news from a Spanish-language paper.

In 1978 Cuevas and Manteiga were still working in Ybor City; but thousands of their old neighbors, uprooted by urban renewal and displaced by a shifting neighborhood economy, had departed. Government programs in the 1960s razed thousands of houses, forcing families out of cherished homes, leaving behind empty blocks where only an occasional mango tree stands. Federal officials promised immigrants and their children new housing in Ybor City, but the Great Society trimmed its commitments and, in doing so, accelerated an out-migration that began after World War II. An interstate highway, completed in 1974, destroyed what remained of an entire section of Ybor City.

Walking along the abandoned stretch of Tenth Avenue, we tried to imagine what the neighborhood had been like with wooden houses, the *bolita* (numbers) dealer, the *pirulí* (candy) man, and numerous small groceries. We came upon a large, low-income housing complex, La Hacienda de Ybor. The nondescript, concrete-block apartments with occasional slashes of terra-cotta represented one of the few promises that the government had kept. José Vega Díaz greeted us, his sprightly gait disguising his ninety-four years. He explained how bureaucrats had forced him and his wife, Blanca, from their nearby home. Blanca wailed in grief on eviction day, "I can't. I can't!" She was dead by sunset. The couple had survived the rigors of immigration, revolution, radical politics, and union strife, but they could not endure the wrecking ball.

José's life story read like the history of Ybor City itself. His Spanish father had emigrated to Cuba in the nineteenth century, choosing in 1892 to take his family to Tampa. "We came to Ybor City, not Tampa!" José carefully insisted. He pointed to the now empty spot where his family homestead once stood. "No screens, no lights then," he sighed, as he reminisced about the strikes and work, community and family. He was perhaps the last survivor of the 1899 weight strike. "Oh, *la huelga de pesa!* . . . What a strike. . . . We make a union. That's how we started la Resistencia. That was our worker's union, the first. We won that strike."[1]

As we looked at the buildings along Seventh Avenue, we were exhilarated by the thought of what they had meant to the community and depressed by their present condition and what this said about the people and the activities that once gave them life. There was a sense of scale as motifs transplanted from Barcelona, Havana, and Palermo transformed granite and concrete into cathedrals for the working class. Hexagonal sidewalk designs, cast-iron street lamps, and the smell of deviled crabs provide a backdrop to this immigrant community.

Seventh Avenue was once the heart of Ybor City; its mutual aid societies have always been its soul. Such organizations were hardly novel to urban America, but in Ybor City these associations assumed roles of remarkable responsibility, size, and humanity. In the late 1970s Spaniards, Cubans, and Italians still maintained five mutual aid societies, their clubhouses all on or near Seventh Avenue. El Centro Español, founded in 1892, housed the oldest of these societies; members erected the present clubhouse in 1912. A lavish dance floor, a theater, and elegant spiral staircases speak of former glory, but in 1978 El Centro's future was gloomy.

Two blocks away is the four-story home of L'Unione Italiana. Built in 1918 after its predecessor burned down, the club anchored Ybor City's Little Italy, providing its more than 2,000 members with medical care, economic insurance, and social comity. Upon entering the lobby, a statue of Garibaldi and an Italian flag are prominent, but such conventional symbols mean less than the activities upon which the statue's lifeless gaze rests. The club's *cantina* (recreation room) introduced a new Italian America to both of us. A haze of cigar smoke hung over the dozens of gaming tables, where elderly men cursed and cajoled, laughed and gesticulated, in pandemonium. Expecting to see spirited rounds of *tresette* or *briscola* (Italian card games), we instead observed impassioned games of dominoes. The origins of this pastime soon became clear while listening—or better still, trying to grasp—the babel of Italian, Sicilian, English, and Spanish.

As the dominoes were formed into myriad patterns, so too did individual life histories unfold. Within the *cantina* of L'Unione Italiana was an immigrant universe, a condensed version of an Ybor City that would soon disappear. Paul Longo, a ninety-year-old Sicilian, rasped, "I came with my father in 1904." He recalled his first impressions of Tampa: "Hhumph! *zanzare e coccodrilli!*" (mosquitoes and alligators). Dressed as always in a three-piece suit, he explained how he had rolled cigars for twenty years before turning to insurance and real estate.[2]

If Longo represented the cigarmaker turned businessman, Joe Maniscalco personified the eternal *tabaquero*. His hair long ago whitened, Maniscalco elaborated about his first days in Tampa: "Ybor City was great. When I came here in 1910, great. The best thing in the world I ever saw. . . . And I never saw people so friendly—you used to sleep with the door open at night, people in the street at night. Musicals, serenades. Oh, it was terrific. Everyone was like a family. . . . today it's all gone."[3] Of course, he remembered the better times rather than the worst, but that is as it should be among the old.

The impressions gained from this first exposure to Ybor City tantalized us as historians and as heirs of that immigrant experience. We had certainly never witnessed anything quite like this in our own backgrounds, even though we had both grown up in Italian American settings. George Pozzetta was born in a New England town and raised among a small group of northern Italians who had emigrated from the province of Piedmont. His subsequent research into Italian immigrant life in New York City, with its numerous densely populated "Little Italies" and its extensive network of ethnic institutions revealed a world remarkably different from his own. Gary Mormino spent his youth amid a large cluster of Sicilian Americans in Wood River, Illinois, an industrial suburb of St. Louis. Ironically, the subject of his doctoral dissertation was "Dago Hill," the Lombard enclave in St. Louis, a neighborhood that his grandfather had earlier rejected as a place to settle because the northern Italians there were so unfriendly toward Sicilians.

The diversity we saw all around us in Ybor City heightened a sense of uneasiness about prevailing conceptions of how immigrants have created—or recreated—their new social worlds. Very different communities in the United States have come into existence, often composed of immigrants from the same regions, even the same villages. The relationships existing between class, culture, and community lay at the heart of the diverse outcomes, central issues that blended in different combinations and intensities over time, but whose interplay remained at the core of immigrant destinies and identities. Alan Dawley has written that historians should seek "a recognition of the dialectical interaction between ethnic cultures and the conditions of working class life, a process in which both the cultures and the conditions were transformed."[4] Yet the complex ways in which this give-and-take actually worked is only imperfectly understood.

Fortunately, scholars have discovered many pieces of the puzzle. Over the past twenty years historical scholarship dealing with America's immigrant past has advanced both in size and sophistication, and this literature has often singled out Italian immigrants for particular attention. Indeed, from the work of Rudolph Vecoli to that of Virginia Yans-MacLaughlin, John Briggs, and Robert Harney, among others, Italians have figured prominently in some of the field's most innovative and lively work.[5] New approaches and fresh theoretical advances now at hand have presented a rich portrait of Italian immigrants in the Americas. But these immigrants have been seen in isolation too often.

The Italian diaspora created hundreds, if not thousands, of immigrant communities and subcommunities around the globe, each one reflective of the economic, social, and cultural conditions underlying its birth, growth, and, in some cases, demise. Nearly every North American city of any size, and many smaller towns, housed one or more "Little Italies" during the late nineteenth and early twentieth centuries. In each place residents erected an institutional framework designed to sustain some sort of immigrant culture.

Asa Briggs has observed that "to understand how people respond to change it is important to understand what kind of people they were at the beginning of the process."[6] Anthropologists and historians thus have sought deeper analyses of the specific old-world origins of immigrants. We now possess a substantial body of literature that has examined sending societies with accuracy, sensitivity, and detail. Dino Cinel's study of San Francisco's Italians, for example, devotes nearly half of its pages to a discussion of very precise old-world developments.[7] By focusing on the point of contact and exposing the nature of both sending and receiving societies, recent scholarship has advanced our understanding of the complicated strategies immigrants devised to confront their new environments.

The same precision employed in analyzing European villages, however, has not always characterized the study of immigrants after they arrived at their new-world destinations. Rudolph Vecoli has pointed out, for example, that on landing immigrants did not at once take on such generalized labels as Italian American or Polish American. In fact, newcomers tended to retain individualized identities, often framed in very local contexts, for many years after initial settlement.[8] How these people coped with problems here reflected the attitudes and styles brought with them, which in turn were transformed in the very act of articulation. Inevitably, the process of immigration shaped the character of American communities as they evolved to account for the presence of newcomers. Just as certainly, the nature of life in the home villages was altered as well. At the core of this process rested people who, either as individuals or as members of families and kin groups, attempted to deal with the new demands imposed by migration. The closer we can come to comprehending how immigrants fashioned strategies and adjusted mentalities over time, the clearer understanding we will have of the immigrant experience.

Since the majority of immigrants who entered the United States after 1890 came in search of work—in most cases industrial work—their relationship to the labor performed assumed a special importance. The vast portion walked through the portals of the New World with preindustrial cultural values and confronted a bewilderingly complex urban-industrial economy. Immigrants proved remarkably flexible, adapting their traditional values to the workplace and neighborhood. Immigration and industrialization, we now realize, did not result in wholesale cultural disintegration and social anomie. Far from it. Yet the challenge has been to chart the exact ways by which immigrant cultures survived the transition and created new social and institutional forms.

The shift to an industrial setting, E. P. Thompson noted, "entailed a severe restructuring of working habits—new disciplines, new incentives, and a new human nature upon which these incentives could bite effectively."[9] Immigrants have figured prominently in the scholarly endeavor to understand how American industrialization evolved and matured. More specifically, they have occupied a conspicuous place in the effort to comprehend the formation (or lack thereof) of an American working class. As working men and women in turn-of-the-century America, immigrants faced a complicated set of life possibilities which challenged their identities, cultural loyalties, and careers.[10] To show how these diverse influences came together to produce specific outcomes, one needs to examine change and continuity in the context of the physical and mental world that bounded immigrant lives.

"Working-class behavior," John Bodnar wrote, "was not merely a reaction to economic conditions, but was also influenced by various subcultures confronting industrial America."[11] Urban America contained a kaleidoscopic range of immigrant groups, living amid and beside one another. Scholarly research has often noted this basic fact but seldom has taken it fully into account. Put simply, most examinations of immigrant life have not focused upon the adaptations and interrelationships stemming from the coming together of diverse immigrant groups in North American urban centers.[12] Immigrants most often encountered multiethnic settings that put them into initial and most immediate contact with other immigrants, not some idealized "American society." The resulting interaction among immigrant groups and groupings contributed to the shifting composition of class and culture in America.

The preceding views about the formation of class, culture, and community provide the intellectual basis of this volume. Ybor City's particular experience induced us to explore some of the wider implications of our understanding of the immigrant world. In order to do so, we recognized that the immigrant community must not be perceived in isolation from its larger environment, which in this case meant most immediately the greater Tampa metropolitan area.

In many ways Tampa is an attractive setting in which to observe the dynamics of migration, settlement, community formation, class relations, and ideological division. What began as a sleepy southern coastal village of approximately 800 people grew in about twenty years, with the arrival of the cigar industry in 1885, to a port city of over 30,000, fueled by immigration from Cuba, Spain, and Italy. By 1905 Tampa and its suburbs had more than 10,000 foreign-born residents. Community size and the immigrant population make the city a desirable laboratory. Group numbers remained manageable for microexamination; Tampa's foreign-born Italians, for example, totaled 3,000 in 1920. Not only was each immigrant community small, but they were also relatively homogeneous —most Italians, for example, came from only a handful of villages in southwestern Sicily. One community, Santo Stefano Quisquina, supplied more than 60 percent of the total Italian population in Tampa. Hence, opportunities for both control and generalization were present, unlike situations most commonly encountered in much larger and more diverse urban areas.

What was true of Italians was also true of their immigrant neighbors in Ybor City. Cuban and Spanish migrations also were relatively small in number and these groups underwent experiences similar to the Italians. By treating them, as well as Italians, we hope to avoid the narrowing of focus that often comes from concentrating on a single group experience. It has been our intent to go beyond mere comparisons among the various immigrant residents to show how they influenced each other, as rivals and as friends with common concerns.[13] Too many community studies present groups in social and cultural isolation, even when they have lived in the same neighborhoods, as if they failed to affect each other in any way.

Tampa's geographic location suggests other avenues for analysis. Historians of the American South have seldom had the opportunity to examine the phenomenon of immigration and its impact on urban areas. With the notable exception of New Orleans and a few smaller communities, immigrants largely shunned this part of the nation during the late nineteenth and early twentieth centuries. Hence the substantial immigrant presence in Tampa created social conditions different from those found in the majority of other southern urban centers. Located in the Deep South and initially populated by people identifying with the values and attitudes associated with traditional southern society, Tampa faced no simple black-and-white equation in its race relations. Instead the cigar city confronted an array of possible configurations in its social structure and cultural framework. How these accommodations sifted out affords different insights into the social dynamics of race relations in the South.

Ybor City in its heyday was a community of ideas. Anarchism, socialism, and communism, debated and tested in Spain, Cuba, and Italy, thrived here. Immigrants arrived with a heightened sense of class consciousness, which included a deep-seated skepticism of organized religion and the established order. "When in 1902 I landed in Tampa, I found myself in a world of radicals for which I was prepared," wrote Angelo Massari in his autobiography.[14] What happened to immigrants like Massari—who became, of all things, an international banker!—was the result of an interplay between old-world ideas, new-world opportunities, and the uniformly hostile reaction to radical beliefs by native Floridians.

The cigar industry exerted a pervasive influence over Ybor City. Virtually everyone fell under its shadow, for it employed more than 12,000 individuals at its peak in the 1920s. A distinctive culture of work evolved from the cigar benches and factories, shaped and nurtured by the extraordinary influence of the *lectores* and the searing collective experiences of labor strikes.

Concepts of class solidarity enjoyed a broad-based popularity throughout much of Ybor City's history. In this sense notions of class went beyond concerns of struggle and revolution to include a whole set of values and experiences arising out of economic location and workplace realities. It is clear, however, that levels of acceptance varied within the community. Committed leftists steadfastly maintained attachments to class goals and ideologies. Cubans, Italians, and Spaniards of this type joined together in radical groups, cooperatives, and unions to advance working-class causes. Among these individuals there existed a multifaceted class culture. Yet tension always existed between the pull of class-based collectivist solutions and the tug of individualist approaches to society.

The radical movement in Ybor City, despite trumpeting class war and revolution, never lived up to its rhetoric. In the end the issues of class gave way to those of a culture and community that were increasingly coopted by middle-class American values. Yet a rich associational life flowed in part from the leftist doctrines circulating in Ybor City, resulting in group endeavors of extraordinary proportions. The degree to which immigrants dedicated themselves to constructing mutual aid societies and militant unions, and the extent to which diverse immigrant groups cooperated, were remarkable. Over time these institutions and loyalties became infused with intense social meaning. In contrast to the communal organizations of Ybor City, which operated with an unusual lack of racial or ethnic prejudice, stands the record of local, state, and federal authorities, who conducted a mounting crescendo of nativist assaults against Ybor City's immigrant population.

The major crucible of cultural formation in Ybor City was labor unrest. The turbulent strikes of 1899, 1901, 1910, 1920, and 1931 helped transform clusters of Italians, Spaniards, and Cubans into a distinctive "Latin" community, to use the local expression. While this community coalesced in part because of hostility from native "Anglo" Tampa, the interaction between ethnic groups and their institutions was far more creative. Sharing occurred in many realms but never more persistently or pervasively than in the mutual aid societies and the workplace.

By the 1920s Ybor City's inhabitants had evolved from disparate collections of immigrants to established groups with roots in and commitments to Tampa. Like the Rome of Caesar Augustus, Latins had founded Ybor City on a bed of sand and left it a city of bricks. Many of the first generation had died by this time, and a second generation began to show signs of change. Formal schooling had become increasingly important. Most Italian families had left the cigar factories and invested their energies in trades and businesses. One of the great ironies of Ybor City is that the material success generated by Latins blunted the radical messages in which they had once fervently believed. "There is no such thing as economic growth," observed E. P. Thompson, "which is not at the same time, growth, or change of culture."[15] Ybor City evolved out of this change into a series of contradictions: free enterprise versus the solidarity of the proletariat; individual freedoms versus the demands of family, neighborhood, and group.

The fulcrum upon which this study balances is its focus on the interaction between Italian immigrants and their Latin neighbors. There is also a recognition of the importance of the dynamic exchange between immigrants and the urban-industrial ecology. We have largely structured this work along thematic lines on the assumption that this organizational framework illuminates most clearly the texture of the immigrant world of Ybor City.

The first three chapters establish the necessary groundwork for the ensuing analysis of ethnic interactions. Chapter 1 places Tampa's Italians in their old-world villages, exploring their premigration experiences. Here we learn of their traditional culture, economic skills, ideological leanings, shared adversities, and motivations for emigration. Such details permit an examination of what was lost, gained, or mutated in the New World. Chapter 2 establishes the city of Tampa and accounts for its evolution as an industrializing urban center. Chapter 3 provides for the origins and settlement of Ybor City and treats the inception of the cigar industry, the first Cuban and Spanish immigrations, and the appearance of early Italian arrivals in the city.

Once Italians are established in Ybor City and placed in the wider urban-industrial structure, the factor of immigrant interaction is engaged directly. The intensity and importance of interactive situations has determined the ordering of subsequent chapters. Hence the workplace and unions, mutual aid societies, and radical groups receive first priority. These contexts ultimately determined the major contours of Italian immigrant adjustments and the nature of the community's broader social relations. Those confluences follow which were less crucial in community formation and group development and were to an extent derivative from the earlier ones (religion, neighborhood, mobility). Each of the six thematic chapters contains its own internal chronological framework. Chapter 10 traces the period since World War II, which witnessed the disintegration of Ybor City as a Latin neighborhood and its evolution as a black residential area.

This volume employs a broad range of sources. Archives in Italy and the United States yielded valuable information about the immigrants who settled in Ybor City. But had this study relied solely upon census schedules, statistical abstracts, newspapers, and other written historical sources, important dimensions of the Ybor City experience would have been missing. For these elusive areas we made extensive use of oral history interviews, fully aware of the limitations of these materials as historical sources. We feel strongly that oral accounts must be scrutinized and tested like any other document; an interview stands as no more or less legitimate than a newspaper article or government report.[16] As a consequence, every effort has been made to test oral testimony for its accuracy and authenticity.

In many cases Tampa's humid climate, perfect for cigarmaking but terrible for preserving records, has led to major gaps in the traditional historical sources. No school records for the city before the 1940s have been discovered. The archives of the Office of Licenses and Permits and the court records have disappeared. Voting lists and police records are completely nonexistent prior to 1935. No one has been able to determine where the naturalization petitions of Tampa's aliens have gone. Incredibly, for a city that cigars made famous, there survives not one complete set of company records for any of the 200 firms active between 1886 and 1960. On March 1, 1908, a great fire completely destroyed seventeen square blocks of Ybor City and thousands of irreplaceable records were lost forever. Oral accounts, therefore, constitute an indispensable link to the immigrant world.

The taping of Ybor City's past should not be viewed as an end in itself. History from the bottom up allows one to challenge the conventional wisdom, not only as it applies to the local scene, but also as it fits into wider patterns of national development. We encountered numerous instances where oral history contradicted secondary accounts—which does not necessarily mean that conventional sources are inaccurate, or that the immigrants misrepresented the truth, but simply that if enough people believe in a doctrine, even if it is incorrect, then it becomes the truth, at least for those who hold it. This is often the only means of charting out the mental worlds in which people operated.

Many immigrants and their children shared their experiences with us. Labor leaders and workers, politicians and *bolita* players, housewives and peddlers, all gave distinct impressions and memories of the workplace, neighborhood, and family. Interviews provided unique insights, perspectives to be analyzed as historical documents. The fact that Julio Cuevas, José Vega Díaz, Victoriano Manteiga, Paul Longo, Mary Italiano, and Joe Maniscalco—even El Centro Español—have died since our research began in 1978 poignantly dramatizes the urgency of collecting oral histories. The dominoes in the *cantina* now skid across the table with a tempo more adagio than allegro. Soon the immigrant generation will be gone.

NOTES

1. Interview with José Vega Díaz, May 3, 1980.
2. Interview with Paul Longo, June 1, 1979.
3. Interview with Joseph Maniscalco, April 3, 1980.
4. Alan Dawley (review of Bodnar, *Immigration and Industrialization*), *American Historical Review* 84 (February 1979): 268–69.
5. Vecoli's pathbreaking "*Contadini* in Chicago," 404–17, began a vigorous reassessment of immigration history. Among the many recent works that have added to the debate are Harney, "Ambiente and Social Class," 208–24; Harney, "Chiaroscuro," 142–67; Yans-McLaughlin, *Family and Community*; Briggs, *An Italian Passage*; and Gabaccia, *From Sicily to Elizabeth Street*.
6. Asa Briggs (review of Thompson, *English Working Class*), *Labor History* 6 (Winter 1965): 84.
7. Cinel, *From Italy to San Francisco*.
8. Vecoli, "Chicago's 'Little Italies,'" 5–20.
9. Thompson, *English Working Class*, 57.
10. Herbert G. Gutman's work has made important advances in understanding these processes; see particularly his essays in *Work, Culture and Society*.
11. Bodnar, *Workers' World*.
12. Sociologists Richard Juliani and Mark Hutter provide preliminary theoretical conceptions of these issues in "Italian and Jewish Interactions." A few volumes have explored selected dimensions of immigrant interaction; among them are Bayor, *Neighbors in Conflict*, which deals primarily with conflict situations during the depression decade; Greene, *Slavic Community on Strike*, which examines the interactions of Slavic miners in the Pennsylvania coalfields; and Bodnar, *Immigration and Industrialization*, which at times integrates the experiences of several disparate groups.
13. A good example of the strengths and weaknesses of the comparative approach is Barton, *Peasants and Strangers*.

14. Massari, *Wonderful Life*, 56.
15. Thompson, *English Working Class*, 97.
16. Hareven, *Family Time and Industrial Time*, 371–82, contains an extended discussion of interviewing techniques and oral history usages. See *Amoskeag*, by Hareven and Langenbach, for a rich collection of oral interviews illustrating many of these concepts.

1 "We Live in Order Not to Die"
The Origins of Tampa's Italian Community

> Sicily, o signore, is not Palermo, it is not even the Palermo countryside, for the real Sicily is in the interior, especially near Bivona, in the province of Girgenti (Agrigento).
>
> Testimony by Calcedonio Inghilleri,
> *Inchiesta Agraria sulle Condizioni dei Contadini*

Angelo Massari scribbled a message on the family gate, pondering between spasms of doubt the importance of the occasion. In chalk he wrote, "13 *ottobre* 1902." For the eighteen-year-old, it was a moment of profound importance.[1] Massari had already met head-on a series of turbulent events that had significantly altered his life in Sicily: the bankruptcy of Italian agrarian policy; the brutal suppression of the *fasci* (workers' leagues); and the exodus to the Americas of men from his own Santo Stefano Quisquina, an agrotown in southern Sicily. Now he too was to leave.

After feverish consultation with *americani*, villagers who had immigrated to Tampa, Florida, and returned, Massari prepared himself for departure. "How crowded my home was that evening!" he reminisced sixty years later. The next morning, he and a half-dozen *paesani* (countrymen) left Santo Stefano by donkey cart for the harbor of Palermo. For Massari the journey was a baptism into a mysterious and exhilarating world beyond the confines of his village; for the others, all seasoned travelers on the emigrant trail, the ride was simply tedious. One fellow traveler, Giuseppina Spoto, had planted the emigrant seed in the impressionable

Massari. She had reluctantly returned to Sicily, dutifully accompanying her homesick husband, after they had accumulated a modest fortune in Ybor City. In the New World, she had proclaimed to Massari, "there was no scarcity of anything." Zia Peppina explained in graphic detail the *buona vita* (good life) in America, "how in Ybor City they used to make coffee in a big pot. Such a thing was not to be dreamed of in Santo Stefano."[2]

Massari's departure captures the quintessence of the emigrant experience and offers insights into the means for entering it. Here, at the local level, one can best appreciate how people made their choices and undertook to find a new life, decisions that propelled thousands of Sicilians from their *paesi* (villages) to the Americas. Although it may seem that epidemic "American fever" had ravaged all of Italy and Sicily, in retrospect the phenomenon was actually more particularistic, striking certain villages and towns with varying degrees of intensity. The dynamics at work can be examined in a cluster of Sicilian hill-towns in the province of Agrigento, all of which were swept into the vortex of the emigration process.

The roots of Tampa's Sicilian community sink deep into the island's troubled past. The villages sending emigrants to Florida are contained in the Val di Magazzolo, one of many valley systems in the midst of southwestern Sicily's mountainous terrain. Beginning at the northern end with Santo Stefano Quisquina, the settlements stretch out like beads on a string—Bivona, Alessandria della Rocca, Cianciana. Perched on hilltops away from malarial bottomlands, the villages, though different in important particulars, shared a long history of contact and interaction.[3] Santo Stefano was neither the most civically important of the villages (the courts, central police station, and subprefect's offices were in Bivona), nor the largest in size, nor even the most economically diverse. Yet it was by far the most significant community for the Tampa experience. Santo Stefano Quisquina accounted for approximately 60 percent of Tampa's Sicilian population at its height and virtually all of its earliest settlers. The social, political, and economic forces stimulating migration and change in this one locale, therefore, assume special importance.

King Federico II of Aragon, in 1296, designated Giovanni di Caltagirone the first Baron of Santo Stefano. A succession of powerful families followed—Ventimiglia, Sinisi, Anzalone—until the Belmonte family dominated the town in the nineteenth century. The Belmonte castle, overlooking the town fountain in the central square, symbolized the power of the lord over his possessions, which included thirteen large fiefs in the surrounding countryside and numerous buildings.[4]

The physical environment played a major role in the lives of the Stefanesi and their neighbors. The village rests at the southwestern end of the formidable Madonie Mountains, which range across central Sicily to Cefalu in the north. Pizzo Carbonara represents the highest point (2,000 meters) of this massif.[5] Santo Stefano lies 732 meters above sea level, a critical factor shaping the village economy and social outlook. Although large *latifondi* (estates) once dominated the region, there existed subtle differences among the village economies. The Santo Stefano uplands proved unsuited for vines and fruit trees; instead, those inhabitants with the means to do so carried on the pastoral trades of goat and sheep herding. Stefanesi *pecorino* (cheese) and *lana* (wool) acquired enviable reputations. Small numbers of *contadini* (peasants) harvested sumacs, almonds, pistachios, and limited quantities of olives and flax.[6] The lower-lying villages specialized in the growing of these crops but most particularly in the mainstay of Sicilian agriculture, hard-grained wheat. Sprawling *latifondi* (or *feudi* in Sicily) dotted the valley floor and slopes. Cianciana, the southernmost of the villages, had its own economic specialty: large sulphur mines employing hundreds of workers, many of whom were young children. The misery existing among the miners, especially the indentured children, was remarkable even for Sicily.[7]

Patterns of trade among the villages evolved, albeit slowly. The exchange of goods and services followed well-defined routes. Dairy products from Santo Stefano found markets in the squares of Alessandria della Rocca and Bivona, while young male Stefanesi worked in the fields of neighboring villages. Annual agricultural fairs drew people together for social and commercial purposes. All residents of the valley shared elements of a common dialect, confronted identical problems of poor soils, worried about malaria and bandits, suffered under the same limited access to outside services and information. Young men and women found marriage partners in neighboring villages as the links extended outward. Although certain aspects of *campanilismo* (highly localized loyalties) existed, residents of the Magazzolo valley knew each others' problems and idiosyncrasies well. This shared web of experience later proved important in shaping the adjustments these people made in Tampa.[8]

Santo Stefano and its neighbors evolved into classic agrotowns, urban-ecological responses to a cluster of historical circumstances. Urban vil-

Map 1. Magazzolo Valley and Villages of Origin, Southwestern Sicily.

lages developed, with some peasants walking long distances each day to their carefully tended and extensively cultivated plots in the Magazzolo valley. As a young boy in Alessandria della Rocca, Tampan Paul Longo remembered men leaving the village in the morning. "They go when the sun come up," he recalled, "and they come [back] at sunset." Herders, orchard tenders, and harvesters—who by necessity acquired rudimentary economic skills—peddled surpluses in the marketplaces of Corleone, Palermo, and Termini Imerese. Tenuous contacts with the world outside the valley existed, bound by primitive cart tracks and *fondaci* (country shelters or inns).[9]

The sheer physical presence of the mountains dominated the lives of the Stefanesi and their neighboring villagers. The pioneering social historian Fernand Braudel wrote, "Mountains are mountains: that is, primarily an obstacle, and therefore also a refuge." He noted that the practice of vendetta flourished only in mountainous regions where the inhabitants "had not been molded and penetrated by medieval concepts of justice."[10]

Santo Stefano, like much of Sicily's interior, was accessible only by mule paths until quite recently. Stefanesi lived in a densely populated town, but once beyond the *comune* (municipality), a forbidding and uninviting landscape greeted the visitor. "You can ride for five or six hours, from one town to another . . . but the scene is always the same: everywhere solitude and a desolation which wrings the heart," lamented the Florentine observer Baron Sidney Sonnino in 1876.[11] Carlo Patricio testified during the 1875 *Inchiesta Agraria sulle Condizioni dei Contadini*, "It is a fact that one cannot travel from Bivona to Sciacca." So primitive were transportation routes as late as 1910 that the Lorenzoni Report found many residents of interior villages who had never seen a wheeled cart. Yet the countryside was not completely empty. Wolves still prowled around Santo Stefano in the twentieth century, and as late as 1911 the city council paid bounties for their destruction. One early source described the Sicilian interior as "a land without roads, rivers without bridges."[12] By the twentieth century little had changed, except that there were more Sicilians.

The number of children spiraled upward in the late nineteenth century as a demographic time bomb ticked away. The population of Sicily rose from 1,000,000 persons in 1800 to 2,408,521 in 1861 to 3,568,124 in 1909. During the 1880s the birthrate soared to 42.1 births per 1,000 persons, an increase that pressed the capacity of the island to sustain itself. Santo Stefano can serve as a case study. Baptismal and census records, preserved in the parish and communal archives, suggest a village in transition. In 1570 the community numbered 1,639 persons; the *comune* grew to 2,959 inhabitants in 1653 and climbed to 5,262 by 1831. After a cholera outbreak in 1837 the population increased slowly until the mid-nineteenth century, when Stefanesi fecundity began its dramatic upward climb.[13]

In 1861 Santo Stefano had grown to 5,464 residents; by 1881 that figure had risen to 6,315, a steady but not spectacular increase. Twenty years later, however, the total had dipped to 6,097, and by 1931 the town could only count 5,897 residents. Local records reveal a much more dynamic demographic profile. During the thirty-year period following Garibaldi's conquest of Sicily in 1860, the baptistry of the central church in Santo Stefano registered an average of 254 births per year.[14] Santo Stefano's birthrate of more than 40 births per 1,000 inhabitants resembled that of the island, a demographic figure associated with developing nations or frontier societies.[15] In the same period records reveal only 180 deaths per year. More children were surviving childhood, further intensifying the economic crisis gripping the countryside. Santo Stefano confirmed historian Frank Thistlewaite's thesis of a direct correlation between the rates of emigration and the natural increase twenty years previously.[16]

In 1881 Sicily contained 348 *comuni*, and Santo Stefano Quisquina typified the interior, latifondiary agrotown.[17] Wages for landless dayworkers averaged 1.30 lire in the valley, less than the provincial average for Girgenti of 1.36 lire, according to the parliamentary agricultural investigation of 1883–84. Powerful absentee landlords who resisted any hint of reform had long since claimed the very best lands. Santo Stefano consistently ranked among the leaders of Sicilian towns having the highest percentage of lands given over to *latifondi* (twelfth in 1929, with 64.7 percent).[18] The population base was large enough, however, to support a crude but important class of artisans and merchants. Santo Stefano's involvement in the raising of goats and sheep, and the sale of products resulting from these activities, gave the community a noticeable mercantile dimension often absent from other latifondiary *comuni*.

For those working the land, a rigid system of sharecropping, the *mezzadria*, had evolved by the nineteenth century into what critics labeled the "second serfdom." The *gabelloti*, a class of ruthless rural entrepreneurs, controlled rents, capital, tools, animals, mills, and markets. They typically rented extensive acreage from landlords, in turn subdividing the property into slivers of land, derisively called *fazzoletti* (handkerchiefs) by the *contadini*.[19]

Peasants, defined by Eric Wolf as "rural cultivators whose surpluses are transferred to a dominant group of rulers," anchored the village economy.[20] The Stefanesi work force was devoted almost exclusively to the production, processing, and distribution of foodstuffs. These laborers, however, engaged in a wide variety of rural-commercial tasks, and there were fine gradations of status and prestige existing within the village social structure. The distribution of the local work force stood at 40 percent *contadini* in the 1880s (the same average as Sicily as a whole), followed by *braccianti* (unskilled laborers), *giornalieri* (day laborers), *artigiani* (artisans), and *borghesi* (businessmen/merchants).[21]

During the late nineteenth century free-world markets increasingly expropriated the fruits of peasant labor. Sicilian products became less competitive as foreign goods circulated with greater ease and efficiency. The pernicious squeeze by landlords and the mafia further reduced the margin for survival. In 1877 the mayor of Santo Stefano wrote to his superiors that the town was "absolutely in a critical condition, actually in the most extreme misery." By 1880 peasants working on the huge estates bordering Santo Stefano sagged under the load of an incredible burden of taxes: *il seme* (a tax on seed), *l'aggio* (interest on the seed tax), *la cuccià* (*gifts to the landlord*), il *guardiania* (a tax to pay the field guards), and *il Santo* (gifts to wandering monks), among others. So effectively did the tax collector accomplish his job that a local proverb described the *contadini* as "*mancu l'occhi pi chianciri*" (lacking the eyes with which to cry).[22]

Wolves may have roamed the hills of this part of the island, but still worse were the human predators. The villages lay in the heart of the mafia district of western Sicily. During the Inchiesta Agraria of 1875, Giuseppe Rossi, the prefect of Girgenti, testified that the interior villages of his province were hopelessly dominated by the rural underworld. "The maffia [*sic*]," he confessed, "is a native institution and although the name is new, the system is old."[23] As Anton Blok has pointed out, the mafia exploited "the gaps in communication between the peasant village and the larger society."[24] It also exploited those who sought to close these openings in the interests of the peasantry, as the village of Santo Stefano was to learn with brutal clarity.

Even *mafiosi* were not immune from a collapsing agrarian system, however. A worldwide glut of wheat and grapes depressed Sicilian markets, an economic disaster worsened by blunders in Rome. Prices plummeted in the 1870s and 1880s. Italian diplomats, angered over French advances in Tunisia, declared a tariff war against French farmers, resulting in devastating losses of markets for the *contadini*. Competing exports from the Black Sea region and the Americas further dropped the price of wheat from thirty to thirteen lire per quintal between 1880 and 1894. Similar forces adversely affected those peasants growing citrus fruits and mining sulphur, the latter constituting a particularly severe blow to the residents of Cianciana.[25]

If landholding peasants reeled from the blows inflicted by the vicissitudes of international politics, landless dayworkers suffered worse deprivation. In 1875 a Monreale bureaucrat reported that unskilled workers typically labored only during harvests, two or three months a year. "They make nothing. They make not enough to hold onto life."[26] Incredibly, wages, depressed by a surplus of labor, fell even further as the century drew to a close. In Santo Stefano residents expressed their growing sense of fatalism: "We live in order not to die."[27]

Peasants in the valley once prayed to the church for mitigation of their misery. Indeed, a remarkable line of religious figures, including Santa Rosalia, the patroness of Sicily, was born in Santo Stefano. But by the 1880s a virulent brand of anticlericalism had taken hold. Generations of prelates and priests preferred the task of building a temporal empire in Sicily to ameliorating the peasants' plight. In Santo Stefano the church commanded huge assets, including extensive landholdings and three handsome convents and monasteries. So well stocked was the monastery of Quisquina that the Bishop of Girgenti himself regularly came there to spend his summer vacation. This structure was only one of nine church buildings within the borders of Santo Stefano. Some peasants claimed that priests were in league with the mafia, and stories of bodies conveniently disappearing behind walled-up nooks in church buildings circulated in local legend.[28]

L'Asino (The Donkey), a caustically anticlerical newspaper, found a ready audience among the people of Santo Stefano. Young Angelo Massari recalled how the paper shaped his early opinions. He also remembered with rancor how a certain priest, Father Favati, forced the plebians to kneel for hours on the cold floor while awaiting the annual Easter confession, yet routinely welcomed the *prominenti* to the head of the line.[29] Massari, and others like him, ceased to attend church. There was a village proverb: "Monks and priests hear the masses and then kick you in the kidneys."[30]

In large part priests became the principal target of local discontent because they controlled substantial amounts of property and other large landowners were absent. The Prince of Belmonte lived in Palermo, visiting only occasionally to check on his extensive holdings. The fate of the Cannella family, the prince's representatives in Santo Stefano, however, gives some indication of feelings toward the upper classes. In 1860 when Giuseppe Garibaldi unleashed revolution on the island, peasants attacked the Cannellas, forcing them to seek refuge first in Bivona and then in Palermo. When the family returned after some months, a crowd assaulted their home and killed everyone within.[31]

By the 1890s Sicily in general and the Magazzolo valley in particular were sitting on social and political volcanoes. "One finds in the provinces of Palermo, Girgenti, and Caltanisetta," wrote Adolfo Rossi in 1893, "an ominous state of affairs, a peasant movement that breeds a new reign of justice, reminiscent of Spartacus. Peasants are carrying red flags with socialist inscriptions and are imbued with religious zeal."[32] Another functionary reported fatefully, "The word 'Ireland' is on the lips of many."[33] To nervous officials the explosive potential of the *fasci dei lavoratori* (workers' leagues) after 1893 seemed to confirm their worst fears of social revolution.

In communities throughout Sicily local groups rose to challenge traditional authorities and address long-standing grievances. The remarkable expansion of the *fasci* represented a militant outgrowth of the worker-peasant organizational movement that appeared in Sicily after unification. By the 1880s the mutual aid momentum had gained in popularity and activity; between 1860 and 1890 organizers had formed 285 groups in Sicily. In 1881, for example, Stefanesi established the Circolo Agricolo-Operaio di Mutuo Soccorso (Agricultural Workers Circle of Mutual Aid). Housed in an abandoned communal jail, the Circolo attempted to provide various educational and self-help services to fieldworkers, but it produced few results.[34] These meager seeds of collective action soon received nourishment from outside the village. With the peasantry embittered over the declining standard of life, disillusioned about the future, and desperate because of a serious drought, the *fasci* movement exploded over Sicily in 1893.[35] The crusade burned brightest in the Sicilian interior.

A remarkable character emerged in Santo Stefano, a figure destined to lead the local *fascio* and influence profoundly those in neighboring villages. Ultimately he embodied the tragedy of the wider movement. Lorenzo Nicolò Panepinto was born in 1865, the son of a moderately successful artist and teacher. When their father died, Lorenzo's older brother, Giuseppe, taught elementary school to support the family, but after some years he entered the priesthood. Lorenzo acquired a modest formal education but followed an autodidactic path to a fervent belief in socialism. Like his father he exhibited a talent for painting and teaching, and for most of his life he earned a living as a teacher in the public schools of Santo Stefano.[36]

In 1887 the young Panepinto entered the Italian army and volunteered for the disastrous Eritrea campaign in Africa. The Italian government's imperial folly and the needless slaughter brought on by the African venture profoundly affected the young intellectual. He published *A le Vittime di Satti* (1887), turning over all profits to families of deceased Italian soldiers, and later a book of art, poetry, and prose, *L'Africa Italiana*.[37] Panepinto's exposure to the inhumanity of war and the brutality of Italian government policy decisively shaped his worldview. He was now convinced of the injustices existing in the Italian social order.

Lorenzo Panepinto returned to Santo Stefano in 1889, becoming a town councilman (the youngest on the board) in that year. Quickly he acquired a reputation as a dissenter and a troublemaker, at least in the eyes of government officials. Between 1889 and 1893 his disillusionment with a system he felt incapable of reforming was hardened. On several occasions royal commissioners threatened him with arrest for his statements and activities among the *contadini*; ultimately officials dismissed him from the town council.[38]

The initial impetus to begin a *fascio* in Santo Stefano resulted from a visit on May 28, 1893, by three representatives from the *fascio* of Prizzi and messengers from groups in Palermo.[39] After a slow start the newly formed group, with Panepinto as its elected president, sent forty mounted men to the Prince of Belmonte's largest estate in September and called all *contadini* working there out on strike. Groups of *fascio* members soon visited the remaining *latifondi* in the area, sometimes carrying clubs for emphasis, and produced similar results. By October the organization counted 1,028 members, almost all of whom were *contadini*, and proudly flew a large red flag with its name handsomely emblazoned across the face.[40]

The organization's constitution appears quite moderate today, but in

1893 any criticism of the status quo smacked of revolution. Santo Stefano's *fascio* advocated reforming the *mezzadria*, requiring landlords to assume a greater burden of the costs. Ultimately, suggested Panepinto, landlords should give seed and land to the peasants. Other goals included the "betterment of the economic, moral, and intellectual condition of the working class," to be achieved by struggling "within the legal means and without leaving the orbit of established institutions." The constitution further provided for the establishment of night schools and Sunday lectures to make educational instruction available. "We need bread for the stomach," preached Panepinto, who possessed an almost mystical faith in education, but "we also need bread for the brain." Workers, advised the *fascio*, should take part in political struggles and elect their own candidates.[41]

Political activism and agricultural strikes continued in Santo Stefano, quickly spreading outward to include other towns in the valley. The *contadini* were receiving an education in the benefits that organization and class action could bring. One after another the Magazzolo villages established *fasci* and joined the movement sweeping the island.[42] Soon similar organizations could be found in nearly every corner of Sicily; total membership figures stood in the hundreds of thousands.

In Santo Stefano, Panepinto swung decisively to the side of the Socialist party, publicly signaling his conversion in September by ending his eulogy to a deceased *fascio* member with the words, *"Viva il Socialismo!"* His schedule of organizing and protest activities soon included areas far beyond the confines of his home village and valley. He became, in the words of one of his supporters, "the eternal nightmare of the patricians and priests of all the regions of Girgenti."[43]

To the authorities, talk of socialism and rent strikes conjured up the specter of the Paris Commune and Spartacus. When the moderate government of Giovanni Giolitti fell in 1893, the fate of the *fasci* was sealed. The new prime minister, Sicilian-born Francesco Crispi, determined to crush the movement. In Parliament, Crispi lectured that socialism was indistinguishable from anarchism, that the *contadini* were "corrupted by ignorance, gnawed by envy and ingratitude, and should not be allowed any say in politics." On January 3, 1894, a royal decree declared the island in a state of siege; 30,000 Italian troops, supported by wealthy landowners, proceeded to suppress the "rebellion."[44] In Caltavutoro troops opened fire on a crowd of workers, killing 50; in Caltagirone landowners declared that education had become too dangerous and must be prohibited.⁴⁵ Everywhere soldiers marched.

Elite squads of *bersaglieri* (sharpshooters) grimly accomplished their objectives in the Val di Magazzolo as well. Between January 9 and 17 the *fasci* of Bivona, Alessandria della Rocca, and Cianciana shut their doors in compliance with government orders, and a series of arrests succeeded in closing the workers' circle of Santo Stefano. Yet as late as January 30, Santo Stefano's *fascio* continued to fly its red flag proudly. A troop of well-armed soldiers arrived on February 2, 1894, and carried out a new series of arrests which led to the *fascio*'s official closing.⁴⁶ Even nature played a hand in the misery, as a powerful earthquake struck Santo Stefano shortly after the troops departed (and before damage caused by a similar quake several years earlier had been repaired). Elsewhere on the island military tribunals tried and convicted leaders and followers of the *fasci*, sending them to jails or into exile.⁴⁷ For hundreds of Stefanesi and thousands of Sicilians the search for alternative solutions to the problems besetting their lives assumed a new intensity. Many Sicilian villages were soon to cease the export of wheat and intensify the export of people.

The historian Giampiero Carocci has written that the Sicilian countryside responded to the travail of the 1880s and 1890s with "resignation, socialism and emigration."⁴⁸ Most studies of Sicilian settlement in America have concentrated on the last of these strategies. This is not unusual, since that option had the most direct and observable impact on American society. A popular view of Sicilian emigration has closely associated emigration rates with landholding patterns, social structures, and collectivist activities. In southern Italy and eastern Europe, the thesis holds, landless peasants and propertyless laborers were conspicuously absent from the ranks of emigrants. Those who had nothing to lose did not emigrate. Where landholdings were concentrated and worked by a propertyless peasantry, a collectivist ethos expressed itself in organized resistance but low rates of emigration. High emigration resulted in those areas where a high percentage of proprietor-landholders prevailed and, coincidentally, in locales of limited political-collectivist action. John S. MacDonald has theorized that with the *fasci* suppression the hopes of peasants in the Sicilian interior disintegrated and emigration resulted. Prior to this time Sicilian peasants pursued collectivist solutions to their problems, much like the organized responses that characterized areas such as Tuscany, and exhibited low rates of emigration.⁴⁹

Historian Donna Gabaccia has questioned the MacDonald model as it applies to Sicilian emigration patterns. Her examinations of Sambuca di Sicilia, a village resting approximately thirty kilometers west of Santo Stefano, have found that Sicilians followed strategies of both emigration and socialist (collectivist) agitation after the suppression of the *fasci*. For the villagers of Sambuca these two solutions were not contradictory alternatives but rather viable choices that shaped, in a complementary fashion, social change on both sides of the Atlantic. Key actors in Gabaccia's studies were village artisans, who not only initiated and built migration chains, but also forged links of collective action.[50] This view of Sicilian emigration suggests various possibilities for analysis, recognizing as it does the varied nature of Sicilian village life and the impact of intensely local social patterns on migration.

The villages of the Magazzolo valley reacted to the crises of the 1890s by selecting from a range of responses that were appropriate to their particular histories. As some villagers departed, others remained at home and agitated for reform in the local arena. The two approaches existed in different combinations and intensities during the period under review, but both exerted influences on those who stayed and those who left. Indeed, it is difficult to explain fully either phenomenon without reference to the other, as often there existed a clear dialectical relationship between the two.

To imagine that pressure for social change in interior Sicily ceased with the suppression of the *fasci* would not only be mistaken but naive. In addition to being a reaction to profound social and economic problems, the *fasci* also resulted from fundamental political considerations; they built upon a legacy of agitation that was already well established. A social ferment continued to shape the dynamics of village life and by doing so affected the experiences of those who chose to leave the homeland, even if only temporarily. Lines of communication with overseas settlements continued to operate and developments on both sides of the Atlantic resonated with what were mutual strands of causality. Ideas, money, and personalities flowed back and forth between old and new worlds, molding the texture of the societies in both locations.

In Santo Stefano, for example, Lorenzo Panepinto remained after the *fascio* was disbanded and continued his activities. He organized several cooperative agricultural societies to serve the needs of workers, refining and extending his socialist proselytizing. By July 1894 the subprefect of Bivona already included him prominently on his "List of Most Dangerous

Socialists."[51] Panepinto's lecturing and writing generated a considerable following which radiated well beyond the confines of Santo Stefano. In 1901 he sponsored the Lega di Miglioramento fra i Contadini (Peasant Betterment League), an organization mirroring the aims and goals of the earlier *fascio*. The league and its sister institution, the Unione Agricola (Agricultural Union), led *contadini* on strikes and lobbied in town politics.[52] Villagers residing in Tampa gave evidence of their support for these initiatives by purchasing 101 shares in the agricultural union on its opening day. By 1903 a Sezione del Partito Socialista (Socialist party local) in Santo Stefano, with Panepinto as president, proclaimed its existence and proudly hosted the first Provincial Socialist Congress of the region.[53]

Imitating Santo Stefano, other workers' leagues and socialist locals soon dotted the neighboring villages, and combined meetings frequently took place. One such gathering in Bivona led to Panepinto's arrest, following his vigorous denunciation of a recently passed public security law. So threatening did the crowd in attendance become that authorities quickly released him, allowing completion of his speech (followed by impassioned addresses by socialists from Bivona and Alessandria della Rocca).[54] Out of a similar meeting came a decision by the Santo Stefano league to rent a nearby *latifondo* and farm it collectively, one of the first such actions taken in Sicily.[55]

Panepinto worked at a remarkable pace, serving on various government commissions, publishing a newspaper, *La Plebe*, to spread his views, organizing additional self-help associations, and even visiting the overseas communities of Stefanesi in 1907–8 (at their invitation and expense). Socialist luminaries, including Nicolò Barbato, Bernardino Verro, and Napoleone Colajanni, came to Santo Stefano to discuss political strategies and confer with Panepinto.[56] His socialism consisted not of the somewhat simplistic peasant notions often found in *fasci* villages but rather was a well-integrated, systematic ideology that frequently was at the advance edge of Sicilian socialism.

Lorenzo Panepinto's tireless efforts on behalf of the peasants came to an abrupt end on the evening of May 16, 1911, when two shotgun blasts killed the champion of the *contadini* at his doorstep. His death attracted national attention. Correspondent Italo Zingarelli, who traveled to the village to cover the funeral, observed, "The crowd was crying like a wild tribe that had lost its old chief. . . . In the farm road I have spotted many men slain."[57] Tampa resident Frank Giunta, a young boy in Santo

Stefano at the time, remembered the wailing and grief caused by the death. "I was terrified," he recalled, "for several weeks people came from all the villages of Sicily with black flags. . . . they paraded through the streets and bands would play mournful tunes. It continued with people making speeches amid gatherings of black flags. I still remember, I used to tremble, see, because of the way the old people used to talk. Nobody seemed safe anymore. They could kill anybody!" To this day Giunta can recite verse and song of the composition written to commemorate Panepinto, and he recalls the erection of a handsome plaque donated by the Tampa Stefanesi in remembrance of the "Apostle of Socialism."[58]

Although no convictions ever resulted from the murder, local residents knew with certainty that mafia assassins hired by local powers had committed the crime. "His enemies," wrote one Stefanesi, "the feudal owner and renter, together with the clerics, had no rest until they killed him." The number of murders, cattle rustlings, beatings, and threats increased dramatically in the valley as wealthy landowners reasserted their dominance.[59] In an attempt to replace the leadership supplied by Panepinto, Socialist party leaders sent Sebastiano Cammareri Scurti to Santo Stefano, but he soon died of natural causes. Momentum temporarily stagnated and some village leagues began to close their doors.[60] Yet the vision of Lorenzo Panepinto did not die as easily as the man.

Mass emigration resulted from an intricate relationship between a complex cluster of social, psychological, political, and economic factors. Choices existed in even the most remote villages. In most cases emigrants were not simply pushed out by crippling disaster; alternatives existed. Most Stefanesi and their fellow Sicilians in neighboring villages chose to stay. Moreover, those who migrated often viewed emigration as a means of assisting those who remained behind, most often family members. This relationship between temporary migration and familial goals has long been recognized. To be sure, many villagers conceived of migration as a way of obtaining money to increase family landholdings in the *paese* and acquire or increase the status accorded to property owners.[61] Others, however, came to see the act of migration in a broader context. Just as Stefanesi in America who opted to support agricultural unions by purchasing shares were signaling their emotional ties to the homeland and their probable intentions of returning, so too were they demonstrating a willingness to support organizations that looked beyond the individual or single family in their social orientations. The worldview and sociopolitical values championed by associations such as the *fasci* and the *leghe* (leagues), therefore, possessed a social force and class-based message that went beyond the groups themselves or their physical setting in Sicily. These sentiments were carried to the New World by emigrants who had, in many cases, assisted in their creation.

Emigration from the Magazzolo valley prior to the traumatic *fasci* revolt of the early 1890s had been moderate but nonetheless substantial enough to establish the first rough signpost along the trail that later would be worn smooth. After the violent suppression of the *fasci* and the reaffirmation of power by the dominant classes, large numbers of emigrants left for the Americas. Ultimately, thousands of artisans and peasants moved outward to find new opportunities elsewhere, including locations in central Florida. Movement from Santo Stefano reached a high point in the years 1898 to 1910.

Emigration functioned as a sensitive barometer of the social and economic climate of Sicily and Florida. In 1876 only 141 emigrants left the province of Girgenti, a figure which fell to 29 in 1880. Beginning in 1883, though, large numbers of Sicilians from this province began leaving the island: 211 in 1884; 891 in 1887; 2,267 in 1889; 2,154 in 1898.[62] By 1900 Girgenti claimed 138 emigrants per 10,000 inhabitants, the second highest rate among the provinces of the island.[63] Santo Stefano and the other villages supplying Tampa closely resembled the patterns of Girgenti: 184 villagers departed Santo Stefano in 1891, followed by 236 in 1892, 160 in 1893, and 63 in 1894—a depression year in the United States; the total for 1903 reached 501. For the period 1891–1913, some 7,557 emigrants had left Santo Stefano, 119.6 percent of the village's 1881 population (see Table 1).

Emigration from this Sicilian hill-town proceeded in carefully delineated stages, each step measured by the social and economic yardstick of individual survival and familial improvement. In the earliest stage pioneers explored opportunities abroad, probing new economies and pathways, mastering the maze constructed by steamship agents, labor brokers, and immigration officials.[64] For the Magazzolo villages the precise details of the very earliest out-migrations are largely lost to the historical record. Sometime in the 1870s pioneers left the valley, possibly using informational networks that had long been forged between Sicily and places like New Orleans. Some pathfinders made their way to the mining frontier of America, working in the silver, gold, and lead fields of Colorado and Utah. Others trickled into the coal regions of Pennsylvania, ending up in places like Pittston, Keyston, and Swearton. Still others

TABLE 1 Emigration from Santo Stefano, 1891–1913

Year	Total	Year	Total
1891	184	1903	501
1892	236	1904	303
1893	160	1905	440
1894	63	1906	243
1895	118	1907	347
1896	46	1908	62
1897	154	1909	188
1898	215	1910	211
1899	289	1911	87
1900	303	1912	129
1901	180	1913	147
1902	385	TOTAL	7,557

SOURCE: Ministero dell Agricoltura, Industria e Commercio—Direzione Generale della Statistica, *Statistica della Emigrazione Italiana* (Roma, 1892–   ); Messina, *Caso Panepinto*, 33, 141.

found their way to such locations as Santa Fe (Argentina), Carthage (North Africa), New Orleans, and Chicago. Early in this process New York City attracted a small beachhead of semipermanent residents.[65]

The first contacts with Florida are more clearly etched in the local history of the villages. According to oral accounts derived from the pioneers' children and a scattering of documents, a vanguard of young peasant males left Santo Stefano in 1882 and landed in New York City. Here labor agents for the Atlantic and Gulf Coast Canal and Okeechobee Land Company recruited them. Castrenze Ferlita, one of the original argonauts, told the story of his odyssey to a friend, who transcribed the tale. Traveling by rail from New York, the group was destined for employment on a sugarcane plantation at St. Cloud, located in central Florida's Kissimmee Valley. Lacking anyone who spoke English or the funds to purchase food, the group went hungry for two days. They finally relieved their plight by obtaining a meal of fried fish from a black vendor in Savannah, Georgia. Eventually they arrived in Kissimmee. "We had to sleep on the hard floor of the station on an empty stomach," Ferlita related, "and when we reached St. Cloud, we were made welcome with a repast of sweet potatoes."[66]

After "four long months of beating hearts and tears," the first letter from the group arrived in Santo Stefano, telling of the St. Cloud plantation and its employment possibilities. The news set into motion other peasant adventurers who made the trek to central Florida and back.

Philip Spoto's father came in 1888 on the first of five trips, during which he spent time in New York and St. Cloud, now called the "sugar place." Joe Valenti's father followed the same process, making three trips in all before finally settling in Florida. A large group of sojourners arrived in 1891 and included villagers from Alessandria della Rocca and Bivona. By this date a cluster of about 100 male laborers were filtering in and out of St. Cloud, subsisting mainly on boiled sweet potatoes and a simple flour-based lasagne.[67]

The migrants first worked on the St. Cloud and Sugar Belt Railroad, laying track through the virgin forests. In the lore of local history the St. Cloud years were known as "the starving time." Upon completing the fifteen-mile railroad managers shifted the Sicilians to grueling labor in the sugar fields. Treated as human chattels, much like the blacks alongside whom they worked, Sicilians accepted their lot as part of the price to be paid for the opportunity to make enough money to return to Santo Stefano and live a decent life.[68] "Work hard, work hard or you will die like a dog," warned a Sicilian proverb.[69] The rigors of St. Cloud had not been unexpected, but some events were unforeseen. Philip Spoto's father related the story of one workday that began as he headed for the sugar fields armed with his shovel. He soon encountered a huge *coccodrillo* along the path. The hysterical Spoto, imagining such beasts lurking only in Dante's *Inferno*, thrust his shovel down the alligator's mouth. Unfortunately the giant clamped down on the tool and remained immobile. The foreman, hearing the hapless worker's tale, shrugged and announced, "No work, no pay."[70]

The St. Cloud experiment, with its isolation, exploitation, and ruthless passion for saving, typified the sojourner stage of emigration. The labor camp supplied a source of employment for the Stefanesi, whose expectations changed as they adjusted to the new economic order. By the late 1880s several hundred individuals had trekked to the remote reaches of central Florida and returned to Sicily, bringing tales of the strange new land with them. The same probing for economic opportunity that brought these men to the sugar fields of St. Cloud, however, operated to ensure that they would not long remain satisfied with the opportunities found there. Events were unfolding elsewhere in Florida that soon drew them with magnetic force out of the cane stands.

The story of John Cacciatore is illustrative of how these intertwined networks operated within families and villages. Cacciatore was born on May 12, 1860, in Santo Stefano. In his own words his father "was a farm peasant working the soil for a land owner." As a youngster he labored in the fields helping his parents. He married a village girl in 1882, leasing a plot of land to plant wheat, oats, potatoes, and vegetables. That same year saw the departure of the contingent of peasant migrants that ultimately arrived at St. Cloud, Florida. Included among the four pioneers who blazed the trail to the central Florida sugar plantation were John's cousins, Antonio, Salvatore, and Angelo Cacciatore.[71]

In 1885, for some unrecorded reason, John decided to leave for the New World as well, but he went to New Orleans, not to Florida. The stay in New Orleans proved a brief interlude. Soon Cacciatore began to hear of the movement taking place from St. Cloud to Tampa. Several friends urged him to go. As he explained, they "described Tampa to me with such glowing colors that I soon became enthused." Taking a train to Mobile, Alabama, and then a steamer to Tampa, Cacciatore arrived with the expectation of seeing a flourishing city. His hopes were dashed immediately. "There was nothing; what one may truthfully say, nothing," he reported.[72]

The sugar fields of St. Cloud and the limited opportunities available in early Tampa exerted a pull that primarily attracted landless peasants from the Magazzolo valley. The types of work, skill requirements, and possibilities for advancement offered were not particularly attractive to artisans or the better-off peasantry, who typically went to New Orleans or New York if they migrated. Angelo Massari's peasant, but landowning, family was indicative of this split. When the youngster agitated in the early 1890s for permission to emigrate to Tampa, his mother recoiled at the thought of sending him there, explaining, "Emigration [is] for poor people and not for members of our family!"[73]

When Tampa changed, so too did the migration stream flowing to it. As the city expanded, adding to its urban infrastructure and industrial base, the size, permanence, and composition of Sicilian immigration responded. By the late 1890s more artisans and landholding peasants came to Tampa, both directly from the villages and from other new-world outposts. The settlement in Tampa came to replicate more closely the social structure in Sicily.

The "successes" achieved by the sojourning Stefanesi generated a momentum that reached infectious proportions in their old-world *paese*. The funneling of several thousand Sicilians to Florida involved an intricate network of unwritten rules, oral confirmations, formal trusts, and financial transactions. The second stage of movement forged the links of chain migrations. Returnees, their tote bags filled with the promise of abundance and showing a willingness to display their new possessions as ostentatiously as possible, dazzled the home villagers. Domenico Giunta witnessed the effects in Santo Stefano. "Word spread like wildfire of the wonders of America," he recalled, "and they [his fellow villagers] began to have the courage to migrate."[74] Soon—in the piazza, around the water fountain, on the mule paths—Stefanesi and their neighbors debated the future, particularly their future in Florida. Angelo Massari, born in 1885, remembered that while he was a young boy in Santo Stefano children dreamt and played fantasy games of emigrating. The *americani* even tutored Massari in the rudiments of the English language; among other things, they taught him the magic phrase, "*Se misti, gari giobba fo me?*" (Say mister, got a job for me?).[75]

Emigrants left the Val di Magazzolo by donkey cart, guiding *carrette* (carts) along narrow paths to Corleone or Lercara Friddi, where a train waited to take passengers to Palermo. Many, however, wishing to economize, steered their carts ninety miles to the great port city, selling produce along the way and spending nights at selected *fondaci* (shelters), or sometimes even sleeping under cart beds when accommodations were not to be had.[76] Paul Longo remembered leaving Alessandria della Rocca as a fifteen-year-old, sitting proudly on a one-horse cart, traveling first to Bivona and then to Palermo, where he stayed at a hotel arranged for by an immigration agency. "Yes, so many people coming from Alessandria then," he sighed.[77]

From Palermo emigrants boarded steerage for New York or New Orleans, or sailed to Naples for transfer to other ships sailing to America. Veterans of the watery trek warned greenhorns of bunko artists and *il truffatore inglese* (the flimflam man). Fakirs and false Franciscans, quacks and patent medicine hawkers prowled the wharves, preying on the superstitious and the unprotected. Since the Italian government regulated the export of wheat with more sensitivity and scrutiny than the traffic of human freight, villagers relied upon a sophisticated yet unwritten cluster of premigration values that were imported to America: a suspicion of strangers and a distrust of government officials, the codes of *onore* (family honor), *furberia* (shrewdness), and *amicizia* (friendship). A dogged capacity for hard work also accompanied these Sicilians.[78]

Santo Stefano's parish records dramatically record the demographics of emigration, how Florida stripped the town of young members, taking with them the next generation. In 1877 there were 299 babies born in

TABLE 2 Births in Santo Stefano, 1877–1920

Year	Total	Percent/variation
1877	299	100.0
1880	254	85.0
1885	305	120.0
1890	269	88.2
1895	227	84.4
1900	197	86.8
1905	177	89.9
1910	168	95.0
1915	180	107.1
1920	174	96.3

SOURCE: *Liber Baptizatorium Parochiale Ecclesiae, Santo Stefano ad Quisquinam,* 1877–1920.

Santo Stefano; in 1910 only 168 births occurred, the smallest number in three generations. The downward spiral induced by emigration bottomed out in 1911, when only 110 births were recorded (see Table 2). What emigration did not take away the cannons of Caporetto and the Piave did: a somber memorial to the sixty-two Stefanesi who died in World War I stands in Piazza Panepinto, an ironic blending of tragedies.[79]

If Stefanesi found the beginnings of prosperity in Florida, the same could not be said of those who remained on the island. Emigration may have spared Sicily an explosive social revolution, but life remained desperately difficult for Sicilians. World War I brought only suffering and loss to the Magazzolo valley. In addition to the human toll, blockades and submarines cut off markets for agricultural goods and left many families divided between America and the homeland. Francesca Adamo Tagliarini remembered spending the war years in Santo Stefano while her husband was in Florida, each unable to reunite with the other. The only commodities the village possessed in plentiful supply were northern Italian refugees who had been displaced by the great battles with Austria. Sleeping in horse stables and eating from a common soup kettle, the refugees only taxed slender village reserves further as the government failed to supply sufficient funds for their support.[80]

The postwar period brought no relief. Peasants throughout the valley cried out for land reform, at times occupying estates and fields that were lying unproductive. The *lega* (league) continued to exist, protesting increased taxes and mafia depredations while urging greater use of cooperative ventures among the peasantry. The messages of class-based action began to bear tangible fruit in 1921, when a socialist mayor took office in the village and a section of the Communist party appeared.[81] The rise to power of Benito Mussolini, however, dissipated any immediate hopes for meaningful change. Perhaps the most ignoble slight of all occurred in 1922 when Mussolini incorporated the name of the *fasci* to fuel his cause. Yet the leftist orientation of the community did not permanently disappear. The first government in Santo Stefano after World War II was communist, and it remained so until 1961. Indeed, as early as February 1945 the liberated village had formed an agricultural cooperative, named Lorenzo Panepinto, which took over vast amounts of abandoned land.[82] Stefanesi clearly had not foresaken the socialist teachings of Panepinto, with their appeals to cooperation and militance on behalf of class interests. Ironically, those villagers who cast their lot with Ybor City had by then deserted such directions, despite a lengthy experimentation with them in the New World.

Throughout this period the primitive roads leading out of the valley continued to be marked by the dusty footprints of emigrants seeking new opportunities elsewhere. Even today remittances supply a major source of the Magazzolo valley economy, only now money orders arrive postmarked Antwerp and Brussels, not Ybor City. Santo Stefano continues to attract notice. A recent feature article in *Giornale di Sicilia* documented the village's history of "peasant struggles" but somberly concluded that poverty still envelops the Stefanesi. The *latifondo* system has resisted, and continues to defy, complete dissolution.[83]

Summary

Between 1880 and 1920 more than three million emigrants left Sicily, constituting one of the greatest mass migrations in history. In general, peasants and artisans fled the island in search of alternatives to a steadily deteriorating agrarian economy; more specifically, several thousand men and women left the agrotowns located in the folds of the Val di Magazzolo due to the push of restricted economic mobility, an accelerating birthrate, the unfulfilled aspirations of the *fasci* movement, and the pull of opportunities in America. A small stream of Stefanesi, the size of which fluctuated with economic and social conditions in Sicily and America, tested the waters of the New World and established a beachhead at St. Cloud, Florida, in the 1880s. Originally these sojourners came with expectations of earning enough money to return to Sicily and resume their lives with an enhanced dignity and respect. However, the concomitant successes of these vanguard migrants and the worsening agricultural situation in Sicily encouraged further movement to America. An active chain migration connected the economies and peoples of Florida and Sicily.

In the homeland, vigorous efforts at social change continued under the leadership of Lorenzo Panepinto, a committed socialist. The collectivist solutions to social problems which he proposed reflected the outlooks and values of the Stefanesi who both stayed and left. In addition, neighboring villages became drawn into the spiraling momentum of migration and the hope it spawned. A steady deterioration of life in Sicily ensured that movement out of the villages would continue. Events of a different sort were unfolding in the New World. By the late 1880s the Sicilian outpost in central Florida stood poised at a crucial juncture in its history. News began to filter into the remote sugar fields of St. Cloud of the tantalizing opportunities available just ninety miles to the west in a place called Tampa.

NOTES

1. Massari, *Wonderful Life*, 78.
2. Ibid., 70.
3. De Vita, *Dizionario Geografico*, 12, 83, 88, 296–97; Messina, *S. Stefano Quisquina*, 132.
4. Messina, *S. Stefano Quisquina*, 39–81. Sicily remained officially feudal until 1812, but the system did not disappear entirely for many decades. See Hobsbawm, *Primitive Rebels*, 95.
5. Broquet, "Geology of the Madonie Mountains," 201–30.
6. Messina, *S. Stefano Quisquina*, 151–52; de Vita, *Dizionario Geografico*, 296–97.
7. Covello, *Italo-American School Child*, 228; de Vita, *Dizionario Geografico*, 83; Schneider and Schneider, *Culture and Political Economy*, 46.
8. Interview with Francesco Centinaro, May 6, 1981; interview with Emilio Settecasi, March 16, 1981. An insightful paper by Frank Sturino, "A Case Study of Southern Italian Migration to Canada, 1880–1930," given at the Conference on Italian Immigration to Canada, May 11, 1984, redefines the commonly accepted notion of *campanilismo*.
9. Interview with Giovanni Capodici, March 15, 1981; interview with Paul Longo, March 13, 1980; *Storia di Alessandria della Rocca: dalle Origine al 1905*, typescript copy in authors' possession.
10. Braudel, *Mediterranean*, I, 38–39.
11. Franchetti and Sonnino, *Inchiesta in Sicilia*, II, 15.
12. Jacini, *Inchiesta Agraria*, 593; Braudel, *Mediterranean*, I, 154. Lorenzoni's observations are cited in Mack Smith, *Modern Sicily*, 475.
13. Messina, *S. Stefano Quisquina*, 46–66; Giarrizzo, "La Sicilia e la Crisi Agraria,"

in Giarrizzo and Manacorda, *Fasci Siciliani*, I, 7, 9; Maggiore-Perni, *Popolazione di Sicilia*, 526–27, 532–33.

14. Istituto Centrale di Statistica, *Comuni e loro Popolazione*, 266; *Liber Baptizatorum, Sancti Stephani ad Quisquinam*, La Madre della Chiesa; Archivio Comunale, Santo Stefano, Provincia di Agrigento.

15. *Liber Defunctorum Parochialis Ecclesiae, Sancti Stephani ad Quisquinam*, La Madre della Chiesa.

16. Thistlethwaite, "Migration from Europe," 90.

17. Giarrizzo, "La Sicilia e la Crisi Agraria," 15.

18. Messina, *Caso Panepinto*, 238.

19. Foerster, *Italian Emigration of Our Times*, 72–78; Schneider and Schneider, *Culture and Political Economy*, 59–67.

20. Wolf, *Peasants*, 3–4.

21. U.S. Congress, *Immigrants in Industries*, Tables 130, 132; Giarrizzo and Manacorda, *Fasci Siciliani*, I, 17; Briggs, *Italian Passage*, 4–5. Italian agriculturists generally possessed a cluster of supplemental job skills such as stone working and shoe repairing in addition to their farming talents.

22. Barbagallo, *Lavoro ed Esodo nel Sud*; Messina, *S. Stefano Quisquina*, 74; Messina, *Caso Panepinto*, 30. Perhaps the most hated tax of all was the *macinato* (grist mill tax).

23. Jacini, *Inchiesta Agraria*, 563; King, "Sicilian Mafia," 21–34.

24. Blok, *Mafia of a Sicilian Village*, 8.

25. Sereni, *Capitalismo nelle Campagne*, 223–41; Mack Smith, *Italy*, 150–62. For a discussion of the increasing supply of wheat and grapes and the consequent decline of prices, see Giarrizzo and Manacorda, *Fasci Siciliani*, I, 5–65.

26. Testimony of Calcedonio Inghilleri, counsel of the Appeals Court of Palermo, Deputy of Monreale, in Jacini, *Inchiesta Agraria*, 381.

27. Quoted in Massari, *Wonderful Life*, 45. Anton Blok found similar folk wisdoms: "People have to work in order not to die" (*Mafia*, 48).

28. Messina, *S. Stefano Quisquina*, 74–75, 89, 96; Panteleone, *Mafia and Politics*, 204–5, 209, 211–12.

29. Massari, *Wonderful Life*, 50, 55–56.

30. Messina, *Caso Panepinto*, 29–30.

31. Messina, *S. Stefano Quisquina*, 59, 68–71; Massari, *Wonderful Life*, 41. Of course, agrarian revolutionism had been endemic in Sicily long before 1860. See Hobsbawm, *Primitive Rebels*, 94–96.

32. Quoted in Angiolini, *Socialismo e Socialisti*, 235.

33. Jacini, *Inchiesta Agraria*, 32.

34. See Briggs, *Italian Passage*, 18–19, for the wider mutual aid movement; for the workers' circle in Santo Stefano, see the deliberations of the city council, February 12, 1881, Archivio Comunale.

35. Renda, *Fasci Siciliani*; Spampinato et al., *Fasci Siciliani*; Hobsbawm's sprightly assessment of the *fasci* is found in *Primitive Rebels*, 93–107.

36. Messina, *Caso Panepinto*, 11–12.

37. Ibid., 12–15.

38. Meetings of the municipal council, Santo Stefano, February 2, 1891, February 14–15, 1892, Archivio Comunale. Panepinto's election reflected long-standing class and political conflicts characterizing village life. Indeed, the later creation of the *fascio* can in part be seen as an extension of these much older divisions.

39. Renda, *Fasci Siciliani*, 74; Messina, *Caso Panepinto*, 34. Messina's study indicates the presence of messengers from Palermo; Renda's does not, although both use the same reports from the subprefect of Bivona as evidence.

40. Messina, *Caso Panepinto*, 34-35; Renda, *Fasci Siciliani*, 74. Soon after the formation of Santo Stefano's *fascio*, Panepinto made trips with Bernandino Verro and Nicolò Barbato to many of the neighboring villages. The *fascio* built upon a legacy of radical political movements occurring in the 1860s and 1870s. Cerrito, *Radicalismo e Socialismo*, notes that in 1874 Santo Stefano had an Associazione Internazionale dei Lavoratori, while police in Cianciana, Bivona, and Alessandria della Rocca complained about Internazionale influence. Cianciana had a section of the Internazionale around 1876.

41. Messina, *Caso Panepinto*, 38-41. The *fascio* was open to "all workers of any trade or anyone concerned with the betterment of the working class." Forbidden from membership were "those who had betrayed the scope of the *fascio*" and "all who had become unworthy of public esteem, including vagabonds, *maffiosi* [sic], and all men of bad deeds."

42. Renda, *Fasci Siciliani*, 83, 121, 125, 155. Renda's excellent study curiously misses the formation of a *fascio* in Bivona (note especially his chronological listing of *fascio* formation, pp. 339-43). See Messina, *Caso Panepinto*, 50, and the *Acts of the Subprefect of Bivona, 1893-94*, folio 107, Archivio di Stato di Agrigento, for activities in Bivona.

43. Statement by Giovanni Vaccaro, a socialist activist in Tampa, in *Il Martire*, May 16, 1912.

44. Speciale, "La Stampa Nazionale," in Giarrizzo and Manacorda, *Fasci Siciliani*, II, 177-207; Mack Smith, *Italy*, 174.

45. Renda, *Fasci Siciliani*, 303-4, 329; Mack Smith, *Modern Sicily*, 485.

46. The official files of military and political decisions taken with reference to the *fasci* of the Magazzolo villages are contained in folio 107, Archivio di Stato di Agrigento. See also Messina, *Caso Panepinto*, 50-51. "In case of resistance," wrote the local prefect, "you must proceed to arrest any person resisting, together with pertinent correspondence. . . ."

47. Folio 107, Archivio di Stato di Agrigento; Mack Smith, *Modern Sicily*, 485. Among the lists of arrested individuals appeared names that would soon become familiar in Florida: Pitisci, Cannella, Castellano, Reina, Zambito, Giunta, Guggino, and Massaro, to name a few.

48. Carocci, *Storia d'Italia*, 68.

49. MacDonald, "Italy's Rural Social Structure," 437-56; MacDonald, "Agricultural Organization," 61-75; Barton, *Peasants and Strangers*, 27-47.

50. Donna Gabaccia, "Migration and Militance: A Case Study," paper presented at the American Historical Association meeting, San Francisco, December 29, 1984. Also see Gabaccia, "Padrone Slaves."

51. Messina, *Caso Panepinto*, 56. Hobsbawm was perhaps the first to note that socialists were not completely crushed after the *fasci* were disbanded; see *Primitive Rebels*, 101-4.

52. Messina, *Caso Panepinto*, 73-77, 77-78. An extended discussion of the peasant league phenomenon is contained in Marino, *Movimento Contadino*, 28-34. In Santo Stefano workers released balloons and cried, *"Viva il Socialismo!"* at their league's inauguration. Also see de Stefano and Oddio, *Storia della Sicilia*, 402, 405-7, 410, for more on the cooperative movement and the *leghe*.

53. The socialism espoused by many Sicilians, including Panepinto, was the "rural

socialism" of Cammareri Scurti. This particular brand championed programs that sought to better the wretched conditions of *contadini*, especially in terms of land redistribution, increased access to credit, and improved educational opportunities. See Marino, *Movimento Contadino*, 30–32, 95, which labels Panepinto as "one of the most characteristic exponents of Sicilian 'rural socialism'"; Renda, *Socialisti e Cattolici*, 280.

54. Messina, *Caso Panepinto*, 96; *Il Martire*, May 16, 1913. The membership of Alessandria della Rocca's League of Democracy was present at this gathering.

55. Messina, *Ricerca Municipale*, 58–59.

56. Nicotri, *Storia della Sicilia*, 203; Renda, *Socialisti e Cattolici*, 74. Panepinto's newspaper began in late 1902 and received its support from the Circolo Socialista Bivonese of Santo Stefano, among other area groups.

57. Nicotri, *Storia della Sicilia*, 204; Messina, *Caso Panepinto*, 187–212. The Stefanesi in Tampa formed a Gruppo Lorenzo Panepinto to carry on Panepinto's work and published a commemorative journal, *Il Martire*, on the anniversary of his death for a number of years (copies are available at PKY).

58. Interview with Frank Giunta, July 20, 1980. Some sources have spoken of Panepinto's "messianic" qualities. See Marino, *Movimento Contadino*, 84.

59. *Il Martire*, May 16, 1912; Messina, *Caso Panepinto*, 156; *L'Ora*, May 16, 1911.

60. Messina, *Caso Panepinto*, 229–30. *Il Martire*, May 16, 1913, reports the details of collections taken in support of the work of Scurti.

61. Cinel, *Italy to San Francisco*, 5–99, contains an extended dicussion of the motivations underlying return migration. Also see Cerase, *Emigrazione di Ritorno*, and Balletta, *Banco di Napoli*.

62. Ministero di Agricoltura, *Statistica della Emigrazione Italiana*, 86–87.

63. Renda, *Emigrazione in Sicilia*, 52. Additional discussion of Sicilian emigration rates is contained in Martellone, *Siciliani fuori*, 30–36.

64. Harney, "Boarding and Belonging," 8–37. Harney's pioneering studies are among the few to explore this formative period of emigration.

65. See, for example, *Liber Baptizatorum, Sancti Stephani ad Quisquinam*, La Madre della Chiesa, which includes baptismal records sent by emigrants from various southeastern locations and from Ybor City, West Tampa, Elizabeth Street (New York), and Pensacola. Artisans were heavily represented in the movement to New York City. Donna Gabaccia's contention that peasants and artisans tended to select different destinations and consequently produce distinct new-world communities appears to be born out by the Santo Stefano experience. See Gabaccia, "Padrone Slaves," and "Migration and Peasant Militance," 67–80.

66. Massari, *Comunità Italiana*, 697–707.

67. *Atlantic and Gulf Coast Canal*, 35; interview with Philip Spoto, June 30, 1979; interview with Joe Valenti, March 27, 1980; Massari, *Wonderful Life*, 63–64.

68. Dodson, "St. Cloud Sugar Plantation," 356–70; interview with Philip Spoto, June 30, 1979.

69. Salomone-Marino, *Customs and Habits*, 46.

70. Interview with Philip Spoto, June 30, 1979.

71. FWP, "Life History of Mr. John Cacciatore"; Massari, *Wonderful Life*, 63.

72. FWP, "Life History of Mr. John Cacciatore."

73. Massari, *Wonderful Life*, 41, 69–70.

74. Interview with Domenico Giunta, May 18, 1984.

75. Massari, *Wonderful Life*, 46–47.

76. Interview with Giovanni Frisco, March 18, 1981; interview with Alberto Capodici, March 18, 1981.

77. Interview with Paul Longo, June 1, 1979.

78. Schneider and Schneider, *Culture and Political Economy*, 81–109. The Schneiders examine the key cultural codes of honor, friendship, and cleverness in their study of Sicilian society.

79. *Liber Baptizatorum, Sancti Stephani ad Quisquinam*, La Madre della Chiesa. The authors saw the War Monument during their research trips.

80. Interview with Francesca Adamo Tagliarini, May 22, 1982; interview with Nina Ferlita, April 25, 1980.

81. Messina, *Caso Panepinto*, 233–36; Salvemini, *Origins of Fascism*, 226–27; Mack Smith, *Modern Sicily*, 502–9.

82. Messina, *Caso Panepinto*, 239–40. Also see Sicily Presidenza, *Elezioni in Sicilia*, 451–70, for returns in other elections and villages. The 1947 election, for example, saw 63 percent of Santo Stefano's voters favoring the leftist Blocco del Popolo (composed of the Socialist party and the Italian Communist party).

83. Interview with Antonio Ferlita, May 6, 1981; Bugea, "S. Stefano di Quisquina."

2 Tampa's Evolution as an Urban Center

Tampa is politically southern, industrially northern, and has a distinct Spanish atmosphere.

Florida: A Guide to the Southernmost State

By 1900 Tampa had become the leading manufacturing city in Florida. Its claim to that title rested not with its production of steel, automobiles, or shoes, but rather with cigars, millions of pure Havana cigars. By virtue of its industrial bookends of Ybor City and West Tampa, it stood as the leading center in the United States of high-quality, hand-rolled cigars. Tampa had become the celebrated "Smokeless City of Smokes," attracting thousands of immigrants, including Sicilian hill villagers, to its environs. Its development as a complex urban center determined much of the social, economic, and physical world that both immigrants and industrialists confronted upon their arrival in Florida.

Tampa's evolution from an obscure port town into an urban-industrial center was neither unique nor unusual in this era which some historians have designated the "Rise of the City." The character of Tampa's industry and the composition of its work force, however, shaped the city in distinctive ways. From the perspective of labor, social, and southern history, the city was an island: it boasted an impressive manufacturing plant located in an overwhelmingly agrarian state; its skilled industrial work force was comprised almost exclusively of immigrants who resided in a region dominated by southern white Protestants and Afro-Americans; its industry, financed and designed by Spaniards and Cubans, existed in an economic climate increasingly controlled by northern wealth; its cigar factories accentuated preindustrial rhythms in an economy obsessed with time clocks and schedules. Cigars so dominated the area that when Ybor City—a company town built anew, a town without Irish or German immigrant predecessors—sneezed, Tampa caught pneumonia. The history of Tampa after the settlement of Ybor City is largely a chronicle of a southern city struggling with the dynamic changes that an expanding industry and a diverse immigrant work force introduced. Yet to know Ybor City one first must comprehend the larger milieu within which it evolved.

Tampa owes its modern origins to the federal government's decision in 1824 to build a military cantonment, Fort Brooke, as a bulwark for south Florida.[1] The fort evolved from a primitive beachhead into a crude community, one that grew increasingly important each year, both in military and economic terms. Militarily the outpost served as a deterrent to the disgruntled Seminoles; economically the bivouac functioned as a trading post and social center, and as the leading edge of a Florida frontier not yet conquered.[2]

After the Second Seminole War (1835–42) Florida's first families, future dynasties of power and prestige, began to develop their small fiefdoms. Captain James McKay, Howell Lykes, William Hooker, and Jake Summerlin inaugurated a profitable cattle trade with Cuba and oversaw commercial empires fed by territorial growth, rising beef prices, and timely marriages. The last confrontation with the Seminoles, the Billy Bowlegs War (1855–58), was fought largely to decide whether the future of south Florida would be determined by Indians or cattlemen.[3]

One can never isolate Tampa from the Deep South, especially in terms of power structure—the slave-holding cliques—and Old South values. Slaves constituted one-third of Hillsborough County's population in the period 1840–60, and slavery also occupied an important niche in Tampa. When the Deep South seceded, white Tampans marched lockstep with the Confederacy.[4]

Tampa, a community of only 885 persons in 1861, braced for the inevitable blockade. The people adjusted to a war fought hundreds of miles away. When blockade runners brought their screw steamers and clipper ships through Union lines—and they usually did—Tampans wanted for little. But increasing sacrifices demanded from Richmond and scarcity resulting from a long war determined the rhythms of the city. When Tampa finally fell, more with a whimper than a bang, on May 6, 1864, northern troops discovered a sickly, half-deserted town. After one day the conquerors left. "The appearance of Tampa is desolate in the extreme," wrote a Union officer.[5]

The war cost Tampa little in physical terms; in emotional and economic terms, however, the defeat drained the community. For decades, like Southerners elsewhere, Tampans mourned the Confederate dead and cursed Black Republicans and Radical Rule during Reconstruction. To dull the memories of the bitter present Tampa organized elaborate chivalric festivals. Yet this retreat to a halcyon past that never was could not erase the realities of depression, yellow fever, and poverty.[6]

By any index bad times gripped Tampa in the 1860s and 1870s. The town's basic economic structure remained unchanged: yeoman agrarianism supported by village mercantilism. The population mirrored the malaise, falling from 885 inhabitants in 1860 to 796 in 1870, then to 720 in 1880. Adding injury to insult, a succession of yellow fever epidemics scourged the community.[7]

The decade of the 1870s saw the nadir of Tampa's misfortunes. Few visitors rhapsodized the present; no Chamber of Commerce championed the future. "I am prepared to state that the means of transportation to and from Tampa are so limited and uncertain," moaned a treasury agent in 1875, "that people are leaving there and going to other places. . . . it seems to me that of necessity, that port [Tampa] must continue to go backwards for years to come."[8] Naturalist Kirk Munroe recorded his impression of the city in 1882: "Tampa once reached is found to be a sleepy, shabby southern town, with wide streets innocent of other pavement than that offered by deep, loose, white sands. . . . [Some] 800 inhabitants . . . transact whatever business they may have on hand in the leisurely manner peculiar to southerners, with whom neither time nor money seems to be an object."[9]

Tampa's misfortunes reflected the general hard times of Florida. If the state escaped the ravages of Sherman, it was because it had too little to be destroyed. The Sunshine State's principal assets to the Confederacy —salt and cattle—would be of little help in building a new order. Florida's major weaknesses—a scarcity of people and the absence of industry—augured a bleak economic future.

Florida's composition mirrored the postwar South: a dependence upon agricultural pursuits and extractive industries; a high percentage of black inhabitants who strode the bottom rail and faced a rigid color line; and an absence of cities in general and immigrants in particular. The state's most important urban centers in 1880 included Key West, Jacksonville, and Pensacola, none of which numbered more than 10,000 persons in 1880 and all of which lay at the state's periphery. Immigrants constituted less than 4 percent of the state's population; fewer than 1,600 German and Irish immigrants lived in Florida, a remarkably low figure even for the South.[10]

In 1880 the 58,560-square-mile peninsula contained 269,493 persons; only Nevada, Oregon, and Delaware claimed fewer residents. The state capital at Tallahassee, little more than a village, counted only 2,494 inhabitants. Most Floridians lived in the Panhandle and in northern Florida. Had Frederick Jackson Turner looked southward rather than westward in 1880, he would have discovered a state emotionally and physically tied to the frontier. The vast territory south of Tampa and Orlando was still largely uninhabited, with only a handful of Seminole Indians and plume hunters living in the subtropical region.[11]

If Florida had a scarcity of people it certainly possessed an abundance of land. State leaders had long defined poor transportation as Florida's greatest handicap to development, and they determined to solve this nagging problem by utilizing the state's land reserves. In 1855 the General Assembly organized the Internal Improvement Fund as the agency to promote railroads, dig canals, and reclaim swamplands. But grandiose antebellum dreams were dashed upon the rocks of unscrupulous railroad promoters and the exigencies of war. By 1881 Florida teetered on the edge of bankruptcy, a result of scant revenues and avaricious railroad promoters who left the Improvement Fund with an encumbered debt of one million dollars. To rescue the state's faltering finances, Governor William B. Bloxham urged European and American financiers to invest in Florida's future, holding out as an incentive fifteen million acres of the public domain.[12] The great 1880s barbecue followed.

Hamilton Disston, a thirty-six-year-old scion of a Philadelphia tool empire, struck a most lucrative deal with the governor of Florida in 1881. The trustees of the Internal Improvement Fund accepted Disston's offer of one million dollars for four million acres of south-central Florida real estate. Disston had previously visited the state to fish for tarpon; he now announced more ambitious plans to reclaim the Everglades, dredge the Kissimmee River, and establish agricultural colonies. Soon crews of black and immigrant workers began cutting canals, experimenting with thirty varieties of sugarcane and rice, and constructing rail lines south to Kissimmee and Narcoossee, heretofore cow towns. In time Disston established the agricultural community of St. Cloud and the narrow-gauge St. Cloud and Sugar Belt Railroad. Italian immigrants arrived during the 1880s to harvest sugarcane and labor on the railroads. Disston's greatest accomplishment would ultimately be not what he did in the Kissimmee River valley but what he achieved for Florida in opening the state to outside investors.[13]

Few individuals watched Disston's maneuverings more closely than the financier Henry Bradley Plant, who in 1881 was preparing his own investment invasion. Plant, like most shapers of Florida history, was born somewhere else. His upbringing in Connecticut, where he worked as a cabin boy for the New Haven Steamboat Company, cast him in the classic mold of a New England robber baron. His career began in the Northeast, with the New York and New Haven Railroad, but culminated in the Southeast, where he revolutionized the transportation industry.[14]

In early 1882 Plant acquired charter to the South Florida Railroad Company, which had just completed a track between Orlando and Kissimmee. Soon thereafter company officials negotiated land rights to the Jacksonville, Tampa, and Key West Railroad. The latter's charter promised lucrative rewards—13,840 acres of land for every mile of track laid; however, the grant would expire in late January 1884. "It is said the railroad is about to pierce this wilderness," rejoiced the *Tampa Sunland Tribune*. Driving his crews relentlessly from Sanford and Tampa, Plant finished the Jacksonville-Kissimmee-Tampa connection with only hours to spare. "Tampa never saw so many strange faces," remarked the local paper.[15]

The Plant system continued to crisscross the state, and Florida richly rewarded the company with two million acres from the public domain. By the time of its founder's death in 1899, Plant's company had laid nearly 1,200 miles of track, transforming transportation and communication in Florida. "How the railroad kills time and space!" exclaimed the *Ocala Banner*.[16] Plant astonished everyone when in 1887 he proclaimed his latest undertaking—construction of the ornately lavish, Moorish, three-million-dollar Tampa Bay Hotel. The city never did become the Newport of the South; and if his hotel became a white elephant, he was able to make his fortune in other financial spheres.[17]

Plant announced plans in 1887 to extend his rail line along Old Tampa Bay and unveiled his latest creation, Port Tampa. Despite its aesthetic

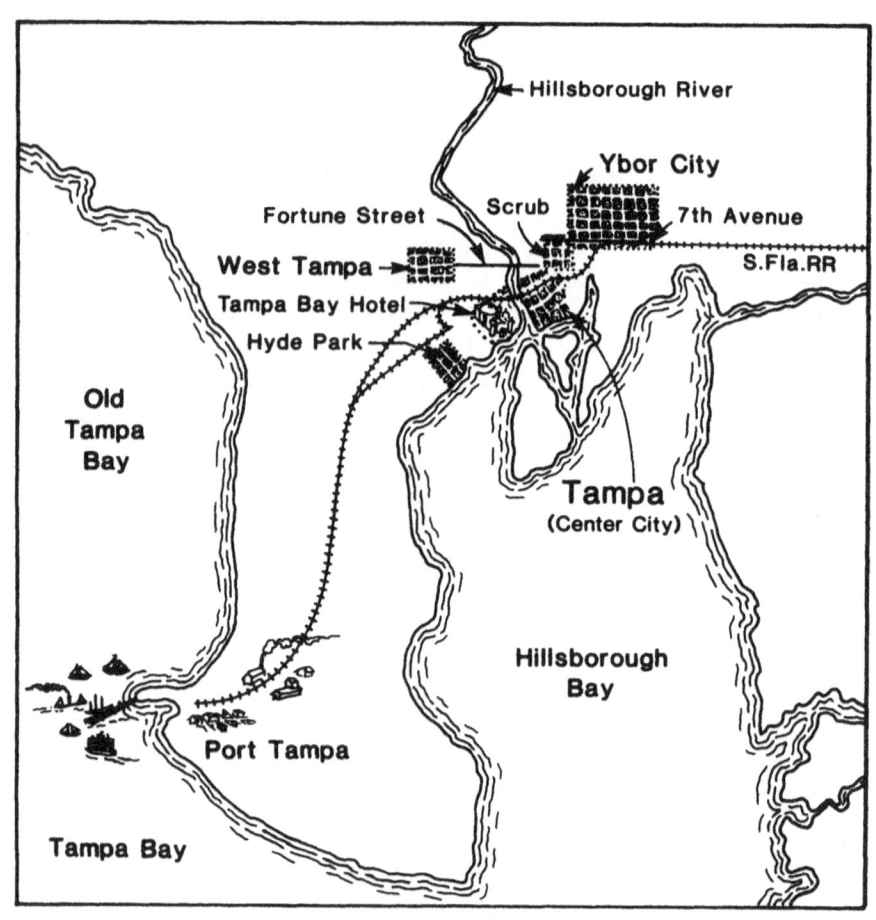

Map 2. Tampa and Vicinity, 1900.

attributes, Tampa Bay was quite shallow. The peninsula at Black Point, however, offered a deeper natural harbor, and at the end of this desolate tip six miles from Tampa a port city was erected. With some astute lobbying by Congressman Stephen Sparkman, who also happened to be the attorney for Plant's railroad, and a national defense scare generated by the Spanish-American War, Port Tampa received generous appropriations. It served as Tampa's Ellis Island, customs house, quarantine station, and phosphate docks. Port Tampa remained a separate, unincorporated city, not merging with Tampa until 1961.[18]

In 1880 Tampa stood as an isolated provincial village, "an island community," in Robert Wiebe's paradigm. Beginning in the 1880s a transportation revolution (internal and external), demographic increases (international and domestic), technological advancements, and industrial developments helped transform Tampa from an obscure, self-contained village into a city boasting factories, trolleys, and frequent exchanges with the outside world. Many of Tampa's struggles during the next half century resulted from the collision between the city's traditional elites (entrenched families, commercial and civic leaders) attempting to retain power and those elements threatening to alter the status quo (immigrants, blacks, and industrialization).[19]

Rapid demographic change, the creation of new neighborhoods and subcommunities, and the rise of a city with a modern infrastructure characterized the period 1880–1930 in Tampa. From a village of 720 persons in 1880 the city climbed rapidly to 15,839 inhabitants in 1900 and over 100,000 residents in 1930 (see Table 3). In 1884 a visitor had bewailed the plight of the struggling village, but two years later the same person expressed astonishment at the new Tampa: "Trim vessels sail away to sea from new wharves. New sidewalks, new hotels, new railroads, waterworks, a Board of Trade, an Opera House, new manufacturers, new business blocks, fast steam presses for newspapers are the order for the day."[20]

A new business era dawned in Tampa—begun in New York, perfected in Chicago, tempered by Washington, D.C., and tailored to local mores. Increasingly the decisions made on Wall Street, State Street, and Pennsylvania Avenue shaped Tampa's economic fortunes. The rise of the corporation signified a shift of power from family hands to new economic entities—witness the transition of the Plant Investment Company to the Atlantic Coast Line Railroad Company in 1902. National and international events affected the course of the city. In the spring and summer

TABLE 3 Tampa, Population Growth, 1880–1940

Year	Population	Percent increase by decade
1880	720	—
1890	5,532	668
1900	15,839	186
1910	37,782	137
1920	51,608	36.6
1930	101,161	48.8
1940	108,391	7.00

SOURCE: *Tenth Census*, Table 3; *Eleventh Census*, Table 20; *Twelfth Census*, Table 27; *Fourteenth Census: Population*, Table 10; *Fifteenth Census: Population*, Table 2; *Sixteenth Census: Population*, Table C-40.

of 1898 Tampa served as the port of debarkation for 66,000 soldiers destined for Cuba. Chaos reigned, but the alarming lack of preparedness and natural limits of the harbor brought an unexpected windfall of federal grants and subsidies. Following the war Congress deepened the harbor and helped modernize the rail and port facilities. World War I also stimulated the local economy.[21]

During the late nineteenth century Tampa acquired the trappings of a modern city. Street lights, gas mains, and sidewalks provided urban amenities and services to a new Tampa. By the 1890s residents and businesses could reasonably expect fresh water pumped from the newly completed waterworks. A succession of bond issues addressed the pressing needs of an urban population. Tile sewers carried away effluent, although it continued to be emptied into the Hillsborough River. After experimenting with cypress paving blocks (which popped up when wet) and Bartow clay (made from phosphate pebbles which became soggy with rain), the city inaugurated an extensive campaign in 1904 to pave the streets with vitrified brick.[22] Soon electric lights and telephone poles, automobiles and trolleys, sewers and skyscrapers altered the city's landscape and life-style.[23]

Just as Plant's railroad fueled the economic expansion of Tampa, so too did the electric trolley facilitate the city's internal growth. In 1892 C. W. Chapin, a New York financier, helped organize the Tampa Suburban Company, which in 1894 consolidated into the Consumers Electric Light and Street Railway Company. The trolley, proclaimed the *Morning Tribune* in 1895, "reaches the limits of every portion of the city, and as it extends its projection of steel it carries the town with its extension."[24] In the late 1890s the Consumers Company was sold to the Tampa Electric Company (TECO), a firm controlled by Stone and Webster of Boston. Peter O. Knight became TECO's first vice-president. By 1900 over twenty-one miles of track carried passengers to every corner of the urban landscape, and on the eve of World War I, Tampa boasted an urban grid of forty-seven miles of trolley line, which included sixty-seven coach cars.[25]

The trolley and later the Model T served a social purpose as well. Their arteries recast living patterns, created new neighborhoods, and further segregated Tampans into distinct enclaves.[26] Spatially the Tampa of 1900 was very different from the community of 1880. Since the founding of Fort Brooke in 1824 the city center had clustered around a few square blocks. The trolley and new social dictates changed that. Tampa was becoming a city of neighborhoods, where residency depended upon ethnic background, religion, economic status, and race. Hyde Park, Tampa Heights, Seminole Heights, Palma Ceia, and New Suburb Beautiful offered the city's middle and upper classes a peaceful setting, made attractive by its schools, well-built bungalows, and access to good roads.[27]

Tampa's urban-ecological portrait differed sharply from the metropolitan growth of the Northeast and Midwest. In cities such as Chicago and Cleveland a diversified industrial work force, a heterogeneous population, and fragmented residential patterns accompanied urban expansion.[28] Tampa's immigrant population was relatively homogeneous in comparison to other industrial communities. Virtually no immigrants settled in Tampa prior to the 1880s; hence Cubans, Spaniards, and Italians faced no competition from entrenched groups. Moreover, one can argue that Ybor City's Latins were culturally sympathetic to one another, at least when compared to the disparate ethnic elements of Detroit, Chicago, or Cleveland. Finally, Ybor City evolved as a clearly defined residential locale exclusively inhabited by Latins, unlike the mixed use of space characterizing much of urban America.

Tampa's political structure between the Bourbon era and the 1920s represented what social scientist Daniel Elazar described as a "traditionalistic political culture." Rooted in the Old South's paternalism and the New South's acquisitiveness, this political culture embodied "an older, pre-commercial attitude that accepts a hierarchical society as part of the ordered nature of things."[29] Politics offered a sounding board for certain established groups (old entrenched families), a springboard for certain factions (the new middle class of professionals and businessmen), and a closed door to minorities (Afro-Americans and Latin immigrants). To be sure this system resulted from conflict, but debate raged over the means, not the end, of economic-political control. Tampans vigorously argued over such issues as the city manager system of government and even experimented with the commission system for a brief period, managing to convert it to their conservative objectives.

Although the Democratic party reigned supreme in Florida, it exercised little power or discipline because of the decentralized nature of the state and the lack of any real opposition. Debates therefore occurred between elite-dominated factions and personalities within one party. The commercial-civic elite comprised a coalition of pioneer families—owners of the powerful establishment papers, the *Tampa Morning Tribune* and the *Tampa Daily Times*; leaders of newly organized corporations; and members of organizations such as the Tampa Board of Trade (the forerunner of the Chamber of Commerce) and the Cherokee Club (a private association of leading businessmen). This coalition espoused change, especially new economic growth, but wished to retain strict control over new development.

Peter Oliphant Knight embodied the power of the modern Tampa establishment, providing a transitional link between the old Tampa family network and the new bureaucracies. Born in Pennsylvania, Knight practiced law briefly in Indiana before journeying to the frontier outpost of Fort Myers, Florida, in 1883. His oratorical ability and legal mind quickly marked him as a rising star: he became the first lawyer to try a case in Fort Myers, helping to incorporate that embryonic coastal village as a city in 1885; he later became its mayor and representative in Tallahassee. In 1891 Knight moved up Florida's west coast to Tampa and in a remarkably short time established himself as one of the city's most powerful attorneys, a courthouse lawyer with considerable clout at the state capitol as well. In particular he demonstrated special expertise in his work for large corporations. During World War I the federal government persuaded Knight to construct a shipbuilding facility; and in 1919, as counsel for the area's major phosphate owners, he led a vicious campaign against the miners who were then on strike.[30] In June 1919 Knight commented, "To hear some of the flannel-mouthed, pin-headed, brainless anarchistic, bolsheviki labor agitators talk about questions of this kind [the War Labor Board], you would think we were living in Russia."[31]

If Peter O. Knight typified the new civic leader, Donald Brenham

McKay personified the old Tampa establishment. The grandson of Captain James McKay, a legendary seaman-financier who established a dynasty in Florida, D.B. inherited his grandfather's money and demonstrated remarkable talents in two consuming enterprises: journalism and politics. He became the editor, publisher, and owner of the *Tampa Daily Times*, from 1898–1933, in addition to serving as mayor of the city for a record five terms. McKay first reached office in 1910, on the White Municipal party ticket, a "reform" intended to eliminate the "corruptible" black vote and allow "responsible" whites to debate the real issues. During a bitter 1901 cigar industry strike he led a citizens' committee that forcibly kidnapped union leaders and shanghaied them to Honduras. As mayor he pledged to act with the same vigilance.[32]

The typical city officeholder during this period was a businessman of southern or midwestern background who worked in the downtown district and lived in Hyde Park. Although mayors or city councilmen generally reflected Anglo backgrounds, it was possible for others to succeed—if they conformed to the social and economic value systems. Such was the case of Herman Glogowski. Born in Prussia, he immigrated to New York City in 1859, later migrating to Gainesville, Florida, where he married Bertha Browne. In 1883 the couple moved to Tampa, opening a clothing store. Glogowski, a German Jew, moved freely and comfortably within Tampa's power structure, not an uncommon phenomenon in southern seaport communities. He became the first president of Tampa's German-American Club, joined the Knights of Pythias, and ascended to a thirty-second-degree Mason. He served three times as Tampa's mayor between 1889 and 1895.[33]

New routes to political power emerged as the city changed under the impact of industrialization and immigration. Nowhere was this more clearly seen than in the symbiotic relationship that evolved between politics and crime. Beginning in the late 1880s *bolita* (Spanish for "little ball"; a version of the numbers game) captivated Latin immigrants. By 1900 *bolita*'s popularity had spread to other neighborhoods, particularly Afro-American sections. Gambling had become a profitable cottage industry. *Bolita* was dependent upon one commodity which only Anglo Tampa could supply: protection. The key individual in this intricate accommodation was Charlie Wall.

Born in 1880, the son of the distinguished physician and civic leader, Dr. John P. Wall, Charlie appeared destined for a promising career. An uncle by marriage and an early city powerbroker, Dr. Howell T. Lykes, extended his connections. For reasons that psychobiographers might answer better, Wall became drawn to the gambling dens of Ybor City. Early in the twentieth century he ceased being merely an interested observer and became a leader. With important familial contacts at the city and state level, Wall came to exercise formidable power. Standing six-foot-two and garbed in expensive linen suits, he was an imposing figure.[34]

An early portrait of Wall's *bolita* empire survives. In 1912 Claude L'Engle, the crusading editor and publisher of the *Jacksonville Dixie*, dispatched Charles E. Jones to investigate *bolita* in Tampa. In his subsequent article, subtitled "Sodom or Gomorrah—or Both," Jones expressed outrage at what he saw. "Tampa is reeking in crime, and gamblers in the open operate in various parts of the city." He outlined his findings: "Gambling with its plain and fancy trimmings was flourishing in Tampa under an agreement between Mr. Charlie Wall, . . . and the executive branch of the city of Tampa, by virtue of which Mr. Wall was assured a monopoly in the gambling line. . . ." Jones visited several gambling parlors in Ybor City and purchased *bolita* chances. His investigation ended when a spectator identified him as a reporter. "A crowd of fully 200 had gathered about this time and I [had] been knocked to my knees. . . ." The police intervened, arresting Jones for carrying a weapon. Tampa, concluded Jones, justifiably deserved the sobriquet of "the most wicked city in the United States."[35]

Reformers may have decried the wickedness of *bolita* but little was done to curb its influence. *Bolita* and politics made comfortable bedfellows. Ybor City, with its densely populated neighborhoods and a citizenry that viewed politics cynically, supplied gangsters and politicians with a suitable environment. Profits generated by expanding markets and new businesses (prostitution, bootlegging, slot machines) secured the election of compliant candidates at city hall, the sheriff's department, and the state's attorney's office. A coalition of Latin *bolita* barons, Charlie Wall, pliable immigrants, and acquiescent officeholders conspired so efficiently that they virtually controlled both city and county politics between the 1920s and the 1940s. Many observers staunchly believe that during these decades there was not a single honest election in Tampa/Hillsborough County. Wall's creation controlled the electoral process to its own, not the immigrants', benefit, but Anglo elites worried about its impact on their power and Tampa's reputation.

Tampans had always stressed the importance of the city's image. The rhetoric of boosterism that emanated from commercial and civic agencies since before the turn of the century was now unrestrained. "It is an undisputed fact that the Queen of the Gulf [Tampa] is the most progressive city south of the Mason-Dixon line," suggested the *Morning Tribune* in 1896.[36] David Goldfield has asserted that while boosterism had deep roots in American history, its southern variant contained a distinctive style. "Boosterism, like its partner evangelical Protestantism, thus 'purified' the southern city of its class and racial divisiveness, uniting all under the banner of the growth ethic."[37] By the 1920s boosterism reached feverish proportions as papers trumpeted the new Florida of good roads, designed communities, and leisure/tourism.

While boosterism attempted to mask class and racial divisiveness, Tampa's population growth steadily undermined these efforts. The inception of Ybor City in 1886 abruptly transformed Tampa from an economy centered around yeoman self-sufficiency to a dynamic manufacturing base. It also diversified the population mixture (see Table 4). By 1890 Tampa (which then included Ybor City) contained 5,532 inhabitants, over half of whom were immigrants and their children. For the next half century the city's image and economic health depended upon cigar manufacturing. By 1900 almost three-fourths of Tampa's 15,839 residents claimed first- or second-generation immigrant status or were of Afro-American background. In 1900 foreign-born and Afro-American adult males overwhelmed white native adult males, 3,267 to 1,672. If West Tampa, an industrial enclave incorporated into Tampa in 1924, were included, the profile would be even more dramatic. In 1910 only 626 residents of West Tampa's 8,258 inhabitants were native whites of native

TABLE 4 Tampa Population Characteristics, 1890–1940

Year	Native white–native parentage	Native white–foreign parentage	Foreign-born white	Black	Foreign-born Cubans	Foreign-born Spaniards	Foreign-born Italians
1890[a]	2,473	742	1,427	1,632	2,424	233	56
1900	4,557	2,497	4,371	4,382	3,533	963	1,315
1910	12,037	6,857	9,896	8,951	3,859	2,337	2,519
1920	17,542	11,837	10,666	11,531	3,459	2,726	2,817
1930[b]	43,096	22,296	14,521	21,172	5,112	3,457	2,817
1940	50,201	23,760	11,082	23,331	3,317	2,600	2,684

SOURCE: *Eleventh Census*, I, Table 23; *Twelfth Census: Population*, II, Table 27; *Thirteenth Census: Population*, II, Table 21; *Fourteenth Census: Population*, III, Table 10; *Fifteenth Census: Population*, III, pt. 1, 15; *Sixteenth Census: Population*, Table C-40.
[a]1890 figures are for Hillsborough County.
[b]Includes West Tampa, incorporated into Tampa in 1925.

parentage.[38] Yet while Tampa's industrial prestige was due to its immigrant workers, the city's native white power structure jealously guarded and retained control, and thus resembled its New South counterparts.

Three distinctive traits characterized the southern urban experience: ruralism, biracialism, and the lingering handicap of economic dependency. Tampa's experience deviated sharply from this formula, but the vestiges of the city's southern traditions and environment must be understood within the context of these attributes. The commencement of cigar manufacturing in the 1880s did not suddenly divorce the city from its rural environment. Indeed, industrial development remained restricted to the tightly defined barrios of Ybor City and West Tampa. If one examined Tampa in the absence of these immigrant industrial enclaves, the city would have resembled a typical southern community. Instead Tampa was an urban-industrial island in an agrarian South.

Geographically Tampa existed as a relatively small-sized city within an immense county. In 1910 its boundaries encompassed a meager 8.6 of Hillsborough County's 1,655 square miles. Through annexation Tampa grew to 26 square miles by 1930, while Hillsborough, through losses from the creation of Pinellas County, had stabilized at 1,235 square miles.[39] Vast portions of the county consisted of stretches of cypress stands, hardwood hammocks, swamplands, and pine flatlands. However, until the post–World War II era the vast majority of the county's residents lived in Tampa. Consequently, the county's rural-agrarian environment played a major role in allowing residents to invest in relatively inexpensive land and to expand outward with minimal difficulty.

Many Tampans reacted violently to changes occurring within the city and the county. Hillsborough County cattlemen, who historically had exercised great influence in the future of the area, felt estranged by the influx of immigrants, capital, and technology. They successfully fought the closing of the open ranges until the 1940s, so potent were their numbers in the legislature. Many powerful Tampa families, such as the Lykes and McKays, controlled considerable amounts of land and cattle in the region. A classic illustration of the town-country tension can be seen in several 1890s incidents in which county cattlemen dynamited electric dams built on the Hillsborough River because they felt the power stations represented an intrusion and a threat to their rural domains.[40]

Drawn by expanding economic opportunities, Tampa received a steady influx of rural blacks and whites, predominantly from north Florida, Alabama, and Georgia. These newcomers helped shape the character of the city and the county. Violence accentuated the rawness of social relations, and it was a rare Monday headline that did not feature a murder or knifing. "Tampa is establishing a reputation for being a very wicked city," complained the *Ocala Mail and Express* in 1897. "She has surpassed all records for brutal fights, desperate deeds, ugly murders. . . ."[41] Tampa was not immune to lynch law and communal justice. In 1882 General Joseph B. Wall, an attorney of local fame, helped a Tampa mob lynch Charles Owens, accused of assaulting a white woman (Wall allegedly tied the noose).[42] Such vindication of "southern honor" was not uncommon in Tampa. In 1899 M. J. Christopher, a black newspaper editor newly arrived from Brunswick, Georgia, antagonized the Tampa police force in a series of published indictments. He was shot and killed.[43] In July 1903 officials released George House, a black man accused of rape, to an awaiting mob who immediately castrated and killed him. "The race question, so far as Tampa is concerned, has been solved," crowed the *Morning Tribune*.[44] In 1910 a mob intercepted a wagon holding two Italian immigrants accused of murder and promptly lynched them.[45]

Tampa's Afro-American community grew rapidly after the Civil War as rural blacks from Georgia and Florida moved to southern cities such as Tampa. In 1890 there were 1,632 blacks in Tampa, a figure that increased to 8,951 by 1910 and 21,172 by 1930.[46] The proportion of Afro-Americans in Tampa has remained reasonably constant, running between 20 and 25 percent throughout the twentieth century.

Jim Crow legislation, not the technology of the streetcar, determined Afro-American residential patterns. By the 1890s a strict separation of the races characterized Tampa's living spaces. Identifiable black sections emerged, typically located in the least desirable sections of the city. An area northeast of the business district, then on the periphery of settlement, became the city's principal ghetto. The Scrub offered its inhabitants few urban amenities. By 1900 several other black neighborhoods had evolved, most notably College Hill, Central Avenue, and Dobyville.[47]

Blacks in Tampa endured a well-drawn color line and abominable living conditions. White city residents rigidly enforced segregation until the early 1960s. As late as World War II blacks had no public parks or playgrounds, and the city's only medical facility serving blacks consisted of the privately run Clara Fry Hospital, an antiquated building with fewer than twenty beds. Housing in black quarters was the city's poorest; disease rates, illiteracy, and infant mortality were the highest.[48]

In 1930 virtually all of Tampa's 4,200 servants, maids, and laundresses were black; and the city's 20,000 Afro-Americans could muster 67 clergymen but only 18 teachers, 4 dentists, and 2 lawyers. Only in the stevedore trade did blacks gain a union foothold. Tampa's biracial society in the 1870s, and multiethnic society after 1886, had virtually eliminated blacks from contributing to and participating in the city's economic and urban development. The influx of immigrants, moreover, supplanted blacks from such "traditional" trades as barbering, carpentry, bootblacking, and truck farming.[49] The solid entrenchment of the black community at the lowest end of Tampa's social and economic scale meant that immigrants entered at a level above at least one major segment of the local society, a fact that proved significant in framing the initial reception and mobility of immigrants. In Tampa the open hostility toward blacks deflected some of the nativism and discrimination immigrants commonly encountered elsewhere.

Tampa's power structure resolved to make sure that the city's Afro-Americans never threatened the status quo. Southern progressives identified reform with racial segregation and black disfranchisement. Promising efficient and honest government, the progressives offered an all-white primary which became law in the early twentieth century. Proponents argued that if blacks could be removed from the political arena, white unity could be maintained, a broader white democracy achieved, and issues debated free of the divisive, corrupting influence of blacks.[50]

A series of legal hurdles blocked black attempts to vote. Florida's 1889 poll tax law required voters to bring tax receipts for the two years prior to the election. In spite of poll taxes and threats, Tampa's Afro-American residents had persistently attempted to exercise their franchise. Candidates for the city council sought support from prominent black citizens, and in 1908 a black man, Z. D. Greene, attempted to run for municipal judge.[51] But the new White Municipal party unveiled in 1909 and designed to eliminate black voters from the all-important city primaries, served to effectively crush black political activism for forty years. On the eve of the party's first test in 1910, the *Morning Tribune* editorialized, "In Florida the negro has no voice whatever in the selection of U.S. Senators, Representatives in Congress, Governor, Statehouse offices. . . . In only one municipality in the State—Tampa—does he have any voice in the election of city officers. He has had, by the way, his last voice in this city. . . . His voice has ceased to be either an asset of civilization or valuable commercial commodity. His right of suffrage is only a name."[52]

The paper promised that "the primary [would] be an honest, free and full expression of the white electorate of the city." The effect of the white primary can be dramatically seen in the absolute drop in registered voters in Tampa between 1910 and 1912, from 5,675 to 3,987. Blacks could vote in general elections, but in Florida, as in much of the South, winning a primary was tantamount to an election victory. As late as 1939 blacks still represented less than 5 percent of the city's registered voters yet constituted roughly one-quarter of the population.[53] The *Morning Tribune* smugly surveyed the political landscape after the 1910 test of the white primary and concluded, "For the first time in the history of Tampa, candidates for office have not found it necessary to go down into the dives of the 'Scrub' to hobnob with the festive colored brother on his own ground."[54]

Summary

For most of its early history Tampa languished as a backwater frontier outpost with much promise but little development. Beginning in the 1880s, however, rapid demographic, economic, and territorial expansion produced explosive urban growth and increased social complexity. Tampa resembled other New South cities as it acquired the trappings of a modern urban center. The introduction of streetcars, a rural-to-urban migration of southern whites and blacks, and the growth of new transportation and economic networks reshaped Tampa's living space and work environment.

As it underwent the metamorphosis to an industrial city Tampa sorted out its new social order. By the early years of the twentieth century white Tampans had determined the position of blacks in the local society. Segregated into well-defined residential zones, circumscribed by rigorous Jim Crow laws, and effectively excluded from politics and many job areas, blacks faced an uncertain future. So solidly were they stuck on the lowest rung of the occupational, social, and economic ladder that the point of entry for incoming immigrants was moved upward.

Tampa's business and professional elites sought a measure of social and political control that went beyond the elimination of blacks from meaningful participation in community affairs. They successfully integrated newly arrived whites from other states, allowed them selective access to the levers of power, and infused them with a vigorous booster mentality. By the turn of the century control of the city rested in the hands of a few dozen families for whom the protection of Tampa's image as a prosperous, trouble-free metropolis assumed major importance. The fact that this conception papered over serious racial and class divisions—separations that would, in fact, increase with time—only made the effort to maintain it more precarious and prone to social conflict.

It is in the context of these developments that the most fundamental transformation of Tampa—the creation of Ybor City—must be viewed. A German visitor to Tampa in 1931 caught the essence of the changes that already had taken place: "I go to Tampa. . . . one half of Tampa, the one every tourist gets to see, is rightly called a paradise. . . . For lo and behold, the lack of money quickly banishes me from the paradiscal [sic] half of Tampa. [The other half] is even more interesting. Here they have Italian opera houses with balconies, cock fights, bullfights, houses with balconies, incredibly numerous coffee shops where Italians, Spaniards, Creoles gesticulate wildly. . . . We are in Ybor City."[55] Just as this German observer stared across the economic and cultural boundaries separating native Tampa from Ybor City, so too did thousands of other foreigners, among them transplanted Sicilians, who had been attracted to this part of the Florida peninsula. Those who had participated in the founding and development of Ybor City as an immigrant community knew just how firmly these lines of division were etched in history.

NOTES

1. *Niles Weekly Register*, March 24, 1821. See also ibid., June 30, 1821: "From what we hear of Tampa Bay, though its shores are not now inhabited, it will probably contest with Pensacola the honor of being ultimately fixed upon as the southern naval depot of the United States."

2. Covington, "Life at Fort Brooke," 319–30; Chamberlin, "Fort Brooke"; McCall, *Letters from the Frontiers*.

3. Covington, *Billy Bowlegs War*; Akerman, *Florida Cowman*; Will, "King of the Crackers," 31–39; Otto, "Florida's Cattle Ranching," 71–84; Pizzo, "James McKay," 6–19.

4. *Florida Peninsular* (1855–61); Bayless, "Invisible Pioneers."

5. *War of the Rebellion*, XXXV, 389–90; Davis, *Civil War and Reconstruction*, 303.

6. *Florida Peninsular* (1867–69), specifically May 26, 1866, May 16, 1868, June 23, 1869; *Tampa Sunland Tribune* (1877–78), specifically July 7, 1877, November 20, 1878; Grismer, *History of Tampa*, 150–54, 167–68; Wilson, "Hard Times and Long Faces."

7. Barker, "Seasons of Pestilence"; McFarlin, "Diary: Tampa"; *Ninth Census*, I, Table 3, p. 98; *Tenth Census*, I, Table 3, p. 118.

8. Treasury agent quoted in Shofner, *Nor Is It Over Yet*, 268.

9. Munroe, "Gulf Coast City."

10. *Tenth Census*, I, Tables 3, 13. On March 17, 1896, the *Tampa Morning Tribune* commented that Tampa must be one of the few cities in America where St. Patrick's Day would *not* be celebrated.

11. *Tenth Census*, XXVII, Table 3.

12. Shofner, *Nor Is It Over Yet*, 109–18; Williamson, *Florida Politics*; Dovell, "Railroads and the Public Lands," 236–58.

13. Dodson, "St. Cloud Sugar Plantation," 356–70; *Atlantic and Gulf Coast Canal*; Rose, "Disston Sugar Plantation," 85–88; Sitterson, *Sugar Country*, 361–63.

14. Smyth, *Henry Bradley Plant*, 42–53; Johnson, "Henry Bradley Plant," 118–32.

15. *Tampa Sunland Tribune*, March 7, 1881, January 13, 1882; Pettengill, *Florida Railroads*, 68–78.

16. Prince, *Atlantic Coast Line Railroad*, 21–22; Johoda, *River of the Golden Ibis*, 205; *Ocala Banner*, October 12, 1881.

17. Covington, "Tampa Bay Hotel," 3–20; *Tampa Weekly Tribune*, February 12, 1891; *Tampa Journal*, July 13, November 22, 1888.

18. *Tampa Morning Tribune*, December 22, 1897, June 22, 1947; *History of Port Tampa*.

19. Wiebe, *Search for Order*.

20. Webb, *Jacksonville and Consolidated Directory*, 519; *Twelfth Census*, II, Table 27, p. 214.

21. Mormino, "Tampa and the New Urban South," 337–56; *Tampa Morning Tribune* and *Tampa Daily Times*, 1895–1918; Schellings, "Tampa, Florida"; Grismer, *History of Tampa*, 245–56; Buker, "Tampa's Municipal Wharves," 37–47.

22. For controversies over city improvements see *Tampa Morning Tribune*, August 16, 1895, August 11, 19, 1896, July 12, 1902, May 10, 1907; "Pioneer Florida," in *Tampa Sunday Tribune*, September 16, 1951; Long, "Making of Modern Tampa," 333–46; Grismer, *History of Tampa*, 190–212.

23. *Tampa Morning Tribune*, January 22, 1897. For school essays honoring the Confederacy, see ibid., May 23, 1909, February 27, 1911.

24. Ibid., June 23, 1895.

25. See Tampa newspapers, 1895–1920, especially ibid., June 23, 1895, May 10, 1907.

26. Ibid., May 10, 1907.

27. Goldfield and Brownell, *Urban America*, 205–10; Hays, "Changing Political Structure," 6–38.

28. Mohl, *New City*, 53–64.

29. Elazar, *American Federalism*, 99–103.

30. Rerick, *Memoirs of Florida*, II, 584–85; Rachaels, "Peter O. Knight," 2–6. Rowland Rerick's 1902 volume on Florida affairs inventoried Knight's extensive power as director and/or attorney for the following corporations: the Exchange National Bank, Tampa Gas Company, Tampa Electrical Company, the Tribune Publishing Company, the Tampa Building and Loan Association, the Florida Brewing Company, the Ybor City Land and Improvement Company, the Florida Central and Peninsular Railroad Company, and the American Cigar Company. See Rerick, *Memoirs of Florida*, II, 585.

31. *Tampa Morning Tribune*, June 29, 1919.

32. Ibid., March 25, 1910; McKay, *Pioneer Florida*, I, II.

33. *Tampa Morning Tribune*, December 4, 1909.
34. Mullen, "Florida Close Ups."
35. "Dixie's Little Journey to Tampa," *Jacksonville Dixie*, June 27, 1912.
36. *Tampa Morning Tribune*, November 25, 1896.
37. Goldfield, *Cotton Fields and Skyscrapers*, 160.
38. *Twelfth Census*, Table 27, p. 214; *Thirteenth Census*, Table 4, p. 332.
39. Polk, *Tampa City Directory*, 1914, XIII, "Preface"; ibid., 1930, XIX, "Statistical Review."
40. *Tampa Morning Tribune*, January 9, 1897, December 14, 1898, January 24, 1899, January 27, 1900.
41. *Ocala Mail and Express*, quoted in ibid., August 10, 1897; *St. Petersburg Times*, June 3, 1897.
42. Ingalls, "General Joseph B. Wall," 51–71.
43. *Tampa Morning Tribune*, June 25, 26, 27, 1899. The paper editorialized, "Other agitators of his stamp who are deceiving the negroes of the South should read well the turbulent story of Christopher and mark the lesson well."
44. Ibid., July 31, August 2, 1903.
45. Ibid., September 25, 26, 1910.
46. *Eleventh Census*, Table 23; *Thirteenth Census*, II, Table 2; *Fifteenth Census: Population*, III, Table 15.
47. Raper, *Negro Life in Tampa*. This study, compiled during the spring of 1927, was actually written by Benjamin Mays, then director of Tampa's Urban League. See Mays, *Born to Rebel*.
48. Mays, *Born to Rebel*; *Tampa Morning Tribune* and *Tampa Daily Times*, 1920–40.
49. *Fifteenth Census*, Table 12, pp. 363–64.
50. Grantham, *Southern Progressivism*.
51. *Tampa Morning Tribune*, May 31, 1908; Shofner, "Custom, Law, and History," 287.
52. *Tampa Morning Tribune*, April 5, 1910. See also ibid., May 4, December 3, 1909.
53. Ibid., April 5, 1910, April 1–3, 1912; *Tampa Daily Times*, April 1–6, 1912; Bureau of Elections, records for 1935–40, HCC.
54. *Tampa Morning Tribune*, April 5, 1910.
55. Leitner, *Frau Reist*, 101–2.

3 Ybor City and the Beginning of a Latin Community, 1886-1900

> This was once a small Cuba . . . but Tampa began to cosmopolite itself. The Italians and Spaniards began entering here, and now it is a mixture.
>
> Pedro Barrios, "Early History of Ybor City"

Off the island of Manhattan, in 1886, workers put the finishing touches on the magnificent Statue of Liberty, a belated centennial present from the people of France. Few realized it then, but the Lady symbolized the changing of the immigration guard. Record numbers of immigrants would soon pass by the statue; but it was not merely the total count that signified change so much as the origins of these newcomers. Whereas previous generations of Americans looked to northern and western Europe for their ancestors, these "new" immigrants arrived from southern and eastern Europe. Slavs and Jews, Italians and Greeks would supply the human resources for America's ascendancy.

The year 1886 also heralded the creation of a new industrial enterprise: Ybor City, in Tampa, Florida. In its own way Ybor City fit perfectly the era's values, as businessmen and immigrants came together to launch an industry that fed the emerging middle-class values of leisure and consumption. Observers also saw an industrial city serving as a magnet for migrants seeking new opportunities. But Ybor City's experience would, in some ways, take different paths from the mainstream of this larger current.

The founding of Ybor City suggests a tenpenny opera: Spanish agents search mythical forests for exotic fruit; émigrés plot a revolution abroad; a cast of thousands embark on a *völkerwanderung* (national migration), eventually congregating at a small town on Florida's west coast that had been discovered by a conquistador four centuries earlier. But the genesis of Ybor City also represented the culmination of less romantic sentiments: a quest by foreign businessmen seeking a protected industrial sanctuary; an asylum for Spanish and Cuban workers amid the tumult of revolution; and an opportunity for groups of Sicilians from the Magazzolo valley, probing the world economy for bread and work.

In November 1884 two unusual visitors arrived in Tampa. Bernardino Gargol, a Spanish purveyor of jellies and fruits in Cuba, and Gavino Gutiérrez, a gifted Spanish civil engineer and businessman, had come in search of groves of guavas and mangoes believed to exist on Florida's west coast. Disappointed by their failure to locate sources of guava paste, they were nonetheless impressed by what they saw. Returning by sea to New York, the Spaniards stopped over at Key West, where they called upon their countryman, Vicente Martínez Ybor. Ignacio Haya, a Spanish cigar manufacturer from New York, who by chance was visiting with his old friend Martínez Ybor, listened intently as Gutiérrez painted an alluring portrait of Tampa. "I have just come from a place which I believe would be an ideal location for this industry," Gutiérrez exclaimed. Martínez Ybor had long wrestled with the inadequacies of Key West. The island possessed no fresh water supply, could be reached only by sea (the railroad did not arrive until 1912), and could offer little land for future expansion. But a more compelling reason to relocate may have centered around his and Haya's inability to control the increasing labor militancy of their workers, at that very moment engaged in a bitter strike. Key West's strength—its accessibility to Cuba—was also its drawback, the impossibility of controlling the labor supply.[1]

Martínez Ybor and Haya had already begun inquiries into the availability of land at Galveston, Mobile, and Pensacola. They added Tampa to the list and soon visited the place themselves. Plant's railroad and steamships provided ideal transportation facilities, and the region's notorious humidity supplied a natural humidor suitable to tobacco leaf. The city fathers pledged to underwrite capital should labor agitation threaten investment, using the police if necessary. Returning in September 1885 Martínez Ybor and his business associate, Eduardo Manrara, sought to negotiate a final agreement on a plot of land two miles northeast of downtown Tampa, a swampy and uninhabited tract of real estate. Townsfolk rejoiced over the prospect. "The benefits that would inure to Tampa from the establishment of such an industry cannot be too deeply impressed on our citizens," commented the *Sunday Tribune*.[2]

Specifically Martínez Ybor expressed interest in forty acres of land only recently purchased by Captain John T. Lesley, son of a prominent Tampa pioneer. Lesley agreed to sell the land for $9,000, a price the Spaniard felt was exorbitant. Into the negotiations stepped the Tampa Board of Trade, organized in May 1885 to promote business interests in the city. The board called a meeting in early October, arriving at a plan to placate Martínez Ybor and pay Lesley his asking price: Martínez Ybor offered $5,000 and local businessmen subsidized the remainder. Additional purchases of property in the area soon followed. The October 21, 1885, minutes of the board recorded the historic agreement in stark fashion: "arrangement had been consummated to secure the cigar factory of Ybor and Co."[3] Tampa would never be the same.

Martínez Ybor and Haya set out to build a company town. In time there would be hundreds of factories and firms, diluting control of any single company, but for the first few years the pair maintained complete mastery of their development. During the late nineteenth century George M. Pullman's planned industrial community outside of Chicago and various southern mill towns appealed to visionaries and realists who wished to achieve financial success, co-opt labor militancy, and retain absolute power over the employees' homes and work.[4] Whereas nature endowed a climate suitable for cigar rolling, and Henry B. Plant supplied railcars moving northward, only the townspeople themselves could provide what Martínez Ybor and Haya needed to complete the triangle: control. On March 8, 1887, the Tampa Board of Trade codified what had been promised: "Resolved: that the Board of Trade hereby assures Mess. Ybor and Company and Sánchez Haya, as well as the citizens of Tampa, generally, that they will guarantee their full support and protection for their lives and property by every legitimate means." Tampans would come to interpret that document very broadly.[5]

"On the 8th of October 1885," reported the *Tampa Guardian*, "the first tree was felled which covered the site on which Ybor City is now building."[6] Martínez Ybor and Haya had persuaded Gavino Gutiérrez to lay out the planned community, which by the fall of 1886 consisted of 111 acres of land. Gutiérrez borrowed liberally from a variety of sources in designing Ybor City: grid-patterned streets, a surveyor's dream, derived from his American training; brick factories with courtyards, from Havana; generous use of wrought iron in the railings and balconies, reflecting his Spanish heritage; simple workers' shotgun cottages, which had long been used in the South and were perhaps of African origin. "The mammoth three-story brick cigar factory of Mssr. V. Martínez Ybor and Co. is nearing completion," observed the *Guardian* in the spring of 1886. "There is not a more substantial structure in the State of Florida. None but the very best material has been used in any part and no expense spared to make it both handsome and convenient."[7]

To build the factories and drain the swamps Martínez Ybor hired local laborers; to man the factories he attracted Cubans and Spaniards to this remote outpost. In the spring of 1886 the first Cubans arrived aboard the sidewheeler SS *Hutchinson*. Martínez Ybor's inauguration of triweekly steamship service to Key West and Havana proved farsighted. A disastrous fire in Key West on April 1 suddenly made Ybor City more attractive, as displaced cigarworkers searched for jobs. By May 1886 the founder had recruited nearly 220 cigarworkers.[8]

The prize for the first cigar produced in Ybor City would not go to its namesake but rather to Ignacio Haya. Cuban workers at Martínez Ybor's El Príncipe de Gales factory had gone on strike because he had hired a Spanish bookkeeper. The vignette provided an ominous first act in what was to become a turbulent labor drama. The factory of La Flor de Sánchez y Haya captured the honor of producing the first cigar, on April 13, 1886.[9]

Boosters may have lauded Ybor City as a planned industrial enterprise, but the enclave's early years reflected the rawness of a mining camp and the dangers of a frontier presidio. Carved from palmetto scrubland, pineflats, and lagoons, pioneer José García remembered the settlement in 1886 as "wilderness."[10] Another stalwart, Fernando Lemos, recalled an infestation of insects so severe that inhabitants "were forced to go about with goggles to keep the gnats from your eyes."[11] Giovanni Cacciatore, who arrived in the late 1880s from New Orleans, remembered his first impression of the outpost: "What I saw before me almost brought me to tears." When Cacciatore's bride arrived later, she too was dumbfounded. "She burst out crying at what she saw," he recalled. "Wilderness, swamps, mosquitoes and open closets." She then posed what must have been a frequent question, "Why have you brought me to such a place?"[12]

To attract skilled cigarmakers to a primitive outpost, Martínez Ybor offered workers inexpensive homes unobtainable in Havana or Key West; to entice cigar manufacturers to move from New York, Cuba, or Key West, he offered his fellow capitalists generous inducements of free land and factory buildings. Typically Martínez Ybor and Haya encouraged manufacturers with a free ten-year lease on land and a new factory built to their specifications. In return these firms guaranteed to manufacture a quota of cigars and furnish a fixed number of workers who would rent or buy houses from their benefactors.[13]

After 1890 announcements of new cigar factories became commonplace. "Little Havana is all the rage now," exclaimed the *Morning Tribune* in 1895.[14] Devastating fires in Key West in 1886 and 1896 caused many manufacturers to relocate to Tampa, whose industrial and demographic base was expanding rapidly. By 1900 the city approached Key West in population (15,839 to 17,114), exceeded it in the number of factories (129 to 92), and far surpassed it in Latin (Cuban, Italian, and Spanish) inhabitants (5,811 to 3,130).[15]

Ybor City's cigar industry created a whole set of related operations, such as cedar-box factories, lithographic studios (for production of labels), and other support services. So successful was Ybor City that it even spawned an imitation, West Tampa. Conceived in 1892 by the Scottish-born attorney-financier Hugh Campbell Macfarlane, West Tampa also became an immediate success. Following Ybor City's promotional formula, Macfarlane purchased several hundred acres of cypress wetlands, drained the swamp, and lured the Del Pino brothers to his domain. Unlike Ybor City's founders, Macfarlane successfully fought annexation to the city of Tampa; hence West Tampa remained a fiercely separate city from its 1895 incorporation until 1925.[16]

In 1895 West Tampa boasted ten cigar factories, a $20,000 opera house, and streetcar service. The *Daily Tampa Tribune* observed that "quite a number of Cuban families have moved to the West Tampa cigar town . . . [including] 116 cigarmakers and 80 strippers."[17] Alfredo Prende, one of the last pioneers, reminisced: "West Tampa was just like the wild west, a frontier town. There were cock fights, boxing matches, horses tied to hitching posts in front of *cantinas*. . . . West Tampa was called '*La Caimanería*' (place of gators)."[18] Others nicknamed the site "El Cerro" because the Cuban work force missed the old neighborhood of that name in Havana.[19] Italians shared in the settlement as well. Mary Italiano remembered her first introduction to the community: "When I moved to West Tampa after I got married, my heaven! It was like a wilderness over there. I really cried. . . . I was scared you know, at night they had no lights in the streets."[20]

The growth of West Tampa kept pace with the popularity of cigars at the turn of the century. By 1900 the community had 2,355 inhabitants, more than the state capital of Tallahassee; a decade later West Tampa was the fastest growing city in the fastest growing state east of the Mississippi, its population having climbed to 8,258, of whom only 626 were native whites of native parentage.[21] Thus by 1910 the ethnic complexion of the area was fully established. Native Tampa sat uneasily astride two islands of Latin culture, enjoying the benefits that flowed from the economic prosperity of the two centers but harboring steadily escalating fears.

Ybor City expanded as literally billions of cigars followed the historic first smoker. Immigrants survived the rigors of the formative years to witness the rapid and uninterrupted growth of an industry from 1886 to 1900. Neither the travail of yellow fever nor foreign competition could dislodge the primacy of cigars in Tampa. Every indicator after 1886—from customs revenues to payroll receipts—points to the symbiotic interlinkage of cigars and the growth of Tampa, the "Cigar City." To the outside world deluged with labels bidding for "Tampa Life" or "Tampa Girl," cigars and Tampa became forever synonymous.

The sheer weight of statistics underscores the integral role of cigars in Tampa's economy. In 1886 customs receipts (the value of import fees) at the Port of Tampa totaled $2,508; by 1900 the duties (almost exclusively tobacco products) approached $1 million a year, tenth highest in the nation. In 1900 Tampa's internal revenues accounted for two-thirds of Florida's total revenues. Quantum gains marked the growth of this expanding industry. In 1900 Tampa received 1,180 tons of Cuban tobacco, valued at nearly $3 million, which workers transformed into $10 million worth of cigar exports.[22]

When compared to the rest of Florida, Tampa's industrial profile loomed even more impressively. In 1900 Tampa cigarmakers earned $2 million in wages, making them the highest paid per capita and the most concentrated work force in the state. Only the vast and unintegrated lumber and naval stores industry accounted for more value-added manufacture.[23] The growth of the cigar industry continued unabated after 1900. By 1911 customs house receipts had more than doubled to $2,299,473. Even more dramatic was the increase in total product: in 1886 Ybor City operatives produced 1 million cigars, which climbed to

20 million in 1900 and peaked at 410 million in 1919. In one week in 1911 nearly 8 million cigars left Tampa by rail and ship.[24]

While the proliferating numbers of premium cigars added to the coffers of the U.S. Treasury, growing payrolls earned by Latin workers buttressed Tampa's economy. The *Journal* gushed in 1888 that the weekly payroll at V. M. Ybor and Co. had reached $4,000.[25] In 1894 weekly paychecks for workers at twelve factories averaged $12.90, an impressive figure for this era. A record book from V. M. Ybor and Co. in 1897 indicates that packers averaged $27 a week, followed by selectors at $20 a week, and cigarmakers at $12.50.[26] "In the magic city by the great gulf lies the Havana cigar center for the world," exulted the *Morning Tribune* in 1895, adding, "the cigarmakers of Tampa receive more than five million dollars a year in wages."[27]

Ybor City, confessed the *Tribune* in 1895, contained the city's "financial soul."[28] "The cigar industry is to this city what the iron industry is to Pittsburgh," remarked the paper in 1897.[29] But with the growing importance of cigars came also the danger to a city's health in being a one-industry town. "The cigar industry of Tampa is its very backbone and muscle," wrote one observer. "Any hand raised to do it harm is an enemy to the people. . . . So woe to those who ought to damage this industry. . . ."[30]

The number of cigar factories and operatives continued to grow. From 2 factories in 1886 the number expanded to 120 cigar factories and 4,783 workers in 1895, plus innumerable storefront shops employing small groups of workers.[31] By 1920 Tampa's sprawling cigar industry employed more than 12,000 workers directly and furnished a livelihood for thousands more in ancillary trades and jobs.[32] "Tampa without its cigars would not be Tampa today," commented the *Daily Times*.[33] Amid the economic boom of 1906 a spokesman pleaded for the addition of 2,000 cigarmakers. Two years later officials believed 3,000 more cigarworkers could easily find employment in Tampa.[34] The problem facing the industry was not overproduction but rather the recruitment and retention of enough skilled hands.

The men and women who fueled the burgeoning industry's first years of growth came from Spain and Cuba. Many of these pioneers had shared a history of work and accommodation before arriving in Ybor City. This did not mean, however, that harmony would prevail in their new settlement. As Cubans and Spaniards descended the gangplanks at Port Tampa, deep fissures appeared in the fault lines of Ybor City, divisions deepened by nationalism, racism, and radicalism. Yet along with their tote bags, Cubans and Spaniards brought a cultural vitality that helped create an ethnic *paella* unique for the South.

Spaniards

The major points of origin for Tampa's Spaniards lay in the northwestern Spanish provinces of Asturias and Galicia. Heralded as the "Birthplace of the Reconquest," Asturias prides itself on its racial purity and the recounting of myths, such as how Gothic nobles under Don Pelayo repulsed the Moorish invaders at Covadonga. "Asturias is the only real Spain," explained a Spanish immigrant, "the rest is just reconquered territory."[35]

Yet the unification of Spain did little to ameliorate harsh living conditions among the poor. The causes for the impoverishment of the Spanish peasantry are complex. While the climate of Galicia is moist, its granite-strewn soil is only marginally fertile. One source described sixteenth-century Galicia as a barren land, where the coarse rye bread was indigestible.[36] Landholding patterns squeezed the *campesinos* (peasants) between an unyielding environment and a regressive social system. The disentailment of Catholic church lands beginning in the late eighteenth century, which in France had benefited land-hungry peasants, only aggravated the plight of the landless Spanish. Unlike southern Spain, where the *latifondi* ruled, northern Spain was characterized by hopelessly small family farms. The region's notoriously primitive roads only intensified the burdensome laws of tenancy, exemplified by the antiquated system of *foros* (hereditary quitrents). Peasants exercised little control over their lives, since the village elite—the banker, lawyer, and priest—generally held power. Symbols of Spanish backwardness, the *caciques* (bosses) consolidated power in Asturias and Galicia, functioning as political bosses, grain brokers, and intermediaries for absentee landlords. The church, as it forfeited more of its lands in the late nineteenth century, lost interest in its most fervent supporters, the third estate. "Pray to God and the Saints," suggests a Spanish proverb, "but put fertilizer on the crops." To many the church's defense of the established order epitomized the inequities gripping Spain. Declining agricultural prices cruelly coincided with a spiraling birthrate. Between 1768 and 1900 Spain's population doubled to 8.6 million persons; the population density in northern Spain approximated that of Belgium, the highest in Europe.[37]

Spaniards reacted to the social and economic upheaval caused by agrarian decline, colonial failure, and emerging industrialization in a variety of ways. At home, workers and intellectuals activated a number of movements, most notably the spread of anarchism. Spanish anarchism held a special attraction to *los desheredados* (the disinherited), landless laborers, tenant farmers, and displaced artisans, groups who felt the sting of class hatred. Temma Kaplan has also noted the appeal of anarchism to small-scale producers and independent peasants. The anarchist movement quickly spread from doctrinal debates in cafés to the city and the countryside.[38]

The writings of Mikhail Bakunin attracted a following in Spain. His philosophy emphasized the inherent good of humankind and the repressive nature of institutions and hierarchies. Bakunin and Marx passionately disagreed over the means and ends of the revolution; if people are naturally good, argued the former, the evils of collective life stem from institutions, which must be purged. In place of Marx's centralized committee Bakunin believed in the spontaneity of the rural masses; and he possessed an unshakable faith in the restoration of community as the core of society. The specter of direct action also appealed to people who had long venerated the social bandit. Between 1890 and 1912, despite the fact that terrorism was never more than a minority doctrine, acts of violence riveted Spain. Propaganda by deed resulted only in splintering the anarchist movement and increasing civil repression.[39]

Not all Spaniards hoisted placards at home. Responding to the tumult of the late nineteenth century, thousands selected a different path of social change: emigration. Asturians and Galicians have carried to the far-flung parts of the Spanish empire their cherished *sidra* (cider) and *gaita* (bagpipes). Aptly referred to as the "Nursery of Spanish emigrants," Asturias and Galicia have been sending their sons and daughters to the New World for nearly half a millennium; their ranks even included Pedro Menéndez de Áviles, the founder of St. Augustine, Florida.[40] Today in Ybor City, in the *cantinas* of Centro Asturiano and Centro Español, one immediately surrenders to the quickening tempo of dominoes and proverbs. "The Asturians do not leave Spain because of money, but for the sheer adventure of it," assured coffee merchant Julio Cuevas.[41] But the elderly Cuevas, who left his beloved Asturias in 1918, later confessed that the proverb romanticized the cruel reality that forced 820,000 Spaniards like himself to emigrate to the Americas between 1880 and 1920, of whom 130,000 came to the United States.[42]

Cuba had long served as both a magnet and a safety valve for Spanish society. Lured by the boom brought by the rapid expansion of sugar, tobacco, and coffee plantations, and driven by the repressive Spanish government, *peninsulares* (Spanish-born subjects) had been prominent in Cuba since the early days of the conquest. The full spectrum of political ideologies in Spain came to be found on the island. As the Spanish empire diminished in the New World, increasing tensions between *peninsulares* and *criollos* (in this case Cubans) resulted.[43] To seek an alternative to African slave labor, Spanish officials imported 125,000 Chinese laborers between the 1850s and the closing of the coolie trade in 1874. In the 1850s authorities also approved a plan to import 50,000 Galicians—called "Spanish Irishmen"—but official corruption and a mutiny by the first arrivals caused a rethinking of the idea.[44]

On the island of Cuba a rebellion broke out in 1868, at Yara, convulsing the colony in a ten-year struggle. The Treaty of Zanjón in 1878 spelled a truce, albeit a short one. The Ten Years War of attrition had exacted a terrible toll: the countryside lay wasted and perhaps 100,000 Cuban expatriates remained dispersed in the Americas and Europe. Irreconcilable Cuban émigrés abroad and committed revolutionaries within pledged themselves to the idea of *Cuba Libre*. One result of the war was the emergence of Key West, Florida, as a vibrant Cuban community.[45]

The peace treaty of 1878 ushered in two decades of social unrest and economic instability in Cuba, coinciding with a period of domestic convulsion in Spain. The abolition of slavery in Cuba in 1886 disrupted an already fragile economy. Displaced rural workers battled the unemployed in overcrowded Cuban cities, while in the countryside social banditry and vagrancy were on the rise. Spain's solution to the vexatious Cuban problem was to entice transient laborers as well as settlers to embark for the already overcrowded island colony,[46] which they did in increasing numbers during the 1880s and 1890s. While official statistics vary, Duvon Corbitt, who worked in the Havana archives, contends that between 1882 and 1894 nearly 250,000 emigrants arrived from Spain. In a half-desperate, half-benevolent gesture, the Spanish government offered to pay the passage of any white Spaniard who agreed to work in Cuba for one year, in the hope that the influx of emigrants would relieve pressures at home while strengthening the loyalist cause abroad. The policy, above all, aimed to buttress the white *peninsulares* in Cuba. Following the disruption of war, which broke out in 1895 and ended with

Cuban independence in 1898, Spanish emigration continued unabated. Between 1899 and 1905 approximately 150,000 Spaniards went to Cuba. Many of them, troubled by the instability of the Cuban economy and enticed by new opportunities in the United States, soon trod increasingly familiar pathways to New York City, Key West, and Tampa, where expatriate cigarmaking centers had crystallized during the ten-year Cuban struggle.[47]

Perhaps the most remarkable of these expatriate outposts was Ybor City, the capstone to the career of the extraordinary, even visionary, capitalist Don Vicente Martínez Ybor. Born to wealthy parents in 1818 in Valencia, Spain, Martínez Ybor, in a fashion customary to his class, immigrated to Cuba as a young man to avoid compulsory military service. There he followed and then directed the spectacular rise of the cigar industry, climbing the ladder from apprentice clerk to broker to manufacturer. Displaying a deft touch and a good entrepreneurial instinct, he helped to modernize the primitive Cuban tobacco industry. Seizing what was, upon his arrival, a cottage industry, he persuaded rural workers in the lush Vuelta Abajo region to specialize in rolling cigars, later moving them to Havana and recruiting others to work at his factories.

Martínez Ybor rationalized the Cuban cigar industry, creating new markets and expanding operations to meet an insatiable world demand for premium hand-rolled, pure Havana cigars. In 1853 he anticipated the genius of James Buchanan Duke by a generation when he introduced his El Príncipe de Gales (The Prince of Wales) label. As of 1859 Havana boasted a thriving cigar industry, which included hundreds of factories and shops claiming 15,000 workers. By the eve of the Ten Years War, finished tobacco products had become a three-million-dollar-a-year industry.[48]

The gathering storm of Cuban independence swept Martínez Ybor into its vortex. His less than secretive support of the separatists stemmed principally from economic motivations—a free Cuba would lift burdensome Spanish restrictions—but he also felt a geniune sympathy for the Cuban cause. Alerted that the government had issued an order for his arrest, the manufacturer went into hiding, later fleeing to Key West in 1869.[49]

Martínez Ybor may have sparkled as the brightest luminary among the *patrones de tabaqueros* (tobacco magnates) but the careers of a number of like-minded countrymen were strikingly similar. Born in the post-Napoleonic era and sensing diminishing opportunity on the peninsula,

Spaniards such as Ignacio Haya, Enrique Pendas, Peregrino Rey, Manuel Sánchez, Vicente Guerra, Angel La Madrid Cuesta, and Serafín Sánchez left first for Cuba and eventually for Martínez Ybor's experimental community. Highly conscious of their dependence upon a Cuban proletariat, these *patrones* retained their chauvinistic attitudes, almost always preferring Spaniards for the upper-echelon positions in the industry.[50] Unlike the Spanish and Cuban cigarmakers who huddled together in Ybor City, the owners often preferred to mingle and live among the elite of English-speaking Tampa, and they or their children frequently intermarried with Anglos. Gavino Gutiérrez, for instance, married Nelly Daly; his daughters, Aurora and María, entered into the upper crust of Tampa society with their betrothals to Donald Brenham McKay and Dr. L. Mitchel, respectively.[51] The daughter of Martínez Ybor married a financier, Hugo Schwab.[52]

The great majority of Tampa's Spaniards first immigrated to Cuba, where they apprenticed in the cigar industry centered in Havana. Generally they followed a pattern of migration characterized by the flow of skilled labor to opportunity and long periods of sojourner status. Many Spaniards in the New World "commuted" between Spain and the Americas for extended time periods, maintaining separate households on both sides of the Atlantic. Large numbers came with designs of eventually accumulating enough money to purchase land in the *patria chica* (old-world village).[53]

Asturian and Galician villages such as Ferrera de los Gavitos, Las Villas, Cándamo, Moutas, Infiesto, and Pintueles sent steady streams of Spaniards to Cuba and Florida. A small group of Catalans also appeared in Tampa. Spaniards, too, left the Old World in chain migrations, assisted by a complex and well-organized network of kinfolk, compatriots, and ideologies. Typical was the path chosen by Fermín Suoto. "I was born in the little village of Ferrol de Galicia in June of 1858," he told an interviewer in 1935. "My father was a stone cutter . . . my mother was born and raised in the country. I am, therefore, a plebian. My parents were poor people, and in those days a poor man could only look forward to a very meager education. On October 30, 1879, a friend took me to Havana, Cuba."[54] Half a century later María Ordieres followed the example of Suoto. "I was born and raised in Cándamo, Asturias. My father heard that in Tampa, Florida, the cigar industry was in need of workers. So in 1923 he left for Tampa. My brother and I followed since we were the oldest and could work."[55]

The Spanish settlement in Tampa manifested a distinctive demographic profile that affected its social and economic behavior. Persistently high male-to-female ratios characterized the Spanish presence, especially during the colony's formative years. "Fully 85 per cent of the total Spanish population of Tampa is composed of males who have reached maturity," reported the U.S. Immigration Commission in 1910. The imbalance of males over females, so typical of the earliest stages of immigration, characterized Ybor City's first decades.[56]

In 1900 about 33 percent of Tampa's Spaniards lived in boardinghouses, a percentage that was unchanged a decade later. In 1910, for instance, census takers noted 810 Spanish boarders, 352 Cubans, and 45 Italians.[57] According to the U.S. Immigration Commission, slightly less than 50 percent of the Spanish males over the age of twenty were married, as opposed to 72 percent of the Italians and 66 percent of the Cubans.[58] Not all boarders, however, were single men. The career of Modesto López typified that of many Spaniards. In Cudillero, Asturias, López worked as a tenant farmer and later as a doorman at a Madrid hotel. His wife, Faustina Vásquez, was a Gallega. After their marriage the López family moved to Havana in the 1890s. The elder López, through kinship ties, became a selector in a Havana cigar factory, but the López family decided that only Tampa offered *tabaqueros* a future. So the family, including seven children, remained in Havana while the husband departed for Tampa. "After he was here for six to eight months [1906], he decided to send for the family," explained his son Alfonso. Modesto López, as did hundreds of like-minded Spaniards, used the boardinghouse as both a temporary refuge and a social and economic bulwark.[59]

From the mountainous villages of Spain and the barrios of Havana a remarkable center of Hispanic culture evolved in Tampa. The Spanish population, though relatively small in Tampa during the formative years, exercised enormous influence. In 1890 the U.S. Census estimated there were 233 Spaniards in Tampa, a figure that grew to 963 in 1900 and 2,337 in 1910. Held together by a vibrant Latin culture, infused with a set of distinctive work rhythms, and accentuated by a heightened political consciousness, Ybor City offered its Spanish residents contrasting values and alternatives: solidarity buffered by individuality; an isolated community beset by revolution and unrest; an elite work force challenged at every point by a Cuban proletariat.

Cubans

Beginning with a vanguard of workers in 1886, Cuban immigrants emerged as the most numerous ethnic group in Ybor City. Within four years of the founding of the settlement, 1,313 Cubans had settled in Tampa; their number grew to 3,533 by 1900. The census count was almost certainly underestimated. As one city official complained in 1895, "many of the town's Cubans lived in very small apartments and come and go like blackbirds."[60] On another occasion a newspaper editorialized that "practically no count was made of the Spanish [-speaking] residents in the census."[61]

By any definition Cuban immigrants were remarkably mobile. The physical proximity to Cuba, the ease of travel between Havana and Tampa, and the interchangeability of work skills melded, in the words of one Cuban historian, "a world of the cigarmakers on both sides of the Florida straits into a single universe."[62] Peripatetic Cubans returned to their homeland during slack periods of employment and during holidays, frequenting social clubs with branches in Tampa and Havana and slipping on a work apron, if necessary, to roll cigars.

Ramón Williams, American consul general to Cuba throughout the 1880s and 1890s, testified before a congressional committee in 1892: "The people here [Cuba] look upon Florida as so much a part of their own country." Refuting the idea that Cubans were mere "birds of passage," he elaborated: "They have more attachment for the U.S. than that sort of people. . . . I should say that there is no emigration from the island of Cuba in the European sense of the word, i.e., there is no emigrant class. There is steerage, but they go as regular passengers. Between Key West and Havana, people go as between Albany and New York. . . . They go back and forth as those French laborers go from Canada into New England. . . . There is daily intercourse between the people of Havana and Key West and Tampa, Florida."[63] The investigating committee estimated that between 50,000 and 100,000 persons passed annually between Cuba and the United States and back again. Typically Cubans did not pass through a customs or immigration clearinghouse. One cigar manufacturer testified he had employed the same Cuban three separate times during a period of one year. In his reminiscences about early Ybor City, the Cuban author José Rivero Muñiz pointed out that, when he landed at Port Tampa in 1899, there was still no formal customs check. "We landed without anyone asking either me or my brother where we intended to go or how long we intended to stay in the city."[64]

Cubans emigrated principally from Havana and from a small cluster of towns outside the capital, including Bejucal, San Antonio de los Banos, Santiago de las Vegas, and Cardenas. Cuban tobacco farmers from Pinar del Rió also came to Tampa. Movement most commonly involved families, in large part because of the unsettled conditions in Cuba and the facility of travel. Many Cubans were second-generation Spaniards, such as José Vega Díaz. Born in Havana in 1884, the son of an Asturian immigrant, Díaz accompanied his father to Ybor City in 1892 aboard the *Olivette*. "We came to Ybor City not Tampa!" Díaz insisted. His father became president of the Cigar Makers Trade Union, and Díaz followed kith and kin into the cigar factories.[65]

The volume of traffic to and from Cuba fluctuated wildly according to the barometer of international politics and labor relations. Over 500 workers, for instance, arrived at Tampa in one week after a strike in Key West in 1889. "I arrive in Tampa in August 1912," mused José de la Cruz, a Cuban immigrant. "A strike among cigar makers in Havana forced me to leave Cuba in search of work elsewhere. I arrived in Ybor City in the middle of a torrential rainstorm. . . . And on that night, my first night in Tampa, I vowed I would return to Cuba within the year."[66]

Strikes in the Cuban cigar industry were becoming all too common. By the 1870s Cuba already was home to committed anarchists and socialists who labored tirelessly in support of the working class. An important early influence in the spread of anarcho-syndicalist ideas was José Llunàs, publisher of *La Tramontana* in Barcelona, who wrote a series of small pocketbooks dealing with various aspects of anarchist ideology. Supporters sent large numbers of these volumes to Cuba, where a fellow Catalan, Enrique Roïg San Martín, distributed them.[67] Roïg San Martín, who became the island's most noted anarchist, in his early career had worked as a *lector* in one of Havana's cigar factories and had received his sociopolitical indoctrination at the hands of militant cigarworkers.[68]

By the early 1880s Roïg San Martín had participated in the founding of several workers' groups, including the Junta Central de Artesanos de la Habana, an organization that precipitated a series of violent strikes. In 1887 he began publishing Cuba's first anarcho-syndicalist newspaper, *El Productor*. He was also instrumental in forming the Circle of Workers

(1888), an organization that suported a wide variety of workers' agencies, including evening schools, day-care centers, orphanages, and other social welfare institutions for the working class.[69]

Socialists and anarchists played critical roles in the creation of a Cuban labor movement. Radicals were important in forming the first effective workers' groups and in structuring the broader agenda of organization and ideology. This was particularly true of the cigarmaking trades, which organized early and possessed leaders of exceptional ability and militance. So dynamic and effective were these artisans that they soon came to occupy something of a leadership position in the wider labor movement. Within the Cuban cigar industry itself a steady upward spiral of strike activity after 1880 gave witness to the increased radicalization of the work force.[70]

The 1892 Congreso Obrero in Havana proved to be an important step in the developing relationship between the Cuban workers' movement and radicalism. Guided by the principles of revolutionary socialism and influenced heavily by cigarmakers, the congress proclaimed a vigorous proletarian ideology, urging, among other things, the adoption of the general strike as a potent weapon and declaring unequivocally that *"los obreros formamos una sola clase"* (workers form a single class).[71] For years, however, the pursuit of working-class goals often found itself at loggerheads with the continuing struggle for independence that periodically convulsed the island.

The disruptions in Cuba meant that Ybor City was becoming, in the vernacular of the times, a "Little Havana," or *La Pequena Asturias*. If the colony had not yet measured up to the grandeur of Havana, the community's cast reflected a microcosm of a Cuban barrio. Nothing accentuated Ybor City's distinctiveness—perhaps its uniqueness in North America—more than the presence of Afro-Cubans, who worked side-by-side with white Cubans, Spaniards, and Italians and lived among them in integrated housing.

Afro-Cubans

The Afro-Cubans in Ybor City had emigrated from Havana and the surrounding towns, especially Bejucal. They brought with them cultivated cigarmaking skills and a rich culture, which was a mixture of African rituals, Caribbean customs, and Hispanic traditions. Afro-Cubans were represented in the vanguard of Ybor City. By 1890 their numbers had already grown to 367; by 1900, 791 Afro-Cubans and their children, of whom 540 had been born in Cuba, had settled in Tampa.[72] These people represented a "minority within a minority," in 1900 constituting 13 percent of the Cuban population. Afro-Cuban men filled an important niche in the cigarmaking ranks; indeed, no male group concentrated their labors more heavily in that profession. By 1900 there were fewer than a dozen Afro-Cuban males laboring outside the cigar factories; the women, however, tended not to work for wages.[73] Black Cubans, like white Cubans, were extremely mobile geographically, shuttling frequently between Tampa and the island.

Within the sheltered confines of Ybor City, race relations between Afro-Cubans and other Latins appeared remarkably tolerant and harmonious. "In those days we grew up together," reminisced Hipólito Arenas, an Afro-Cuban. "Your color did not matter—your family and their moral character did."[74] Anglo Tampa accepted this breach of state, regional, and local customs as long as such racial interrelations occurred only within the colony. In part this acceptance reflected Tampa's tendency to derisively classify all Latins as "Cuban niggers."

The Cuban Revolution

No single event defined the values and shaped the thought of early Ybor City more than the struggle for Cuban independence. Afro-Cubans such as Ruperto Pedroso and Bruno Roïg spearheaded the formation of local patriotic clubs, and revolutionary leaders such as José Martí preached the unity of races in a greater Cuba. By 1896 Tampa's Cubans had formed forty-one patriotic clubs.[75]

While rank-and-file Cuban workers were the foot soldiers of the Cuban revolution, a handful of intellectuals served as generals for the all-consuming crusade of *Cuba Libre*. Articulate and forceful leaders such as Ramón Rivero y Rivero, José Dolores Poyo, Fernando Figuerado, and Elegio and Nestor Carbonell edited the earliest newspapers of Ybor City *(El Yara, La Contienda)*, organized political cells (Los Independientes, Club Ignacio Agramonte), and read stories of the French Revolution, San Martín, and Simón Bolívar from factory pulpits.[76]

The arrival of José Martí in November 1891 galvanized the Cuban community. Contrary to local myth, Martí did not act alone in stirring revolutionary fervor; rather, he fashioned with others in Tampa and Key West a successful movement, the Partido Revolucionario Cubano, in

February 1892. *"El dia de la Patria"* (one day's work for the homeland) became the theme song of Ybor City's Cubans in the 1890s. A contemporary speculated that "the insurgents received as much financial aid from these people [Tampans] as from all other American sources abroad."[77]

Inspired by emigrant cigarmakers, the revolutionary junta in Cuba signaled *el grito de guerra* (cry to arms) on February 24, 1895. The news that the insurrection had begun convulsed Ybor City into wild demonstrations, kindling "the sacred flames of patriotism on every Cuban altar in the city." To consecrate the moment, a crowd of 3,000 Cubans gathered in front of the Martínez Ybor factory.[78]

The impassioned battle over Cuba shaped the terms for debate and organization in Ybor City from 1886 to 1898. Almost from the beginning the frontier outpost bristled with Cuban and Spanish radical political groups and debating societies, most of which resulted from the repression on the island and many of which gravitated to the independence cause. The anarchist Carlos Baliño, a friend of the Cuban patriot José Martí, was the man most responsible for the popularity of radical doctrines among Cubans. He had gained an early introduction to government suppression when his father disappeared after being deported from Spain for his political activities. Baliño had spent time in Key West before coming to Tampa, where he worked as an *escogedor* (cigar packer) to earn his bread while subscribing to anarchism as his way of life. He founded at least six clubs in and around Ybor City and was instrumental in creating the Centro de Propaganda Obrera, an agency that regulated the distribution of radical literature among the city's Spanish-speaking people. For a time he published the radical journal *La Tribuna del Pueblo*.[79]

Caught in a vicious crossfire between defenders of empire and torchbearers of independence were the Spanish radicals, particularly the more numerous anarchists. Some Cuban radicals distrusted them, perceiving anarchism as a Trojan horse designed to confuse patriots over the true goals of the revolution. Still others believed that the Spanish government hired anarchists to foment strikes as a means of stopping the flow of support funds to the rebels.[80] Yet the patriot José Martí worked assiduously to enlist the aid of anarchists and socialists of all nationalities for the war effort. Most believed, as did Ybor City's noted Spanish anarchist Pedro Esteve, that "it is good to love *'la patria'* but it is better to love liberty and justice." In further support of this view, Carlos Baliño explained that there existed a symbiosis between anarchism and independence. It would be absurd, he urged, to endorse individual liberty and oppose collective liberty.[81]

The Cuban revolution brought profound change to Ybor City. The war absorbed vast sums of individual resources that might have financed family and community enterprises. For the Cuban community the era of exile would end with the passing of Spanish colonialism; émigrés would become immigrants. An era of working-class militancy dawned as laborers, disenchanted by American control of Cuba and frustrated by the changing nature of the cigar industry, organized. New union heroes would replace Martí and Maceo. But the Ybor City to which another generation looked for a new beginning also changed. Many of the first-generation *patrònes* such as Martínez Ybor had died. New leaders would not only have to deal with new owners but also with a new immigrant group.

Sicilians/Italians

At Martínez Ybor's funeral in 1896, ten mutual aid societies marched in the cortege as Cubans and Spaniards mourned the passing of Ybor City's founder. A new ethnic element, Sicilians, also joined in the procession.[82] Martínez Ybor had not planned for their employment, nor had Sicilians themselves previously figured to be part of Ybor City. Unlike the Cubans and Spaniards who had arrived with logical and necessary skills and from predetermined paths, the infusion of Sicilians came about through testing and chance.

By the late 1880s the St. Cloud sugar plantation that had first attracted Sicilian sojourners to Florida was only one part of a wider mesh of economic possibilities existing in the region. New Orleans, with its intricate network of markets, information, and immigrants, served as a conduit for prospective laborers from the Magazzolo valley. St. Cloud acted as a regional staging center; Sicilians worked in the cane fields there and traveled to other harvesting and work sites as opportunities availed. Workers shifted between Florida and Louisiana and points west with seasonal regularity, occupying the role of migrant laborers but frequently placing their families in a permanent location. Documenting the wanderings of the initial waves of pioneers is exceedingly difficult. The fact that census takers reported only one Italian immigrant in St. Cloud in 1890—at the very height of their presence in Osceola County—reveals the problem of sources.[83]

The unattractive work climate at St. Cloud and the simultaneous expansion of the south Florida economy enabled Sicilians to explore the potential of other locales. A number of them signed on to construct Peter Demens's Orange Belt Railroad during the summer of 1887. By September the threat of yellow fever and the fact that Demens had yet to pay his workers nearly led to a riot.[84] W. H. Reams recalled his boyhood in Winter Park, Florida, through which the Orange Belt Railroad passed in the 1880s, "watching the Italian laborers with their wheelbarrows and shovels building the grade."[85]

In May 1892 the Italian consul at New Orleans reported that Italian nationals were leaving the cane fields of Osceola County. He noted that while 80 of his countrymen still remained at St. Cloud, 250 of them already resided in Tampa.[86] The sugar plantations had served their purpose, supplying an expedient source of employment for needy workers, whose expectations changed as they became knowledgeable about and acculturated to the American economic scene. In reality St. Cloud had never evolved into an immigrant community but merely functioned as a labor camp and temporary refuge. Yet Sicilians reluctantly cut the economic umbilical cord at St. Cloud. As late as 1896 the *Kissimmee Valley* reported, "About 50 Italians came up on this morning's train from Tampa on their way to St. Cloud to cut cane."[87] The plantation's ultimate demise, however, signaled the shift from sojourners to immigrants.

The St. Cloud sugar experiment collapsed in the late 1890s, a victim of declining sugar prices, a national depression, and Hamilton Disston's suicide in April 1896.[88] Long before then Sicilians had begun leaving for Tampa, eighty miles away, a city that offered unskilled labor on railroads and building projects. Even before Ybor City began, Sicilians labored in the phosphate mines to the south of Tampa and on construction crews at the magnificent Tampa Bay Hotel; St. Cloud veteran Gaetano Ferlita, for example, was a construction helper at the site of Henry Plant's hotel. The information network adjusted to these economic shifts. Carlo Spicola, born in Tampa in 1892, explained how his father, Gaetano, having harvested sugarcane in Louisiana, headed for St. Cloud before *paesani* diverted him instead to Tampa.[89] Nicolò Capitano followed a familiar path from Sicily to Houma, Louisiana, where many Stefanesi cut cane, and he too moved from St. Cloud to Tampa during this period.[90]

Local events often changed immigrant patterns. The infamous "Mafia Riot" in New Orleans, culminating in the brutal lynching of eleven Italians in 1891, precipitated the migration of a cluster of families to Tampa, although the incident must be understood as part of a larger process.[91]

Prominent among those arriving in Tampa in the aftermath of the New Orleans incident were immigrants from Contessa Entellina, a Sicilian town with deep roots in the Crescent City.

Contessioti, or "Geg Gegs," added another unique subgroup to the Ybor City milieu, distinctive even within its Sicilian population. In Tampa the Geg Gegs became a minority faction within the greater Sicilian community. Whereas in New Orleans the Contessioti could support and sustain their own mutual aid society, in Tampa they joined other Sicilians to form a single club. Although Geg Gegs largely accommodated their culture to the pan-Sicilian and Latin value systems, they retained their distinctive dialect and many of their particular customs. As late as the 1930s the Catholic church in Tampa kept a special listing of *Italo-Albanesi di Contessa Entellina*.[92]

The career of Pietro Pizzolato typified the Contessioti experience in Tampa. Pizzolato left Contessa Entellina in the 1870s, arriving first in New Orleans and eventually moving on to Socorro, New Mexico, as foreman at a gold-smelting plant. Enriched by his American travels, Pizzolato invested his money wisely, eventually making fourteen trips between Sicily and America. He moved to Tampa in 1892 and opened a livery stable and grocery store. His days in the Southwest had given him experience in handling horses, which he put to good use in Ybor City.[93]

Nothing exerted a more powerful impulse for emigration than the reappearance in Sicily of a Pietro Pizzolato or Angelo Massari, laden with American gifts and sporting store-bought suits and hats. Massari related that when he and Castrenze Ferlita returned to Santo Stefano, a marching band met them at the railroad station twenty miles away. The gifts of a phonograph and Caruso records dazzled the next generation of Stefanesi.[94]

The crystallization of a "Little Italy" in Ybor City occurred precisely at the moment a new cycle of despair paralyzed Sicily in the mid-1890s. Crispi's brutal suppression of the *fasci* shattered any illusion that Sicily might be reformed. To peasants and artisans of the Magazzolo valley the bitter legacy of 1894 spelled a bleak future and the need to reassess short- and long-term goals. Some emigrants had hoped to return as landowners but soon realized how impractical that prospect was. Emigration, once thought to be a sensible means toward a realizable end, now became an end in itself. Sicilians quickly learned of a new destination—Tampa. Sojourners became emigrants, involving not only an adjustment in motivation but also a substantial change of scale.

The stabilization of the family and the reconstitution of relationships marked the second stage of migration. Stefanesi and Contessioti sailed for Tampa, not as anonymous individuals, but rather as links in a chain of migration. "Chain migration," according to Louise Tilly, "moves sets of individuals of households from one place to another via a set of social arrangements in which people at the destination provide aid, information and encouragement to new migrants. . . . At the destination, they also tend to produce durable clusters of people. . . . At the extreme, the migrants form urban villages."[95] Few Stefanesi sailed for Tampa without the guiding support of *americani*, well experienced in the emigrant process.

Prepaid steamship tickets, bought by family or *paesani* in America, hastened a feverish traffic from the Magazzolo valley. "Come to Tampa and I will help you," Francesco Coniglio wrote Pietro Longo in 1903.[96] The Longos departed, leaving behind, as did so many others, elderly parents and grandparents. Emigration clearly belonged to youth. A survey of Ybor City Italians in 1900 revealed only one person—Annetta Vencento—over the age of sixty-five.[97]

The histories of the Cannella and Pizzo families illustrate how much America occupied the thoughts of those left behind. Salvatore and Domenica Cannella operated a small dry goods store in Santo Stefano before relocating their business to New Orleans. They soon returned to Sicily, content to enjoy the fruits of their American labors. Unfortunately the wealthy repatriate died. By custom, Sicilian widows were doomed to a life of mourning in black. "But my mother, she was used to the business all the time," explained Rosalia Cannella Ferlita, Domenica's daughter. "Well, in Italy she had to stay in the house. There was nothing to do . . . there was no communication. Sit and sit. Finally she decided to come back to America. But she didn't want to go back to New Orleans . . . too many memories . . . so she came to Tampa."[98] Thus emigration offered an alternative inconceivable to earlier generations and greatly expanded the opportunities for villagers. In many ways this was particularly true of Sicilian women, whom an Italian official in Girgenti had described in 1861 as "bearing resignedly to their poverty. . . . they earn nothing and rarely leave the province."[99]

Antonio and Giuseppe Pizzo left Alessandria della Rocca in 1882, arriving in New Orleans. Giuseppe headed for Houston while Antonio migrated to the sugar parishes. After accumulating money while working in the cane fields, Antonio opened a grocery store in Jennerette, Louisiana. He invested his money well and returned to Sicily intent on living out his life as a man of status. In Alessandria he bought land, almond groves, and the Albergo Cosmopolitano, the village's only hotel, installing his family on the top floor. Tragedy struck when a kidnapping took the Pizzo family's eldest daughter, who was never returned, despite a ransom payment. The children who had been born in Louisiana were unhappy in Sicily, and daughter Angelina persuaded her father to allow her and her younger brother Paolo to emigrate to Tampa. They arrived in 1901, followed a year later by their reluctant father, who eventually repatriated again to Alessandria.[100]

Although the emigrant experience shaped the collective destinies of Sicilians, the ordeal seared individuals with inescapable memories. "The minute I saw the Statue of Liberty," rhapsodized Nina Tagliarini Ferlita, "I left everything behind." She described her bittersweet indoctrination into American life:

It was like stepping on a piece of ice and by the time you're on the other side, it's melted. . . . It was something, beautiful. . . . Unfortunately, there was a man who died on the boat and they had to fumigate everyone who came in. Imagine a fourteen-year-old kid disrobed in front of adults . . . when you are developing and wanted to hide yourself. They threw on us all kinds of disinfectant. The stink, I still smell it. They got those hose like the firemen have and swish—all over the place. Ohhh, that was the most ungodly thing. But that did *not* give us a bad impression of America. . . . It was just one of those procedures![101]

Ybor City quickly became a central receiving station for Sicilians who had landed elsewhere in the migrant universe. Immigrants laboring in the agricultural fields of the South and the railroad and mining towns of the East and West received news of Ybor City—exactly how we do not know, but oral history reveals some clues. Born in Santo Stefano in 1882, Giuseppe Traina joined his uncle in New Orleans in 1890 and from there the two obtained employment in Houma, Louisiana. Giuseppe earned twenty-five cents a day carrying water to the cane workers. The Panic of 1893 disrupted the sugar industry, dispersing workers, and Giuseppe headed for Chicago, where he sold newspapers on State Street. In the late 1890s he heard about the Stefanesi settlement in Ybor City and migrated to Tampa.[102]

The third stage of the migrant experience involved the building of a community. Sicilians coalesced in a sparsely populated section east of the original Cuban and Spanish settlements in Ybor City. Their choice of residence reflected economic necessity (they accepted the most menial jobs offered in a dynamic Ybor City economy) and social circumstance (it is unlikely that Tampa natives, given their attitude toward all Latins, would have welcomed a separate Sicilian colony outside Ybor City). The nucleus of "Little Italy" centered around Seventh Avenue and Eighteenth Street, which remained the settlement's core for the next seventy-five years. The 1893 city directory recorded more than a dozen Sicilians residing in this area and a scattered few others residing outside the settlement.[103]

Although the directory's stark listing completely missed substantial numbers of sojourning laborers, it does provide at least a hazy outline of the emerging community. All but two of the fifteen individuals in the listing were from the Magazzolo valley, and all but two of the remaining thirteen were from Santo Stefano; only three of the fifteen resided outside the confines of Ybor City. The businesses appearing in the directory were those that most commonly anchored the early stages of community formation. As scholars such as Robert Harney and John Zucchi have pointed out, such businesses as bakeries, groceries, and saloons often shaped the permanence and character of immigrant clusters.[104] These enterprises were far more than simple commercial ventures. The range of services and materials they supplied could become the catalyst for an immigrant consciousness and coalescence. Moreover, these occupations frequently supplied the first contingent of community leaders, as they did in Ybor City.

Two events in 1894 pointed to the awakening of a communal awareness. A dramatic murder early in the year focused attention on the emerging Sicilian settlement. Late one night an unknown assailant killed Ignazio Camparito, who had just sold a piece of real estate for $150. Police soon arrested four suspects in the murder. As headlines of "mafia activities" swirled in the local press, a native citizenry that had not yet forgotten the events in New Orleans grew anxious. To quiet fears and help ensure that Tampans would not resort to mob rule, as so recently had happened in Louisiana, sixteen "prominent Italians of Ybor City" began a subscription for Camparito's children and published an appeal in the newspaper: "Reference having been made by newspapers to the effect that the atrocious crime committed at Ybor City . . . was the act and deed of the dreaded Mafia, and knowing that it is liable to injure the reputation, business standing and character of the Italian residents in the city of Tampa, therefore, we repudiate and deny having any such organization, and we hereby pledge ourselves to help and give the authorities our support in ferreting out the criminals of such act."[105] Included among the signers of the document were, not strangely, a number of the businessmen who appeared in the 1893 directory. Of more interest, perhaps, is the fact that six of the other names appearing were men who had been among the very earliest St. Cloud sojourners.[106] That they were now concerned about their "reputation, business standing and character" in Ybor City attests to the alterations that had taken place in their goals.

The darker side of this incident helps, in part, to explain the second development. In the atmosphere of anxiety and uncertainty, community leaders sought the extra measure of security that organization could bring. Thus began La Società Italiana di Mutuo Soccorso (changed in 1906 to L'Unione Italiana). Composed initially of 124 members drawn almost entirely from the Maggazolo villages, the club had as its first president Bartolomeo A. Filogamo, a cigar factory bookkeeper who had earlier migrated from Castellammare del Golfo.[107] The founding of the club had far ranging consequences for the young community, but few implications were more noticeable during the early years than those that touched upon questions of identity. The naming of the club pointed to the direction this fledgling community was taking in its attempts to frame a public personality. By using "Italian" in its incorporated name, the club may have been trying to deflect some of the negative connotations surrounding "Sicilian" that existed in Tampa. It may also have been a logical choice given the fact that the organization cast a wide membership net—individuals from all parts of the Italian peninsula joined the club from the beginning.

Whatever the motivation of the club's founders, after 1894 virtually no public reference, by immigrant or native, to this overwhelmingly Sicilian settlement used any term but "Italian." An example of this phenomenon occurred in 1896 when the *Morning Tribune* featured a story purporting that the Cubans, Spaniards, and Italians of Ybor City were "in great distress and suffering." Twelve Italian immigrants penned an open letter protesting the article. Giuseppe Licata, who had recently arrived from Santo Stefano, spoke for the group, responding that "after having made my most strenuous effort to find any of them [relief cases], I have failed to discover a single case of distress among the resident Italian colony."[108]

Ybor City's Italian quarter remained relatively small until 1900, when large numbers of newcomers began to arrive in the district. During the late 1880s and early 1890s natives directed little media attention toward the enclave's Italianate character; however, by the late 1890s the *Morning Tribune* characterized Ybor City's eastern district as "Little Italy."[109]

The 1900 census found 1,315 Italian immigrants in Ybor City and West Tampa.[110] Successive streams of new arrivals added a vitality to the colony. According to *Bolletino dell' Emigrazione*, almost 250 Italians arrived in Florida (almost exclusively Tampa) each year between 1900 and 1903, a figure increasing to 600 between 1904 and 1908.[111]

The pace of Italian development did not go unrecorded in local papers. "A large number of Italian citizens are on the tiptoe of expectancy for a colony of emigrants . . . ," observed the *Morning Tribune* in August 1903, adding: "By the way, since these Italians have decided to spend their lives here, they have gone to building substantial houses and spending their money for permanent homes. Becoming more Americanized, they are developing into a desirable class of citizens. The hoarding of money to carry back to Italy is a thing of the past with them."[112] In June 1905 the *Morning Tribune* commented that, during the previous year, perhaps as many as 750 Italian immigrants arrived in Ybor City. "They still wear native garb," the paper reported.[113] In December 1905 the paper estimated "the local Italian colony has increased 100% in two years. . . . It can be verified at any time. Parties from 25 to 100 Italians are arriving in Tampa every week. Not one of them is out of work."[114]

If Ybor City served as a magnet for Sicilians who traveled to distant points only to return to their natal villages, so too did it attract small numbers of Italians born outside the principal Sicilian villages of origin. Some of these locations, such as San Biaggio, Prizzi, Camporeali, Palazzo Adriana, Lecca, and Lecara Friddi, were not far from the core villages; others, such as Castellammare del Golfo, Trapani, and Siracusa, were located further away. Interestingly, Ybor City seemed to have attracted no one from Termini Imerese, a Sicilian seacoast town that sent emigrants to virtually every Italian settlement in the Americas. Other locations in southern Italy were represented, principally Naples and its surrounding small communities.[115]

The individuals who filled these minor streams came to Tampa for a variety of reasons, most of which defy easy explanation. Generally these travelers responded to perceived opportunities existing in Tampa, gleaning knowledge generated along immigrant channels. These conduits of information flowed between the mother country and the new-world outposts, transmitting news about economic conditions, living standards, and transportation routes. Emigrants responded to these networks in ways that afforded expression of individual choice and daring. Not all movement followed the classic lines of *campanilismo*, kin networks, or chain migration; chance, quirk, and human agency sometimes intervened. As news about Tampa circulated, alternately attracting and repelling persons who sampled the possibilities, constant infusions of newcomers filtered into Ybor City. Many left immediately; others stayed for brief periods; and some chose to settle down. This "immigrant grapevine" operated in part from personal exchanges—word of mouth, letters and messages from friends. The Italian American press also generated news about outlying "colonies" existing throughout North America. Whatever its precise mechanism there existed a corpus of knowledge about the nature of the Ybor City settlement that allowed individuals to gauge its desirability for themselves.

Interviews with pioneers and descendants of the immigrant generation evoke a number of powerful images, among them a tenacious loyalty to the homestead and a sense of steady upward mobility. Historically, local observers have explained the "success" of the Italians in Ybor City in terms of restricted options—immigrants allegedly could not easily return to Sicily on the next boat. Yet if one probes deeply, the portrayal of early stability and upward mobility is dispelled by the reality of trial and error, movement and migration. The 1900 census, for instance, revealed Italian immigrant parents in Tampa with children who had been born in Louisiana, New York, Cuba, Argentina, France, and Turkey.[116]

The processes of sojourning, chain migration, and community building brought a varied mix of individuals to Tampa. The life histories of a few illustrate the point. Born in 1876, the son of a Neapolitan engineer, Giovanni Andrea Grimaldi conventionally should have followed in his father's footsteps. His college career ended, at least according to family accounts, when the young student quarreled with a fellow pupil, the Prince of Savoy. Grimaldi sailed for Boston and from there, for unknown reasons, migrated to Ybor City in the 1890s. In a remarkably short time he emerged in the role of *prominento*, a broker between Italians and the rest of Tampa. He learned English and provided information about jobs, steamship connections, currency exchange, and the city bureaucracy. He translated and wrote letters for unlettered immigrants, charging them a fee for his services. In 1905, as his career branched into insurance and travel agencies, he helped found the Bank of Ybor City.[117]

The Rumore family also came to Ybor City in the 1890s, but class and circumstances dictated a different path for them. Giuseppe Rumore left Santo Stefano after the collapse of the *fasci* in 1894. He hoped that Scranton, Pennsylvania, would reward his ability to cut and lay stone.

After a trial of one year Rumore brought his family to Ybor City, where there were no stones but a future for builders. His son Giovanni, born in Sicily in 1891, remembered that his father bought a cow and sold milk to America soldiers at Port Tampa in 1898. "We came to Tampa to survive," said Giovanni Rumore in 1984, then ninety-three years old and still laying bricks the way his father had taught him.[118]

Salvatore Greco came to the United States courtesy of an uncle who forwarded thirty dollars for a steamship ticket. Greco worked in the Louisiana cane fields for seventy-five cents a day, followed by stints with railroads in St. Paul, Minnesota, and in Pennsylvania. In 1907 he returned to Italy, married, and after a few years immigrated to Ybor City with his wife and two children.[119]

Castrenze Ferlita, a sixteen-year-old peasant, and his uncle Gaetano Ferlita left Santo Stefano for St. Cloud in the late 1880s. Gaetano had worked as a stable boy to support his widowed mother in Sicily. The two soon rose to positions of leadership in St. Cloud and later in Tampa, largely because of their ability to arrange for desired foodstuffs. Gaetano opened saloons in Ybor City and downtown Tampa, and in 1904 he became the sole distributor in Tampa of Schlitz beer. He later branched into the import-export business. Castrenze, after working in the cigar factories, joined his father-in-law's dairy and soon bought three cows and a parcel of land east of Ybor City, where he began his own dairy. In 1915 he opened an ice factory, incorporated as the Cosmopolitan Ice Company.[120]

The formative years of Ybor City gave rise to what native Tampans regarded as a well-defined community. More precisely, what existed by the turn of the century were the nuclei of four distinct immigrant subcommunities: Cuban, Afro-Cuban, Spanish, and Italian. In reality the internal histories of each group were never that simple. Most Spaniards, for instance, defined themselves by their Galician or Asturian origins, while the *patrones* considered themselves apart from the proletariat. Cubans and Italians also retained distinctive identities that shaped their internal histories in important ways. Primitive conditions and physical isolation intensified ethnic identities from within, while racial and nativist hostility imposed a sense of shared community from without.

By 1900 Ybor City's social structure, which had initially crystallized around the twin poles of Cubans and Spaniards, had accommodated the later-arriving Italians, who joined black and white Cubans at the lower levels of the cigar industry, the very bottom of the status hierarchy. Lingering images of stiletto-wielding mafiosi engendered by the New Orleans lynching incident dogged the initial years of Italian settlement. Moreover, Italians remained identified with such low-status occupations as farm labor, peddling, and construction work. Most often they mixed residentially with Cubans, the group that Italians came into most frequent contact with in their efforts to break into the cigar industry. Highly skilled Cuban cigarmakers ranked above these groups because of their contributions to the industry, but their positions were precarious due to their growing labor militancy. At the top of the social ladder were the Spaniards, especially factory owners and foremen, who were quickly able to overcome the negative stereotypes of the Spanish-American War era. Not only were they the elites of the immigrant cosmos, but they also moved easily into the upper reaches of Anglo society. Cigar industrialists achieved a rapid and near complete acceptance of their power, status, and social position in Tampa, a fact made all the more remarkable given the Spanish background of most of them. The identification of native Tampans with manufacturer interests included the willingness of local citizens to use any means necessary to keep the industry in Tampa and to ensure its prosperity.

Summary

Through the alchemy of finance capitalism, colonial insurrections, international migrations, suppressed rebellions, agrarian collapses, and a transportation revolution, disparate immigrant groups converged upon Tampa, Florida, between 1886 and 1900. Like Dr. Johnson's Amazing Dancing Dog, the remarkable thing was not that the groups danced so well but that they danced at all. This exotic mixture survived its initial blending and thrived in the cultural hothouse of Ybor City. Instrumental to the survival and sustainment of Martínez Ybor's planned community experiment was the willingness of Cubans, Spaniards, and Italians to remain in Ybor City and to erect institutions that laid the foundation for a Latin community. The period 1886–1900 did not realize the creation of a unitary Latin community but rather witnessed the formation of several subcommunities which, in certain respects, have endured to this day. It would not be until the twentieth century that a more fully developed Latin society evolved.

By 1900 Ybor City's major immigrant groups had arrived, settled, and staked out their first claims to land and power. The struggle to persist in this new environment produced something of a "we-ness"; the hostile attitudes of Tampa's host society reinforced this tendency. As long as prosperity induced by cigars settled over Tampa, the Anglo population would tolerate its foreign neighbors. But the mere threat of disruption to the crucial cigar industry evoked a virulent brand of nativism, demonstrated in verbal abuse, physical harrassment, and even vigilante terrorism. The chasm separating Ybor City from Anglo Tampa assisted in the making of an Ybor City community and a Latin culture. In the end, however, nothing galvanized immigrants into members of a community more than the pervasive influence of the work culture generated by cigar factories and the searing, generational experience of labor unrest.

NOTES

1. Keene, "Gavino Gutiérrez," 33–38; "Pioneer Florida," *Tampa Sunday Tribune*, November 4, 1951; Pizzo, "Gutiérrez"; "Gutiérrez Dead," *Tampa Daily Times*, March 15, 1919. McKay, the son-in-law of Gutiérrez, has supplied a rich vein of history surrounding the founding of Ybor City.
2. "Pioneer Florida," *Tampa Sunday Tribune*, November 4, 1951.
3. Minutes, Tampa Board of Trade, October 21, 1885.
4. Buder, *Pullman*.
5. Minutes, Tampa Board of Trade, March 8, 1887.
6. *Tampa Guardian*, April 14, October 27, 1886.
7. Ibid., June 9, 1886.
8. García, "History of Ybor City"; Lemos, "Early Days of Ybor City"; *Tampa Guardian*, May 19, 1886; del Rió, *Yo'Fui Uno de los Fundadores*, 6.
9. Muñiz, *Ybor City Story*, 11–12.
10. FWP, "Life History of José García"; Muñiz, "Tampa," 337.
11. Lemos, "Early Days of Ybor City."
12. FWP, "Life History of Mr. John Cacciatore."
13. Westfall, "Martínez Ybor"; Muñiz, *Cubans in Tampa*, 18–19.
14. *Tampa Morning Tribune*, January 30, 1895.
15. *Twelfth Census: Manufacturers*, II, Table 4, p. 125; ibid.: *Population*, II, Table 34, p. 742.
16. Minutes, Tampa Board of Trade, September 29, 1905; Westfall, "Hugh MacFarlane," 20–24; *Daily Tampa Tribune*, July 22, September 28, 1892; *Tampa Morning Tribune*, March 7, 1911.
17. *Daily Tampa Tribune*, September 28, 1892; *Tampa Morning Tribune*, January 6, June 23, 1895; Muñiz, *Cubans in Tampa*, 59, 97.
18. Interview with Alfredo Prende, September 12, 1979.
19. *Daily Tampa Tribune*, May 21, July 22, 1892; *Tampa Daily Times*, August 28, 1894; *Tampa Morning Tribune*, November 8, 1900.
20. Interview with Mary Pitisci Italiano, April 20, 1980.
21. *Tampa Morning Tribune*, November 8, 1900; *Thirteenth Census: Population*, III, Table 4, p. 332.
22. Rerick, *Memoirs of Florida*, II, 222; Sabe, "Early Days of Ybor City," 61–70;

Tampa Morning Tribune, January 24, 1896. In 1900 customs revenues collected in Tampa exceeded those of the states of North Carolina, South Carolina, Georgia, Alabama, and Mississippi combined. Ibid., December 21, 1900.
  23. *Twelfth Census: Manufacturers*, II, 126–29.
  24. Baer, *Economic Development of the Cigar Industry*, 137; *Tampa Morning Tribune*, February 6, 8, 1900, June 11, December 31, 1911; *Tampa Daily Times*, July 6, 1910.
  25. *Tampa Journal*, January 12, 1888.
  26. *Tampa Tribune*, May 23, 1894, cited as Appendix L in Westfall, "Martínez Ybor"; Mss., V. M. Ybor and Company Book, THS.
  27. *Tampa Morning Tribune*, June 23, 1895.
  28. *Tampa Tribune*, June 23, 1895.
  29. *Tampa Morning Tribune*, July 30, 1896.
  30. Ibid., June 4, 1908.
  31. Ibid., January 6, 1895.
  32. Ibid., December 17, 1922, June 5, 1927.
  33. *Tampa Daily Times*, July 6, 1901.
  34. *Tampa Morning Tribune*, October 22, 1907, October 31, 1909.
  35. Interview with Julio Cuevas, July 29, 1983.
  36. Braudel, *Mediterranean*, I, 588.
  37. Suárez, *Asturias*, 92–104; Herr, *Spain*, 115–22; Brenan, *Spanish Labyrinth*, 93; Carr, *Spain*; Pescatello, *Power and Pawn*, 30.
  38. Ward, *Truth about Spain*, 133–36; Joll, *Anarchists*, 207; Woodcock, *Anarchism*, 356–57; Kaplan, *Anarchists of Andalusia*.
  39. Saltman, *Michael Bakunin*; Madariaga, *Spain*, 146–51; Bookchin, *Spanish Anarchists*; Herr, *Spain*, 128–29; Florencio, *Terrorismo Anarquista*; Savatar, *Para la Anarquia*, 119–28.
  40. Gómez, "Spanish Immigrants," 59–77.
  41. Interview with Julio Cuevas, July 29, 1983.
  42. Gómez, "Spanish Immigrants"; "Spaniards," in *American Ethnic Groups*, 950–53.
  43. Thomas, *Cuba*, 193–271; Foner, *Antonio Maceo*, 7–88.
  44. Corbitt, "Immigration in Cuba," 302–3. Also see Orovio, "Emigracion Española a Cuba," 505–27.
  45. Pérez, *Cuba Between the Empires*, 4–97; Muñiz, *Cubans in Tampa*, 47–61; Poyo, "Key West," 289–308.
  46. Poyo, "Key West," 289–308; Pérez, *Cuba Between the Empires*, 4–97.
  47. Ibid.; Corbitt, "Immigration in Cuba," 304–5.
  48. Westfall, "Martínez Ybor"; Gallo, "Tabaquero," 108; Gallo, *Tabaco Habana*; "Don Vicente Martínez Is Dead," *Tampa Daily Times*, December 17, 1896.
  49. "Don Vicente Martínez Is Dead," *Tampa Daily Times*, December 17, 1896.
  50. *Tampa Morning Tribune*, April 10, 17, 1895, November 17, 1896, May 11, 1906, November 12, 1915, March 17, 1926.
  51. Keene, "Gavino Gutiérrez," 36, 40; *Tampa Daily Times*, December 17, 1896.
  52. *Tampa Morning Tribune*, April 17, 1895.
  53. Gómez, "Spanish Immigrants," 59–77; Carr, *Spain*, 10–11; "Emigración," in *Gran Enciclopedia Asturiana*, VII, 78. After Tampa became a port of entry, Spaniards were able to come directly from Spain to Florida. See Thistlethwaite, "Atlantic Migration," 264–78, for an analogous phenomenon.
  54. FWP, "Life History of Fermín Suoto," 3–5.
  55. Interview with María Ordieres, June 11, 1981.

56. U.S. Congress, *Immigrants in Industries*, 191; *Eleventh Census*, Table 23.
57. Weltz, "Boarders in Tampa." This paper utilized the U.S. manuscript censuses of 1900 and 1910 and itemized all immigrant boarders.
58. U.S. Congress, *Immigrants in Industries*, Table 175, p. 244.
59. Interview with Alfonso López, April 24, 1980.
60. *Tampa Morning Tribune*, June 23, 1895.
61. Ibid., November 8, 1900.
62. Pérez, "Cubans in Tampa," 137.
63. Testimony of Ramón Williams, in U.S. Congress, *Cuba and Florida Immigration Investigation*, 65–98.
64. Ibid., 66; Muñiz, "Tampa," 339.
65. Interview with José Vega Díaz, May 3, 1980.
66. Interview with José de la Cruz, ca. 1978; *Tampa Journal*, November 7, December 5, 1889.
67. Sánchez et al., "Antecedentes del Movimiento Obrero," 266.
68. Hidalgo, *Orígines del Movimiento Obrero*, 101–2. Roïg San Martín later became a sugar technician. See Thomas, *Cuba*, 291.
69. Muñiz, "Tabaquero," 300–302; Muñiz, *Movimiento Obrero*, 211.
70. Estrade, "Huelgas de 1890," 27–51; Gallo, "Tabaquero," 108.
71. Dumoulin, "Movimiento Obrero," 96; García Gallo, *Biografiía del Tabaco Habano*, 139.
72. The authors wish to express their appreciation to Susan Greenbaum, assistant professor of anthropology, University of South Florida, for sharing her research. See Greenbaum, "Afro-Cubans in Exile," 59–73. See also *Eleventh Census*, Table 23.
73. Cordero, "Afro-American Community." Mr. Cordero has compiled a complete listing of Tampa's Afro-Cuban immigrants from the 1900 and 1910 U.S. censuses.
74. Interview with Hipólito Arenas, November 1, 1982.
75. Pérez, "Cubans in Tampa," 134.
76. Steffy, "Cuban Immigrants of Tampa," 31–78; *Tampa Morning Tribune*, July 14, 1892; Johnson, *"Partido Revoluciones Cubano."*
77. Day, "Cuban Settlers in America," 347; True, "Revolutionaries in Exile"; Pérez, "Cubans in Tampa," 134.
78. *Tampa Morning Tribune*, February 25, 1895.
79. Steffy, "Cuban Immigrants of Tampa," 63–69; *Tampa Tribune*, May 25, 1984; Toca, "Tabaqueros Cubanos," 13–23.
80. Fernández, "Anarquistas Cubanos," 4–5; Martí, *Obras Completas*, I; Pérez, *Cuba Between the Empires*, 4–38.
81. *Carlos Baliño, Documentos y Artículos;* "Our Havana," *Tampa Tribune*, May 25, 1894. There was a long-standing link between anarchism and feudalism in Spain.
82. *Tampa Daily Times*, December 17, 1896.
83. *Eleventh Census*, Table 33; interview with Dottoressa Serafina Castellano, March 20, 1981. For evidence of Italian laborers at St. Cloud, see FWP, "Cruize [sic] on the Minnehaha."
84. Pettengill, *Florida Railroads*, 89.
85. Letter to D. B. McKay, "Pioneer Florida," *Tampa Morning Tribune*, May 24, 1953.
86. Motta, "Nuova Orleans," 464.
87. *Kissimmee Valley*, November 11, 25, 1896. On November 25, according to the paper, "about 30 more Italians came up from Tampa and went out to St. Cloud to strip cane."

88. Sitterson, *Sugar Country*, 363–64.
89. Interview with Carlo Spicola, September 22, 1984; Massari, *Wonderful Life*, 64; Spicola, *Spicola Story*, 1–3.
90. Interview with Giuseppe Capitano, October 15, 1984. See *Passenger and Crew Lists*, VIII, March 13, 1905, for the list of alien immigrants aboard *Città di Napoli*. This ship landed in New York, on its way to New Orleans, carrying several hundred Sicilians, many from the Magazzolo valley, almost all heading for Louisiana.
91. Gambino, *Vendetta*.
92. *Contessa Entellina Society;* Wonk, "Sons of Contessa Entellina," 11–15; "Censimento preso degli Italo-Albanesi di Contessa Entellina," 1931, Ms., Archives, St. Augustine Diocese. Also see *La Parola dei Socialisti*, August 6, 1910.
93. Interviews with Tony Pizzo, 1978–84; McKay, *Pioneer Florida*, III, 772.
94. Massari, *Wonderful Life*, 274–78.
95. Tilly, "Migration," 53.
96. Interview with Paul Longo, June 30, 1980.
97. U.S. Manuscript Census (Tampa), 1900, HCC.
98. Interview with Rosalia Ferlita, May 18, 1980.
99. Carpi, "Condizioni delle Donne," I, 38.
100. Interviews with Tony Pizzo, 1979–84; McKay, *Pioneer Florida*, III, 772.
101. Interview with Nina Ferlita, April 25, 1980.
102. Interview with John L. Traina, October 23, 1984.
103. *Tampa City Directory*, 1893. The individuals listed, with occupations: Di Bona, Frank, bartender, Central Avenue*; Ficcarotta, Giuseppe, salesman, 1705 8th Avenue; Filippo, Gullo, laborer, 1710 8th Avenue; Filogamo, A. B., bookkeeper, 1121 11th Avenue; Gullo, G., shoemaker, 1408 8th Avenue; Licata, Antonio, grocer, 1700 7th Avenue; Mortellaro, Pietro, baker, 1706 7th Avenue; Patella, Antonio, groceries and fruits, 1433 7th Avenue; Pitisci, Philip, clerk, 1628 8th Avenue; Pitisci, Salvatore, grocer, 1628 8th Avenue; Reina, Joseph, salesman, 311 Tampa Street*; Reina, Salvatore, tailor, rooms at Laezar*; Salvaria, Norsiro, cigarmaker, 1726 9th Avenue; Silva, A., cigarmaker, 1817 8th Avenue; Zambito, Frank, baker, 7th Avenue and 8th Street. (*indicates Sicilians living outside Ybor City)
104. Zucchi, "Italian Immigrants"; Harney, "Ambiente and Social Class," 208–24; Harney, "Chiaroscuro," 143–68.
105. The entire affair is recounted in *Jacksonville Times Union*, June 24, 1893; *Tampa Daily Times*, June 12, 1918.
106. *Jacksonville Times Union*, June 24, 1893. Included among them were Gaetano Ferlita, Santo Gullo, Gaetano Cacciatore, Salvatore Pitisci, and Ignacio Reina.
107. Club records, L'Unione Italiana, L'Unione Italiana Collection, USF; Massari, *Comunità Italiana*, 709.
108. *Tampa Morning Tribune*, September 22, 1896.
109. "Considerable headway has been made on the erection of new buildings at the Seidenberg Cigar Company in Ybor City. . . . dwellings will be occupied by a colony of Italian cigarmakers." Ibid., March 28, 30, 1899.
110. *Twelfth Census*, Table 34.
111. "Gli Italiani," 217–18.
112. *Tampa Morning Tribune*, July 8, 1903.
113. Ibid., June 20, 1905.
114. Ibid., December 12, 1905.
115. Family membership rates, in membership directories, L'Unione Italiana Collection, USF. Many interviews mention villages of origin.

116. Hendry, "Revisionist View," 11. Only ten households had children born in Louisiana.

117. Interview with Ray Grimaldi, November 9, 1978; "Tony Grimaldi Can Really Cook," *Tampa Morning Tribune*, November 9, 1978.

118. Interview with Giovanni Rumore, October 21, 1982, October 9, 1984.

119. Massari, *Comunità Italiana*, 791.

120. Ibid., 780; interview with Rosalia Ferlita Anello, October 25, 1984; *Tampa City Directory*, 1900–1920.

4 Italians and the Culture of Labor in a Latin Community

> The *Journal* is a friend of the cigarmakers when they are in the right and reasonable . . . but they must not expect sympathy and encouragement in any unreasonable demands nor in efforts to stir up trouble in the community.
>
> *Tampa Journal,* January 16, 1890

"Never again!" exclaimed the crowd gathered in front of Tampa's classically designed southern courthouse. Placards in Spanish and Italian demanded justice, while orators exhorted the crowd to maintain unity and courage in the strike then convulsing the cigar industry. Policemen surveyed the demonstrators, nervously measuring their behavior. Should trouble arise, they knew their duty; the previous year they had imprisoned hundreds of such protestors.

The background of the confrontation lay in a series of seemingly trivial events taking place at the Bustillo Brothers and Díaz cigar factory in West Tampa. In late October 1902 cigarmakers struck the factory, a not altogether uncommon event in the turbulent industrial center. The work stoppage stemmed not from wage grievances or work hour disputes but rather from an assault directed at a cherished institution of the proud cigarmakers. Workers demanded that management "consent to our establishing the reading in our shop." *El lector,* the reader, symbolized the independence, distinctiveness, and artisan character of cigarwork. Cigarmakers hired and paid the *lector* to read to them during the workday (and, essential to the argument, they selected the literature to be read from the reader's platform). Such privileges were not taken lightly.

Bustillo deferred to custom and so did his workers, who soon hired a Cuban, Francisco Milián, as their reader. In addition to his oratorical talents, Milián was also politically shrewd; he was serving as mayor of West Tampa at the time. His place in municipal politics, however, ranked second in prestige behind the respected position of *lector*. So esteemed were these men that they customarily did not collect their fees personally. Rather, cigarmakers elected a *presidente*, an intermediary whose job it was to screen potential readers, solicit inquiries for future literature, and, every Saturday, collect the *lector*'s salary from the workers as they left the factory. Mr. Bustillo, however, forbade the *presidente* from collecting fees in the workroom, insisting that he stand in the street to perform his duties. Milián, his dignity slighted, resigned, and a factory-wide strike soon followed.

What began as a minor disagreement quickly spread to workers at other factories in the area, especially after assailants kidnapped Milián from West Tampa's city hall. Milián's captors took him to rural Hillsborough County, where he was stripped, beaten, and placed under guard. His tormentors then presented him with a Hobson's choice: exile to Cuba or death. They explained that Milián was "an agitator, a dangerous character, that he must leave, never to return. . . ." So Milián departed for Havana, his mysterious absence convulsing West Tampa and then Ybor City. Cigar factories faced a general strike. The embattled *lector* cabled his supporters from Key West and signaled his desire to return. He received a pointed reply: "RETURN MEANS CERTAIN DEATH," signed the "Committee." Undaunted and defiant, Milián came back to a hero's welcome as crowds mobbed him at the Tampa train station. A throng of over 2,000 cheered his speech at the Labor Temple, the cigarworkers' union hall, which ended with a demand to restore the reader to his former position. In short order the Bustillo factory surrendered to this ultimatum.[1]

The brief imbroglio typified Tampa's labor movement. Milián's terrifying deportation was no aberration. Rather, it served as another example of how Southerners reacted against aliens and agitators. The workers' outburst against Milián's troubles at the hands of management was not a sample of Latin temperament; instead, it revealed how much trust workers placed in ideas, individuals and institutions. Nor was the concerted protest by Italians, Spaniards, and Cubans a 1902 event staged to draw superficial public attention; rather, it demonstrated a continuum of ethnic interaction and unity.

In Tampa, as elsewhere, the forces of industrialization profoundly altered many of the local society's most fundamental habits and values. Communities often found themselves struggling with vast social changes as citizens searched for secure mooring posts. Tampa welcomed the arrival of a cigar industry which promised prosperity and growth. Along the way the industry blended European peasants, Hispanic artisans, displaced American farmers, and other preindustrial migrants into an urban work force. It also gave birth to a vigorous working-class culture, a commingling of various traditions, customs, and worldviews. The process was neither swift nor easy, and some participants questioned whether the price was worth the payoff. Scholars such as Herbert Gutman have shown that the social modifications resulting from such conditions did not necessarily end in the rapid destruction of familiar cultures and institutions.[2] Rather, these entities possessed a remarkable ability to transform themselves to meet new challenges.

Italian immigrants, who had formerly worried about the *padrone* or the mafia, selected options from a vastly different set of life and work choices in Tampa. In this world they would have to deal with a multiplicity of ethnic, class, and urban challenges that were largely alien to their oldworld past. They would ultimately have to adapt old institutions to meet their needs. The Italian work experience in Ybor City was not solely a history of trade unionism, with its failures and triumphs, but a complex blend of families, adjustments, and opportunities. "We won, you know," mused one immigrant cigarmaker while reflecting on his years in the cigar trades. "I know what history is going to say, but I want you to know that it is not so. We were not beaten. We have never surrendered."[3] This observation touches the essence of what the labor experience of any immigrant group rests upon—not just unions and organizations but the social lives of workers, where victories and defeats are more difficult to gauge.

The earliest Italian arrivals to Ybor City would hardly have participated in such demonstrations as the Milián struggle. For them employment in the cigar industry seemed a remote, unattainable goal. Arriving with no cigarmaking skills and held in contempt by the Spanish, the elite of the cigar industry, Italians were unlikely candidates for the factories. The steps that brought them to apprentice galleries, integrated them into the cigar work force, enlisted them in unions, and ultimately placed them in leadership positions among workers require explanation. A necessary prerequisite is an understanding of the work environment confronted by these pioneers.

The Cigar Industry

The cigar industry that arrived in Tampa in 1886 specialized in the making of high-quality, hand-rolled cigars by the "Spanish method." This process required skilled workers who crafted each smoker by hand, obtaining the correct length, circumference, density, and tightness by a sure sense of feel gained through long practice. Using only the finest materials, "Clear Havana" tobacco from the Vuelta Abajo region of Cuba, the best Tampa factories produced the most expensive and well-crafted cigars in America.[4] More important was the special work ethos that distinguished the industry. Dominated by a craft mentality and possessing a full complement of artisan work styles and outlooks, the cigar trade created an industrial ethic based on individual craftsmanship much like the standards of the old-world artisan guilds.

Although individualism reigned in the *galería* (workroom) a clear status and occupational hierarchy existed in the factories, a structure firmly organized in the early years along ethnic lines. The first major division existed between salaried and piecework employees. The former category consisted of foremen, managers, skilled clerical staff, salesmen, and accountants, most of whom were Spaniards. The salaried staff also included *resagadores* (wrapper selectors) and *escogedores* (packers), highly trained men who sorted the tobacco leaves sent to cigarmakers on the basis of color, maturity, and texture, and then selected uniform lots of finished cigars for packing in boxes. Spanish men filled these ranks almost exclusively, as one 1910 report noted: "The manufacturers, who were Spaniards, chose the managers, a majority of the foremen, the selectors, and the pickers and packers from among their own group. In the factories owned by Spaniards in Tampa this rule is adhered to almost absolutely. Even in other factories the managers are most often found to be Spaniards."[5]

The next level began with skilled cigarmakers, who were ordered in status by the size, difficulty of production, and particularly the rate of pay corresponding to different types of cigars. In 1910, for example, *per-*

fectos paid at a rate of twenty-eight dollars per 1,000, while the lowly *cherutos* earned only eight dollars per 1,000. To be good a skilled cigarmaker not only had to be fast but also accurate, making each cigar exactly the same and in conformity with established sizes. A rare cigarmaker who blended both talents could make upwards of 2,000 cigars a week; average weekly production for individuals was somewhere between 1,100 and 1,300. Banders, strippers (workers who removed the center stems from tobacco leaves), casers, and bunchers fulfilled distinct, and less prestigious, roles in the economic hierarchy.[6]

In Tampa, Spaniards generally made the more expensive cigars, and the coveted trade of *chavatero* (knife sharpener) was always in Spanish hands. Cubans rolled the less expensive cigars and filled the ranks from casers to banders. As women began to filter into the cigarmaking outpost they typically labored at the stripping tables. At the bottom of the occupational ladder were those individuals who did not work directly with tobacco but merely dealt with physical tasks such as sweeping, hauling, portering, and doorkeeping. Unskilled Cubans, most of them Afro-Cubans, early arriving Italians, and some local Afro-Americans usually occupied these positions.[7]

Skilled cigarworkers followed distinctive work styles, reflective of an artisan status that was in part an inheritance from Seville and Havana and in part an ethos articulated forcefully over decades of development. No rigid schedules bound their days; they largely came and went as they pleased, often taking extended coffee breaks at nearby cafés that catered to their special tastes. "I loved to make cigars," exclaimed eighty-year-old Alex Scaglione, an Italian immigrant. "I did love it because I had plenty of freedom. I knock off whenever I wanted to. If there was a [base]ball game, I quit and go to the ball game."[8] Workers jealously guarded an assortment of fringe benefits which further accentuated their status. Varied relationships, privileges, and perquisites ordered the workplace, and wherever possible cigarmakers asserted their independence. No other industry permitted blacks, Latin Americans, European immigrants, and women to labor side-by-side at the same workbench. Many cigarmakers controlled apprentices, who performed a host of personal services in return for instruction. Between frequent steaming cups of *café con leche* cigarmakers sampled their craft at will; owners allowed them to take home five free cigars each day.[9]

The world of the cigar workshop offered a curious mixture of old-world traditions and new-world opportunities, a blend of modern economic circumstance and venerable cultures. At its heart cigarmaking remained an art form in which workers carefully controlled the trade they had mastered through a grueling apprenticeship. In this sense cigarmakers resembled other preindustrial craftsmen such as coopers, carpenters, and potters.[10] Since cigarmaking required almost no tools, workers retained the vital secret, the techniques and means of production, in their minds. Only a handful of gifted ones could transform a lifeless scrap of vegetation into a *puro Havana*, called by Lord Byron "sublime tobacco!"[11]

Most symbolic of the special ambience of the cigar industry was the institution of *el lector*. The custom of reading to workers from a raised platform *(la tribuna)* began in Cuba, but the practice had often run afoul of Spanish colonial authorities. In Tampa it became a cherished right, more so because the cigarmakers chose factory readers, paid their fees, and selected the items to be read.[12] The reader served as an important disseminator of worker information, international news, and radical ideologies. As one *lector* reminisced, "The *lectura* was itself a veritable system of education dealing with a variety of subjects, including politics, labor, literature, and international relations."[13]

Readings tended to focus on proletarian themes of the class struggle. "We had four daily shifts," explained Abelardo Gutiérrez Díaz, a Spanish-born *lector*. "One was used to read national news. Another was devoted to international political developments. The third concerned itself entirely with news from the proletarian press. And lastly the novel."[14] Particular favorites among novelists were Emile Zola, Victor Hugo, Miguel de Cervantes, Benito Pérez-Galdós, and Alexander Dumas. The philosophical works of Karl Marx, Errico Malatesta, Peter Kropotkin, and Mikhail Bakunin appeared frequently, as well as reports from contemporary newspapers such as *Tierra y Libertad* (an anarchist paper published in Barcelona), *El Despertar* (anarchist, Key West), *El Machete* (communist, Key West), and the *Daily Worker*.[15] Readers therefore provided the underpinning for a militant class consciousness that took root in Ybor City, a fact not lost on owners and elected officials, who waged an unremitting war to abolish the system of reading and gain greater control of the work force and the workplace.

Despite the perceptions of manufacturers, readers did not, in fact, create the radical temperament of the work force, but they did sustain and amplify it. "You know, when we read in the factory, we were not choosing for the reader, but for the worker," explained Wilfredo Rodríguez, who was in 1984 the last surviving *lector*.[16] Honorato Henry Domínguez, a reader during the 1920s, reminisced, "They [the owners] say we became too radical, reading the news from labor organizations and political groups. We read those things, it is true, but we read only what the cigarmakers wanted us to read." Italian cigarmaker Carmelo Rocca remonstrated, "If we wanted the reader to lecture us, we'd gone to a private hall."[17]

The readers' platforms of the factories became, in José Martí's phrase, "advanced pulpits of liberty." The institution itself reflected the democratic spirit of workers. Each factory elected a *presidente de la lectura* and provided him with a workers' committee, which nominated candidates for the reader's position and entertained auditions from aspirants. The *presidente* also served as a bargaining agent for the workers in fixing the reader's salary, which generally ranged from ten to twenty-five cents per cigarmaker per week, collected every Saturday. A popular reader such as Manuel Aparicio or José Rodríguez earned fifty to seventy-five dollars a week, a princely sum from which they purchased their books and papers and paid the *presidente* a 10 percent commission.[18]

Readers commanded an almost reverential respect. Dr. Ferdie Pacheco remembered Don Victoriano Manteiga, a reader, as "*un intelectual* . . . an impressive man in any society." Manteiga represented a segment of the reader corps that gravitated between the platform and the editor's bench. A half century after the last reader, cigarworkers vividly recalled their favorites. "I remember El Mejicano [Rodríguez]," exclaimed retired cigarmaker Tina Provenzano. "Sometime he read a novel, he read so good that people stand . . . stand and look at him." Joe Maniscalco, a cigarmaker for over sixty years, still marveled at how the best readers could control their voices and mimic characters. So passionate were attachments to certain readers that in 1904 a murder actually occurred in Ybor City following a heated debate over who was the city's best *lector*.[19]

The reader's words reverberated beyond factory walls as information disseminated from the platforms filtered outward into the wider immigrant community via a series of informal networks. Family and friends at the evening meal discussed the day's readings, thus extending the range of contacts. "What happened in my family no doubt happened in every other family," explained Frank Giunta, whose older sister worked in a cigar factory. "The members of the family that heard these novels went home and made known what the day's readings consisted of. These were always items of great social value that we appreciated in those days. Each evening my sister would come home and give us verbally what had taken place. We stuck around the family table some thirty minutes or so after supper to hear my sister give us the episode of the day and the news she had heard from the *lector*." A loose system of meetings among Italians allowed those who did not have family members in the factories to enter this communication network.[20] Yet in their earliest encounters with Ybor City's highly politicized cigarmaker community, Italians found even this tactic difficult to implement.

Italian Adjustments

Upon arrival Italians initially moved into areas of Tampa's occupational structure where vacuums existed, allowing them to seize competitive advantages. Such a strategy promised less overt conflict with immigrant neighbors and represented a realistic assessment both of the employment possibilities available in the local area and the skills they could bring to the marketplace (see chap. 9). Many immigrants, however, made initial employment selections with an eye to the cigar factories.

Some Italians started small cafés catering exclusively to the unique clienteles the cigar work force supplied. Each large factory attracted a satellite formation of cafés, food stores, restaurants, and boardinghouses. Italians quickly saw the potential markets and proceeded to supply appropriate goods and services. Hence they learned how to grind coffee in the Cuban style for shops catering to Cuban cigarmakers; they brewed Spanish brands for those cafés serving Spanish selectors; they supplied the Cuban sweets and desserts, and so on. These small enterprises often resulted in personal contacts with foremen and skilled cigarmakers that later prompted cigar factory employment. As a young man freshly arrived from Alessandria della Rocca, for example, Paul Longo obtained his first cigar industry job through friendships established while working in a restaurant owned by his father and located next to the Coruña factory.[21] These connections also assisted in providing the contexts for the linguistic adjustments so essential to success in Spanish-speaking Ybor City.

Italians entered the cigar factories literally and figuratively through the back doors. Those who first gained employment—almost always in the lowest positions available—took home bits and pieces of tobacco at the end of the workday. Then they practiced making hand-rolled cigars under the eyes of sympathetic Cubans, who provided the service to challenge Spanish owners and foremen.[22] Suspicious because of the mafia incident in New Orleans, Spaniards had prohibited such practices in their efforts to keep Italians out of factories. Cuban cigarmaker Domingo Ginésta remembered how acceptance came about. "When the Italians first came to Tampa," he recalled, "the Spaniards were adversed [sic] to allowing them to settle here, and they tried to keep them from working in the cigar factories. At this time we were in revolt against Spain, and we thwarted every move made by the Spaniards."[23] The Senate Dillingham Immigration Commission noted the same general pattern, observing that Italians faced resistance in their attempts to gain entry. "Nevertheless, they accepted the rougher jobs, always with an eye to the main chance, and for the next few years they did the janitor work, swept the floors...." This description of enterprising Italians doggedly devoted to hard work with an eye to opportunity conforms to their practices in other industrial cities. Tampa's Italians also resorted to the code of *furberia* (shrewdness) evinced by the smuggling of tobacco scraps from the factories to teach cigarmaking to aspiring kin and *paesani*. "In spite of every opposition," a reporter concluded, "a few learned to make cigars and these in turn taught their friends and relatives."[24]

Italians aspiring to cigarwork gained further benefit from the Cuban-Spanish rivalries existing in Ybor City. A few Spanish-owned factories in the 1890s grew so tired of persistent conflicts characterizing Cuban-Spanish relations that they hired Italians exclusively. The Seidenberg factory made such a decision, attracting to its surrounding streets a cluster of twenty-six Italian homes and small businesses.[25] Management also perceived the employment of Italians as a way to divide Latin workers. As more and more Italians gained the necessary skills, the number of routes into factory employment broadened.

The pattern of self-help eventually became more formal through the institution of the buckeye, or *chinchal*. "As soon as I arrived [1896] I started to make cigars," reminisced Alfonso Coniglio. "First my father brought tobacco, and he and the man next door would teach me at night, but in two weeks they found a place for me as an apprentice at a *chinchal* on 7th Avenue. How I loved the wit of cigarmakers. The word *chinchal* for example. It comes from the Spanish word for bedbugs and so is a place where bedbugs gather.... That's how I learned to speak Spanish. In fact I learned Spanish and proper Italian in Ybor City and it has always seemed to me that to speak a language properly is to talk of freedom."[26] For other Italians the *chinchal* proved not to be as memorable an experience. "When I was fifteen, Papa put me up as an apprentice," recalled Paul Longo, whose family came to Tampa with funds forwarded by the Coniglio family. "I did not learn to make cigars at a factory, but at a buckeye. My father pay ten dollars to . . . an old lady, Antonia, a Spanish woman. She requests that all the apprentices clean the house, clean this, do that. One day I told Pepe, her husband, 'My father give you ten dollars to teach me to make cigars, not to be a servant!' . . . I left. Daddy then find me a factory to make cigars."[27]

By the turn of the century an informal system of entry into factories already was effectively in place. Angelo Massari traveled just such a path in 1902 when he arrived in Tampa. A cousin of Massari's spoke to Castrenze Ferlita, one of the earliest Italian arrivals to enter the cigar trades, and secured an apprenticeship position for the young man at Antonio Rico and Company. Massari arrived at the factory door knowing no English or Spanish. The doorman, a Sicilian from Bagheria (Palermo), turned him over to Luigi Bassetti, a Piedmontese cigarmaker who had two apprentices already working under him. In league with these two youngsters, a white and a black Cuban, Massari performed the tasks common to all apprentices in the industry—wetting tobacco, spreading out the leaves, blending materials, sweeping the work area, preparing mucilage, and so on. In return he received instruction in the techniques of cigarmaking from Bassetti and Pietro Giglia, a Stefanesi. At home in the evenings he studied Spanish and practiced his cigarmaking skills. Soon he was earning twenty-four dollars a week and making plans to leave the factories for the grocery business.[28]

By 1898, an important year for Ybor City because of the Spanish-American War, Italians had made substantial inroads into cigar factories, though they still constituted a minority of the work force and lagged behind Cubans and Spaniards in the overall population. As early as June 1900 two-thirds of all gainfully employed Italians in Ybor City labored in the cigar industry in some capacity. By 1910 Italians accounted for almost 20 percent of the total cigar work force.[29] "The Italians are gaining ground in the cigar industry," observed a foreman that year, adding his opinion that they would soon outnumber Cubans in the factories. If one added the numbers involved in the buckeyes and backroom workshops, the figures would be even higher."[30] Significantly, Italians accomplished their movement into the cigar trades in a very distinctive pattern, one that clearly revealed cultural differences among the Latin work force.

"A woman who becomes a worker is no longer a woman," wrote the

TABLE 5 Employment of Italians by Age Group, Ybor City, 1900

Industry	Age 40–60+	Age 20–39	Age 5–19	Total	Percent
Cigar industry	37	196	99	332	70.0
Italian males	18	96	27	141	
Italian females	19	100	72	191	
Non-cigar industry	71	68	4	143	30.0
Italian males	70	67	4	141	
Italian females	1	1	0	2	
Total employed Italians	108	264	103	475	100.0

SOURCE: Adapted from Hendry, "Revisionist View," and based upon U.S. Census Manuscript Schedules for Ybor City residents, located at PKY. The figures do not include Italians who lived outside Ybor City but in the greater Tampa area.

Frenchman Jules Simon, but such advice failed to guide the actions of Ybor City's Italian women. Indeed, what made the Italian entry into factories unique was the unusually heavy incidence of women obtaining such employment.[31] The 1900 census revealed the trend unmistakably: Italian women outnumbered all other Ybor City women at factory workbenches. Census takers counted 191 Italian women, only 75 Cuban women, and a mere 2 Spanish women employed in cigarwork. Equally surprising, Italian males from Ybor City could point to employment in the cigar factories (see Table 5).[32]

In 1900 the great majority of Italian women working in cigar factories labored as cigar strippers, widely regarded as the least desirable position in the industry. Tobacco stripping involved the removal of hard stems from tobacco leaves, a job that many observers felt was particularly suited to the "nimble fingers" of women. Because of meager pay, unhealthy working conditions, and lowly status, the position of stripper often fell to those women who could find no other employment. One Tampa labor paper observed that stripping attracted "orphan girls, maids who have no male helper, widows with young children, the victims of divorce, the daughters of large families, the victims of vicious men, or of sick and disabled men."[33] Italian women, however, belied these generalizations. The majority were married women, and those who were single, according to manuscript census schedules, were daughters helping to supplement family income. Most Italian women sought stripping tables in the early years as points of entry into the ranks of cigarmakers.

To become skilled cigarmakers many Italians underwent apprenticeships lasting a minimum of eight months but sometimes extending to two years. An Italian consul once suggested that this requirement reduced the number of prospective Italian cigarmakers because, while apprenticed, candidates received no pay. Joe Maniscalco recalled learning the cigarmaking art as an apprentice at the Arguelles-López factory. "They used to pay me, after six months I worked there, they used to pay me two dollars a week. . . . But it took me two years to become a cigarmaker."[34] Having endured the training period, however, Italians could expect handsome wages for making hand-rolled cigars. Prior to the 1920s, when industry scales changed radically, workers averaged sixteen to eighteen dollars a week, but particularly gifted artisans could take home twenty-five dollars or more. As early as 1910 there were reports that Italian women had gained such skills and were consistently earning more than twenty-two dollars a week. The indication that, apparently, Ybor City's Italian women earned more than Italian men (certainly a rarity in industrial history) was buttressed by a 1913 report in *Bolletino dell'Emigrazione* that Italian men averaged fifteen to eighteen dollars a week, while Italian women averaged fifteen to twenty dollars and some "even to twenty-three dollars a week."[35]

If women were limited in their work roles—very few became managers or selectors—a remarkable number of Italian women nonetheless did work. In 1910, 16 percent of the foreign-born women in America were employed for wages; in Tampa just under 40 percent of the Italian-born women in Ybor City were engaged in the cigar industry; fully 60 percent of the foreign-born, Ybor City women employed in the cigar industry were Italian.[36] Italian women in the Cigar City were twice as likely to hold jobs as Cuban women, three times as likely as Spanish women, seven times as likely as immigrant women in Philadelphia, and twelve times as likely as Italian women in Buffalo (see Table 6).[37] Why?

On one level women (and children) worked because it was necessary—as one bander explained, "I need to work because at home there is not enough money." An Italian cigarmaker cited the grim realities of his youth in Ybor City: "My mother used to work making four or five dollars stripping tobacco, my father used to work in the farm cutting celery, planting, and all like that for a dollar and a quarter, a dollar and a half a day. So you couldn't support a family . . . so, the kids, we had to go out and make a few dollars extra."[38] But to understand why these women worked one must comprehend not only the meaning of work but also its significance in the local, structural, and immigrant group con-

TABLE 6 Nativity of Cigar Industry Employees by Gender, 1910

Nativity	Male	Female	Total
Native-born of native father:			
white	711	305	1,016
black	80	10	90
TOTAL	791	315	1,106
Native-born of foreign father, by father's country of birth:			
Cuba	195	—	195
Spain	36	—	36
Italy	50	—	50
Other	31	—	31
TOTAL	313	—	313
TOTAL NATIVE-BORN	1,104	315	1,419
Foreign-born:			
Cuban	3,013	532	3,545
Italian, North	13	12	25
Italian, South	833	791	1,624
Spanish	1,881	127	2,008
Other	117	16	133
TOTAL FOREIGN-BORN	5,857	1,478	7,335
GRAND TOTAL	6,961	1,793	8,754

SOURCE: Adapted from U.S. Congress, *Immigrants in Industries*, 405.

text. Virginia Yans-McLaughlin has concluded that Italian women in Buffalo, New York, preferred seasonal occupations, such as canning, fruit picking, and homework, rather than more lucrative and steady industrial employment. In this view cultural imperatives directed them to such work. "Italian immigrants," she wrote, "transformed the canning factories into communities where Old World social attitudes and behavior could continue, maintained by kinship ties."[39] The contours of Tampa's industrial economy differed substantially from those of Buffalo, and Italians were able to adjust their underlying strategies to account for a different opportunity structure. In Tampa cigar factories sought out females for the stripping rooms and Italian women answered the call, utilizing these avenues to reach familial goals.

Tampa's cigar industry marched to a different rhythm compared to northeastern mills and foundries. Cigar factory interiors offered a work atmosphere punctuated by frequent doses of strong *café con leche*, dramatic readings from a popular novel, the companionship of *paesani*, and ultimately the heady solidarity of popular unions. As elsewhere Italians utilized family ties and kinship to influence hiring patterns, frequently filling stripping rooms or cigar benches with fellow immigrants.[40] Traditional Italian values could survive, albeit in altered forms, and rapid economic development could take place within the context of social traditionalism and political radicalism.

Even the city's dramatic labor history failed to dislodge Italian women from the cigar factories. They solidified their place in the rank-and-file by supporting a variety of militant labor unions. In this sense they easily merged into a pattern of female involvement in union activities that was well established in Ybor City. During a strike in 1901 observers noted a "woman named Herrerra, who is secretary of the Resistencia Stripper's Union. Whenever and wherever she can secure an audience of cigarmakers, she delivers herself of the most vituperative language against the manufacturers. . . . she has even attempted to incite the strikers to arson."[41] Reports of female speakers at union rallies and strike meetings became commonplace, as did certain forms of more direct action. One 1916 walkout saw a group of strikers rush into a large factory "deriding with hoots and boos the workers. The women leading the mob called the men at work 'females' and offered their skirts to those who refused to quit."[42] According to some sources the male fear of being insulted by female co-workers was a powerful force in inducing unity during strikes.[43]

Yet in historical perspective the essential group experience of Italian women embodied a conservative life-style. The relationship between labor radicalism and domestic traditionalism represented a delicate balance. The work choices made by Italian women, which took them out of their homes, often gave them higher wages than their menfolk, and placed them in active unions, must be understood in the context of their family connections. As evidenced by numerous family histories, the individual's identity assumed importance primarily as it contributed to the group's advancement. Italian women—and girls—did not work to enhance their individual well-being nor, necessarily, to achieve a share of independence in American terms; rather, they labored to maintain and sustain the family unit.[44]

Italian women in Ybor City's cigar unions proved to be as or more militant than men in strikes once they became involved. As demonstrated in the great textile strikes in Lowell and Lawrence, Massachusetts, and the New York City garment trades, women began using rhetoric that suggested their identification with independence and even militant radicalism. In Lawrence, for example, immigrant women saw this approach as compatible with family and community goals. Perhaps for Italian women in Ybor City the meaning of American independence was a male breadwinner and female "freedom" not to work but to raise children and stay home.[45]

The dominant pattern in Italian families was to utilize cigar factory jobs as a means to an end rather than as permanent employment. While women labored for wages in the factories, often for extended periods of time, men began to move in different directions. Men typically worked for a few years to build a small amount of investment capital, usually put toward some form of property. Women and/or children provided the extra margin of income that allowed these ventures to mature.[46]

Despite the large number of Italian women in factories, at no time were Italian men absent from the workbenches. Although they tended to remain there for shorter periods than Italian women, there were always sufficient numbers of men in the cigar factories to place their distinctive stamp on the character of labor relations in Tampa. In doing so Italians, both men and women, brought to the workplace a cluster of old-world attitudes that shaped their approach to new economic realities. At least in the initial years of entry into the cigar industry, however, Italians accommodated to a labor milieu their immigrant neighbors had largely created.

Labor Relations

A crazy-quilt pattern of radical ideologies, ethnic rivalries, establishment vigilantism, and tumultuous strikes characterized labor relations in Tampa from 1886 to 1931. "People date their lives from various strikes in Tampa," recalled José Yglesias, a native of Ybor City and a noted author.[47] That remains true even today. Older residents of Ybor City measure their family and generational histories by the yardstick of the great strikes of 1899, 1901, 1910, 1920, and 1931.

Almost from the beginning labor problems plagued Ybor City, an irony considering that Martínez Ybor came there in large part to avoid such quarrels. Indeed, the very opening of Martínez Ybor's factory misfired because of Cuban protests over his hiring of a Spanish bookkeeper.[48] In January 1887 the first major labor disturbance struck Ybor City. Led by Ramón Rubiera, a fiery Cuban labor organizer, the strike began over the selection of a foreman at Martínez Ybor's factory. Rubiera's Cuban Federation of Trade Unions urged the hiring of Santo Benites, a Cuban, to blunt Spanish control of the industry. A local of the Knights of Labor, dominated by Spanish selectors, called for a strike, demanding the removal of Benites. Following the dismissal the Cubans held their own strike, precipitating several acts of violence resulting in the death of a Cuban cigarmaker and injury to four others. Throughout the trouble Tampa papers reported polemical debates between anarchists and socialists within the local labor movement. Significantly the *Tampa Journal* blamed anarchists for the strike, labeling them "evil men, agitators, revolutionists" who sought to "gratify their morbid ideas of distinction, heroism and fame by imposing upon the ignorant prejudices of the masses."[49]

The *Journal*'s concern about radicalism was not simply baseless xenophobia. Cuban and Spanish cigarworkers brought to Ybor City a well-developed proletarian consciousness and a strong tradition of union militancy which frequently put them into adversarial relationships with their employers. Anarchist and socialist labor organizers had been active in Cuba among cigarworkers from the 1880s, and these individuals often found themselves in the migration streams that arched between the island and Ybor City.[50] Indeed, the expatriate centers of Spanish-Cuban cigar manufacturing received a growing number of these men as the century drew to a close.[51] Cigarmaker José Ramón Sanfeliz caught the spirit of these years: "At about that time [1891] I became somewhat enamored of radical ideas in the proletarian field. These advanced ideas were, at the same time, a sort of 'epidemic' among the cigarmakers."[52]

Anarchism and socialism shaped much of the character of early labor relations in Ybor City, influencing profoundly the reception immigrant workers received from the natives. In January 1887 Tampa's police expelled more than seventy-five cigarworkers then engaged in a strike, the *Tribune* predicting that this aggressive policy "will no doubt have a most salutary effect upon any other . . . citizens of anarchist tendencies who still may be lurking in our midst."[53] Ybor City's first May Day celebration in the same year featured a mass parade in which, according to Cuban historian José Rivero Muñiz, "the greater part of the demonstrators were Spanish anarchists. . . ." The presence of black flags and class-based rhetoric grated on the nerves of the American community from the earliest years. An 1899 *Morning Tribune* article stressed themes that were already very familiar: "Left to himself, the cigarmaker is a fairly good citizen. But unfortunately there is another class which takes evident delight in meddling between the employer and employed. It is this class of mischief-breeding, anarchist agitators that causes the differences which result in frequent strikes. It would be entirely correct for the people of Tampa to force this undesirable element to abandon their abode in this city."[54] On more than one occasion Tampa's citizenry took this advice close to heart.

Anarcho-syndicalism, with its strong emphasis on education, local control, and nonpolitical direct action, found advocates among the Ybor City work force. To some Ybor City offered an ideal environment in which to test radical methods such as sabotage, obstruction, and the general strike. Just as anarchism and socialism appealed to village-oriented peasants in Spain and Cuba, so too did anarcho-syndicalism supply a reservoir of strength at the factory level.

At first union growth in Ybor City made very little progress. Cigarmakers carried their fierce individualism to the debate over working-class issues and were unable to agree on any unified organization. Moreover, prior to the Spanish-American War the Cuban cigarworkers devoted themselves to the struggle for independence. Even committed labor radicals temporarily put aside their internal disputes to support the revolution.[55]

There existed in the city as well a cluster of work patterns, attitudes, and traditions that tended to pull cigarmakers away from collective action. Many highly skilled workers, especially those who controlled apprentices, considered themselves a "class apart" and resisted changes that threatened this status. Moreover, in Tampa the cigar industry manifested its own brand of upward mobility. Workers could, and often did, become bosses and owners in their own right. Because the trade required no expensive machinery or specialized buildings, enterprising cigarmakers often aspired to open their own small shops. These one- or two-man *chinchales* were always plentiful, supplying graphic evidence of this process at work.[56] Although Tampa was essentially a one-industry town, it was never a one-company town, an important fact in understanding its economic evolution.

The divergent messages of class conflict enunciated by labor radicals, on the one hand, and capitalist enterprise exemplified by the *chinchal*, on the other, coexisted in an uncomfortable balance. During times of labor strife radicals frequently played important roles in shaping union destinies. Socialists, syndicalists, and anarchists joined with their fellow cigarworkers, often in leadership positions, and struggled against the forces of management. Their appeals to class consciousness and worker solidarity were effective in organizing workers and promoting strike efforts. During periods of tranquility the influence of these individuals waned. In these circumstances cigarworkers may have listened with interest to dicussions of the class war, but many apparently were making plans to become factory owners themselves.

Prior to 1898 the Knights of Labor had organized a short-lived society (1887), and the American Federation of Labor began a struggling local (#336 of the Cigar Makers International Union, 1892), but these groups possessed almost no influence in the city or among the work force. This was true despite the fact that the CMIU consistently tried to organize in Tampa during the 1880s and 1890s. Field reports of 1889, for example, complained that "white men" were not welcome in the Tampa factories, and the general consensus among organizers was that little hope existed for union success. Not much had changed by 1896, when one fieldworker concluded in disgust that "an American citizen had as much chance of being hired as being elected Senator."[57]

Labor relations in this context tended to be an unpredictable blend of wildcat strikes, work stoppages, and impassioned marches, usually occasioned by some perceived slight to established custom or by some event connected to the Cuban struggle. When, for example, news broke on February 24, 1895, that an insurrection had begun in Cuba, nearly 3,000 Cubans left their work stations to gather in front of the Ybor factory for lengthy celebrations.[58]

Indicative of the chaotic nature of labor relations was the fact that between 1887 and 1894 there were twenty-three walkouts, but no effective organization resulted.[59] A variety of aggravating circumstances stemming from the minor (brittle tobacco, tepid drinking water, breaches of etiquette toward the *lector*) to the serious (contract violations, nonpayment of wages) could empty a factory. Tina Provenzano, an Italian immigrant, recalled the passionate moment of the walkout. "Someone say, 'We're gonna go the Labor Temple. *Compañeri, para la calle!*' [Comrades, to the street!]."[60] These tactics infuriated the Tampa business community, which charged Latins with being fickle pawns of radical agitators, whom they usually described as "outsiders." The *Tampa Morning Tribune* stated the prevailing mood in 1892: "If Tampa could rid itself of these mischief-breeding anarchists, the cigar industry could harmoniously and profitably proceed."[61] In reality cigarmakers grasped at any opportunity to control their lives and assert their independence. Given the individualized factory structure within Ybor City, control—for an hour or a day—was easily realized. Retaining power was something else.

The weight strike in 1899, called *la huelga de pesa*, marked an important early watershed in Ybor City's labor relations. Cigarmakers, the bulk of whom were still unorganized in 1899, met stiffening resistance to their growing militance. Cubans, rejoicing in the revolution's success, now threw their energies into labor organization.[62] The industry itself was also changing. The introduction of weight scales in the Martínez Ybor factory symbolized a new era. Ostensibly the scales were designed to weigh a specified amount of tobacco for each cigarmaker as a means of controlling costs, but in reality certain principles were at stake: power and custom. Long-established practices dictated that filler was never weighed; to question a Latin's integrity challenged not only his dignity but also the more crucial issue of control over workplace and production. Many of the pioneer *patrones*, including Martínez Ybor himself, were dead, and a new age had arrived in Ybor City that was personified by modern efficiency and corporate rationality. A clash was inevitable.[63]

Cigarmakers refused to comply with the new order and owners countered with a lockout. By July 1899 some 4,000 workers were on strike, with many leaving the city for Cuba. Characteristically the local newspapers bitterly resented this disruption of Tampa's fortunes. The *Morning Tribune*, leading mouthpiece of the city's business community, cautioned its readers: "If the blame must rest on one particular element, it should fall upon the anarchistic leaders who have urged the strikers into this defiance and its results."[64] To define the matter more clearly, the paper ominously warned, "Tampa is afflicted with one of the most dangerous and obnoxious classes of people just now that ever has been tolerated by a civilized community. It is the professional agitator . . . those people are regular anarchists. Tampa can afford to lose cigarmakers. Tampa cannot afford to lose cigar factories."[65]

The resolution of the weight strike came with surprising swiftness. In August management conceded to the workers' every demand, even their insistence on a uniform level of wages. The wage list (or *cartabón*) meant the setting of a standardized scale of payment for each grade of cigar made in city factories. Workers did not oppose all rationalization moves —they embraced those that worked to their benefit. Previously cigarmakers in one factory might earn more money than those in another shop on the same grade of cigar, but under a uniform scale collective action was stressed. Workers were not acting in competition with each other but rather were acting together for the good of all. In this sense the demand was a demonstration of class unity.[66]

The weight strike was significant for three other reasons: it marked the first and last major strike won by the workers; it underwrote the birth of an important union, La Sociedad de Torcedores de Tampa, commonly called La Resistencia by its members;[67] and it led to the creation of the Cigar Trust, capitalized at fifteen million dollars, to be succeeded two years later by the even larger and more powerful American Cigar Company. Thereafter in labor struggles the workers faced the formidable power of a tightly controlled combination that bound together the major factories in Tampa.[68]

Largely unaware of these developments, workers eagerly enrolled in La Resistencia. By November 1900 the union claimed a membership of 1,558 Cubans, 550 Spaniards, and 310 Italians. The organization, created and led by immigrants, particularly appealed to those cigarworkers who professed leftist ideologies. La Resistencia's goals represented a repudiation of the American Federation of Labor's narrow brand of trade unionism, which aimed at organizing only skilled workers and emphasized only work-related issues such as wages and hours. Blasting the AFL's "pure and simpledom" approach, the new union declared that its rival was "pernicious to the goals of the worker." La Resistencia instead aimed at organizing all cigarworkers, and its very formation was a rejection of the AFL's injunction against dual unionism. Much of its rhetoric was syndicalist in nature, calling on workers "to resist the exploitation of labor by capital," and it aimed to organize laborers into one central union.[69] Many socialists and anarchists in Ybor City found these goals attractive. Alfonso Coniglio, soon to become Ybor City's most famous Italian anarchist, remembered with pride that he held union card #245 in an organization that came to number well over 5,000 members. Local Italian anarchist newspapers also gave La Resistencia their warm support. As *L'Alba Sociale* (The Social Dawn) proclaimed, "We are not partisans of partial strikes anyway, it is our conviction that the general strike is a revolutionary motto."[70]

Coniglio was representative of the early Italian entrants into the labor movement of Ybor City. Born in Alessandria della Rocca on January 3, 1884, he came to Tampa with his parents in 1896 as part of the exodus following the suppression of the *fasci*.[71] He remembered the heady experience of socialist idealism in the local *fascio* and the pervasive disillusionment after 1893. His attachment to leftist ideologies, first whetted in the homeland, flowered in Ybor City, where he became a proponent of anarchism. Coniglio worked in the cigar factories and credited readers with supplying his "formal" education. "It was at La Rosa Español that I first heard the reader," he reminisced. "It was a small factory but we had our reader. Oh, I cannot tell you how important they were, how much they taught us. Especially an illiterate like me. To them we owe particularly our sense of the class struggle."[72]

In 1901 La Resistencia attempted to establish a closed shop in Tampa, a policy opposed by the powerful "trust" factories in the city.[73] A protracted, tumultuous, four-month strike ensued, marked by mass evictions, extralegal violence, and collective suffering. Leadership was in Spanish and Cuban hands, but Italians were active in the ranks, both in supplying streetcorner oratory, which helped to maintain worker morale, and in molding strike strategy. Late in the struggle, for example, Italians devised a plan to extend slender union resources. Strikers formed a committee to visit Italian families in the city and persuade them to take union food supplies only when absolutely necessary. According to one account, the spirit of sacrifice engendered by these acts induced Ybor City grocers and landlords to allow further credit and prolong the strike.[74] The Italian anarchist press gave consistent support to the strike, with *L'Alba Sociale* taking the lead in announcing the necessity of establishing *cocinas economicas* (soup kitchens operated by the union) to feed striking workers.[75]

Meanwhile Tampa's business elite grew impatient over mounting losses caused by salaryless cigarmakers and became frightened by immigrant solidarity. In November 1900 nearly 1,500 Cuban, Spanish, and Italian women had packed the Liceo Cubano to express their unity. The *Tribune* editorialized that perhaps a show of force would expedite matters, specifically the closing of soup kitchens, the arrest of strikers on charges of vagrancy, and vigilante raids.[76] Thus inspired, a citizens' committee composed of local business leaders abducted thirteen union leaders on the evening of August 5, 1901. These men were put aboard a steamer, warned never to return to Tampa on pain of death, and dropped off on a deserted stretch of coastline in Honduras. Since the deportees included the president and treasurer of the union, strike funds conveniently were frozen.[77]

Landlords then began wholesale evictions of overdue tenants. Even the nation's most famous cigarmaker, Samuel Gompers, refused to send aid, claiming La Resistencia failed to conform to American trade union principles. The CMIU adamantly declined to assist or amalgamate with its rival and allegedly even offered to supply strikebreakers.[78] Meanwhile manufacturers appealed to cigarworkers in Key West and Cuba to come to Tampa. They apparently were able to induce a few Italians to enter the factories, as that group emerged from the strike with something of a reputation as strikebreakers. By late November 1901 the strike had collapsed and La Resistencia dissolved as an active organization.[79]

The destruction of La Resistencia left the CMIU atop the Tampa labor field, and the latter made strenuous efforts to expand. In 1902 organizer James Wood arrived to plan a membership campaign; by 1905 his efforts had succeeded in attracting about 3,000 workers to three CMIU locals. However, a small but vocal minority of those CMIU President George Perkins described as "the old 'dyed in the wool,' never-say-die remnant" of La Resistencia remained opposed to the CMIU.[80] One year later local union officials launched another effort among Italian and Cuban workers, asking the international brotherhood for the services of an experienced leader, adding the entreaty, "The IWW [Industrial Workers of the World] organizer will be here next week so send us a good organizer."[81]

Italians made impressive gains in the cigar industry work force during the years 1902–10, years of dynamic growth within the colony, city, and industry. Although they still failed to occupy the most highly skilled positions, they were solidly represented in the ranks of cigarmakers and very numerous in the lower paid positions. The same growth was manifested in the CMIU locals. By 1910 five such locals existed in Ybor City and West Tampa, representing the major branches of the trade.[82] The increased Italian presence was indicated by frequent notices of them in the union newspaper, *El Internacional*. Begun in January 1904 as a Spanish-language paper, the editors consistently augmented space devoted to Italian-language articles as the years progressed. These are important indicators as local membership lists and union records have not survived.[83]

By 1910 the CMIU had grown to 6,000 members, most of whom worked in the city's largest factories, a considerable achievement. Perkins himself spoke of the "aversion of the cigarmakers here [Tampa] to our movement," and he frequently mentioned the unsettling effect "radicals" had on workers. They were constantly disrupting meetings, attacking CMIU leaders, and urging workers to follow different directions. Some of the most radical were attracted to the IWW, which had profited from a visit in 1908 by William Haywood. Their numbers were small, but Perkins admitted that "they have a rather formidable following."[84]

Despite persistent difficulties with leftist elements the union attracted large numbers of socialists to its ranks after 1901. This fact is borne out by the union paper, which devoted considerable space to socialist authors and socialist group activities. When available, published membership lists of socialist clubs and attendance reports of picnics, banquets, and the like have matched well with known union members. This evidence appears consistent with the socialist tactic then in practice of "boring from within."[85]

The labor field of Tampa was always a crowded one. Alternately vying for the loyalties of workers were a broad variety of organizations often espousing very different philosophies. The CMIU, IWW, and the Knights of Labor represented a range of options, but there were also organizers for various Cuban groups circulating in the community. Committed socialists and anarchists added their own perspectives on working-class strategies, sometimes from within the ranks of organizations, sometimes from without. Although the CMIU organized the greatest number of workers and granted considerable autonomy to its locals, it never silenced dissent and bickering. A common pattern saw workers flock to the CMIU during times of unrest—particularly when special recruiting drives offered low entrance fees. When strikes were over, however, it appears that large numbers let their memberships lapse. Given the tendency to strike often, this practice was a constant source of complaint at national headquarters, which often found itself having to support cigarmakers in the next strike who were not technically due benefits.[86] In this sense cigarworkers usually seemed to outsiders to be more organized than they really were.

It was from a situation such as this that the CMIU locals confronted owners in a second general strike. Cigarworkers claimed that owners precipitated the strike of 1910 as a means of testing their open-shop demands and squelching increasing union power. The first direct confrontation came in June 1910 when manufacturers belonging to the Clear Havana Cigar Manufacturers Association (the "trust") began dismissing selectors belonging to CMIU Local 493. Grievances accumulated and by August 1910 more than 12,000 cigarmakers were out of work.[87] That month a *Morning Tribune* reporter covered a strike meeting of over 5,000 demonstrators, including "bevies of gayly dressed Spanish, Cuban, and

Italian women" waving their red bandanas. "It was a demonstration such as has reared its head within the gates of Old Barcelona, that hot bed of Latin civic disturbance."[88]

Representatives of the international union arrived quickly to assist in planning the strike. Their ranks included Italian interpreter Antonio Cabrera, who reflected the increased Italian presence on both union rolls and picket lines. As in previous confrontations many Cuban cigarworkers left for Cuba and locations in the Northeast in search of employment.[89] These individuals sent money back to Tampa to assist the cause. Unlike earlier strikes the level of violence in the city was high.

In September 1910 the killing of an American bookkeeper employed at Bustillo and Díaz Company electrified the city. The shots that were fired at the man had come from a crowd of Cuban and Italian strikers gathered at the factory.[90] Soon authorities arrested two Italians on suspicion of murder. One of them had been the subject of *Morning Tribune* reports because of his alleged criminal past. Before the two could be brought to trial a mob seized them and lynched both men. The English-language press pictured them as hired assassins, "tools of anarchistic elements in the city," describing their fate as a "rebuke to lawlessness."[91] In fact both did possess rather unsavory reputations, but only one appears to have belonged to a cigar union. Gaetano Moroni, Italian vice-consul at New Orleans, on orders from the Italian ambassador, visited Tampa and conducted an investigation. His confidential report probably comes as close to the truth as possible, concluding: "The lynching itself was not the outcome of a temporary outburst of popular anger, but was rather planned, in cold blood, to the most trifling detail, by some citizens of West Tampa with the tacit assent of a few police officers, and all with the intention of teaching an awful lesson to the strikers of the cigar factories who had passed from quiet protest to acts of violence against the manufacturers and, at the same time, of getting rid of two 'terrible ruffians'."[92]

A crescendo of violence followed the lynchings. Arsonists burned the Balbín Brothers factory on October 4, and the Tribune building narrowly missed the same fate. On one occasion nine Italian women paraded with clubs in front of the Arguelles-López factory in Ybor City, threatening to beat to death anyone who reported to work there.[93] Mary Italiano remembered: "The 1910 strike! Well, that strike was supposed to last a couple of weeks and it lasted seven months. And that strike really about cleaned everybody up. . . . The workers and parades, they were marching up and down the streets. We little girls used to have our umbrellas with names and slogans on them."[94] Joe Maniscalco arrived in Tampa in 1910 and stepped immediately into the vortex of the strike. He recalled painfully the memories of *paesani* forced to leave town and "fights between laborers and the strike-breakers on Twentieth Street and Tenth Avenue."[95] Soon police arrested several strike leaders, including the Spaniard José de la Campa, president of the unions' joint advisory board. So distrustful of the constituted authorities had strikers become that eleven Italians armed themselves and camped near the county jail to ensure that the arrested board members were not also lynched.[96]

Cigar factories reopened in October 1910, protected by armed patrols organized by a newly formed citizens' committee. Branded by socialists in the city as the "Cossacks of Tampa," these patrols engaged in arbitrary arrests, illegal searches, routine physical beatings, and flagrant violations of civil rights. On one occasion a patrol entered the Labor Temple in Ybor City, where they smashed furniture, broke up a meeting in progress, confiscated union records, closed down the building, and placed a sign overhead reading, "This place is closed for all time." Patrols also raided the union newspaper's offices, destroying its presses, arresting its editor, and intimidating its staff.[97]

Efforts to induce workers back to the factories met with little success. This was particularly true of Italians. One November 10 article in the *Morning Tribune* enthusiastically, but erroneously, reported "great numbers of cigarmakers" returning to work, adding a revealing postscript: "It is notable that among those returning to work there are no Italians, and in many quarters this is construed as representing the Italian as being the backbone of the strike. Many in a position to know say that were the Italians to resume employment at the factories, workers of all nationalities would follow at once, and within two weeks there would not be a man or woman in the cigar trades idle."[98] Responding to the rallying cry *"Morire di fame, ma vincere!"* (To death from hunger, but to victory), Italians emerged as the shock troops of the strike forces.[99]

Owners frequently attempted to split workers along ethnic lines, and they clearly viewed Italians as the key to their efforts. On November 18 the union newspaper announced that "our worthy comrades, the Italians," had been addressed by manufacturers in an open letter that warned they would have no work after the strike if they continued to follow union leadership.¹⁰⁰ When this move failed to bring results, owners tried another approach. Late in December they circulated a bogus manifesto, allegedly signed by Italians, which proclaimed the willingness of Italians to return to work on management's terms. Italian cigarworkers hurriedly distributed a counter-manifesto, signed by 460 of them (lack of space reportedly required leaving off several hundred additional names), which labeled the first claim "utterly without foundation in fact" and pledged a continuation of the strike.¹⁰¹

The reason why Italians occupied such a central place in the union and its strike activities has much to do with the quality of the leadership available to them. To some extent gifted Cuban and Spanish unionists had made special efforts to recruit Italians. José de la Campa, for example, consistently preached the benefits of worker solidarity irrespective of national background. His linguistic and organizational talents allowed him to preach a forceful message. The *Morning Tribune* ironically had spotted the twenty-year-old de la Campa at a rally in 1908, which marked the activist's first public speech. "In less than four years," the paper remarked, "he has learned to speak English, German, French, Italian and Spanish. His friends pick for him a brilliant future."¹⁰² Yet Italians had become important in union affairs principally because of their own leaders who had joined the ranks in the years 1901–10. Indicative of these men were Giovanni Vaccaro, Carmelo Rocca, and the aforementioned Alfonso Coniglio. In their respective careers they illustrate the range of ideological diversity existing in the Tampa labor movement. Following the tenets of socialism, AFL trade unionism, and anarchism, these three men were representative of the individuals who rallied Italian cigarworkers to the union cause.

Giovanni Vaccaro was born in Sambuca di Sicilia in 1882, the son of a carpenter father who wanted him to become a priest. The youngster dutifully enrolled in a seminary, but when Vaccaro was only nine years old his father died suddenly of pneumonia. That death tested the younster's faith, and after attending his father's funeral Vaccaro declared that he would not return to his clerical training. His older brother Filippo had earlier gone to the United States, living and working with a cousin in New York. Shortly after 1900 Vaccaro himself made the ocean voyage, landing first in New York and then moving to Ybor City, where relatives of his mother (a Stefanesa) lived.¹⁰³

Although born in Sambuca, Vaccaro was a great admirer of Lorenzo

Panepinto, whom he met in Santo Stefano while visiting his mother's family; he had been attracted by Panepinto's moral strength and his teachings. The encounter began for him lifelong beliefs in socialism and the workers' cause, beliefs so strong that they came to dominate his entire existence. His feelings for Panepinto were only slightly less powerful. The assassination of Panepinto in 1911 so moved Vaccaro that he began a drive in Ybor City to collect funds for a commemorative statue to be erected in Santo Stefano. For a number of years thereafter he also published and largely wrote a eulogistic journal, *Il Martire* (The Martyr), on the anniversary of Panepinto's assassination. Vaccaro's career, and those of men like him in Ybor City, calls into question Edwin Fenton's assertion that the old-world experiences of Italian labor organizers failed to affect materially their lifework in America. On the contrary, as Rudolph Vecoli has suggested, these backgrounds often rested at the very center of their motivations and strategies.[104]

Giovanni Vaccaro witnessed the 1901 strike and shortly after its bitter conclusion became active in the CMIU as a recruiter. "He went from corner to corner trying to organize people," recalled eldest son Frank. "It was pretty rough." At the same time that he enrolled new CMIU members, Vaccaro threw his soul into Socialist party work. In these years he was a tireless organizer for both groups, devoting nights, weekends, and every spare moment to his two great causes. "In fact, he was rarely home," recalled his son. "He was very busy going to the Union Hall and to socialist meetings. He would come home and we would be in bed. On Sundays, he was gone to meet with people. We really didn't see much of him."[105]

A prolific correspondent for socialist journals around the nation, Vaccaro carried on a particularly extensive communication with *La Parola dei Socialisti* of Chicago. He organized at least two socialist locals, one each in Ybor City and West Tampa, which under his leadership contributed to a variety of workers' causes. So that the connection with Sicily would not be missed Vaccaro named the Ybor City local Gruppo Lorenzo Panepinto.[106] On a more personal level, he hosted a seemingly endless series of visitors from the wider socialist and workers' movements, including Socialist party leader and presidential candidate Eugene V. Debs and Giuseppe Bertelli, founder of the Italian Socialist Federation.[107]

The strength of the CMIU during the 1910 strike owed much to the efforts of Vaccaro. His long reports to Italian socialist newspapers around the country kept outsiders informed of events in Tampa and aided in keeping the flow of contributions strong. In the city Vaccaro recruited many Italians to the CMIU ranks and was instrumental in working the picket lines throughout the struggle. "I remember seeing him late at night when nearly everyone was gone," mused John Massaro. "But he would still be at the Union Hall first thing in the morning to work out plans for the next day."[108]

Carmelo Rocca, still spry and mentally acute in 1984 at age ninety-three, was born in Texas, the son of a lumberman working in the small town of Rockland in the southern part of the state. Rocca's father came from San Biaggo, Sicily; his mother from Alessandria della Rocca. The elder Rocca followed a classic sojourner pattern of migration. Arriving alone in New York City in 1883, he soon found work in Illinois laboring on railroads. From there he drifted to various jobs, spending time in Louisiana and ultimately settling in Texas. The family joined him there. After some years Rocca's mother wrote home to Alessandria to inquire about her family, learning that they had all left the village for various locations, including Argentina, Africa, and Ybor City. A letter in 1905 to John Grimaldi, a well-known Ybor City banker, determined that a sister was indeed residing there.[109]

In 1907 the family moved to Florida and Carmelo went to work in the cigar factories, beginning as an assistant to a Spanish *cafetero*. "In those days in the big factories," he explained, "about 10 or 11 in the morning, there was a man who sold coffee. We had two big pots of coffee (one with hot milk) from where we put them in cups. The Spaniard gave me a couple dollars a week." After a stint as an apprentice in La Rosa Español he became a cigarmaker and a member of CMIU Local 336. He recalled the free intermixing of groups and races in the streets, union halls, and workrooms. "Black Cubans lived and worked with ease along with everyone else," Rocca explained. "It was not till later that 'we had to get civilized'." The wizened old union man could not yet utter the last words without a sardonic look to show his contempt for southern racial policies.[110]

The 1910 strike saw Rocca at the center of the controversy. He remembered vividly the lynchings ("Do you know what they did to those boys!"), the citizen patrols ("They intimidated us, those Georgia crackers rode up and down Seventh Avenue with rifles on their shoulders"), the arrest of José de la Campa ("We were shocked, we feared he would be lynched too"), and a tense private meeting with Mayor D. B. McKay

("I took two men with me, posted at front and back—told them that if anyone came out with me, come and give me help"). Rocca was one of the Italians who camped near the county jail to ensure that de la Campa was not harmed while under arrest.[111]

Alfonso Coniglio was already a hardened veteran of the labor scene in Tampa by 1910. After the defeat of La Resistencia he shifted his organizational energies to the CMIU, where he remained for the rest of his life. Coniglio's brand of philosophical anarchism accommodated his attachment to trade unionism, and he was able to attract many Italians to the union ranks. "As far as the workers were concerned," explained his son Bruno, "he had a tremendous following because my father was considered to be honest and if he had anything to say, he said it no matter what. . . . There were Catholics, non-Catholics, Protestants, people with or without ideas . . . some socialists, communists, and so on. But when it was for the worker's movement, everyone banded together, and naturally there were people that participated in that and had different ideas . . . but he had that following."[112]

Exemplifying a "leadership of protest" style, to use John Higham's construct, these men did not agree on a single strategy to pursue in the workers' struggle.[113] Each man, however, preached the necessity of confronting the power of owners and community elites with the force of an organized working class. From such a base workers could improve conditions in the workplace and ultimately affect wider social change. Yet in the context of 1910 neither these leaders nor their unions could withstand the power arrayed against them. Manufacturers managed to enlist the support of Tampa's business and professional elites, its municipal authorities, and the state's court system and government; they apparently intimidated the only federal agency in the city able to check their plans —the immigration office. On January 26, 1911, the CMIU's joint advisory board called off the strike with the prophetic words, "We simply give up the fight."[114]

The strike had important consequences for Italians. The front-line role played by them removed permanently any stigma remaining over their identification as strikebreakers. Their activities also ensured a prominent position for Italians in future union affairs. Unlike La Resistencia, the CMIU did not disappear but instead slowly rebuilt its fortunes in anticipation of further struggles.

Discouraged, but not humbled, CMIU cigarmakers returned to work following the strike collapse. By then, however, their locals were not the only union options available in Tampa. IWW activists had been at work as early as 1906. A visit by William ("Big Bill") Haywood in 1908 spurred memberships, drawing to the fledgling group the most radical elements of the work force.[115] Factory owners may have secretly cheered the IWW arrival, realizing that workers would have great difficulty in presenting the same united front they could muster in their dealings with unions.

By early 1911 IWW Local 102 was fully operative in Tampa, publishing its local newspaper, *El Obrero Industriale*, holding theatrical performances, renting meeting space, and sending its collectors to factory doors. Numbering some 100 dues-paying members in 1913, the local impressed CMIU President Perkins during a visit to Tampa in that year. As he explained in a letter to AFL Secretary Frank Morrison: "Tampa is a splendid field for IWW propaganda. The workers of Tampa to a considerable extent are permeated with socialist ideas, and many of them at least think they are socialists. In reality they are more inclined to be anarchists if anything. Hence the IWW brand of organization naturally appeals to them."[116] Italian anarcho-syndicalist Carlo Tresca and his companion, Elizabeth Gurley Flynn, arrived the same year. Flynn was struck that "men and women—Cuban, Italian, Mexican, Spanish—worked in factories," and she was particularly attracted to the readers. They "read papers, pamphlets and books in Spanish and Italian," she recalled, "and the contents were usually extremely radical." The couple spoke at a cigarworkers' picnic on May Day, finding enthusiasm for their cause among the large crowd that had come to hear "the IWW from the North."[117]

The IWW local doggedly fought against the CMIU, decrying its policies and personalities in the city. It refused to support several CMIU strikes, and, if one is to believe the claims of *El Internacional*, occasionally supplied strikebreakers: "We learned that any unscrupulous worker under the name of 'radical,' 'bolshevist,' or 'anarchist' can break any strike and not be a scab."[118] IWW membership was composed primarily of Cuban and Spanish cigarworkers who resented what they felt was the "reactionary" approach of the CMIU, aimed at only "partial improvements" of the workers' condition. They were also critical of AFL policies that brought the union into a close working relationship with the government during World War I. Alfonso Coniglio, among others, responded to these charges, claiming, "We consider ourselves radical enough to appreciate the highest sociological values, but the influence of radicalism should be constructive, not defamatory." Few Italians appear to have joined the IWW ranks.[119]

As part of the continuing struggle for membership the CMIU authorized formation of an Italian-language local, 464, in January 1917. Spearheaded by Giovanni Vaccaro, the new local began with 200 members and quickly grew under its founder's guidance. It financed its own newspaper for several years and sponsored the usual range of speeches, theatrical performances, evening classes, and picnics.[120] Vaccaro served as secretary of Local 464, the chief executive post, but his influence went beyond his administrative duties, for he provided the intellectual underpinnings and limitless reserves of energy that gave the organization its early vigor.[121]

During the period 1910–20 numerous confrontations occurred between the recovering CMIU locals and manufacturers. This was particularly true after 1916, when the pressures of World War I began to cause the national economy to fluctuate wildly. Cigarworkers felt increasingly squeezed by owners, who, faced with rising costs, began to hurry the introduction of molds and machines, to increase the numbers of children, women, and apprentices in factories, to break agreements on standardized rates for cigar sizes, and to oppose firmly any wage increases.[122] Skyrocketing increases in the cost of living during the war years underwrote several union-led consumer boycotts in Ybor City, drawing severe criticism from native Tampans, who compared these initiatives to bolshevism. Small successes achieved in these efforts and in short strikes during 1916 and 1918 underwrote a substantial CMIU growth and set the stage for Tampa's third general strike in less than twenty years.[123]

Buoyed by prospects for postwar prosperity, owners determined to resolve permanently the union-shop issue in Tampa by crushing the union movement. Factories began dismissing union collectors and other key members in early 1920. More significantly the Cigar Manufacturers' Association cornered the city's cigar-box supply and resolved to deny supplies to any factory not supporting its positions. On April 14 some 6,400 union workers walked off their jobs; owners quickly responded with a lockout that sent thousands more to the streets.[124]

Having learned the counterproductive results of violence in 1910, union leaders preached the necessity of peaceful protest. Union policy severely curtailed picketing and one joint advisory board announcement advocated allowing those workers who wished to return to the factories to do so.[125] If individual and collective acts of violence did not equal previous struggles, other events were altogether too familiar. The Tampa establishment quickly rallied to the side of the manufacturers, approving at one point an open-shop resolution. Wild stories of "radical agitators" circulated freely in the English-language press, with the usual complement of allegations concerning the "unrealistic demands and un-American character" of these men. Cigarworkers also adopted the World War I–era rhetoric, referring to employers as the "Kaisers" or "Huns" of the cigar industry.[126]

The Italian worker once again emerged as something of a labor bellwether, at least in the eyes of native Tampans. One embarrassingly premature report in August indicated that Italians were returning to their workbenches and that the worst of the strike was over. The last expected fixture of Tampa's strike scene, a citizens' committee, also made its appearance, although the 1920 organization was less active than its predecessors.[127]

In the end the resources and power of owners proved stronger than union will. After ten months of struggle the workers capitulated and returned to the factories, forced to accept work rules determined solely by the Cigar Manufacturer's Association. The installation of cigarmaking machines now proceeded unhampered, as did the opening of new apprentice "schools" run by owners and the employment of American women. The fact that the association's factories no longer permitted readers most clearly revealed the new balance of power.[128] Never again would workers mount a serious challenge to the dominance of owners, although there would be continued efforts to rehabilitate CMIU fortunes and the incidence of short, wildcat strikes remained high throughout the 1920s.

New Realities of the 1920s

The ten-month-long strike marked a major watershed in the Tampa cigar industry and for the Italians within it. Many smaller factories, beset by increased competition and economies of scale, closed their doors permanently; even larger factories lost long-standing orders and some suffered unrecoverable losses. To make up ground the owners accelerated the introduction of cigarmaking machines, already begun before the war, and sped up the hiring of more tractable American women and children to operate them. Exemplifying the new conditions was the rapid growth of Eli Witt's Hava-Tampa Cigar factory. Specializing in antiunionism and machine-made cigars, Witt perfected twentieth-century practices such as free matches with purchases and pioneered the wooden tip and cellophane wrappings.[129] A new era for Tampa's cigar trades was at hand, and the position of Latin cigarworkers who relied completely on factory jobs deteriorated badly in the Twenties. Many workers who had left Tampa during the strike never returned, and large numbers who did found no jobs awaiting them. The CMIU locals languished, with declining memberships and increasing apathy. Union meetings often drew less than a dozen people.[130]

The 1920 strike closed another chapter in the history of labor relations in Tampa: it signaled a ten-year eclipse of the radical element in the work force. Those socialist and anarchist cigarworkers who had never reconciled with American trade unionism already found their position badly eroded by the events of 1910. Opposition to the CMIU, which had supported the strike generously, dimmed their influence, particularly among Italian cigarworkers who were very conscious of job security and believed that CMIU policies were the most effective route to these goals.[131] Although the strike resulted in another loss, CMIU support had been even more liberal, and some workers blamed the defeat at least in part on the destructive sniping and opposition of radicals.[132]

The hysteria of the red-scare era also diminished the workers' position. Linking the Tampa radical community to the same worldwide conspiracy allegedly originating in Russia, the U.S. Justice Department anxiously scrutinized the Ybor City labor movement in microscopic detail. Reports indicated, for example, that Vaccaro "has very bad ideas; he is very revolutionary; is one of these communists that cover themselves under the Socialist Party 'shadow' to be free. Here in Tampa he is known by everybody to be one of the most active radicals. During a [labor] conflict . . . he went to work always with his gun in his pocket."[133] Agents arrested and deported a number of immigrant labor radicals, including the editor of *El Obrero Industriale*. Arrest warrants forced Alfonso Coniglio to flee temporarily to Jacksonville. Deportations, seizures, and intimidations seriously weakened the local union movement, which continued to count Italians as prominent members. Tired of harrassment and convinced that "there was no hope that the union was going to come up again," Giovanni Vaccaro moved with his wife and family to New York City, never to return to Ybor City. Carmelo Rocca soon followed. He lived in a colony of Stefanesi in Brooklyn, earning his living making cigars in several small shops and keeping active in union circles.[134]

The labor defeat in 1920 also signaled a change in the wider Italian relationship to the cigar industry. Italian men accelerated their movement out of the factories, seeking the stability and security that came from property ownership, small businesses, and other skilled trades. Women, too, left the cigar benches, either returning to domesticity or helping in fledgling businesses. A dwindling number remained in the cigar factories and the CMIU locals.[135]

Although the balance of power during the 1920s had decisively shifted to owners, the usual pattern of walkouts and disputes continued, not infrequently with violence. This served simply to accelerate the movement of Italians out of the industry. In late November 1921, for example, after "twelve months of hunger and penury," several dozen Italian women tobacco strippers participated in a wildcat strike protesting working conditions. This sparked a series of similar walkouts affecting men and women in several larger factories, and the authorities quickly arrested eight strike leaders. In the case of one unfortunate man, vigilantes took him to a lonely spot in the woods near where the 1910 lynchings had taken place, showed him a rope, and promised he would also swing from the trees. The strike soon collapsed, with none of the Italians returning to the factories.[136]

The cigar industry remained as volatile as ever, but important changes were taking place in Tampa's business community. The *Morning Tribune* signaled these alterations when it shifted its policies with regard to labor problems. Tampa's business elite was attempting to change the basis of the city's wealth and prosperity. The wave of the future was tourism and development, not cigars, and such a prospect mandated the best possible public image of Tampa. City boosters therefore publicly ignored strikes and suppressed all possible adverse publicity resulting from the violence and vigilantism occurring locally. As one editorial explained, the "best cure" for strike activity was "a policy of silence by all." The space publishers previously gave to labor problems now was filled with tributes to Tampa as a tourist paradise.[137]

When Tampa's last great general strike took place in 1931 there were few Italians left in the cigarworkers' ranks. By then their places had been largely filled by American women and Afro-Americans. Cubans remained, the last of the three immigrant groups still to count heavily in the cigar factories.[138] But the industry was a pale shadow of its former self, already seriously diminished by the Great Depression. Interestingly, the final mass march to the streets represented the last attempt of Tampa unionists to follow a radical union banner.

The cruel reality of the depression struck at the Tampa cigar industry with particular force. The market for high-priced, quality cigars quickly dried up as the nation slipped into the worst economic downturn in its history. Cigarettes, long anathema to the Tampa cigar industry, captured more and more of the tobacco market as the depression deepened. An announced wage cut in January 1931 fueled worker discontent and gravitated them to a new union organized by the Communist party, the Tobacco Workers International Union (TWIU).[139]

As organizing efforts by the TWIU showed evidence of success the usual reaction took place. Vigilantes kidnapped one communist organizer, took him to a remote section of town, and whipped him brutally with leather straps. Police later violently dispersed a huge rally celebrating the anniversary of the Russian Revolution, producing several casualties and numerous arrests. Workers from four of Tampa's largest factories walked out in protest over the police action, and the owners responded by tearing out all remaining readers' platforms in the city (manufacturers had allowed a few to return in 1927), explaining that "all of the trouble is originating from the reader's stand where fiery Communistic translations from anarchistic publications have been constantly poured into the workers."[140] The general strike was at hand.

A familiar pattern of establishment suppression and worker militancy characterized the 1931 strike. José Yglesias remembered it clearly: "The strike left a psychological scar on me. I was in junior high school and a member of the student patrol. I wore an arm band. . . . my mother was in the strike. . . . During the strike, the KKK would come into the Labor Temple with guns and break up the meeting."[141] When owners agreed to reopen their factories after a few short weeks (officials had arrested virtually all strike leaders), dispirited workers returned to the benches. Defeat erased the TWIU from Tampa. Also permanently gone were the readers. Manufacturers replaced them with radios, the final symbolic victory of the new industrial order over the cherished artisan privileges that had for so long sustained Tampa's cigarworkers.[142]

The final irony rested with other, less visible changes in the relationship of Tampa's cigar industry to its Latin population. Italians, once identified as the most ardent unionists in the city by both Anglos and Latins, now perceived the cigar work force from different perspectives. Having exited the cigar factories with varying degrees of speed over the past thirty years, they now overwhelmingly rested in the small businesses and trades begun earlier. Many of these enterprises had evolved from pushcarts and one-horse delivery wagons to well-constructed stores with high overheads. Like longer-established businesses, these operations were increasingly losing ground to the forces of the depression, and labor strikes only further threatened their precarious positions. Italian voices could be heard speaking against their former union comrades. Frank Giunta, whose father had worked in the cigar factories but had left to pursue truck gardening, remembered the prevailing mood among these kinds of Italians: "Sometimes you lose a lot of money—the grocery man, the bread man, the milk man and so on—you just about go bankrupt. Everybody would suffer, there would be wide suffering in Ybor City." When asked who led the workers, Angelina Comescone, a veteran of the 1931 strike, replied with irritation: "Radicals, people who thought they were smarter than the others. . . . they marched them all out, they sit around and sometimes they go to the other factories and march them out. Then somebody asks, 'Why are we here for?' Nobody there to explain why we are out on the streets, no one wanted to be a strikebreaker. You didn't know why you were going out."[143]

Although labor radicals remained and their worldviews helped shape certain elements of Ybor City life, Italians as a group had selected the pathways they would follow to security and stability. By the end of the 1920s these routes no longer included a passionate acceptance of the workers' struggle against management.

Summary

The Italian encounter with cigar factories in Ybor City was never a facile adjustment. The cigar industry dominated not only the economic structure of Tampa but also determined much of the social and cultural interaction taking place within the city. As such, Italians could not insulate themselves from its influence, even if they had chosen to do so. The earliest arrivals suffered from a lack of appropriate skills and an ethnic background that opened few doors. Thus they did not assimilate easily into the cigar work force. As in other parts of the Americas, however, they learned to adjust. Along the way they never lost sight of the cultural imperatives pushing them to provide a secure and stable base for their families.

In the cigar industry the Italians closely encountered Cuban and Spanish immigrants. They learned Spanish, found ways to enter cigar factories, came to join Latins at workbenches as skilled cigarmakers, and ultimately played important roles in the city's labor movement. They also confronted the Anglo community in their positions as cigarworkers and union members. But from the start Italians defined for themselves the place and function that the cigar industry would play in their lives.

First- and second-generation Italians regarded the cigar industry as a means to reach their goals. They used factories to provide a base from which to launch other enterprises that could more faithfully produce the desired end of family security. The Italian case illustrated some of the relationships existing between worker radicalism and capitalist enterprise. These immigrants generally set their sights on the latter and used the former to speed up their efforts to gain their own businesses. By the 1930s and the maturing of the second generation, direct connections with the cigar industry were coming to a close for Italians. The great defeat in the ten-month-long strike in 1920 only propelled forward at a faster pace a process that was well underway. When the final union defeat occurred in 1931, Italians observed the event with interest and perhaps disappointment, due to emotional connections with neighbors and friends, but for the most part not as participants.

A distancing from factories, however, did not immediately translate into a dissociation from the orbit of Ybor City. The stormy history of labor relations in the cigar industry had engendered in Ybor City's Latin residents a sense of community and "fellow feeling." What resulted was, in important particulars, very much like the working-class "peoplehood" that scholars such as Leon Fink and Harry Boyte have found in the work cultures of the Knights of Labor and the political associations existing among Populists.[144] To be sure there existed serious divisions among Latin cigarworkers as to proper union policies and organizational forms, and ethnic cleavages persisted in other spheres of Ybor City's world; but all Latins faced the stark realities of vigilantism, repression, and prejudice from native Tampans and adamant opposition from manufacturers. Driven inward by owners and community leaders seeking to control the cigar industry, Italians and their Latin neighbors made profit from circumstance and forged a set of social and institutional bonds that decisively shaped the contours of their community.

NOTES

1. The details of the Milián affair are in *Tampa Morning Tribune*, November 4, 13, 15, 1902, and *El Federal* (a Tampa cigarworkers' newspaper), November 4, 7, 14, 1902. A controversial episode ended Milián's quixotic career in Tampa. In 1908, apparently afraid that his young bride would leave him, he committed suicide. Over 5,000 cigarmakers and their families filed by his coffin, and all cigar factories in Ybor City and West Tampa closed for the funeral. The September 25, 1908, issue of the *Morning Tribune* gratuitously editorialized: "Most Mayors will decline to adopt the Milián method of resigning from office."

2. Gutman, "Work, Culture, and Society," 559. For the labor experience of Italian immigrants, see Vecoli, "Italian Immigrants," 257–306; Vecoli, "Pane e Giustizia," 55–61.

3. Quoted in Pérez, "Ybor City Remembered," 171.

4. On the handcraft techniques, see Cooper, "Hand Craft to Mass Production," 48–87. On the mystique of the Vuelta Abajo, see Davie, *Cuba*, 219.

5. FWP, "Trade Jargon"; U.S. Congress, *Immigrants in Industries*, 204.

6. *El Internacional*, June 19, 1920. Workers and management agreed to the *cartabón*, or scale of prices, established after the 1910 strike, a list that enjoyed nearly a decade of acceptance and constituted the base from which many negotiations proceeded.

7. U.S. Recovery Administration, *Tobacco Study*, 142; *Tampa Morning Tribune*, October 30, 1955.

8. Interview with Alex Scaglione, April 2, 1980.

9. Some 2,500 workers walked off their jobs in September 1911 when management wanted them to pay ten cents per week to cover their "free smokes." Manifesto, "To the People of Tampa," September 28, 1911, PKY; *Tampa Morning Tribune*, September 15, 29, October 3, 1911.

10. Leon, "Cigar Industry," 76–83; Cooper, "Hand Craft to Mass Production," 48.

11. Campbell and McLendon, *Cigar Industry of Tampa*, 17–20; Scaglione, *Cigar Industry of Florida*.

12. Muñiz, "Lectura en las Tabaquerías" *(Revista)*, 190–272; Muñiz, "Lectura en las Tabaquerías" *(Hoy)*, 78. Ortiz, *Cuban Counterpoint*, 89, claims that Cuban cigar factories copied the practice from similar customs existing in the refectories of convents and the dining halls and workrooms of prisons in Cuba.

13. Pérez, "Reminiscences of a *Lector*," 445.

14. Ibid., 445–46; interview with Victoriano Manteiga, September 2, 1978. One of the most famous readers in Tampa, Manteiga had come to the city from Havana in 1913. He went on to edit Ybor City's *La Gaceta*, a trilingual newspaper still appearing on newsstands.

15. FWP, "Study of the Church," 15; Stelzner and Bazo, "Oracle of the Tobacco Bench," 124–31.

16. Interview with Wilfredo Rodríguez, April 1, 1982. Onofrio Palermo was one of the few Italians elected to the post of reader. His grandson, Nelson Palermo, a fruit and vegetable wholesaler, recalled: "He would put himself in any part he read. . . . he was much beloved." Interview with Nelson Palermo, March 6, 1982.

17. Interview with Honorato Henry Domínguez, September 12, 1980; interview with Carmelo Rocca, July 30, 1983.

18. Interview with Frank Giunta, July 20, 1980; interview with Paul Longo, June 1, 1979; interview with Mary Aparicio Fontanills, March 5, 1982.

19. Interview with Ferdie Pacheco, June 12, 1984; interview with Tina Assunta Provenzano, March 13, 1982; interview with Joe Maniscalco, April 3, 1980.

20. Interview with Frank Giunta, July 20, 1980.

21. Interview with Paul Longo, July 2, 1980; interview with Alex Scaglione, April 2, 1980.

22. Westfall, "Martínez Ybor," 116–17.

23. Ginésta, "History of Ybor City," 3. The tremendous expansion taking place in the cigar industry muted Cuban fears of job competition by Italians.

24. U.S. Congress, *Immigrants in Industries*, 191–92; *Tampa Morning Tribune*, July 18, 1895; interview with Paul Longo, June 1, 1979.

25. *Tampa Morning Tribune*, March 28, 30, 1899.

26. Yglesias, *Truth about Them*, 209. Yglesias, a native of Ybor City and a close friend of Coniglio, obtained this autobiographical interview.

27. Interview with Paul Longo, June 30, 1980.

28. Massari, *Wonderful Life*, 87–94.

29. Hendry, "Revisionist View," 10; U.S. Congress, *Immigrants in Industries*, Table 128, p. 195.

30. U.S. Congress, *Immigrants in Industries*, 192. *Tampa Morning Tribune*, November 1, 1901, reported that the cigar factories employed 1,872 cigarmakers, of whom 424 were Italians.

31. Interview with María Ordieres, June 11, 1981; FWP, "Life History of Fernando Lemos." Both give insight into Cuban and Spanish female employment. Simon, quoted in Scott and Tilly, *Women, Work, and Family*, 3.

32. U.S. Census Bureau, *Twelfth Census*, manuscript census schedules, microfilm 170, PKY; Sumner, *Women and Child Earners*, 196–97; Smith, "Immigrant Women."

33. *El Internacional*, March 2, 1917.

34. Interview with Joe Maniscalco, April 3, 1980; C. Fara-Forni, "Gli Italiani di Nuova Orleans," 217–18. The same report indicated that workers often required three years to become fully skilled in the craft.

35. Moroni, "Emigrazione Italiana," 40; des Planches, *Attraverso gli Stati Uniti*, 117. At least one report claimed that Italian men generally earned more than women. See U.S. Congress, *Immigrants in Industries*, Tables 139, 140, pp. 209–10.

36. Krause, "Urbanization with Breakdown," 291–305; U.S. Congress, *Immigrants in Industries*, Table 150, p. 150; Odencrantz, *Italian Women in Industry*, 48–49. In both 1920 and 1930 Tampa ranked first nationally among cities of 100,000 or more residents in terms of the percentage of married women gainfully employed; the overall figure for 1930 was 33.4 percent. *Fifteenth Census*, Table 30, p. 81.

37. Italian women employed in Ybor City cigar factories actually went against the wider trend then operating in Tampa's cigar industry, which saw the percentage of women versus men obtaining employment go downward by 1900. Among Italians, more women than men in Ybor City worked in the factories. Even by 1909 women fell just short of equaling the total male employment (803 to 846). For the larger pattern, see Durward Long, "Women Workers in the Cigar Industry," paper delivered at the Florida Historical Society meeting, Fort Lauderdale, May 8, 1982.

38. Interview with Joe Maniscalco, April 3, 1980; interview with Mary Fontanills, March 5, 1982.

39. Yans-McLaughlin, *Family and Community*, 217.
40. U.S. Congress, *Immigrants in Industries*, 191–92.
41. *United States Tobacco Journal*, August 24, 1901. During the same strike another woman named Altagracia "led the marching strikers down Seventh Avenue [where] the demonstrators were met by a large armed committee of citizens." Her cool-headed reference to the American flag carried by strikers and their rights under it defused the situation. See del Rió, *Yo Fui Uno de los Fundadores*.
42. *Tampa Morning Tribune*, November 11, 1916; *Tampa Daily Times*, September 26, 1913.
43. *El Internacional*, December 1, 1916.
44. See Bodnar, "Immigration, Kinship and Working-Class Realism," 45–65, for a discussion of these trends. Leuchtenberg, *Perils of Prosperity*, 160, was surely not describing Italian women when he concluded: "By 1930 more than ten million women held jobs. Nothing did more to emancipate them."
45. Dubofsky, *We Shall Be All*, 227–54; Dubofsky, *When Workers Organize*, 59–65, 72–84, 93–97; Furio, "Italian Immigrant Woman," 81–98.
46. A complete set of business directories from 1899 to 1935, housed in the Tampa Public Library, and manuscript census schedules for 1900 and 1910, located at the University of Florida, confirm this pattern. One example among hundreds was Filippo Spoto, who came to Ybor City in 1898 and worked a year in a cigar factory. He soon left to become a peddler, but as of 1900 he had two daughters, aged eighteen and fourteen, working as cigar strippers. He ultimately came to own one of Ybor City's largest groceries. See manuscript census schedules, 1900, microfilm reel 150, p. 179A, PKY.
47. Quoted in Terkel, *Hard Times*, 134.
48. Westfall, "Martínez Ybor," 127.
49. *Tampa Journal*, January 24, 26, March 12, 1887; Poyo, "Cuban Émigré Communities," 224–25. The Tampa Board of Trade held an emergency meeting in which it decided to pledge full police power to protect property and to organize a "vigilance committee" to identify troublemakers. The group quickly warned several labor organizers to leave Tampa within twelve hours. Minutes, Tampa Board of Trade, March 8, 1887, ledger 1.
50. Estrade, "Huelgas de 1890," 27–51; Hidalgo, *Orígenes del Movimiento Obrero*, 101–2; Muñiz, *Movimiento Obrero*, 211.
51. Gallo, "Tabaquero," 108; Poyo, "Anarchist Challenge."
52. Ginésta, "History of Ybor City," 2; Steffy, "Cuban Immigrants," 63–69; *Tampa Tribune*, May 25, 1894. More information on the career of Baliño is contained in *Carlos Baliño, Documentos y Artículos*.
53. *Tampa Tribune*, January 24, 26, 1887. Also see, Poyo, "Cuban Émigré Communities," 224–25.
54. *Tampa Morning Tribune*, July 7, 8, 1899; Minutes, Tampa Board of Trade, March 8, 1887, ledger 1. On April 18, 1893, the *Tampa Morning Tribune* called attention to a "Nihilist" club, counting more than 100 members who hung pictures of Haymarket anarchist August Spies and his companions in their club hall.
55. Fernández, "Anarquistas Cubanos," 4–5.
56. FWP, "Trade Jargon"; *Builders of Florida*, 221. One Italian, Val. M. Antuono, followed a rags-to-riches path in becoming the owner of one of the city's largest cigar factories in 1908. See *Tampa Morning Tribune*, February 3, 1906, for a report of three Italian-owned cigar factories.
57. *Cigar Makers Official Journal* 14 (January 1889), 1; ibid. (March 1889), 6; ibid. 21 (August 1896), 14. The irony is that tobacco workers in Cuba were the first Cuban

workers to form associations for mutual protection and advancement. As early as 1865 cigarworkers already were publishing their own newspapers and organizing mutual aid societies, not infrequently with a socialist or anarchist orientation. See Dumoulin, "Movimiento Obrero," 96.

58. *Tampa Morning Tribune*, February 25, 1895. Cigarmakers rolled the famous "Message to Gómez," which triggered the Cuban insurrection, in a cigar at the O'Halloran factory in West Tampa.

59. Long, "Labor Relations," 551.

60. Interview with Tina Provenzano, March 13, 1982. It is interesting to note that Mrs. Provenzano mixed Italian and Spanish words as she recalled the moment of the strike. Indeed, language mixing proved to be a common phenomenon among Ybor City Italians.

61. *Tampa Morning Tribune*, September 8, 1892. Also see ibid., May 7, August 12, 28, 1891, July 8, 1899.

62. Mormino, "New Urban South," 337–56.

63. *Tampa Morning Tribune*, November 17, December 16, 1896, November 11, 1899.

64. Ibid., July 9, 11, 1899. In issue after issue the paper drummed home its message that strike leaders were "professional agitators . . . regular anarchists, roaming the country, perpetrating their diabolical acts in towns."

65. Ibid., July 30, 1899.

66. Ibid., August 25, 1899. Other concessions included liberal supplies of ice water, coal for heating in the winter, thorough cleaning of factories once a month, and reinstatement of striking workers.

67. Interview with José Díaz, May 3, 1980. The authors are indebted to Patricia Cooper for observations on the wage list.

68. U.S. Recovery Administration, *Tobacco Study*, 146; Sabe, "Early Days of Ybor City," 69; Kennedy, *Palmetto Country*, 279.

69. Quoted in Long, "*Resistencia*," 196; *Tampa Morning Tribune*, November 1, 10, 1900. For attacks on the AFL, see *La Federación*, December 14, 1900.

70. *L'Alba Sociale*, August 15, 1901; Long, "*Resistencia*," 196. *La Federación*, the newspaper of the resistance movement, proclaimed its desire to work for the eventual conversion of society into a "free federation of free workers." Its successor, *El Federal*, called for a worldwide general strike. See "Proyecto de bases," *La Federación*, n.d.; *El Federal*, March 28, 1902.

71. "Casellario Politico Centrale," dossier on Alfonso Coniglio. The Italian government kept extensive files on radicals, tracing their movements in America and elsewhere. The Coniglio file, for example, contains agent reports from 1912 to 1937, covering his actions in Ybor City and Italy. The authors wish to thank Professor Rudolph J. Vecoli for supplying this information from his private collection.

72. Yglesias, *Truth about Them*, 209.

73. *L'Alba Sociale*, July 15, August 1, 1901; interview with José Díaz, May 3, 1980.

74. Long, "*Resistencia*," 210–11; Massari, *Wonderful Life*, 104. The union leader during the strike was Manuel Rivera, a Cuban anarchist. See *Tampa Morning Tribune*, November 6, 8, 1900.

75. *L'Alba Sociale*, August 15, 1901; Manifesto, "To the Workers and People of Tampa in General," August 1901, PKY. Strikers established four soup kitchens in Ybor City, including one in grocer Alex Scaglione's warehouse.

76. Long, "*Resistencia*," 205–9; *United States Tobacco Journal*, August 21, 1901; *Tampa Morning Tribune*, August 1, 1901. In spite of provocations, strikers did not an-

swer violence with violence during the confrontation. See *La Protesta Umana*, February 28, 1902, for a discussion of this fact.

77. *L'Alba Sociale*, August 15, 1901, has a long article, entitled "The Seizures," which describes the kidnappings. In June 1902 one of the men, Félix Méndez, returned to Tampa after a harrowing experience in Honduras. Friendly Indians had helped the strikers, who had been wandering aimlessly in the wilderness. Police officers arrested Méndez immediately on his return and refused to answer questions about his whereabouts. The cigarmakers of La Rosa Español, his former place of employment, walked out in protest. Manifesto, June 6, 1902, PKY.

78. *Proceedings*, 1901, p. 19, AFL Records.

79. Long, *"Resistencia,"* 212. One study claimed that Italians filled the places of departed Cubans and when the strike was over bribed foremen to retain their positions. Campbell and McLendon, *Cigar Industry of Tampa*, 49.

80. Samuel Gompers to D. G. Sanford, April 1, 1903; Frank Morrison to Gompers, July 12, 1906; George Perkins to Gompers, June 27, 1901; all three letters in the CMIU Papers. Wood left his duties in Tampa and went to Palatka, Florida, where several small cigar factories were operating. He was followed by two men from Tampa who shot and wounded him so severely that he lost his left arm.

81. Jacob Brodie to Frank Morrison, September 30, 1906, CMIU Papers.

82. The locals in question were #336 (cigarmakers), #500 (cigarmakers), #493 *(rezagadores)*, #440 *(escogedores)*, and #462 (cigarmakers). Although the evidence is unclear, it appears that semiskilled workers (such as strippers) and unskilled workers (such as porters) had access to the cigarmakers' locals but not the more specialized selector locals.

83. This is based upon a close reading of *El Internacional* for the years indicated and a nine-page typewritten report on conditions in Tampa sent by CMIU President Perkins to Gompers, December 1909, CMIU Papers.

84. Perkins to Gompers, July 27, 1910, CMIU Papers.

85. *El Internacional*, January 30, 1904, March 24, 31, 1911; Shannon, *Socialist Party of America*, 44, 261.

86. Perkins to Gompers, December 9, 1909; J. R. Macías to Gompers, November 20, 1909; Joint Advisory Board to AFL National Office, May 5, 1920; R. A. Septon to Gompers, August 21, 1920; all in CMIU Papers. The CMIU experienced its greatest success during a 1909 membership drive when workers could join for only one dollar. President Perkins himself went to Tampa to help in the campaign. Perkins to Gompers, December 7, 1909, July 27, 1910, CMIU Papers.

87. *El Internacional*, June 3, August 5, 1910; *Tampa Morning Tribune*, June 30, July 13, 14, 28, 1910. The manufacturer's position is outlined in *United States Tobacco Journal*, July 16, 1910; the union's position is made clear in Joint Advisory Board to Gompers, June 27, 1910, CMIU Papers.

88. *Tampa Morning Tribune*, August 12, 1910. As early as July, Perkins wrote to Gompers that "some of the more radical hot-headed members dropped out of the union, apparently because they were opposed to the conservative manner" in which the Joint Advisory Board was handling matters. Perkins to Gompers, July 5, 1910, CMIU Papers.

89. *United States Tobacco Journal*, August 6, 1910; *Tampa Morning Tribune*, August 2, 12, 15, 23, 1910.

90. *Tampa Morning Tribune*, April 14, 1909, September 10, 14, 15, 17, October 5, 1910. Frantic editorials in the English-language press pointed out that Easterling was the "first American to be attacked; city fathers pledged he would be the last."

91. Ibid., September 21, 22, 1910. A more extended discussion of the lynching is contained in Pozzetta, "Tampa General Strike of 1910," 29–46.
92. Gaetano Morini to Marquis Cusani Confalonieri, October 11, 1910, p. 1, Department of State, "Tampa Lynching Incident," box 3671.
93. *El Internacional*, November 18, 1901; *Tampa Morning Tribune*, September 15, November 15, 1910.
94. Interview with Mary Italiano, April 20, 1980.
95. Interview with Joe Maniscalco, April 3, 1980.
96. *El Internacional*, October 21, 1910; *Tampa Morning Tribune*, October 17, 18, 19, 20, 1910. Union officials repeatedly wrote to the U.S. Department of Justice to enlist federal aid in stopping abuses. After several months the Justice Department responded that "no federal intervention is justified." J. M. Cheney to U.S. Attorney General, October 6, 1910, Amos L. Hill to William Howard Taft, January 11, 1911, Department of Justice, "Strike File—Cigarmakers, 1911."
97. *Tampa Morning Tribune*, December 23, 1910; *El Internacional*, December 23, 30, 1910. The citizens' patrols were specially noted in many Italian-language leftist newspapers around the country. One Chicago socialist paper decried the arrest of Italian and Spanish strikers and later urged workers to hold firm, indicating that "workers in every part of the North have fixed their eyes on their comrades in Tampa!" See *La Parola dei Socialisti*, October 1, November 26, 1910; *La Cronaca Sovversiva* (Barre, Vt.), January 14, 21, 1911.
98. *Tampa Morning Tribune*, November 10, 1910. One other *Tribune* analysis indicated, "During the last strike they [the Italians] were accused of being responsible for the strike being broken, and it is said to be the remembrance of this taunt that is making them so stubborn this time." Ibid., December 30, 1910.
99. *Il Progresso Italo-Americano*, November 8, 1910, quoted in *Il Martello*, November 8, 1910.
100. *El Internacional*, November 18, 1910.
101. Ibid., December 30, 1910; *Tampa Morning Tribune*, November 19, December 30, 1910.
102. *Tampa Morning Tribune*, August 10, 1908.
103. Professor Donna Gabaccia has generously made information on Giovanni Vaccaro available from her study of Sicilian migration from Sambuca di Sicilia. See also Vecoli, "Pane e Giustizia," for a discussion of the backgrounds of Italian radical labor leaders.
104. Copies of *Il Martire* are available on microfilm at PKY. The drive netted some $400. *Il Proletario*, July 21, 1911; *La Fiaccola*, June 17, 1911. See especially Fenton, *Immigrants and Unions*, and Vecoli, "Italian American Workers," 25–49, in rebuttal.
105. Interview with Frank Vaccaro, February 25, 1984.
106. *La Parola dei Socialisti*, October 2, 1910, July 29, 1911. *La Fiaccola*, July 22, 1911, contains a statement of the goals of Gruppo Lorenzo Panepinto sent to the paper by Vaccaro.
107. Interview with Frank Vaccaro, February 25, 1984.
108. Interview with John Massaro, August 1, 1983. Vaccaro wrote extensive reports and sent them to *La Parola*; for example, see ibid., July 16, 30, September 3, October 2, 1910, February 4, 1911.
109. Interview with Carmelo Rocca, February 25, 1984.
110. Ibid., July 30, 1983, September 15, 1984.
111. Ibid., October 2, 1982, July 30, 1983.

112. Interview with Sirio Bruno Coniglio, May 2, 1976.

113. Higham, *Ethnic Leadership in America*, 3–8. Among other themes Higham's volume explores the tensions between "leaderships of accommodation and protest." Although both were present in Ybor City, those favoring protest consistently dominated community activities during the years under review.

114. *El Internacional*, January 20, 27, 1911; *Tampa Morning Tribune*, January 24, 26, 1911; T. V. Kirk to Commissioner General of Immigration, January 28, 1911, Bureau of Immigration and Naturalization. Many of the more active labor leaders fled the city, among them the anarchist Pedro Esteve, who went to Paterson, N.J.

115. Perkins to Gompers, June 27, 1910, Perkins to Frank Morrison, February 26, 1913, CMIU Papers.

116. Perkins to Morrison, in *El Internacional*, November 2, 1913. All surviving issues of *El Obrero Industriale* are available on microfilm at PKY.

117. Flynn, *Rebel Girl*, 184–85.

118. *El Internacional*, September 28, 1917. This CMIU newspaper constantly complained of the "ill advised disruptions, hasty conclusions, false conceptions, personal attacks and even calumny" that characterized their opponents' tactics. It concluded, "The interests of the working class cannot afford to be exposed to the rashness of a few enthusiastic radicals." See, for example, ibid., January 5, 17, 1917, October 24, 1919, October 22, 1922.

119. Ibid., May 11, 1917. Also see ibid., April 6, May 18, 1917, March 14, June 21, 1919.

120. Ibid., January 5, 19, October 25, 1917; *L'Organizzatore*, January 3, 1920. As David Brody has noted, union locals attempted to encompass the lives of their members with broad-based programs of activities. See *Workers in Industrial America*, 22–23.

121. Interview with Frank Vaccaro, February 25, 1984.

122. *El Internacional*, September 22, 1916, June 22, 1917, March 15, August 9, 1918 (molds and machines), March 2, 1917, February 21, 1919 (women), June 30, 1917 (children), July 28, 1916 (wage cuts), August 18, 1916 (higher costs of living), July 21, 1916 (apprentices). For highly personal reports of a 1915 strike, see José Ramón Avellanal to Evaristo Avellanal, March 12, 1915, Avellanal Family Papers, Special Collections, USF.

123. *El Internacional*, July 15, 21, August 11, 18, October 5, 6, 8, 1916, January 11, 18, March 1, 22, April 28, 29, May 1, 2, 1918 (strikers); Minutes, Tampa Board of Trade, March 10, 1919; *Tampa Citizen*, June 27, July 11, 1919 (consumer cooperatives).

124. Long, "Open-Closed Shop Battle," 105. The actions of Tampa's owners were only part of a nationwide movement against union labor embodied in the "American Plan," which was aimed at checking union gains. See Brody, *Workers in Industrial America*, 44–45.

125. *El Internacional*, August 20, 1920; Sexton to Gompers, July 31, 1920, CMIU Papers.

126. Minutes, Tampa Board of Trade, July 26, November 19, 20, 23, 1920; *El Internacional*, January 20, June 4, September 3, 1920. Workers constantly complained that "advocates of the open-shop continually link it with the American flag."

127. *El Internacional*, August 27, 1920. On August 2, 1920, Arturo Giovannitti, representing the general council of the Italian Chamber of Labor of New York, felt compelled to write to Tampa's mayor to protest announcement of plans by the local citizens' committee to interfere with the strike.

128. Ibid., February 5, 1920; *Tampa Sunday Tribune*, February 6, 1920; *Tampa Morning Tribune*, June 23, 1926.

129. *Tampa Daily Times*, February 6, 1919, January 31, 1947; *Tampa Morning Tribune*, January 17, 1923, February 1, 1947.

130. *El Internacional*, April 8, 1921, June 13, 1922, June 13, 1924. The union dropped travel and sick benefits between 1927 and 1931 and cut death benefits almost in half.

131. Joint Advisory Board to Gompers, June 27, 1910, (?) to Gompers, August 23, 1910, CMIU Papers; *Tampa Morning Tribune*, January 27, 1911. See also "The Attempt to Drive Union Labor from Tampa," *American Federationist* 18 (January 1911), 151, for further details of efforts to aid Tampa's strikers.

132. *El Internacional*, October 22, 1922, July 20, November 2, 1923; Manifestos, "To the Cigar Workers of Tampa," August 29, 1923, and "To the Cigar Workers of Tampa," August 29, 1923, PKY. Union records show that the CMIU spent a total of $1,490,411.84 during the 1920 strike. See *Proceedings*, 1923, p. 2, AFL Records.

133. Department of Justice, ICF #362112.

134. Ibid., #5606; interview with Frank Vaccaro, February 25, 1984; interview with Carmelo Rocca, February 25, 1984. See Department of Justice, ICF #06 20713 and #194147 for reports on Coniglio.

135. Interview with Frank Settecasi, May 18, 1979.

136. Perkins to Gompers, November 29, 1921, CMIU Papers; *El Internacional*, November 22, 29, December 2, 30, 1921. Vigilantes put Luis Díaz, described as a "fiery radical," on a train for Jacksonville and told him never to return.

137. *Tampa Morning Tribune*, October 22, 1924, January 23, September 2, 1926; *El Internacional*, November 17, 1922, January 8, 22, 1926. Cigarworkers protested city funds being used to pay for tourist facilities when public facilities in Ybor City were in poor repair. They also blamed high rents on the willingness of tourists to pay higher rates for housing and accommodations.

138. Department of Labor, *Women in Florida Industries; Fifteenth Census: Population*, IV, 341–42, 352.

139. Ingalls, "Radicals and Vigilantes," 44–57.

140. *Tampa Morning Tribune*, November 27, 1931.

141. Terkel, *Hard Times*, 449.

142. Interview with Alena and Lora Noto, May 4, 1980.

143. Interview with Angelina Comescone, July 18, 1979; interview with Frank Giunta, July 20, 1980.

144. Fink, *Workingmen's Democracy*, 22; Boyte, "Populism and the Left," 58–61.

Citizens of Alessandria della Rocca stroll along the Via Roma, circa 1900. *(Special Collections, University of South Florida Library)*

A bell tower rises over Santo Stefano Quisquina, 1981. The town's profile reflects recent construction, an effort by the Italian government to solve the "southern problem." The town of Bivona can be seen further down in the valley. *(Special Collections, University of South Florida Library)*

West Tampa, 1894. Scaffolding scales Céspedes Hall, home of a Cuban social club and an opera house, named for the island patriot. The O'Halloran factory, notable for producing the cigar that ignited the Cuban Revolution of 1895, looms in the distance. *(Tony Pizzo Collection, Special Collections, University of South Florida Library)*

Model A's line Ybor City's La Gran Séptima Avenida (Seventh Avenue) in 1926, facing east from the 1500 block. *(Tony Pizzo Collection, Special Collections, University of South Florida Library)*

Tampa became synonymous with hand-rolled cigars. Shrewd merchandising and the sophisticated artistry of chromolithography resulted in thousands of distinctive cigar labels. *(Special Collections, University of South Florida Library)*

On April 13, 1886, workers rolled Ybor City's first cigar at the wood-framed Sanchez and Haya factory, located at Seventh Avenue and Fifteenth Street. *(Burgert Brothers Collection, Tampa-Hillsborough County Public Library)*

Opened in 1914, the Perfecto Garcia factory functioned as a barometer of Ybor City's economic health. In August 1926, workers at the Perfecto Garcia factory walked off their jobs in support of Sacco and Vanzetti, precipitating a strike of 15,000 Tampa cigarworkers. The factory closed in 1982. *(Burgert Brothers Collection, Tampa-Hillsborough County Public Library)*

Immigrant women strip the tobacco leaf from the rib, a job that frequently served as an entry point to the cigar industry for Italian women. *(Special Collections, University of South Florida Library)*

Selectors carefully grade and pair the aged tobacco leaves. *(Burgert Brothers Collection, Tampa-Hillsborough County Public Library)*

Cigarmakers at their benches at Cuesta Rey and Company in 1924. Note the presence of Afro-Cubans and women among these artisans. *(Burgert Brothers Collection, Tampa-Hillsborough County Public Library)*

El lector (the reader) gesticulates as he translates the morning newspaper for the cigarmakers at the Morgan City factory in 1929. The institution of the reader was finally abolished in 1931 following a bitter strike. *(Burgert Brothers Collection, Tampa-Hillsborough County Public Library)*

Joaquin de la Llana, dressed in a style befitting his station as a reader, poses for this 1920s photograph. *(Courtesy of Judy Deese)*

Lorenzo Panepinto, artist, author, and socialist leader, was a hero to Tampa's Sicilian community. *(From Gaspare Nicotri, Storia della Sicilia nelle Rivoluzione e Rivolte. New York: Italian Publishers, 1934, p. 192)*

The command post of Ybor City's turbulent labor movement, El Centro Obrero (the Labor Temple), which stood at 1616 Eighth Avenue, survived through the 1920s. *(Burgert Brothers Collection, Tampa-Hillsborough County Public Library)*

José de la Campa exhorts a 1912 crowd estimated at 5,000 during a speech marking his return to the labor movement after serving a year of hard labor on a chain gang for his role in the 1910 strike. *(Special Collections, University of South Florida Library)*

"Strikes marked the passage of time," remembered José Yglesias. *La Huelga de la Pesa* (the Weight Strike) convulsed Ybor City for sixteen weeks in 1899. Workers, black and white, organized soup kitchens to feed the families of striking cigarmakers. *(Special Collections, University of South Florida Library)*

Founded by Rámon Valdespino and José Gregorý, the important Spanish-language newspaper *La Traduccion* (The Translation) was relied upon by readers in the cigar factories. This photograph shows newsboys about to deliver the paper. *(Burgert Brothers Collection, Tampa-Hillsborough County Public Library)*

Conceived as a cathedral to the worker, L'Unione Italiana was dedicated in 1918. The Italian Club, located at Seventeenth Avenue and Eighteenth Street, embodies elements of classical and Mediterranean architecture. *(Tony Pizzo Collection, Special Collections, University of South Florida Library)*

In 1930 El Centro Español sparkled as a jewel amidst urban clutter. Founded in 1892, the building shown here was dedicated in 1912 and closed in 1983. *(Burgert Brothers Collection, Tampa-Hillsborough County Public Library)*

The Recreation Committee of the Italian Club poses for this 1924 photograph. Seated in the front row are the committee's presidents, Helen Scaglione, third from the left, and Paolo Longo, to her right. *(Special Collections, University of South Florida Library)*

The Cuban Club served as a social hub for Ybor City's youth. Cuban Americans, dressed for a club dance, pose for this 1912 portrait. *(Florida Photographic Collection, Florida State Archives)*

Delivery wagons and workers in front of the Pardo and Brother's Bakery, 1900. Note the cigarworkers' cottages to the left and the stacks of wooden paving blocks to the right. *(Special Collections, University of South Florida Library)*

The Parrino family pose with some of their Belmont Heights customers at the Red Front Grocery, 1940. Many Italian American–run grocery stores catered to black residents. *(Courtesy of Donna Parrino)*

5 *Italians and the Radical Culture*
From Contadini *to* Compañeros

In our community, socialism and anarchism were in vogue.

Angelo Massari, *Wonderful Life*

A radical culture of unusual complexity, durability, and diversity came into being in Ybor City. Nurtured by the *lector*, sustained by a tradition of militancy, and tempered by the fires of nativist hostility, radicals imprinted their distinctive stamp on the entire community. Today it is difficult to gain a sense of this leftist orientation, since Ybor City seems becalmed in its new role as a tourist center. "But it wasn't like that when I was growing up there," exclaimed the novelist José Yglesias. "It was extremely radical. Anarchists. Communists. And they were well organized."[1] The visions of a just society held by these individuals frequently clashed with attitudes existing in the wider society and in some cases in the immigrant community itself. When radicals formed debating clubs and political groups, published newspapers, participated in strikes, led unions, and in many other ways attempted to spread their messages, friction resulted. The tensions resulting from these activities had important consequences for all of Ybor City.

Early-arriving Italians stepped into the ideological and organizational ferment of Ybor City with some firm guideposts from their past. Many had listened to the teachings of Lorenzo Panepinto and shared in the experience of the *fasci*. Not a few converted to socialism. All were only too familiar with the harsh lessons of Sicilian life, with its greedy landlords, grasping officials, and self-serving clergy. Angelo Massari spoke for hundreds of villagers as he recorded his first impressions of Tampa: "When in 1902 I landed in Tampa, I found myself in a world of radicals for which I was prepared, and when I listened to speeches against the Catholic Church and the priesthood, I was not at all surprised. In those days in Tampa, anarchists and socialists were many."[2]

In the cigar factories Italians listened to the daily readings, with their stinging criticisms of capitalism; on the closely packed streets and corners of Ybor City and the open-windowed meeting halls of the clubs they heard debates about the working-class struggle; in the newspapers they read the points and counterpoints of radical speakers. They filtered all of this through their own encounter with leftist philosophies in the Old World. It was not long before they gravitated toward existing groups and in some cases formed their own.

By 1900 Italians possessed a radical culture that rivaled in variety and activity that of their Latin comrades. Ybor City and West Tampa contained left- and right-wing socialists, centrists, revolutionary and IWW syndicalists, pacifistic and "propaganda of the deed" anarchists, and a number of others as well. These individuals organized various socialist *circoli* (discussion groups) and *sezioni* (sections), anarchist *gruppi* (groups), debating clubs, speaking societies, and political organizations in both communities. The majority were small entities formed for the purposes of self-education and debate. Typical of these groups was the small anarchist club that attracted Angelo Massari shortly after he arrived in 1902. "In our community, socialism and anarchism were in vogue," Massari observed of the early years. "I associated with a group of friends who had organized a club for social studies. At the club I read pamphlets, newspapers, books, and all kinds of sociological literature. I also attended all the lectures and debates that the two groups, socialist and anarchist, organized, inviting to Tampa the greatest exponents of the two theories who were living in the North."[3]

Each group typically included a secretary who was responsible for corresponding with like-minded individuals elsewhere and for maintaining a small club library. Whether it was a single shelf of books or a collection numbering into the hundreds, every club provided access to some literary material. These collections typically featured a wide assortment of reading matter, ranging from simple spelling and grammar texts to Italian-language editions of the great radical masters. Invariably included among the latter were the works of Mikhail Bakunin, Peter Kropotkin, and Errico Malatesta. Most items in these club libraries were small, inexpensive pamphlets *(opuscoli)* offering polemical essays on various topics or excerpts from larger works.[4] Some were printed in the city, most commonly by La Poliglota Press, owned by the renowned Spanish anarchist Pedro Esteve, and featured the writings of local literati. More numerous, however, were the publications contained in several educational series sponsored by a variety of radical groups. Among the most popular in Tampa were *Biblioteca Socialista-Anarchica, Biblioteca Popolare Educativa,* and *Libreria Sociologica,* distributed from a number of radical centers in the North.[5]

To meet the social and cultural needs of their members, as well as provide for their political education, clubs collected small monthly dues, from ten to twenty-five cents per member, and periodically held various fund-raising functions such as picnics and benefits. More often than not members held meetings in their homes, although some of the larger groups were able to obtain meeting space in the Labor Temple (usually free of charge) or one of the immigrant club buildings. The immigrant press of Ybor City is filled with meeting announcements for these groups, particularly in the years before World War I.[6]

The anarchist Alfonso Coniglio formed a group named Risveglio (Awakening) and held meetings and teaching sessions in his home. His son Bruno remembered them clearly: "We had a long, last room like what we might call a porch, but it was all enclosed, and we had a long table. . . . we always had people come in. And he used that table for, let's see, one, two, three, about four pupils, all grownups who worked during the day. Twice a week they would come over and my father would teach them what little he knew. . . . well, then others did the same thing."[7] Other groups, among them La Voce dello Schiavo (The Slave's Voice), L'Alba Sociale (The Social Dawn), and Gruppo Volontà (Group of the Will), met regularly and, in the case of the first two, for a time published newspapers bearing the same names (see below for an analysis of newspapers).[8]

Socialists also supported a variety of *circoli,* which regularly advertised their meetings and agendas in the local newspapers. The Circolo di Studi Sociali, for example, regularly met at 1702 Seventh Avenue under the sponsorship of publisher Vincente Antinori. In 1911 this group sponsored the creation of a consumer cooperative. The most popular socialist group was Gruppo Lorenzo Panepinto, begun by Giovanni Vaccaro in 1911 after Panepinto's assassination; by that June the organization counted more than 200 members. The club often held joint meetings with other radical groups in the area to raise money for worthy causes, hold debates, and plot strategy. It also pledged a yearly stipend of L1,200 to the socialist section of Santo Stefano Quisquina to assist in its work among the peasantry.[9]

Unlike their anarchist comrades, who banded together in autonomous groups with little or no formal organization, many Italian socialists after 1910 organized into affiliated locals of the Socialist Party of America. Two such groups, designated "Italian locals," were located in Ybor City and West Tampa; they joined company with four other locals operating in Ruskin, Tampa, St. Petersburg, and Palmetto.[10] These other organizations were composed of native Americans, representing the "grass roots socialism" that had made significant gains in the South and Southwest. Like Italians in Sicily, many southerners of this period had experienced agricultural distress and had responded with radicalism. In many ways a heightened class consciousness gripped the South even as class-conscious Italians were entering Florida. The two intersected in Ybor City.[11]

Socialists and Politics

Even before formal affiliation Italians frequently cooperated with other socialists in Hillsborough County. In the years before 1917 socialists were active, if not particularly successful, pursuers of political office. As with most aspects of the radical culture, however, there was substantial diversity of opinion regarding the efficacy of political activity. The majority of local socialists, including Italians, appear to have belonged to the "right" or "constructive" wing of the socialist continuum, to use James Weinstein's terms.[12] They believed that the socialist state could be achieved by the ballot. Giovanni Vaccaro was an eloquent spokesman for this point of view, perhaps influenced by the political activity he witnessed among village socialists in Sicily. He served as secretary of the Ybor City Italian local of the Socialist party and frequently agitated for joint strategy meetings with other groups. In December 1911, for example, he organized a mass political meeting that featured a speech by noted socialist Kate Richards O'Hare. Nearly 1,000 people, including many women, were present, and Vaccaro predicted that the rally would be "a great help for the next municipal election."[13]

These tactics did not go unchallenged in either the Anglo or immigrant socialist ranks. A minority of "left" or revolutionary socialists were contemptuous of the moderates. "All these little [political] reforms lead people astray," explained one such believer. "They leave the great question of emancipation of the wage slave from the capitalist regime forever unanswered, and only offer more laws to confuse the people and make them forget that they are hungry and homeless."[14] Even further estranged from ordinary political reform were anarchists in the city. "You will never convince the capitalists by legislation that they are robbers," shrilled one adherent. "The capitalist system is maintained by force and force will have to destroy it. There is everything on earth to make the people happy if there is no law to obstruct it, and when people are happy it is easy for them to be good."[15]

Despite these existing divisions and the gulf that tended to separate immigrants and Anglos, socialists were able to mount substantial political challenges to the dominant Democratic party on the local scene. The 1904 election, for example, witnessed a socialist ticket offering a full slate of candidates for state, county, and city offices. As an indication of their strength, all candidates made campaign stops at the Italian socialist clubs. In the elections of both 1910 and 1912 socialists came close to winning political office with tickets that included Latin candidates.[16] So effective were these campaigns that the White Municipal party was forced to resort to trickery and fraud to ensure victory. In several cases, for example, the names of socialist candidates failed to appear on the printed ballot, and efforts to contact appropriate city officials for corrections proved unavailing.[17]

Bureaucrats routinely disapproved socialist requests for the appointment of election inspectors, and on one occasion police arrested the socialist candidate for city treasurer when he attempted to monitor the Tenth Ward polling place. As socialist strength increased in 1910 and 1912, Democrats linked the specter of increased black political power to any socialist victory. Their concern was intensified because socialists refused to participate in the white primaries, preferring instead to oppose the White Municipal party in the general election. The *Morning Tribune* in 1912 warned city residents that socialists were planning to attract to their ranks "the negro voters who were denied participation in the white primaries" in order to win. The paper concluded that "no greater calamity could befall this city than the election of socialist administration, or even a partly socialist administration. It is up to the voters of the White Municipal Party to make such a calamity impossible."[18]

Local political elites took the *Morning Tribune*'s admonition to heart. They continued tampering with the printed ballot—reversing the candidate order for the Fourth Ward (Ybor City) in 1912 so as to confuse voters who might have been told to vote for the second candidate (socialist) throughout—and won a clean sweep for the White Municipal party.[19] Among the socialist candidates in this election was Angelo Leto, a union cigarmaker from Ybor City who ran for the city council. Nicholas Lodato attempted unsuccessfully to win a city council seat in 1914, and Giovanni Vaccaro carried the banner in 1916. Although no socialist was victorious in any election from 1904 to 1916, in certain contests the party captured as much as 40 percent of the vote.[20]

The Radical World

Just as Italians rapidly integrated themselves into Ybor City's radical structure, so too did they quickly become part of the worldwide community of Italian radicals. They sought to keep in contact with their fellow leftists who lived in other Italian immigrant centers through a variety of means. Alfonso Coniglio, for example, served as a middleman for the socialist library of Paterson, New Jersey—actually a published series of inexpensive paperbacks covering various radical topics—and supplied volumes to interested individuals. He also operated as a southern distributor for the anarchist newspaper *La Cronaca Sovversiva*, published in various locations but principally in Barre, Vermont. Coniglio received bundles of the weekly newspaper and distributed them by hand to people in Ybor City and West Tampa. He also mailed some to comrades in neighboring southern states.[21] Other anarchists such as Pietro Scaglione, Salvatore Lodato, and Luigi Noto ordered leftist papers, including *Il Martello* (New York), *Il Proletario* (New York), and *La Parola dei Socialisti* (Chicago), and made them available in various club libraries. In time Spanish-language newspapers such as *El Despertar* (anarchist, New York and Paterson) found their way onto the shelves.[22]

The orbits joining Ybor City's Italian radicals with this wider universe went beyond the printed word. Club resources financed radical speakers and authors who participated in the *giro di propaganda* (propaganda tour), a vigorous network which carried personalities and ideas along well-worn routes connecting the radical immigrant world. Again, young Angelo Massari remembered the dynamics of the process as it worked in Ybor City. Socialists and anarchists "vied with each other, and brought in well-known speakers, both of socialistic and anarchistic convictions. There were well-attended lectures and debates."[23] Ybor City became a regular stop for radical luminaries as they circulated throughout the world, visiting the far-flung outposts that immigrants had populated. Between the years 1890 and 1919 virtually every radical of distinction came to Florida to spend time with their Ybor City *campanieri*. Errico Malatesta, anarchist veteran of revolutionary activities in a dozen different countries, visited in February 1900, lecturing and debating for several days while enjoying the warm Florida winter. His talks, delivered in both Spanish and Italian, filled lecture halls to capacity.[24] "Yes, he was a good man," remembered José Vega Díaz. "And although he's no good in Spanish, we understand what he say."[25]

Socialists Arturo Caroti and Vincenzo Vacirca and anarchist Luigi Galleani also responded to invitations and made journeys to Tampa, as did Giuseppe Bertelli, socialist editor of Chicago's *La Parola dei Socialisti*.[26] Bertelli made a ten-day visit in May 1910, publishing several lengthy reports of his stay in his newspaper. He commented on, among other things, the amicable relationships existing in the Tampa area among Italian socialists and anarchists, the nature of the cigar industry and its unions, his public debates with the Spanish anarchist Pedro Esteve, and the status of religion among the city's immigrants. As a parting gift cigarmakers presented Bertelli with a bundle of Havana tobacco marked *"tobacco anarchico per la pipa di Bertelli."*[27]

Despite Bertelli's claim of harmony existing between the adherents of socialism and anarchism, relations were much more often marked by suspicion and hostility. Proponents of one viewpoint or the other attacked those who disagreed in newspaper feuds that often had lengthy runs. These splits spilled over into street-corner arguments and more formal debates in clubs and at picnic grounds. Discussions centering on the proper modes of organization and/or unionization for the working class invariably invoked heated exchanges. Particularly strong disagreements existed between those who advocated working for political solutions through the existing system and those who refused to accommodate, urging instead direct action in the form of strikes and agitation.[28] However, while radicals may have disagreed about doctrine, they seldom, if ever, made distinctions on the basis of nationality. Surviving documents suggest strongly that Cubans, Spaniards, and Italians gravitated to certain groups according to their ideological leanings or the personal magnetism of a particular leader. Although clubs initially may have been composed entirely of one nationality, they typically attracted members of the other immigrant groups to their ranks in rapid order.[29]

The career of Pedro Esteve illustrates these patterns at work. Born in Barcelona in 1866, Esteve played an important role in the developing Catalan anarchist movement. He accompanied the incomparable anarchist spokesman Errico Malatesta during his *giro de propaganda* of Spain in 1891. Esteve worked with the principal anarchist newspaper of Barcelona, *El Productor*, where he learned the printing trade that would occupy his working career. Toward the end of the nineteenth century he emigrated to Brooklyn, where he became active in the publication of the anarchist newspaper *El Despertar*. Soon thereafter he and his paper moved to Paterson, New Jersey, a well-known center of anarchist activity.[30] In 1899 Esteve attracted his old friend Malatesta to Paterson, where a bitter fight was raging between factions of Italian anarchists. From this battle Esteve emerged as editor of the Italian anarchist newspaper *La Questione Sociale*, a position he held intermittently until March 1906, when Ludovico Caminata replaced him. During his career in Brooklyn and Paterson, Esteve had worked with anarchists of several different nationalities, although he was always most closely allied with Italians. When he stepped down from *La Questione Sociale*, the Spanish anarchists of Tampa invited him to join them; with funds collected from various clubs in the city, supporters supplied him with his own printing shop and a residence.[31]

In Ybor City, Esteve guided the fortunes of Antorcha, a cultural center open to free-thinkers of all nationalities. The club offered free classes on many subjects, musical recitals, literary gatherings, a reading room with newspapers from Madrid, Rome, and Havana, and a gymnasium for exercise and sport. Arturo Massolo, a young Italian socialist, also offered fencing lessons for interested individuals, while the ubiquitous Giovanni Vaccaro served as the club's treasurer. "In *Antorcha*," claimed Angelo Massari, "all languages freely blended. English, Spanish, and Italian were common, but Spanish was more or less the official language, and we all understood each other quite well."³² Esteve's other creation in Ybor City, a Francisco Ferrer school, also attracted students from each immigrant group, although Spanish anarchists gave it the most consistent support.³³

It is difficult to gauge the membership of the various radical groups. As historian Paul Avrich noted, anarchists possessed an almost "instinctive hostility toward organization," a factor that worked against formal structures and accurate recordkeeping. Socialist groups were often secretive of their membership lists, fearing police repression or surveillance. Even syndicalists, who joined and/or created unions, are often impossible to identify with any precision since union records are sparse and, when available, do not identify members by ideology. Nevertheless, some sense of numbers is gained from the newspapers these groups published, even if only for a short time, and from oral testimony.³⁴ Anarchist clubs were always small, with a committed core of a dozen or so individuals perhaps representing the average. Socialist groups tended to be larger, and in the case of the locals of the Socialist Party of America, may have numbered into the hundreds. A simple head count, of course, does not in itself give full indication of influence. Many residents of Ybor City attended the speeches, debates, and rallies sponsored by these organizations, and their newspapers surely reached a larger audience than the membership. In addition to these public dimensions of the radical presence, there appears to have been considerable movement in and out of these clubs as individuals experimented with different ideologies.³⁵

In the sense that radical groups provided forums for the disparate elements of Ybor City's population to come together, they served an integrative function for the community. They also supplied strategies that led to various cooperative ventures, ranging from devices to stretch the funds of striking workers to boycotts against Tampa merchants and the establishment of consumer cooperatives. Although radicals differed as to the exact contours of the class ideology they believed to be correct, all agreed that the working class shared a common set of enemies and a common goal of betterment. As in the case of socialists, they also supplied some connective links with segments of the Anglo community. From this perspective radical ideologies worked to pull the community together and provided contexts in which members of the major immigrant groups could interact with each other in face-to-face encounters. As one socialist wrote during a cigar strike, "*A voi lavoratori! Italiani, Spagnoli, e Cubani di Tampa: tutti come un sole uomo, mantenetevi fermi e non tradite la nobile causa"* (To you workers! Italians, Spaniards, and Cubans: All as a single man, keep firm and do not betray the noble cause).[36]

The message of working-class solidarity lent Ybor City a leftist orientation. That the level of acceptance was more than merely superficial or confined to a tiny segment of the community can be seen in the character of Ybor City's unions, its shared club programs, its pattern of consumer cooperatives, its press, and, of course, the profound impact of the *lector*. It can also be charted by the reaction of the community to events outside its borders. Ybor City residents were forever taking up collections and demonstrating to aid one leftist cause after another. One mass rally in 1913 possessed endorsements from the Italian local of the Socialist party, Gruppo Panepinto, Gruppo Risveglio (Italian anarchist), Grupo La Luz (Spanish anarchist), the IWW local, and all of the CMIU locals. Funds to support the 1905 Russian Revolution, the Mexican Revolution, the defense of arrested comrades around the world, and the establishment of various leftist groups and newspapers elsewhere flowed out of Ybor City in a steady stream. Reports of collection committees often included block-by-block itemizations of contributions, revealing the breadth and depth of community support.[37]

Existing alongside these unifying roles, however, were more divisive tendencies. As mentioned, radicals were inclined to split over minor matters of doctrinal orthodoxy. Although the distinctions may have been small, the levels of passion and commitment were not; at times various groups fought each other with as much intensity as they battled the workers' enemies.[38] Radicals also served as lightning rods for the native Tampa community, which frequently attributed problems in their relationships with Latins solely to the presence of radicals. As such they became handy pretexts for intrusions, often violent, into Ybor City life, a fact not lost on many residents of the immigrant community. The case of the cigarworkers' unions is illustrative, as they often spent as much time defending themselves against claims of being dominated by "outside anarchist agitators" as they did in trying to explain their labor positions.[39]

Although the evidence is scanty and at times even contradictory, it appears that Ybor City radicals differed from their counterparts elsewhere in their attitudes toward race relations. According to some scholars, radicals accepted American racist practices; some even advocated complete segregation. Milton Cantor has claimed that socialist interest in blacks did not rise until after World War I, and that southern locals tended to exclude blacks throughout the period.[40] Ybor City radicals operated in a community that precluded any facile acceptance of Jim Crow practices or beliefs. The facts of everyday life gave the lie to the most negative racist assertions about black inferiority and undesirability. The intermixture of substantial numbers of Afro-Cubans in the neighborhoods, workrooms, and union halls accustomed residents not only to the presence of black faces but also to interacting and working with these people on a day-to-day basis. The events surrounding Tampa's 1900 Labor Day parade give insight into the status held by Afro-Cubans. Organized by a committee representing unions throughout the city, the resulting parade drew only "a very small and insignificant" contingent from the cigarmakers, by far the city's largest branch of labor. Several reports claimed that "the desire of the committee to make the parade a white one" caused the cigar unions to abstain from participating. Ultimately, even white Tampa bent to the prevailing customs, allowing, for example, mixed seating on trolleys servicing Ybor City even after the passage of restrictive Jim Crow laws mandating separate black sections.[41]

The position of Afro-Americans in the social world of Ybor City is less clear. After 1900 they found employment in the cigar factories in increasing numbers, although they generally entered and remained at the lower levels. The Ybor City locals energetically supported the decision of the AFL in 1920 to organize black workers. Even earlier the union newspaper had praised the actions of black cigarworkers during strikes, and no evidence exists that points to exclusionary policies for access into cigar unions. Not a few reports of crowds of picketers and strikers mentioned the presence of "negroes." Blacks also tended to gravitate residentially into the streets of Ybor City, particularly into the Italian sections, as very often the small groceries, bakeries, and shops of Italians catered to Afro-Americans.[42]

To be sure Ybor City residents, including radicals, accommodated southern racial practices in some respects. The founding of the all-black Martí-Maceo Club represented such a compromise, at least in part. To flaunt more vigorously the racial mores of Anglo Tampa was to risk even greater manifestations of vigilantism, an ever-present danger. Radicals preferred to work in ways that promised less overt danger—that is, by accepting dark-skinned people as comrades, by working next to them at cigar factory benches, by building strong labor unions with them, and by living near them in the streets and alleyways of the community.

World War I

At no time were Ybor City's radicals and the Italians among them more on the defensive than during the World War I era. The federal government monitored community activities with scrupulous attention, as it honeycombed Ybor City with agents and informants. The file drawers of the Bureau of Investigation brimmed with alarming reports, including allegations of plots to kill President Woodrow Wilson and President Victoriano Huerta of Mexico (an anarchist from Ybor City earlier had killed the Spanish prime minister) and accounts of the public and personal lives of leftists. Documents reveal an unmistakable pattern of government espionage, establishment violence, and deep paranoia over the "Ybor City problem." "It is a fact of common knowledge," one agent confirmed, "that the entire Ybor City, with all its Spaniards, Cubans, Italians . . . are [not] in harmony with this government. This is evidenced by the large number of this class who attempted and in fact did avoid the draft law. . . ."[43] Another agent insisted, "I can state that the Italian Spanish colonies of West Tampa and Ybor City, Florida are the most advanced towards the 'Social Revolution.' I could say that they have established here a Soviet on a small scale. . . . [I] have the impression of being in Russia."[44] Undercover operative A. V. French added his perspective in November 1919 that there "has always been a certain amount of animosity between the American and the Latin American element in this city, due to the fact that public opinion is aroused against the foreign population here on account of their alleged disregard of the selective service regulations."[45] French had noted a sore point in community relations.

No lockstep march to Americanization characterized Ybor City's immigrants during World War I. The war was not popular there, especially among the radical elements. Editorials critical of the lack of enthusiasm in Ybor City for the war effort dotted the English-language press. The *Morning Tribune*, for example, chided the county registration board for not recording the names and addresses of individuals who denied citizenship to avoid the draft: "These husky young aliens are fattening off the wages or the products of the United States and are walking about in pompous indifference, not to say defiance, of the government's pleas. . . . While the American boy is off to camp of training [sic] or in the trenches facing the enemy. . . . The calls for aid to the Liberty Bond fund, the Red Cross, the Y.M.C.A. War Council, and every other demand for money and loyal self-sacrifice have brought no responsive contribution from thousands of these. . . . They should be interned in prison camps and there sent to work for the common good. . . . Many of these alien exempts have fled from the country until after the war is over."⁴⁶ Particularly galling to many natives was the rising curve of strike activity. In 1918 one city lawyer claimed, "The man who quits his job at the present time without just and proper cause is a traitor." More common were complaints about the *lectores*, who allegedly were "reading books condemned by the government" and encouraging disloyalty. Authorities arrested several readers for persisting in such activities.⁴⁷

Italians represented the only major immigrant group whose homeland fought in the struggle, but this hardly translated into greater enthusiasm for the war. Indeed the Italian government viewed Ybor City as a center of opposition to its participation in the war. Unlike some other enclaves, which greeted Italy's entry into the war on May 23, 1915, with wild celebrations and parades, Ybor City experienced no public manifestation of any kind. Nor did Italians rush homeward to enlist in the Italian military.⁴⁸ Rather, they and their Latin neighbors responded to the war in one of several different ways: studied indifference, open hostility, or temporary migration to Cuba.

The bilingual labor paper *El Internacional*, Ybor City's most popular newssheet, provides an insight into the community reaction to the war. During the period 1914–18 the paper contained only three articles reporting on war events in Europe, and these merely transmitted information on important military developments. Chest-thumping jingoism and 100 percent Americanism were completely absent. The great battles in France and Italy failed to change the paper's editorial policies, which continued to stress reports on labor-related news and discussions of strategies to organize the working class.⁴⁹

Since Ybor City possessed no Italian-language commercial press, the usual source of progovernment, prowar campaigns, there were no public efforts to whip up enthusiasm for the struggle. Italian government officials struck a near solid wall of indifference when they arrived to sell Italian bonds, both during and after the war, finding success only among a handful of prosperous Italians, most notably Val Antuono, a cigar factory owner who had earned a reputation as the most determined open-shop advocate in the city. In 1919 Antuono stumped the community in an effort to sell Italian government bonds, explaining that this was an excellent way to show the community's "patriotism." Ultimately he purchased nearly L500,000 worth of bonds himself, in a bid to receive an appointment as Italian consul in Tampa, but he was only able to sell a small amount to several other businessmen.[50] His close identification with the Italian government, his position as a factory owner, and particularly his reputation as an antilabor force doomed his community campaign from the start.

Fund-raising in Ybor City typically went toward very different ends from those desired by Antuono. The activities of Domenico Lodato, secretary of the Italian Socialist Federation of Tampa, revealed the nature of the community's responses. Acting on a complaint from Carlo Papini, Italian vice-consul of New Orleans, federal agents investigated (and confirmed) reports that Lodato had collected money in Tampa by popular subscription "for the purposes of overthrowing the Italian government." Lodato was "spreading bolshevikism in that community," the vice-consul added, urging that this "dangerous menace" be silenced.[51]

Latin radicals were not content simply to ignore the war, especially those who were of draft age. On May 23, 1917, the *Morning Tribune* reported a "considerable exodus of conscription age men (21 to 30 years old) to Havana," a tangible result of antiwar sentiment, and within a week Governor Sidney Catts felt compelled to order deputies to inspect all boats leaving Tampa for foreign countries.[52] One impassioned letter to the Bureau of Investigation detailed more vigorous responses of the Tampa left. Radicals "discouraged enlistments in our Army and Navy and aided those who wanted to evade the draft by giving them money to leave the country," claimed one irate citizen. "After the Armistice, these men affiliated themselves with anarchists from Spain, Cuba, and New York, also with Bolsheviki of Russia. These men were interested in doing bodily harm to our President. They also tried to bring about a race riot by inciting the negroes against the whites. They are also responsible for various strikes."[53]

Radicals paid a heavy price for their opposition to the war. Not only did the government greatly increase its surveillance and control, but the native community's hostility rose to new heights. The socialist locals in particular, perhaps because of their greater visibility and size, increasingly felt the pressure of public opinion. "We resent any effort of enemies of socialism to identify our cause with Pro-German propaganda," protested one socialist.[54] But to no avail. As patriotism grew more shrill, protest took different forms.

Consumer Cooperatives and the Red Scare

The war years saw a resurgence of consumer cooperative and boycott activity in the Tampa area, often led by radicals who infused these movements with their working-class messages. Latins knew well the costs of the war on the local scene: they saw prices for consumer goods shoot upward as wages lagged behind. "Under the pretext of this accursed war," one socialist raged, "the prices of all commodities are rising." Another continued, "We shall soon be seen on the streets barefooted, dressed in rags, almost starving in the service of our masters." A bread strike in 1915 and a potato, onion, and meat boycott in 1917 brought howls of protest from Tampa merchants and retailers but no raise in cigarworkers' wages. The cost of living went even higher in the postwar period. Robert K. Murray has estimated that by late 1919 the purchasing power of the 1913 dollar had fallen from 100 to 45.[55] One well-supported 1919 boycott of Tampa's business establishments urged workers not to buy new winter clothing until costs came down. "It will become a symbol of loyalty and class solidarity," organizers explained, "to be seen wearing last winter's clothing."[56] Blaming conditions on "capitalist greed," Latins finished the year with a seven-month boycott on rent increases, threatening to "let the tenement sections become a barren wilderness . . . before paying another penny for their damnable shacks."[57]

Radicals also channeled their energies into the creation of consumer cooperatives as weapons against high prices and as broad-based instruments of self-help. By 1919 there were some two dozen of them operating in Ybor City and West Tampa (see Table 7). The cooperative La Nuova Vita, organized by Italian Vincenzo Cusumano and Spaniard José Guastella in West Tampa, was typical. Begun in February 1918 the cooperative included fifty members who paid $1 a week into a common fund from which supplies were purchased. At the end of the year each member received $52 and a share of the profits, depending on individual contributions in labor and service to the cooperative. The profits of members ranged from $109 to $120 and were realized largely through economy of management. The cooperative paid no salaries, made no deliveries, rented the cheapest suitable stores or operated out of homes, and promised individuals "good service, full weights and measures, no adulteration or imposition." Stores typically opened every night at seven o'clock, with three members taking turns conducting business.[58]

Tampa merchants saw dangers in the cooperative and boycott move-

TABLE 7 Principal Food Cooperatives in Tampa, 1915–19

Name	Location	Years in existence as of Dec. 1919	Number of members	Average monthly sales
Companía, El Progresso	Ybor City	4	79	$ 4,500
Ybor City Groc. Co.	Ybor City	4	60	3,150
Social	Ybor City	1	53	2,250
La Comune	Ybor City	2	100	4,950
La Latina	Ybor City	2	93	4,050
Ideale	Ybor City	2	74	3,150
Avanti	Ybor City	1	43	1,870
Igualdad	Ybor City	2	36	1,800
El Recurso	Ybor City	1	45	1,400
Palmetto	Palmetto Beach	1	35	1,300
Proletaria	Ybor City	1	22	1,350
Robert's City Groc. Co.	Ybor City	2	73	3,325
Los Provisores	West Tampa	3	34	6,150
Oriente	West Tampa	1	21	2,925
La Nuova Vita	West Tampa	2	50	2,925
La Niveladora	West Tampa	1	93	4,500
Nueva Era	West Tampa	1	48	1,800
La Unión	West Tampa	1	39	1,800
La Defensa	West Tampa	2	18	1,350
El Seg. Professo	Ybor City	1	58	2,250
El Futuro Obrero	Ybor City	1	38	2,250
La Economia	Ybor City	1	45	3,150
La Llegado	Ybor City	2	74	3,850
Nebraska Groc. Co.	1911 Neb. Ave.	2	67	2,925
TOTAL			1,413	$69,970

SOURCE: Minutes, Tampa Board of Trade, J. T. Watson, "Notes for Remarks," Dec. 18, 1919.

ments that went beyond their cash register receipts, especially when they reached the height of their popularity in 1919. The nativist *Tampa Citizen* pointed out that these actions smacked of "collectivism" and "bolshevism" and should be watched very carefully.[59] Special agent A. V. French worried about the possibilities for widespread violence. Undoubtedly aware of the city's past, he reported that citizens "in general have expressed their willingness to forget law and order and take matters in their own hands." One of Tampa's finest was even more direct. Former mayor M. E. Gillett wrote to special agent Frank Burke, explaining, "a number of years ago we deported a bunch of agitators to an island off the coast of Honduras. Would to God that the rest of them were all in the same place!" More to the point, Gillett indicated that "a committee of prominent businessmen have requested me to write you and if possible get you to send us a man, preferrably a Latin who can get into the good graces of the ring leaders here and get us a correct list of the undesirables. We will do the rest."[60] Tampa's elite had always done so.

Gillett's inquiry pointed to a painful fact of life for government agents and police alike—it was often extremely difficult for them to obtain precise information on the radicals they wished to apprehend. In December 1919 French reported to his superiors the methods radicals used to "keep themselves in the shadows." "If a strike is to be called," he indicated, "they let circulate in every factory a piece of paper inciting the men to go out on strike, disgracing those who do not want to obey such order. If a store is to be boycotted; if a meeting is to be held; if any matter is to be discussed, the same method is used. By doing so the leaders are kept secret. . . . When a subscription is to be made for the political prisoners, and that happens very often, a boy is put in the door of a factory who collects the money and gets the name of the contributors. I have spoken with many Cubans and Italians and they unanimously have stated that if in the other centers they would have the same system, it would be better for the working class."[61] In January 1921, when French attempted to track down Alfonso Coniglio for officials who wanted to serve him with a deportation warrant, he was forced to throw up his hands in defeat, complaining, "This entire section of the city is occupied by Spanish, Cuban, and Italian families, making it extremely difficult to secure the slightest information."[62]

Difficult though it might have been, agents ultimately performed their work well. More than a dozen radicals, most of them Spanish anarchists, came under deportation proceedings and departed Ybor City involuntarily. Many others, such as Alfonso Coniglio and Giovanni Vaccaro, found it necessary to go underground or to leave Florida. Several foreign-language newspapers closed down after agents confiscated their records and bolted their doors. Tampans joined ranks to stamp out the "disloyal" elements. In 1919 the *Morning Tribune* explained the situation to its readers: "We must not allow any sentimental considerations for free speech to blind us to the imminent peril of allowing treason and anarchy to be preached in our streets." In a statement that must have amazed socialists and anarchist in the city, the paper concluded, "We have been far too lenient in the past. We should tighten the reins in the future."[63]

As always Tampa's elites rallied to the cause. Local leaders clamoured to make a test case out of the May Day 1919 rally in Ybor City. Police arrested any individual found putting up notices of the gathering, and on the appointed day city officials called in the Home Guard Militia to break up protest meetings. After dispersing a small gathering the militia drilled for three hours, "with shining guns and bayonets," near several large factories in an effort to intimidate workers. "Gone and forgotten are the beautiful daydreams of how wonderful and beautiful the world would be when the German Kaiser had been put out of business," lamented one radical. "Now a greater struggle and more suffering." And so it was. The deportations, seizures, confiscation of records, closing of meetings halls, and intimidation of leaders and newspapers seriously weakened the Ybor City radical community.[64]

The ten-month-long strike in 1920 dramatically revealed the toll the red scare had taken in the Ybor City labor movement. Radicals had lost their influential roles to the more traditional union leaders who fought (unsuccessfully) for the closed shop. With the principal labor unions ascribing to AFL tactics, the radical labor edge of Ybor City had dulled. Radical labor leaders were not unaware of how events had worked against them. The "war and its waves of hysterical patriotism," raged one such leader, "have been used by manufacturers to prevent collective bargaining." Whatever their motives, owners freely branded every effort for improvement as anarchistic, socialistic, or bolshevistic during the 1920 strike and thereafter. So complete was their victory that they imposed their antiunion "American Plan" virtually without check. The leftist presence, which had once pervaded the worker's movement, was reduced to a fading subculture during the ensuing decade.[65]

Sacco and Vanzetti

Although radical influence diminished in the cigar factories after 1921 and the red-scare repression diluted its impact in the wider community, leftists did not wholly abandon Ybor City. The scattered elements of the left rallied around two causes which gave their presence purpose and commitment. The first of these, the celebrated case of Sacco and Vanzetti, galvanized the Ybor City radical community, and particularly the Italian element within it, with an almost missionary zeal throughout the seven-year life of the affair. From its beginning in 1920 leftists scrutinized with intense interest the events surrounding the arrests, trial, conviction, appeals, and eventual executions in 1927. They collected money for defense funds, held rallies, sent telegrams and petitions, and staged protest strikes in support of the two anarchists in Massachusetts.[66]

As in Italian American communities elsewhere, passions mounted as the date for execution neared. One manifesto of July 1, 1926, explained that the "bourgeoisie is trying to kill two comrades. . . . their only crime was to be opposed to the war." The document summarized the details of the case, claiming, among other things, that the two men had been tortured by the police.[67] CMIU Local 464, the Italian local, now headed by Alfonso Coniglio, coordinated a Pro-Prisoner Committee to raise money for the Sacco and Vanzetti defense fund. More militant radicals scoffed at the CMIU's use of peaceful protests, suggesting that the unionists were in fact on the side of the capitalist oppressors. In their view "only a general strike" could help free the men.[68] Despite differences over tactics, wide community support greeted efforts to raise money and organize protests. On April 27, 1927, cigarworkers overwhelmingly approved a strike resolution and left the workbenches en masse for a one-day walkout. Three months later a joint committee headed by Alfonso Coniglio, Vincente Antinori, José Esposito, and Francisco Alonzo organized another one-day strike involving 12,000 workers. When Massachusetts Governor Alvan T. Fuller announced on August 5 that he would not intervene in the case, cigarworkers again struck, this time sending 15,000 people to the streets.

Characteristically the *Morning Tribune* only saw evidence of radical excesses in these disruptions. One editorial on August 6 explained that Sacco and Vanzetti were "defiant of law, hostile to government, murderers at heart" and concluded, "We know of no convicted, condemned men who have enjoyed such exceptional indulgence at the hands of the law."[69] An August 10 walkout again emptied the cigar factories. More than 5,000 cigarworkers, including several hundred women and children, jammed into the Labor Temple to hear speeches in Italian, English, and Spanish. Time after time frenzied applause swept the audience as speakers extolled the condemned men. Ybor City's main thoroughfare, Seventh Avenue, was virtually deserted as every store fronting the street closed for the day after gracing the windows with crudely painted signs —"Save Sacco and Vanzetti," "Help the Innocents," and so on. The last and largest strike on August 23 ended with a memorial to "bid farewell to.

our noble comrades." On this sad occasion some 5,000 Italians gathered at the Italian Club for speeches and memorializing. All of Ybor City's businesses closed, with *La Traducción* suspending publication.[70]

Antifascism

The other great cause that sustained Ybor City's radicals during the 1920s was antifascism. Italian leftists in Tampa viewed Benito Mussolini's turn to fascism as a profound tragedy for Italy. During his early career Mussolini had been an ardent socialist and, in the words of John Diggins, "a thunderous voice in the Italian-American Left." His writings were well known in Ybor City before the war. Factory readers had intoned his socialist teachings from the pages of *Il Proletario* and *Lotta di Classe*, and copies of Mussolini's *L'Avanti* had circulated on the streets and in the clubs of Ybor City. Il Duce's repressive regime therefore evoked a special sense of betrayal and anger in Ybor City—a community-wide depth of feeling that eluded other, less leftist-oriented "Little Italies" elsewhere in the United States. Mussolini's vigorous suppression of the left in Italy, dramatically highlighted by the murder of Socialist deputy Giacomo Matteotti, only added to the hostility existing in the Cigar City.[71] Because of the intense interaction among Latin radicals, opposition quickly spread to the other major immigrant groups. Italian officials charged with spreading the fascist message to Italy's overseas "colonies" quickly learned the results of these attitudes.

As early as April 1923 Giovanni Vaccaro wrote from Brooklyn of the establishment of the Anti-Fascist Alliance of North America. A cluster of labor organizations in the New York area had created the Alliance, which they hoped would become the focus of opposition to Mussolini's government. Vaccaro, serving as chairman of the press committee, urged that Ybor City support the work of the Alliance and begin to organize its own antifascist efforts. During the ensuing years he directed a steady stream of publicity and organizational advice to his comrades in Ybor City, after 1925 as secretary of the Anti-Fascist Federation for the Freedom of Italy, a socialist-led splinter group that had seceded from the Alliance.[72]

Editorials critical of Italian fascism began appearing with regularity in the local press, exhorting workers to participate in protests and to donate funds to support antifascist work. Il Gruppo Antifascista di Tampa soon came to number in the hundreds. Organized by an architect named Ivo de Mincies, the group received backing from CMIU Local 464 and for a time published an antifascist newspaper, *La Riscossa* (The Insurrection).[73] Just as radical notables had earlier circulated through Ybor City as a part of the *giro di propaganda,* now the Cigar City became a regular stopover for a litany of antifascist luminaries. Socialist Arturo Massolo arrived on January 26, 1926, to give lectures and take subscriptions to *Il Nuovo Mondo* (The New World), a fiercely antifascist newspaper.[74] A week-long series of debates and lectures attended the visit of émigré anarchist Armando Borghi in August 1928. Held at L'Unione Italiana, Borghi's lectures drew packed houses, often forcing latecomers to stand in the streets and listen through open windows. The local press faithfully reported the activities of antifascists in the city and elsewhere and reprinted the speeches of many of these individuals. Favorites included the exiled history professor Gaetano Salvemini and former Italian Parliament member Vincenzo Vacirca.[75]

"There were a few Italian fascists in our city," noted the banker Angelo Massari, "but they could not cope with the anti-fascists, who were overpowering." He once related an incident that occurred during a rare visit of the Italian consul general of New Orleans, who upbraided a small group of Italian American businessmen for not doing more against the antifascists in the city, calling them "cowards." Massari responded angrily, pointing out that "the Italian community in Tampa is mostly radical in its political views" and that "it has been nurtured on Mussolini's revolutionary and socialistic tenets. It is not their fault if the Master who taught them how to be subversive has changed his point of view and turned his coat." He challenged the consul general to explain what Italy had done for the poor emigrants who left their homeland and then answered his own question, stating that they had largely been forgotten. "Oh, yes," he added, "we have been remembered when our help was needed to raise funds for the Messina earthquake, for other disasters, for our intervention in Fiume, or to buy Italian bonds." At the end of the heated exchange Massari admitted to a friend that the consul was lucky "he did not meet with the militant antifascists, for they would have made short work of him and his dignity."[76]

The Italian government rightly regarded Ybor City as a settlement of overwhelmingly antifascist tendencies. No internal community struggles between fascists and their opponents took place in the streets and columns of the local press, as so often happened elsewhere in the United States. Mussolini possessed too few supporters to mount even a weak challenge to the antifascist tide. Realizing this fact, the Italian government directed little propagandizing toward this community, preferring to work in areas of the country that held greater promise. The attention Tampa did receive came in the form of careful monitoring of antifascist activities by consular officials. The New Orleans consulate submitted sheaves of reports on individuals and groups in the city, including most notably the anarchist Alfonso Coniglio and an antifascist publication, *Numero Unico*, sponsored by him and a few supporters.[77]

Only a small handful of Italians in Ybor City were bothered by the fact that the Italian government did not have a more favorable view of the community. Among them was factory owner Val Antuono, who proudly supported the fascist government and published several long, praiseworthy articles following trips to Italy. But his word carried little weight in the wider immigrant community.[78] Generally Ybor City residents spoke of Mussolini with open contempt and hostility. When Il Duce appeared in the newsreels playing in Ybor City's movie houses, crowds loudly booed and stamped their feet.[79] The policies of the Italian Club—the very heart of this settlement—perhaps best illustrated the community's attitude toward the Italian regime. As club president Ernesto Palermo explained in 1944, "The Italian Club of Tampa has for the past twenty-two years fought consistently against fascism and its agents who have tried time and again to infiltrate the Mussolini philosophy among the democracy loving Americans of our colony. To date, and since the advent of fascism in Italy, no official representative of the Italian government has been allowed to put foot in our club building."[80]

The twin causes of Sacco and Vanzetti and antifascism, while providing continuing contact points for radicals with the wider community in Ybor City, were not effective substitutes for the much more integral role they had played earlier in the labor movement. A distance remained that was never closed, although the community's center of gravity was still decidedly to the left. As might be expected, the same patterns of development affected the radical society's most public institution, the press.

The Press

As was true of other aspects of Ybor City life, Cubans and Spaniards preceded Italians in publishing newspapers. Cubans in particular had produced a truly large number in the pre–Spanish-American War period, most of which, although representative of a broad variety of ideologies and interests, generally focused on the struggle for independence.[81]

Yet the Cubans did establish a mentality and a market for local newspapers that would later be exploited by different types of publications. They also cemented firmly the use of local papers in the *lector* system.

The practice of reading in the factories played a dual role with reference to the early press in Ybor City. On the one hand it tended to obviate the need for papers, as readers transmitted much information orally in the factories and from there into the wider community. For some papers, however, new markets opened as *lectores* searched for convenient news sources. Such was the beginning, for example, of *La Traducción*, a paper that specialized in clipping items from external newspapers and translating them into Spanish for use in the factories.[82]

Sicilians coming from the Magazzolo valley possessed no formal experience with publishing or editing local newspapers prior to arriving in Ybor City. Until well into the twentieth century, in fact, many could not even read formal Italian. What printed news filtered into Santo Stefano and its neighboring villages came from out-of-town papers and journals, usually emanating from Palermo. Hence among immigrants there existed no reservoir of editorial talent originating in the Old World.

The first Italian-language newspaper to appear in Ybor City, *La Voce dello Schiavo* (The Voice of the Slave), exemplified how these newssheets sprang from new-world soil. Begun by Pietro Calcagno, a self-described anarchist, exiled from Sicily, who had fled the suppression of the *fasci*, the paper was stridently anarchist.[83] Calcagno, apparently a self-educated mason in Sicily, was pressed into service by his comrades in America to take up publishing. *La Voce dello Schiavo* started in 1900 by the same process that underwrote numerous other leftist papers. The gifted anarchist publisher Aldino Felicani succinctly described the process as it worked in New York City: "We just announced that our paper would come out on such and such a date and that we needed money to publish it. That was sufficient to bring us enough money to publish the paper."[84] Although quick to begin, *La Voce dello Schiavo* ceased publication after a few issues.[85]

Similarly short-lived was *L'Alba Sociale* (The Social Dawn), another anarchist paper which appeared in June 1901 and apparently lasted only until August of that same year. Unlike its predecessor, which supporters distributed free of charge, *L'Alba Sociale* carried a subscription fee of one dollar a year. It too utilized a standard four-page, three-column tabloid format and appeared on a biweekly basis.[86]

Italian socialists took more measured steps before entering the publishing field. *La Voce della Colonia* (The Voice of the Colony) appeared in June 1911, under the guiding hand of Arturo D. Massolo. The young Massolo, who migrated in 1906 from the Stefanesi colony in New York, was an ardent socialist. By trade he was a *ragioniere* (certified public accountant), but his immersion in the radical world of Ybor City propelled him into many other activities. He labored tirelessly for the workers' cause, assisting in their unionization and education. During the 1910 strike he participated actively on the picket lines, exhorting workers to remain loyal to the union struggle. "He was one of the leaders," commented his friend Angelo Massari, "and the local authorities went after him. He had to leave Tampa and went north."[87] After his return to Tampa, Massolo's strategies had modified. His newspaper attempted to straddle the militant class-based messages that characterized earlier anarchist papers.

La Voce della Colonia proclaimed that it was not "a business agency, but . . . a vigorous defender and an impartial friend of the best interests of our colony. . . ."[88] As such its focus was on the local Tampa scene, and for the most part its editorial policies manifested a hardheaded realization of what was necessary to adapt to this new land. Intermixed with appeals to class unity and support of socialist causes were much more mundane considerations relating to the practical day-to-day world of Ybor City. One column, for example, criticized a local newspaper for racial inaccuracies in a report of a "fight between Italians and white Americans."[89]

While *La Voce della Colonia* remained concerned about public image, its major appeal centered on the necessity of organization and unity within the community. Witnessing firsthand the effects of cooperation among factory owners and municipal authorities, and realizing that the Italian community was now a permanent entity, Massolo urged the diverse ethnic elements of Ybor City to come together for the common good: "We have therefore need of a strong representative organization that may be the esponent [sic] of all, which if necessary can protect our rights and that can defend us against possible annoyances."[90] In such statements the paper revealed a basic acceptance of society as it existed and a willingness to devise effective strategies within it.

More determined to change the political balance was *L'Aurora* (The Dawn), Tampa's Italian-language organ of the Socialist party. First appearing in May 1912, *L'Aurora* received support from the Socialist Study Circle of Ybor City and the Italian Socialist department of the Socialist party. The paper vigorously entered political frays in the city and county, promoting various Socialist party tickets, and it was particularly supportive of Angelo Leto, a socialist candidate for the city council in several unsuccessful elections.[91] In these respects it stood fully in the New World, recognizing the nature of the political process and the need for representation. Printed by Pedro Esteve's La Poliglota Press, *L'Aurora* served the needs of a community that was bridging two worlds and two generations.[92]

No existing newspaper directory provides accurate data on the circulation or duration of these anarchist and socialist papers, so we can only guess at the size and nature of the audience they reached.[93] What is clear, however, is that they represented the efforts of certain segments of the Ybor City population to articulate their philosophies in printed form and in the native language. Although these newssheets addressed local events, often with substantial intensity, they also spoke to a wider circle of concerns and issues that spiraled outward beyond the immediate community and its environs. They attempted to tie Tampa's Italians into a much wider network of ideas and personalities. Hence they reported on happenings in Italy and Sicily, as well as providing news of workers' struggles and ideological debates from the far-flung corners of the world.[94] In doing so they charted the mental and physical horizons of their readers, who happened to reside in Ybor City, Florida, but whose mind-set propelled them toward a larger world of comradeship, comment, and concern.[95]

No church-based Italian-language publication—a fixture in many "Little Italies" throughout North America—appeared in Ybor City, and a purely commercial newspaper came very late to the Italian community. The first commercial enterprise, *La Voce della Colonia* (not to be confused with the earlier socialist paper of the same name), arrived on the scene in August 1929. This paper, which was edited by Domenico Tagliarini, aimed at the wider audience of Italians in Florida, attempting to capture the loyalties of a growing population in the southern portion of the state. In doing so, however, it failed to obtain a sufficiently broad base in Tampa and lasted only a short while.[96]

The immigrant press in Ybor City reflected the dominant cultural patterns at work within the community. Newspapers shaped their policies according to the city's deserved reputation as a militant union town, which helped to account for the predominance of radical and labor publications in the years before 1920. Because of their ideological bent, the papers often acted as integrative forces among the diverse immigrant groups residing in the community. Many, for example, printed columns in both Spanish and Italian. Virtually all of the Spanish and Italian papers supported efforts to promote cohesion between the various immigrant segments of Ybor City. As one editorial concluded, "Capital is our common enemy. If we were born in different lands, it is not our fault. We must blot out all differences."[97] More specifically, most papers tried to unite immigrant workers and incorporate them into an effective labor movement. Although they might have disagreed over exactly which labor movement served workers best, they were uniform in their calls for organization.

Summary

Overall, the size of the radical element in Ybor City was disproportionate to its influence. Clearly, radicals never comprised more than a minority of residents, but they served important functions as intellectual critics and as leaders of working-class organizations. On the union front they supplied a class ideology that helped to create a labor consciousness of such a broad and flexible nature that members of disparate immigrant groups were able to find common ground. That immigrant workers could strike for protracted periods of time and still maintain their solidarity despite determined manufacturer opposition, vigilantism, and economic deprivation attests in part to the effectiveness of this message. Radicals gave voice to the "class obligations" existing among workers; the dynamics of unionism in Tampa cannot be understood without reference to their presence.

Through their clubs, newspapers, educational work, cooperatives, and debating forums, radicals articulated a leftist orientation to the social problems of the day. They dramatized issues of work and life and often instilled a spirit of pride and class consciousness in their fellow residents. Through these actions they reached not only the immigrant generation but the children of immigrants as well. José Yglesias was only one of many second-generation Latins profoundly affected by the radical climate existing during his youth. In this sense the radical influence extended beyond the years of community building and migration.

Unlike the Labor Temple, which still stands proudly in the heart of Ybor City, little remains today of the radical presence, in part because the causes championed by radicals so often failed to meet with success and because the legacy of repression directed against them still leaves a bitter taste in the mouths of many. Although absent from Tampa now, radicals nonetheless did force the host society to cope with their presence earlier. Tampa's political values, nativist sentiments, propensities toward vigilantism, and antiunion consensus all owe a heavy debt to the reactions radicals generated. To look only at the contemporary terrain, without reference to this earlier experience, is to miss an important formative aspect of Tampa's past.

The fires of labor conflict tempered working-class activism into simple reductions: "Bread and Work" and "Class War." The heady solidarity generated by militant trade unionism and leftist ideology accelerated ethnic cooperation and economic interdependence. But cigarmakers lost nearly every labor battle and radical groups declined. It remained to be seen whether Cubans, Spaniards, and Italians could organize themselves in other ways.

NOTES

1. "He Misses Tampa as It Used to Be," *Tampa Magazine* (October 1981), 74–75.
2. Massari, *Wonderful Life*, 56.
3. Department of Justice, ICF #362112, "Report of A. V. French," September 24, 1919; ibid., "Report of Byrd Douglas," July 14, 1919; Massari, *Wonderful Life*, 91.
4. Pozzetta, "Immigrant Library," 10–12. Alfonso Coniglio came to possess one of the largest collections of Italian anarchist literature in the world. When he died, family members distributed the materials to several locations in Latin America and Europe.
5. For ads see *El Internacional*, October 4, 1906, June 19, 1908, September 23, 1910; *L'Alba Sociale*, August 1, 1901. An example of a locally produced volume is Esteve's *La Legge*, a xeroxed copy of which is in IHRC.
6. *El Internacional*, February 19, 1915, March 10, April 14, 16, 1916; manifesto, "To the Workers of Tampa," April 5, 1913, PKY, advertising a series of lectures on hygiene sponsored by Gruppo Risveglio.
7. Interview with Sirio Bruno Coniglio, May 2, 1976. Giovanni Vaccaro also gave evening instruction in his home to workers.
8. Copies of these newspapers are available on microfilm in PKY. See *La Cronaca Sovversiva*, March 25, 1916, June 3, 9, 1917, for notices of Gruppo Volontà, the only surviving evidence of this particular club.
9. *El Internacional*, April 14, 21, December 8, 1911, February 5, March 9, August 27, 1915; *Il Proletario*, September 15, 1911; *La Voce della Colonia*, June 10, 1911.
10. *El Internacional*, September 23, December 30, 1910, March 31, April 21, 1911; *Tampa Morning Tribune*, August 18, 1910. J. L. Fitts, organizer for the Socialist Party of America, visited Tampa for recruiting work in 1908. Ibid., November 25, 1908.
11. Green, *Grass-Roots Socialism*.
12. Weinstein, *Decline of Socialism*, 5–8.
13. *El Internacional*, March 31, April 21, 1911; *La Voce Della Colonia*, July 15, 1911; *La Parola dei Socialisti*, December 30, 1911. In 1917 Kate Richards O'Hare

chaired the Socialist party's committee on war and militarism, which wrote the strongly antiwar St. Louis Proclamation. See Cantor, *Divided Left*, 58–59.

14. *El Internacional*, January 20, 1911. Also see ibid., October 7, November 4, 1910.

15. Ibid., February 24, 1911.

16. *Tampa Morning Tribune*, January 4, 5, May 18, June 8, July 1, 6, October 5, 1904. One report of a 1910 meeting of local socialist groups added, "the Italian locals were especially well represented." Ibid., August 18, 1910.

17. Petitions to the Tampa City Council, Book 1, #2359, May 17, 1910; *Tampa Morning Tribune*, June 7, 1911. As late as 1916 the practice still occurred. See ibid., November 11, 1916.

18. Petitions to the Tampa City Council, Book 1, #3243, May 21, 1912; *Tampa Morning Tribune*, May 15, 23, 24, 1910, June 4, 5, 1912.

19. *Tampa Morning Tribune*, November 6, 1912. In the presidential election years 1904, 1908, and 1912, Florida had the highest percentage of left-wing votes of any southern state. In 1912 only nine states had a higher percentage of socialist votes among the total votes cast than Florida. For a discussion of these returns see Robbins, "Socialist Party in Florida"; Green, "Florida Politics and Socialism"; Weinstein, *Decline of Socialism*, 24.

20. *L'Aurora*, May 31, 1912; *Tampa Morning Tribune*, January 25, June 5, August 31, 1910, November 7, 8, 1912.

21. Department of Justice, ICF #194147, "Untitled Report," May 17, 1918; Yglesias, *Truth about Them*, 209. Radical newspapers often carried a column entitled *"Piccola Posta"* (Little Post Office) which reported on events occurring in other radical centers. Tampa soon began to appear with frequency in these listings. A good introduction to anarchist papers is contained in Cerrito, "Emigrazione Anarchica Italiana," 269–76.

22. *La Voce dello Schiavo*, August 15, 1901; *Il Proletario*, September 1, 1911; *Il Martello*, February 12, 1921; *La Parola dei Socialisti*, December 31, 1910. Department of Justice, ICF #362112, "Report of A. V. French," December 13, 1919, contains a list of fifteen communist publications identified as being sent to Ybor City radicals.

23. Massari, *Wonderful Life*, 106.

24. *La Federación*, February 16, March 2, 9, 1900; Massari, *Wonderful Life*, 68.

25. Interview with José Vega Díaz, May 3, 1980. Because of its connections with the Caribbean, Ybor City harbored many radicals from Latin America. See *La Parola dei Socialisti*, February 25, 1911, for a report of the visit of "Comrade De Lara" from Mexico.

26. *La Parola dei Socialisti*, May 14, 21, July 2, 1910 (Bertelli), July 2, 1910 (Galleani); *El Internacional*, November 10, 17, 1905 (Caroti), May 14 and October 17, 1915 (Vacirca).

27. *La Parola dei Socialisti*, May 21, 1910.

28. *El Internacional*, November 16, 1916, January 5, 12, February 9, April 6, 1917, March 14, October 24, 1919, October 20, 1922; all give a flavor of these disputes. See Vecoli, "Italian Immigrants," 273–75, for a discussion of the wider pattern of dissension.

29. See *El Internacional*, August 27, 1915, for reports concerning a joint collection involving socialist groups in Ybor City. Membership lists indicate considerable mixing. See also ibid., April 21, 1911, for an announcement of the formation of a socialist cooperative, *La Cosmopolita*, which included four Italians, three Cubans, and two Spaniards on the governing council.

The Radical Culture 171

30. Santillán, *Historia del Movimiento Obrero Español*, 188, 283, 292-93, 392-93; Junco, *Ideología Política*, 632, claims that *El Productor* ceased publication in 1893.

31. Massari, *Wonderful Life*, 107; Carey, "Anarchists in Paterson," 51-56. Emma Goldman also had met Esteve; see Goldman, *Living My Life*, I, 150.

32. Massari, *Wonderful Life*, 107; *El Internacional*, March 1, 1918; manifesto, "Antorcha-Círculo de Instrucción y Recreo," August 26, 1908, PKY. This latter indicated that Antorcha also offered classes in the Esperanto language.

33. *La Parola dei Socialisti*, June 18, 1910; Department of Justice, ICF #374384, "Report of Agent BB," November 22, 1919; *La Fiaccola*, October 7, 1911. Housed at Eighth Avenue and Seventeenth Street, the school published its own bulletin for a number of years. See *F. Ferrer Boletín*, March 26, 1910, September 9, 1911, PKY. More information on Ferrer schools is contained in Avrich, *Modern School Movement*.

34. Avrich, *Russian Anarchists*, 239. Ironically, radical newspapers were almost obsessive in publishing the names of subscribers and supporters; for example, they often carried long lists of individuals who donated funds for various radical causes. Police and government agencies used these lists, often meticulously cross-indexed, in their investigations. See *Il Martello*, March 15, 1920, and *La Cronaca Sovversiva*, October 17, 1903, for two lengthy lists of Ybor City radicals.

35. *La Voce dello Schiavo*, June 17, 1901; *L'Alba Sociale*, August 15, 1901; *La Voce della Colonia*, July 1, 1911.

36. *La Parola dei Socialisti*, January 7, 1911.

37. Manifesto, January 30, 1913, PKY; *El Internacional*, April 14, 28, 1911 (calling for a general strike to support the Mexican Revolution); *La Voce della Colonia*, June 17, 1911 (collection for Panepinto family); *La Parola dei Socialisti*, July 17, 1909 (collections for a defense league for political refugees); *Tampa Morning Tribune*, January 20, 1906 (Russian Revolution), September 27, 1918 (Tom Mooney defense fund), September 28, 1912 (Ettor and Giovannitti defense fund). Department of Justice records relating to Alfredo Rubio Rodríguez (alias Jack Rubio), a Spanish anarchist, give evidence of the immigrant group mixing in radical Ybor City. Rubio's career intersected with Cubans and Italians on many different levels. See especially ICF #374384, "Jack Rubio File," November 6, 14, 1919.

38. *El Internacional*, April 14, 1911, September 28, 1917, February 23, November 2, 1923. Fenton, *Immigrants and Unions*, 157-95, offers an extensive discussion of the issues dividing the radicals.

39. *El Internacional*, March 24, 1911, October 13, 1916; *Tampa Citizen*, July 18, 1919; *Tampa Morning Tribune*, October 4, 15, 1910. As one labor editorial explained, "All is wonderful in Tampa until the cigarmaker stops working. Then everyone rallies around the owner. The cigarmakers must be suppressed because they have been influenced by some *ANARCHIST* who have given them books to read, and read seditious literature to them."

40. Miller, *Radical Immigrant*, 166; Cantor, *Divided Left*, 13-15, 30.

41. *Tampa Morning Tribune*, September 4, 1900; Shofner, "Custom, Law, and History," 288-91.

42. Interview with Philip Spoto, June 30, 1979; *El Internacional*, October 13, 1916, March 5, 1920.

43. Department of Justice, ICF #342696, "Investigation of Spanish Press in Tampa," February 6, 1919.

44. Ibid., reports, January 7, 1920, March 25, 1919.

45. Ibid., ICF #382470, "Report of A. V. French," November 18, 1919.

46. *Tampa Morning Tribune*, November 15, 1917.
47. Ibid., August 12, 1918.
48. Ibid., May 23–30, 1915; interview with John Massaro, August 1, 1983.
49. This assessment is based upon a close reading of the labor newspaper *El Internacional* for the war years.
50. Massari, *Wonderful Life*, 196. When the bonds failed to mature, Antuono lost heavily. No greater success attended efforts to sell American war bonds among Latins. See *Tampa Morning Tribune*, November 15, 1917.
51. Department of Justice, ICF #366198, "Report on D. Lodato," May 29, 1919. Fainsod, *International Socialism*, claims that Italian socialists were instrumental in keeping Italy out of the war in 1914.
52. *Tampa Morning Tribune*, May 23, 31, 1917; Department of Justice, ICF #362112, "Report of Byrd Douglas," July 14, 1919, includes a letter from Mayor D. B. McKay complaining of the number of men leaving for Cuba and Spain to evade the draft.
53. Department of Justice, ICF #362112, "Letter from 'A Citizen,'" October 15, 1919; *Tampa Morning Tribune*, April 24, 1919.
54. Murray, *Red Scare*, 21, details the costs socialists paid for their antiwar stance. Also see *Tampa Morning Tribune*, May 25, 1917.
55. Murray, *Red Scare*, 7; manifesto, "To Workers and Families," January 19, 1915, PKY; *Tampa Morning Tribune*, May 13, 1915; *El Internacional*, August 18, November 24, 1916, March 23, August 10, 1917. Chandler, *Inflation*, 1, indicates that wholesale prices during and shortly after World War I increased about 170 percent above prewar figures. Cigarworkers refused to accept the war as a cause of higher prices and lagging salaries, blaming them instead on greed and "unscrupulous competition" among factory owners which forced them to deny wage increases.
56. *El Internacional*, October 31, November 7, 14, 1919.
57. Ibid., August 29, September 5, 12, 1919. See ibid., December 10, 22, 1916, for discussion of a butter and egg boycott.
58. Ibid., March 16, 1917, February 1, May 3, 1918, January 24, 1919. Italians, Cubans, and Spaniards mixed together freely in forming cooperatives, a practice that was already old by World War I. See *Tampa Morning Tribune*, July 1, 1900 (bakers' cooperative), January 16, 1908 (Italian and Spanish grocers' association), August 8, 1908 (cigarmakers' grocery cooperative).
59. *Tampa Citizen*, June 27, 1919. Also see, Department of Justice, ICF #362112, "Report on John J. Earle," November 18, 1919; minutes, Tampa Board of Trade, March 10, 1919.
60. Department of Justice, ICF #382470, "Report of A. V. French," November 18, 1919; ibid., ICF #362112, "Letter of M. E. Gillett," November 15, 1919. Ultimately the Tampa Wholesale Grocers' Association refused to sell goods to the cooperatives and drove them out of business.
61. Ibid., ICF #362112, "Report of A. V. French," December 2, 1919. Agents had particular problems in finding Spanish-speaking operatives to infiltrate the presses, which were convenient and favorite targets.
62. Ibid., ICF #202-600-697, "Report of A. V. French," January 1, 1921; ibid., ICF #194147, "Report of Agent Douglas," May 17, 1918.
63. Ibid., ICF #374384, "Report of George Lamb," February 26, 1920; ibid., ICF #20713 "List of Aliens," January 10, 1921; *Tampa Morning Tribune*, April 21, 27, 1919. *El Internacional*, May 30, 1919, condemns two editorials in the English-language press that advocated "stamping out Bolshevism with force."
64. *El Internacional*, May 9, 23, 1919, January 9, 1920. Police arrested socialist

Frank Lehti, a shoemaker, on disloyalty charges when he posted signs for the May Day rally. *Tampa Morning Tribune,* April 26, 1919.

65. *El Internacional,* April 11, 1919, March 12, 1920. The goal of the so-called American Plan was an open-shop policy in industry.

66. Ibid., June 10, August 12, 1921, April 18, 21, 27, 1927; manifesto, "To the Workers of Tampa, Pro-Prisoner Committee," n.d., PKY.

67. Manifesto, "Pro-Sacco and Vanzetti Protest Organizing Committee," July 1, 1926, PKY.

68. Manifesto, "Torcedor Bulletin," August 6, 1927, PKY.

69. *Tampa Morning Tribune,* August 6, 1927. The Central Trades and Labor Assembly of Tampa had voted against the protest strike, but cigarworkers acted independently.

70. Ibid., July 7, 8, August 5, 10, 11, 23, 1927.

71. Diggins, *Mussolini and Fascism,* 112; Department of Justice, ICF #342696, "Investigation of Spanish Press in Tampa," February 4, 1919; ibid., ICF #362112, "Report of Byrd Douglas," August 5, 9, 1919. Diggins has pointed out that Mussolini wrote for the IWW's *Il Proletario* before the war and regularly criticized the American middle class in his paper *Lotta di Classe.*

72. Manifestos, "Anti-Fascist Alliance," April 27, 1923, "The Anti-Fascist Movement in America," May 23, 1923, PKY. For more on these groups see Diggins, *Mussolini and Fascism,* 114, and Philip Canistraro's introduction to Salvemini, *Italian Fascist Activities,* xxxvi.

73. Interview with Carmelo Rocca, July 30, 1983; manifesto, "To the Italians of Union 464," August 12, 1926, PKY; *El Internacional,* January 19, September 14, 1923; *La Riscossa,* October 12, November 16, 1940, Special Collections, USF. The group included Spanish and Cuban members as well as Italian.

74. *Il Nuovo Mondo* began publication in 1925 under the direction of Frank Bellanca. Diggins, *Mussolini and Fascism,* 113.

75. *El Internacional,* July 1, 1927; series of handbills advertising the lectures of Borghi, microfilm, PKY. For more on the career of Borghi see Diggins, *Mussolini and Fascism,* 119, 120, 139; Woodcock, *Anarchism,* 354.

76. Massari, *Wonderful Life,* 230–33. For the activities of Italian officials in the United States in general, see Cassels, "Fascism for Export," 707–12.

77. "Casellaro Politico Centrale," file on Alfonso Coniglio, contains a number of reports on antifascist activities in Tampa, including lists of known antifascists. Interestingly, of the individuals mentioned only two were not born in either Alessandria della Rocca or Santo Stefano. The majority were cigarmakers by trade.

78. *Tampa Morning Tribune,* September 13, 1928. See Diggins, *Mussolini and Fascism,* 126–34, for struggles between fascists and antifascists in other communities.

79. FWP, "Interview with Pedro and Estrella"; Kennedy, *Palmetto Country,* 321–22. Diggins, *Mussolini and Fascism,* 116, estimates that antifascists among Italian Americans probably numbered less than 10 percent of the whole. While this represents a valid approximation for the nation, it does not accurately describe leftist centers such as Tampa. One can surmise that locations such as Barre, Vt., and Paterson, N.J., would similarly have had much higher percentages of antifascists.

80. *L'Unione Italiana,* Fiftieth Anniversary Special Commemorative Issue (1944).

81. The numerous papers included: *El Mosquito, El Independiente, El Yara, Libertad,* and *Cuba.*

82. Begun by *lector* Ramón Valdespino, *La Traducción* was a perfect example of immigrant enterprise, as it worked to fill the needs of the hard-pressed *lector* for timely news to disseminate from the factory platform. See Muñiz, *Cubanos,* 37.

83. *La Voce dello Schiavo*, February 4, 1901, microfilm, IHRC. The earliest surviving issue is dated September 29, 1900, listed as year 1, no. 4; the last known issue is March 21, 1901, listed as year 2, no. 12. For a time, a Spanish-language edition, *La Voz del Esclavo*, appeared as well. In 1914 a Milanese socialist, Guido Ciarrocca, began publishing *La Sicilia Rossa* in Santo Stefano. The weekly journal received funding from Gruppo Panepinto in Ybor City.

84. Interview with Aldino Felicani, Columbia University Oral History Project, 26. Felicani published a number of radical newspapers in the Northeast and Midwest.

85. *La Voce dello Schiavo*, February 14, 1901. Calcagno's departure for Sicily may have led to the paper's demise.

86. *L'Alba Sociale*, June 30-August 15, 1901, microfilm, IHRC. This newspaper carried the subtitle *Periodico Socialista-Anarchico*. Woodcock, *Anarchism*, 346, claims that in the United States, Italian anarchists published more expatriate journals than all other groups combined.

87. Massari, *Wonderful Life*, 115.

88. *La Voce della Colonia*, June 10, 1911, microfilm, PKY. Massolo shared editorial duties with Vincente Antinori, another well-known socialist in Ybor City. In 1912 Massolo retired from the paper to move to New York City. Antinori continued publication until 1914, at which time he became secretary of L'Unione Italiana and ceased his newspaper work.

89. Ibid., June 10, July 1, 1911.

90. Ibid., June 10, 1911.

91. *La Parola dei Socialisti*, June 26, 1909, announced the beginning of *L'Aurora* in Ybor City, but no issues of this early attempt have survived. This account attributed the publication to Angelo Leto and recommended it to "our comrades in the South."

92. Issues of *L'Aurora*, May 17, 1912-May 16, 1913, have survived. The first issue is listed as year 1, no. 5. James Weinstein, in his careful study, failed to include Tampa's socialist newspapers in a lengthy list of socialist publications. See Weinstein, *Decline of Socialism*, 94–102.

93. Bryan, "Latin Press in Ybor City," 25, estimates an average circulation of 1,200 for *La Voce della Colonia* but supplies no supporting documentation. The same source also lists another anarchist paper, *Il Risveglio* (The Awakening), published by John DiMaio, beginning in November 1920, but no issues have survived.

94. *La Voce della Colonia*, July 1, 1911, for example, contains several items of correspondence from Santo Stefano. Of interest also is the column *"Piccola Posta"* from *L'Alba Sociale*, August 1, 15, 1901, which contains news items from, among other places, Spring Valley, Ill.; Paterson, N.J.; Hites, Pa.; Victor, Colo.; Groton, Conn.; Saginaw, Mich.; Numa, Iowa; Douglas, Alaska; Dillonville, Ohio; and Cecil, Pa.

95. See Harney, "Ethnic Press in Ontario," 3–14, for a discussion of these patterns.

96. *La Voce della Colonia*, August 3, 1929, microfilm, PKY.

97. *El Internacional*, September 15, 1916.

6 The Cradle of Mutual Aid
Italians and Their Latin Neighbors

Chi rispetta rispettato sarà.
(He who respects will be respected.)

Sicilian proverb

If the cigar factories functioned as the economic heart of Ybor City, mutual aid societies served as its soul. The emergence of these voluntary associations reflected an organizing impulse that left its legacy in wooden dance floors, marble edifices, and modern hospitals. These institutions defined the new world of the Latin immigrants and in the process provided new affirmations of group identity and a buffer to the urban-industrial environment.

Cuban, Spanish, and Italian immigrants brought with them traditions of voluntary associations and mutual aid. In the first half of the nineteenth century thousands of these organizations sprang up throughout Europe,[1] and many of them survived the passage to the Americas. In 1887 a group of Asturians organized an *asociación de beneficiencia* in Havana, known as La Covadonga, after the site of an important battle of the reconquest. Spaniards from Asturias organized similar societies in other Cuban towns throughout the 1880s. On May 2, 1886, members from several of these groups organized El Centro Asturiano in Havana, an institution that came to occupy a position of immense social and economic importance. Cubans drew upon the same patterns of self-help. In

1871 Cuban émigrés in Key West founded the San Carlos Club, a mutual aid society based upon similar organizations existing in the homeland.[2] It was no accident, therefore, that the early immigrants in Ybor City looked to the Old World for solutions to the problems pressing upon them. The clubs that resulted represented a collective means of reconciling individual/family concerns with those of the ethnic group and confronting the stark realities of urban life.

The Birth of Mutual Aid in Ybor City

To comprehend fully the extraordinary associations that evolved in Ybor City, one must understand the milieu from which they emerged. Grafted onto a town which before 1880 boasted scant numbers, Ybor City residents could expect little assistance from Anglo Tampa. A vacuum similarly existed in terms of previous immigrant groups. Whereas in northern urban areas Italians frequently occupied neighborhoods recently vacated by Germans, Irish, or Jews, Ybor City's Latins encountered a very different situation. Expansion often had to await sufficient housing; and, more important, there were no institutions, such as churches or charitable agencies, left behind to minister to newly arrived immigrants.

Local ecological factors contributed in many ways to the character of mutual aid societies. In late 1885 nature grudgingly yielded to workers clearing the palmettos and draining the swamps that would become Ybor City. For decades Ybor City's beleaguered inhabitants battled semitropical mosquitoes, belligerent alligators, and unsanitary conditions. "The mortality of all areas at Ybor during the past year [1889]," reported the *Tampa Journal*, "has been far in excess of that in Tampa proper."[3] In 1893 a *Daily Times* reporter, after visiting Ybor City's Italian quarter, "expressed wonder that some malignant disease had not broken out."[4] Immigrants interviewed during the 1930s Federal Writers' Project offered a litany of health-related problems stemming from the settlement's primitive conditions.[5]

Water problems plagued the lives of early inhabitants. Crudely dug wells and cisterns yielded a substance old-timers jokingly defined as "too thick to drink and too thin to plow."[6] Residents passed drinking water through filters to remove insects and debris. Not so easily removed were former inhabitants of the swamp. "If a person had to travel at night," explained Fernando Lemos, "he provided himself with a lantern in order to avoid tripping over tree stumps or gators."[7] As late as the 1890s the *Daily Tribune* continued to report on Ybor City's "war of extermination on the razor back."[8] The incessant croaking of frogs, growling of panthers, and bellowing of gators made sleeping at night a near impossibility, recalled José García.[9] The terrible yellow fever epidemic of 1887, which may have been caused by mosquito-infested imported Cuban fruit, claimed a number of recent immigrants.[10]

The cigar factories, which at the time were free of dangerous machines, seemed on first impression to be exceedingly safe; in fact they were a breeding ground for tuberculosis. Dr. Charles W. Bartlett, agent for the State Board of Health in Hillsborough County in 1903, complained in his annual report of the total lack of "hygenic precautions in any of them [factories]."[11] Workers spat on the floors or in rare spitoons, a practice which in this warm, moist environment spread the disease quickly. "We have to take a collection every week for some consumptive comrade," observed a cigarmaker in 1917.[12] Until well into the twentieth century epidemics of yellow fever, typhoid, and dengue fever struck Ybor City. *El Internacional* reported in 1922 that the cigarmakers' union had paid thousands of dollars in sick benefits caused by an outbreak of dengue fever. "Ybor City is more unsanitary than [it has been] in years," complained the paper.[13] The social, psychological, and linguistic barriers separating Ybor City and Anglo Tampa aggravated the pressing need for medical and health services.

Mutual aid societies proliferated in urban America. Thousands of Slavic, Italian, and Jewish associations flourished in North America during the nineteenth and twentieth centuries.[14] What strikes one about such institutions in Ybor City is not the sheer number of competing factions but rather the consolidating nature and the encompassing character of five separate societies serving the Spaniards, Cubans, and Italians. In building a model for mutual aid, Italians borrowed heavily from their Latin neighbors.

El Centro Español

In April 1891 a small body of artisans and businessmen in Ybor City gathered to discuss an alarming problem, the "anti-social atmosphere prevailing against the Spanish."[15] Ybor City was becoming increasingly polarized: Spaniards commanded the elite positions in the cigar industry while Cubans occupied the lower economic niches; Spaniards monopolized the Sánchez-Haya factory while Cubans dominated the Martínez Ybor factory. Earlier, Cubans had stoned Ignacio Haya and his America-born wife as they walked down Seventh Avenue. B. M. Balbontín, a pioneer Spaniard, told interviewers in the 1930s that "the Spanish at that time [1890s] were persecuted, abhorred, and were the target of Cuban hatred because of the Spanish government in Cuba."[16] To counteract these conditions Spaniards resolved to organize a mutual aid club.

The state of Florida issued El Centro Español's charter on September 7, 1891. Manufacturer Ignacio Haya, who donated funds for the first building, became the first president of the association; other officers included fellow owner Enrique Pendás as vice-president. Pendás, born in Asturias in 1865, left Spain for Cuba in 1881 and later joined his uncle's manufacturing firm in New York City. Lozano, Pendás and Company became Ybor City's third cigar factory in 1889. Pendás typified the Spanish *patrón* in that his activities and status placed him in the upper social levels of both Ybor City and Anglo Tampa. He became the director of the Citizens Bank and Trust Company and a stockholder in the Tampa Tribune Company.[17]

Once launched El Centro Español served as an organizational model and economic blueprint for future groups. An examination of its constitution allows a glimpse into an immigrant institution's capacity to adapt. El Casino Español, a similar organization based in Havana, restricted its membership to *peninsulares:* only persons born in Spain were eligible for admission; even members' children born in Cuba could not enter. However, the by-laws of El Centro Español in Tampa stipulated that only the president and vice-president need be Spanish-born; for others the constitution read: "It is required of all applicants that they be Spaniards by birth and by patriotic inclination *or* that they be loyal to Spain and to its prestige in America."[18]

El Centro Español dovetailed the needs and demands of its diverse clientele. Typical of immigrant aid societies, members paid twenty-five cents a week in return for social privileges and death and injury benefits. Given the Spanish community's preponderant young-single-male profile, the idea of a mutual aid society with congenial social outlets appealed to individuals living in boardinghouses. "The Spaniards to avoid the monotony of their boarding houses must have clubs," observed an Immigration Commission report.[19]

In 1892 directors organized the Spanish Casino Stock Company to promote further recreational and theatrical activity. The society's original 186 members each pledged stock shares of $10, used to finance a clubhouse at Sixteenth Street and Seventh Avenue. An ornate wooden structure costing $16,000, the finished building contained a theater, dance hall, *cantina*, and classrooms. Dedicated in June 1892, the *Tampa Tribune* described the club's opening as "a great day for the Spanish colony of Ybor City." Ceremonies featured "a hundred dollars worth of fireworks" and several lyric operas.[20]

By 1901 the membership rolls of El Centro Español had grown to 926, expanding to 1,886 in 1907 and 2,537 in 1912. The society tolerated a wide spectrum within its membership, including Galicians and Asturians from Spain, *criollos*—sons born in Cuba—a few Italians, cigar manufacturers, elite artisans, radical cigarmakers, and readers. Different classes and ideologies mixed together. "In those days [his father's]," reflected Frank Juan, who has been a member of El Centro Español for sixty-two of his sixty-four years, "the club was all we had."[21]

The club leadership, confident that a dynamic Spanish community could sustain and support an ambitious building campaign, embarked on such a program in 1909. In that pivotal year El Centro Español's 1,773 constituents owed not one cent and hundreds of new applicants awaited formal membership. So many Spaniards from West Tampa now belonged to El Centro Español that the society pledged to build two magnificent new clubhouses, one in Ybor City and the other in West Tampa.[22]

El Centro Español de Recreo e Instrucción de Tampa offered its membership a wide range of social and cultural attractions. Spanish members imported the custom of the *romería*—a pilgrimage celebration, generally associated with a saint's day—adapting it to the secular humanism of Ybor City. The *romería* picnics generated popular support, often involving thousands of participants. Interethnic gatherings were not unusual, especially when connected with a cause such as fund-raising for the Labor Temple or the cigarworkers' unions. "They'd [Spaniards] pack the open streetcars and hang banners," remembered Sara Wohl Juster, elderly daughter of an Ybor City Jewish merchant, who had witnessed preparations for the gala affairs.[23] Social functions attracted three generations of Spaniards to the Sunday *fandangos* (dances) held at El Centro's magnificent ballroom, which boasted the finest parquet floor in the Southeast. Long-time Spanish member Manuel Valles recalled the affairs: "Ah, there was a day when it was a joy to see the ladies come here all dressed up. That big fan on the wall. We used to stand under it when we were teenagers and watch our parents come through the door."[24]

The mutual aid society, bolstered by new streams of immigrants and an expanding second generation, retained the loyalties of the Spanish community through the Second World War. Membership ebbed and flowed but persistently remained strong despite the cataclysmic impact wrought by a world war, an influenza epidemic, and major labor strikes. El Centro Español's 1901 membership of 926 fell markedly, to 690, after the strike of that year. In 1908 the club boasted 2,687 members, which declined abruptly to 1,299 following the 1910 labor imbroglio. By 1915 El Centro had rebounded, enrolling a pre–World War II peak membership of 2,549; but the pincers' effect of World War I (many Spaniards returned to Cuba to avoid the draft), the red scare, and the 1920–21 labor strike plummeted membership to 1,525 in 1922.[25] The other great challenge to El Centro Español's vitality was the appearance of a rival Hispanic society, El Centro Asturiano.

El Centro Asturiano

Founded for essentially social reasons, El Centro Español deftly balanced the strong regional loyalties of its Asturian and Galician constituents. The early society, unified by real and perceived animosities from Anglo Tampa and the colony's Cuban element, could not retain such loyalties following the conclusion of the Cuban Revolution. The Asturian element steadfastly urged the society to broaden its collective efforts in the medical arena, but the leaders of El Centro Español resisted entrance into such an unexplored area because of costs and the "ungovernable and rebellious nature of the Asturians." Labeled "anarchistic" by the Galician leadership, a large faction of dissident Spaniards seceded in 1902 to organize El Centro Asturiano.[26]

El Centro Asturiano became a North American auxiliary of Havana's most renowned institution. In 1900 *Norton's Complete Handbook of Havana and Cuba* described El Centro Asturiano de Habana: "Its furnishings are splendid. It has a well-selected library of 5,000 volumes and occupies several floors. The staircase is of Mexican onyx, but the most notable feature, perhaps, is the great dancing hall, with its polished marble floor and magnificent chandeliers. . . . The club spent $35,000 in merely fitting up the ballroom."[27]

Affiliates of El Centro Asturiano in Cuba already claimed 10,000 members by 1900. The international by-laws required a minimum of 300 members, a percentage of future dues, and a written constitution before granting a charter to the new American subsidiary. Pioneering members, of whom sixty-five were still alive in 1936, recalled that enraged leaders from El Centro Español—especially the cigar manufacturers—fought against the creation of a rival and potentially radical society, even to the point of dispatching delegates to Havana to plead against the proposed establishment. The Spanish hierarchy in Cuba disregarded the disaffected element and granted a charter to El Centro Asturiano de Tampa on April 1, 1902. According to records meticulously preserved at the clubhouse, 546 charter members enlisted in the new society.[28]

Destined to evolve into the most stable, well-financed, and best-preserved clubhouse in Ybor City, El Centro Asturiano began with a two-room, wood-frame building at 1410 1/2 Seventh Avenue. The organization's ranks swelled to 3,030 by 1907, the same year leaders announced plans to erect a modern facility on the corner of Palm and Nebraska avenues. Dedicated on January 22, 1909, the $75,000 clubhouse stood unrivaled by Tampa's standards. A June 1912 fire completely destroyed the splendid structure, but members resolved four months later to build yet another, more ambitious clubhouse. In a gesture inconceivable fifteen years earlier, El Centro Español offered El Centro Asturiano the use of its facility—with full membership privileges—during the construction period.[29]

The *Morning Tribune* heralded the new El Centro Asturiano, unveiled on May 15, 1914, as "the most beautiful building in the South." Designed by the architectural firm of Bonfoey and Elliot, which held commissions for all other major clubhouses, the structure cost a staggering $110,000. Dedication ceremonies went on for three days, highlighted by original operatic scores and endless balls and banquets.[30] The building still sparkles as an architectural gem seventy-two years later. Its spacious features include a dramatic 1,200-seat theater (each mahogany and red velvet seat conforms to the specific dimensions of its patron), a 27-by-80-foot stage, $4,000 worth of modern lighting fixtures, a *cantina*, a ballroom, and a well-stocked *biblioteca* (library).[31]

Financially sound, socially progressive, and institutionally viable, El Centro Asturiano attracted thousands of members. Between 1907 and 1919 membership stabilized between 3,030 and 3,618. While El Centro naturally promoted the supremacy of Asturian culture, at no time did it exclude other Spaniards or Latins. Italians, Cubans, and Galicians joined El Centro Asturiano because of its facilities and benefits.[32] Economically the club operated efficiently, demonstrated by a surplus income of $165,000 for the period 1902–14.[33] During the 1920 strike the Havana chapter canceled a $5,000 debt in support of the cigarmakers' cause.[34] Asturian officials also established a club bank.

No institution in Ybor City or Tampa generated the crowds and numbers as could El Centro Asturiano. A 1911 picnic at Sulphur Springs attracted 6,000 members, their families, and guests, causing the trolley company to press all of its cars into service. Six months later another picnic drew a crowd of 4,500. "Every nationality was represented," reported the *Morning Tribune*.[35] Such gatherings demonstrated graphically the interactive nature of Ybor City, drawing together members of different groups bound by marriage, work, language, and culture.

The Latin community fostered an intense appreciation for the theater since the earliest days of settlement, and the clubs nurtured this passion. Una Sección de Declamación, an amateur theatrical troupe, presented plays every Sunday at El Centro Español and El Centro Asturiano. The advent of "talkies" and the popularity of movie houses, while drastically curtailing live theater in much of Florida, actually enlivened the Spanish-language theater of Ybor City, since many Latin residents spoke little or no English. "In 1935," observed a student of the Florida theater, "Ybor City seems to have been the only place in Florida which still maintained a type of resident theater company."[36]

El Centro Asturiano served as the headquarters for one of the more experimental programs in American cultural history—the New Deal's Federal Theatre Project. As such the club was the only Spanish-language theater unit in the United States. In addition the unit included an Italian opera company staffed by local talent. Latin audiences, drawing upon the cultural wellspring of Spanish, Cuban, and Italian residents, preferred the popular art forms of *la bufa* (vaudeville), *la zarzuela* (musical comedy), and *las funciones* (musical revues). On March 5, 1936, the federal theater opened with the comedy *El Conde de mi Puchungo* (The Count of My Sugar Lump).[37]

Headed by Manuel Aparicio, one of the most celebrated *lectores* in Tampa, the federally sponsored theater survived until July 1939. Aparicio, a Spanish immigrant, brought to the stage an immense talent, one he later successfully parlayed into a career in radio. In addition to his theatrical abilities, sharpened by his earlier readings at the factories, he spoke seven languages; he also wrote several plays. *El Mundo en la Mano* (The World in His Hand), written and directed by Aparicio, brought huge crowds to El Centro Asturiano. The play consisted of folktales from the villages of Spain, Cuba, and Italy and featured stock characters: *el bobito* (the village idiot), *el maricón* (the homosexual), *el gallego* (the Galician), and so on.

Fifteen plays in all appeared as part of the Spanish-language theater unit, including the Spanish version of *It Can't Happen Here (Esto no lo Pasará Aquí)*. Many of the stock players left suddenly when Congress ordered that all aliens on Works Progress Administration rolls be fired, but throughout its short life the project attracted standing-room-only crowds to El Centro. Between January 1936 and October 1937 the Ybor City theater counted 48,939 customers, compared to only 18,268 in all of Jacksonville.[38]

The vibrant Spanish-language theater dramatized the cultural influence of mutual aid societies. From the beginning groups frequented plays at neighboring club theaters, enhancing the spread of Spanish- and Italian-language drama. Carmen Ramirez de Esperante, a Spanish-born actress, organized a children's theater which performed at local clubs. In Ybor City, remembered José Yglesias, there "were wonderfully active cultural centers, for those cigarmakers knew how to organize more than trade unions. . . . At the Centro Asturiano we saw *zarzuelas* performed by local amateurs. When great international performers, like [Enrico] Caruso, came to Tampa, it was cigarmakers who booked them, not the Americanos on the other side of Nebraska Avenue."[39] Opera stars such as Amelita Galli-Curci, Tito Schipa, and Virgilio Lazzaro also played at the Latin theaters to packed houses. El Centro Asturiano regularly hosted some of the finest talent of the Spanish theater, including the Compagnía de Opera Creatore, doña María Guerrero, and the Compagnía Zarate with María Tabau and Roberta Rey.[40] During labor unrest strikers used the auditoriums for mass meetings and protests.

El Centro Asturiano, like the other clubs, protected and promoted the idea of the supreme Latin male; women's auxiliaries existed to serve the male members. "These social clubs all had libraries, auditoriums, gyms, dance halls and canteens, where the men gathered in the evenings," recalled a Spanish American.[41] Typically, Latin men ate dinner with their families—although many Spaniards remained single—leaving promptly thereafter for the gaming tables of their respective clubs. Spanish men, noted a writer in the 1930s, "see their children only during the evening meal. . . . Anyone who does stay home is considered 'hen pecked' and only half a man."[42] The *cantina* hosted spirited card games, such as *tute*, *substado*, and rummy, but dominoes remained the favorite. El Centro Asturiano also erected a bowling alley and gymnasium for its members, who formed athletic teams and competed against rival clubs. Compared to Nordic women, stated one observer, "they [Latin women] do not take part in civic activities."[43] On Sundays in Ybor City the *cantinas* reverberated with the tumult of Spaniards, Cubans, and Italians playing dominoes and cards, and club halls commonly were filled to capacity.

El Círculo Cubano

During the formative decades of Ybor City, Cubans invested their collective energies in the unremitting crusade of *Cuba Libre*. Organizational talents funded the revolution with unceasing support, leaving a void in their community-based infrastructure. The end of the war signaled a mass return to the homeland, only to discover the disillusionment of an unfulfilled revolution. Thousands returned again to Tampa, determined to reshape and invigorate their "Little Havana" in Ybor City.

The history of Cuban mutual aid societies paralleled the timeline of revolution and reconstitution. The origin of El Círculo Cubano can be traced to the postwar milieu, specifically to a recreational society, El Club Nacional Cubano, founded on October 10, 1899. The welter of labor activism in 1901 arrested early growth of the club, but membership climbed after the strike to 300 in 1902. In honor of the new Republic of Cuba, the society changed its name in 1902 to El Círculo Cubano. The charter expressed the hope, "To bind all Cuban residents of Tampa into a fraternal group, to offer assistance and help the sick."[44] The by-laws prohibited discussion within the society of labor, politics, or religion—surely a much-violated provision!

In 1907 El Círculo Cubano erected its first clubhouse on Fourteenth Street and Tenth Avenue. The two-story building cost $18,000 and included a 900-seat theater. Dedication ceremonies brought out a number of American and Cuban dignitaries. In 1916 the original building burned down, spurring the membership, then numbering 2,600, to rebuild with a more lasting monument.[45]

Mario Menocal, president of Cuba, donated $1,000 toward the new clubhouse, while individual members pledged extra levies during a bond drive. Completed in 1918, the $60,000 structure featured a spacious theater (members were entitled to one free pageant per month), a *cantina*, a pharmacy, a library, and a 100-by-70-foot dance floor lavishly decorated by Cuban painters. Imported tile, stained glass windows, and marble accentuated this "cathedral for workers."[46]

The Cuban Club vigorously promoted recreation and culture. In the rear of the clubhouse members built a gymnasium and a boxing arena. Leaders also constructed a school where professors taught Spanish literature and Hispanic culture. "I remember as a boy going to the free art classes summer evenings at the Círculo Cubano," reminisced José Yglesias.[47]

The vicissitudes of the cigar industry affected every club in Ybor City, but none manifested such stark contrasts between good times and bad as El Círculo Cubano. In 1909 membership stood at nearly 1,000 but pitched to 125 by the end of strike-torn 1910. With characteristic vigor and flux the membership revived to 3,225 by 1919 but fell again due to labor unrest to 1,602. Like a phoenix the club thrived throughout the Twenties, with membership cresting at 5,000 in 1930; but in 1935 the aggravation of depression and dispersion saw the membership decline to 2,492.[48]

La Unión Martí-Maceo

The consuming cause of independence before 1898 co-opted the issue of racial equality. José Martí, during his stays in Ybor City, often spoke to the necessity of a united front, indivisible from racial or political differences. After an incident in which Martí narrowly escaped poisoning by Spanish agents, the "Apostle of Cuban Liberty" stayed at the home of Ruperto and Paulina Pedroso, prominent Afro-Cubans. For her aid to the cause Paulina has been called Martí's "second mother." This symbol of racial unity helped rally supporters of the Cuban Revolution. "White and Negro Cubans lived in harmony," wrote José Rivero Muñiz, a contemporary, "all being admitted without exception to the various revolutionary clubs, none ever protested." Muñiz later added, "The relations between Cuban whites and Negroes were most cordial and there was no racial discrimination. . . . They were mutually respectful. . . ."[49]

José Ramón Sanfeliz came to Ybor City in 1890 from Havana. He assisted in creating the 24th of February Club when war began in 1895; later he helped to organize and became president of Los Vengadores de Maceo (The Avengers of Maceo). In 1899 he became one of the founders of El Club Nacional Cubano, which he remembered as being "composed of white and black members—a sort of rice with black beans. There was no distinction of race. When the Círculo Cubano was formed, however, the negroes were left out."[50]

Cubans who yearned to go home to their now liberated island discovered quickly the disillusionment of peace: Cuba was in ruins, banditry was rampant, and the economy was in a shambles. Newspapers reported many Cubans returning to Ybor City, the result of the social and economic dislocation.[51]

The decade of the 1890s also resulted in a new era of race relations in the American South that was characterized by a proliferation of Jim Crow laws, lynchings, and terror.[52] Ybor City's fluid race relations clearly troubled Anglo Tampa. Afro-Cubans worked alongside white immigrants (male and female), a custom carried over from the integrated residential patterns of the enclave. "In Ybor City, you'd live with an Italian on one side, a Spaniard and a Cuban on the other side," recalled eighty-five-year-old Alfonso Díaz, an Afro-Cuban born in Havana.[53] Juan Mallea, an Afro-Cuban born in 1918 on Twelfth Street and Eighth Avenue in Ybor City, remembered: "The Caltagirones, Scagliones, the Martinos—all these people lived across from us. There was no such thing as a white section and a black section. The only time you encountered discrimination was when you left Ybor. . . ." Anglo Tampa pressured Ybor City's white Cubans to dissociate themselves from Afro-Cubans, resulting in the organization of separate white and black Cuban societies around the turn of the century. "The government [state and local] told them [Cubans] we could not work together, have a society together, and would have to keep the races apart," exclaimed Mallea. "That was the law of the country. So we blacks decided to build our own club."[54] The charter to the constitution of La Unión Martí-Maceo eloquently stated their cause: "to meet outside the house in a way acceptable to men of dignity."

Afro-Cubans at first had organized two separate but overlapping societies. In 1900 they formed La Sociedad de Libre Pensadores de Martí-

Maceo (The Society of the Free Thinkers of Martí and Maceo), patterned after a similar Cuban organization. The Tampa group's first president, Bruno Roïg, had been a member of the Cuban Club. The choice of names amplified the heritage of the revolution: Martí was the voice of Cuban liberty; Antonio Maceo, a black general, represented the movement in action; both men had died on the battlefield. In 1904 a faction within the organization founded a new society, La Unión, for the purpose of economic and medical benefits. In 1907 the two organizations merged, forming La Unión Martí-Maceo.[55]

By 1907 officers of the club had purchased a lot on the corner of Sixth Avenue and Eleventh Street, and within a year members embarked on a building campaign. Completed in 1909, the two-story clubhouse is still fondly remembered by veterans of the society. Razed by urban renewal in 1965—the only major ethnic clubhouse so taken—the structure at one time housed a theater for 300, a dance hall, and meeting rooms. Members paid off the building debt in 1918.[56]

La Unión Martí-Maceo gave a degree of stability to Ybor City's mobile Afro-Cuban community. The club's theater and dance hall sponsored virtually every social and cultural event celebrated by the colony's members. The club also began a school, located next to the facility. "In order to keep our heritage," explained an elderly member, "we organized a school at night to teach the Spanish language and Cuban history." Juan Mallea reminisced that the old-timers, while encouraging his generation to learn English, would not allow English to be spoken in the clubhouse. The club's baseball team, Los Gigantes Cubanos (The Cuban Giants), competed against the Latin clubs. "You see," explained Mallea, "the club was the only offering black Cubans had."[57]

Moving between Tampa, Key West, and Havana with regularity, Afro-Cubans had difficulty maintaining the continuity necessary for stability. José Díaz, in pointing out the problems encountered in supporting a viable club, underscored the flux so prevalent in Cuban residential patterns: "Every Cuban family left for Havana to enjoy the holidays."[58] Another observer noted that, "with few exceptions, [Afro-Cubans] came to this city to work for seasons and would return to Cuba, so it did not matter for them to belong to the club."[59] Between 1904 and 1926 over 700 different individuals enrolled in the club, although at no time did the membership exceed 250. The depression and the accompanying decline in the cigar industry devastated Tampa's Afro-Cuban community.

During the decade of the Thirties, Tampa's black foreign-born population declined by more than half (631 to 311) as individuals such as Juan Mallea left for New York or Havana.[60]

L'Unione Italiana

Immigration forced change, by which emigrants were recast with new identities. "In America he will be an Italian to all members of other nationalities," wrote Charlotte Gower Chapman in her study of the Sicilian village of Milocca. "In Sicily he will be a Milochese. In Milocca, he tends to remain a Piduzzana [clan member] who has moved."[61] Emigrants left the Magazzolo valley as Stefanesi and Alessandrini only to emerge in Ybor City as Sicilians and Italians and later Latins. The mutual aid society was a handmaiden to this conversion.

Founded in April 1894, L'Unione Italiana's original members included 116 Italian and 8 Spanish immigrants. The charter stated that the organization's purpose was "to aid such members of said association as may become sick and to provide for the paying of the burial expenses of such members as may die, and to promote fraternity, charity and social intercourse among its members." Article 7 explained, "This society is founded exclusively by Italians"; however, the club would admit "social members of other groups" as long as they were of good moral standing and between fourteen and fifty years of age. In a blatant show of indifference to organized religion, the society's by-laws set a precedent, which is still followed, that the annual and monthly meetings of the membership would be held the first Sunday of each month at 10:30 A.M.[62]

L'Unione Italiana drew from the leadership ranks individuals familiar to students of Italian immigration as *prominenti*, bearing with them the distinctive imprint of their migration experiences and settlement patterns. Bartolomeo Filogamo, the society's first president, reflected the classic *prominento* profile. He left the Old World in 1885 and settled for a time in New Orleans before relocating to Tampa in 1889, ahead of the major immigrant stream. He quickly exploited the Ybor City economy, using his linguistic and financial talents to become bookkeeper at the Pendás and Alvarez cigar factory. Filogamo befriended the firm's owner, Enrique Pendás, who had pioneered the founding of El Centro Español in 1891. When an embryonic Italian settlement emerged, Filogamo brought Pendás and seven other Spaniards into the charter membership of L'Unione Italiana and consciously modeled the organization after El Centro Español. Born in Castellammare del Golfo, Sicily, not a major source for Tampa's Italians, Filogamo nonetheless was tapped by Sicilians from the Magazzolo valley to head the new venture. It is possible, although there is no clear evidence, that Filogamo intersected with his future *paesani* in New Orleans. His organizational talents and his connections with Spanish elites made him an effective first president, yet the choice of an "outsider" as head of this particular society seems remarkable, given the heavy predominance of Stefanesi and Alessandrini in the early colony.[63]

Filogamo, who guided L'Unione through its first decade, was followed by Filippo F. Licata, who held the reins of power for the next eighteen years (1906–24). Born in Santo Stefano in 1877, Licata emigrated with his peasant parents in the vanguard movements from the Val di Magazzolo in the early 1880s. Like Filogamo the Licatas settled in New Orleans, where they too prospered. Soon Antonio and Providenzia Licata owned a grocery store, while Filippo acquired a rudimentary but valuable education in the New Orleans schools and streets. The Licata family migrated to Tampa in 1891, again representing an early move, bringing with them financial capital, business experience, and a knowledge of English.[64]

Antonio Licata opened a grocery store at 1700 Seventh Avenue, an anchor in the emerging "Little Italy." Filippo earned an apprenticeship in the cigar factories, developing a talent he put to little use; however, the fringe benefit, the addition of Spanish to his linguistic repertoire, allowed him to maneuver freely and early within Ybor City and Tampa. In the early 1890s the teenager was one of only a few Italians who knew English and Spanish. He often spent days in court, translating for his *paesani*, or writing letters and filling out forms. Like Giovanni Grimaldi, Filippo Licata became an early intermediary between the Italian and Anglo communities; but unlike the Neapolitan Grimaldi, Licata's Stefanesi roots allowed him to play a long-term, prominent role in L'Unione Italiana.[65]

Licata's terms as president of the Italian Club paralleled his personal economic successes. Like *prominenti* elsewhere he cultivated business opportunities while leading L'Unione. As a young man he purchased a saloon and a buckeye cigar factory, later broadening his investments to cover insurance and banking. His accomplishments included positions as vice-president of the Bank of Ybor City, president of the Ybor City Merchants Association, and director of the Guarantee Title Company. Socially he widened his associations with memberships in the Knights of Pythias, the Kiwanis Club, and a physical move to adjacent Tampa Heights in 1918. He also became the first Ybor City Italian to serve on the city council, for three consecutive terms.[66]

The leadership core of L'Unione exemplified the rising commercial element within the Italian community. Paul Longo is an example. He and his mother emigrated from Alessandria della Rocca in 1904, joining the father in Ybor City. As a young boy Paul apprenticed in the *chinchales*, graduating as a cigarmaker, at which he labored for twenty years. He came to know Filippo Licata through their association in the Italian Club, finally accepting his offer to leave the factory and sell real estate during the Twenties boom. Longo spent the next sixty years as a salesman (land and insurance) and promoter (Italian Club). He explained recently that serving as an officer in the club aided his career in insurance since the society was, among other things, an insurance agency. In his three-quarters-of-a-century affliation with L'Unione, Longo faithfully worked in all aspects of club life, from pasta cook at picnics to manager of the baseball team to president (1933–34, 1945–46, 1949–50). "Next to my family, L'Unione is my family," he proudly asserted. Until the time of his death in 1985 he rarely missed an executive meeting of the club and continued to make daily treks there to play dominoes.[67]

The statutes of the club borrowed, with appropriate changes, a clause inserted by founders of El Centro Español: "one must be Italian or of Italian descendent to be President, Vice-President, Treasurer or Secretary."[68] Early officers in L'Unione came from peasant backgrounds, most beginning their occupational careers as laborers, usually in the cigar industry. They invested their savings wisely, generally in a saloon or grocery, and rose to positions of mercantile prominence. A number of future officers inaugurated their American lives outside Tampa, gaining valuable experience, exposure, and esteem. All except one were members of the major migration streams from Sicily to Tampa, and many had arrived in the pioneering rivulets. Timing proved important.

If leadership within L'Unione followed paths similar to other immigrant clubs, L'Unione itself diverged from the roles played by the traditional Italian mutual aid society. From the selection of its charter president, to recruitment of members, to a broad definition of purpose,

L'Unione Italiana operated far beyond the narrow constraints often found elsewhere. From its inception L'Unione avoided the provincial battles that drained the energies of so many other Italian societies. What strikes the observer as remarkable is not so much what occurred in Tampa but what did not. Stefanesi, although constituting at least two-thirds of the early colonists and possessing more than enough numbers to form a *campanilismo*-based organization, failed to so organize. In contrast, a Brooklyn colony of Stefanesi founded just such an organization, La Società Santo Stefano Quisquina.[69] What was true of Stefanesi also applied to Alessandrini and Contessioti. The latter group, bound by strikingly different linguistic and cultural ties, did not organize a separate society in Tampa as it had in New Orleans. L'Unione served as a collective umbrella, not only for immigrants and children from the Magazzolo valley, but also for smaller numbers of other Sicilians and Italians and even clusters of Spaniards and Cubans, who for economic, marital, or other considerations were drawn to this ethnic banner.[70]

Rival mutual aid societies met with little success in challenging the hegemony of L'Unione. In 1910 a small number of Italians, disenchanted with the leadership of the main club, formed La Società di Mutuo Soccorso Italia, later erecting a wood-frame building on Eighth Avenue and Nineteenth Street. Club Italia, popularly stereotyped as *la societá di vecchi* (the old-timers' club), was led by the Neapolitan banker and travel agent Giovanni Grimaldi.[71] The organization appears to have attracted only a very limited membership, restricted primarily to the older immigrant generation. In 1914 a number of Italians living in West Tampa, feeling the geographic isolation from Ybor City, founded La Società Sicilia. By 1929 its 500 members had erected a $75,000 structure at Howard and Spruce streets. In 1934 L'Unione absorbed La Società Sicilia in *una fusione*, taking over the building as its West Tampa branch and enrolling its members in the larger organization. In 1935 the club membership, thus bolstered by expansion, passed 3,000 for the first time.[72]

L'Unione Italiana, with its reverence for social custom and its deliverance of mutual aid, quickly came to play a paramount role in Ybor City's Italian community. In this sense L'Unione paralleled its dynamic institutional counterparts, El Centro Español, El Centro Asturiano, El Círculo Cubano, and La Unión Martí-Maceo. Judging from institutional records, oral interviews, and documentary reports, between the 1890s and 1930s some 90 percent of Ybor City's first- and second-generation

Latin men belonged to at least one of these societies. "My father belonged to L'Unione," boasted Domenico Giunta. "Before he ever bought a loaf of bread, he paid his dues. We grew up appreciating that fact."[73]

The mutual aid society appealed to the most basic of human instincts. Immigrants, terrified of dying unattended and unnoticed in a strange land and concerned about the uncertainties facing them, banded together to formalize the rituals of life and death. L'Unione honored customs long revered in Sicily, adapting them to Ybor City. Such customs did not need a formal organization to express immigrant pathos. The *Morning Tribune* noted in October 1893, six months before the founding of L'Unione, an Italian funeral with a "corpse carried by four large men with uplifted hats, followed by a brass band, then an empty hearse and carriage preceding the regular concourse of sorrowing relatives and sobbing friends."[74]

The realization of L'Unione institutionalized the funeral. In 1900 the club purchased and dedicated an Italian cemetery two miles north of Ybor City, at Twenty-sixth Street and Twenty-third Avenue. The cemetery, with its imported cypress trees, inset ceramic photographs on gravemarkers, and tombstones inscribed in Sicilian and Italian script, bears a near exact resemblance to the hallowed grounds in Sicily which it sought to duplicate. "Pioneer Spanish and Italian settlers say that this custom [photographs inset on the tombstones] was followed in their youth in their own countries," observed one researcher in 1938. Asked to explain the custom, an elderly Latin said, "It is probably because he [the Latin] loves life and animation. . . . When we visit a relative's grave and see his life-like picture gazing at us from his monument, it obscures the memory of his death. . . ."[75]

A cherished set of rituals governed every aspect of the Italian funeral. As mortuaries did not appear in Ybor City before the 1940s, the club assumed many of the necessary duties. The corpse was laid out at a private home, often on a bed of ice to prevent rapid decomposition in the Florida heat. The funeral involved hundreds of participants, many of whom walked the entire distance of the procession. The cortege always paused for a final tribute in front of the deceased's house and in front of the Italian Club, where flags of Italy and the United States hung at half-mast. As the procession made its way through Ybor City, merchants, as they had in Sicily, closed their doors in a gesture of respect and superstition. A brass band led the throng to the cemetery, followed by family, kin, and *paesani*.

Club rules required members to march in funeral processions as far as Twenty-second Street and Michigan Avenue (Columbus Drive), at which point they returned to work. "You go to a funeral at two o'clock," recalled Cuban immigrant César Medina, "and you wouldn't get home till seven at night. You had to go and walk the coffin in front of the Italian Club."[76] The cigar industry's flexible schedules easily adapted to such customs. In 1911 the *Morning Tribune* noted the funeral of Pasquale Lazzara, with "300 members . . . in the procession costumed according to the rules of the society."[77] In the early years each member contributed $1 to the bereaved family; later the club instituted a $300 death benefit.[78]

Bolstered by steady streams of newcomers and confident of the future, the leadership of L'Unione in 1910 announced plans for a permanent clubhouse. In March 1911 the club's 450 members turned out to view the architect's rendition of the building. The $40,000, three-story structure on Seventh Avenue between Seventeenth and Eighteenth streets was dedicated on Columbus Day 1912. It featured an athletic room and theater. Paul Longo, one of the few survivors who remembered the original clubhouse, reflected as to its meaning in 1912: "I thought, my God, in Sicilia only the Church and Counts build such a monument!"[79] By erecting lavish clubhouses Italians emulated their Cuban and Spanish neighbors. Club construction became another legitimate expression of ethnic rivalry and status.

The monument, intended to last three generations, stood for three years before a fire destroyed everything. Members unhesitatingly pledged to rebuild. Construction began in April 1917, at a time when "Little Italies" elsewhere were channeling their community resources into bond drives and Red Cross benefits in support of World War I.[80]

The erection of the new L'Unione Italiana signified a profound commitment to Italian communal life in Tampa and an important benchmark in the consolidation of the community. The clubhouse became the focus for virtually all immigrant activity, a source of unimagined pride within the community. "Oh, when that was going up we were all so excited, so thrilled," remembered Mary Pitisci Italiano. "Most everybody that didn't work would go out there and stand around and watch the building go up. It was a beautiful affair, a beautiful club."[81] Built in the Italian Renaissance style, decorated with classic columns, terra-cotta relief, and a profusion of marble, the clubhouse stands today as an impressive monument to immigrant aspirations. The building included a magnificent theater with an auditorium and balcony (later converted to a movie theater), a spacious dance floor, a library, a *cantina*, a bowling alley, and recreational rooms. A local factory owned by Salvatore Capello furnished most of the decorative ceramic flooring. Giovanni Rumore laid all the tile, remembering sixty-five years later, "I made extra certain that my grandchildren would walk on tile laid by John Rumore."[82] With furnishings the building cost $80,000, a considerable sum.

The Italian Club, as the social center for the community, performed myriad roles for its members. For Italian men the *cantina* served as a sanctuary, a male bastion where a women never entered casually. Like their Spanish counterparts Italian men retreated to the club for after-dinner socializing. "We used to come here during the week, all the people who live around here," remembered Joe Maniscalco. "They come here to the club and play dominoes, *briscola, scoppa*—until twelve, one o'clock at night! This [club] used to be paradise."[83]

If the gaming tables of the *cantina* lured male clientele, the banner of L'Unione Italiana attracted families, especially for group excursions. Picnics, outings, and festivals made it possible for the club to raise impressive amounts of money and bring together huge crowds of people. Newspapers frequently noted these excursions, such as one July 1911 affair: "600 Italians left on the *Favorite* yesterday at 9:25 for St. Petersburg and Anna Maria Key." The report added that participants "danced on the way down, waltzed on the Key, and hopped gleefully coming back. Professor Mazarelli's orchestra filled the salty air with many tunes of Sunny Italy, while hungry excursionists ate ice cream, cake, macaroni and spaghetti."[84] Picnics frequently featured athletic exhibitions; in September 1911 an excursion to De Soto Park included a baseball game between club members and soldiers stationed at Fort Dade.[85] Old-timers still delight in retelling the details of a 1912 picnic held at De Soto Park, highlighted by a band concert, fireworks, and a marathon race won by Giuseppe Leto. Manuel La Rosa's second-place finish earned him a gold watch fob, which he proudly carried seventy-three years later.[86] In 1924 the club enjoyed a mammoth picnic to celebrate a membership drive that had successfully enrolled 1,000 newcomers. L'Unione's 1,800 members and their families gathered at the farmstead of F. M. Antuono and posed for a photograph that still hangs at the club.[87]

On Saturday evenings the polished dance floor of L'Unione Italiana came alive. "Talk about dances!" exclaimed Nina Ferlita. "We used to have some of the most beautiful dances . . . cabaret tables all over the hall. And they would have Cuban music, Italian music. . . ."[88] When the second generation began to frequent the club two bands often entertained the crowds, one playing more sedate tunes for the parents, the other performing the more rhythmic rumba and samba for the younger set. A number of youth groups organized as auxiliaries, and in 1932 the Goodfellowship Club made use of the ballroom for a benefit dance.[89] "I remember when the Italian Club was built," reminisced Alfonso López, the son of Spanish immigrants. "It was a nice club. . . . we [Spanish kids] used to go to dances there quite a lot as young boys, the Italian Club, also the Centro Español, Centro Asturiano, and the Cuban Club. It was a perfect setup for a young boy, because you could go there and didn't have to take a date. . . . you could always find some girls that were chaperoned."[90]

L'Unione transcended the dance floor and domino tables, however, to instill a vigorous cultural life. The library housed a diverse collection of literature, especially strong in its emphasis on working-class and leftist themes. Many of the classic works by Mikhail Bakunin, Victor Hugo, and Peter Kropotkin were available in leather-bound editions, reflective of the honored places they occupied in the minds of club members.[91]

In 1920 L'Unione Italiana purchased a three-story brick building adjoining the clubhouse, which President Filippo Licata hoped would one day be converted into an opera house. "We see the day when we will bring the Grand Opera Company here," he predicted.[92] While that never happened (the building served as a medical clinic for members), a flourishing Italian theater did establish roots at the Italian Club. The auditorium for L'Unione attracted numerous prominent opera stars. In 1908 the touring company Empresa Perdomo entertained local audiences with the Spanish musical *Gigantes y Cabezudos* and the popular Sicilian tragedy *Cavalleria Rusticana*.[93] Ybor City became a favorite stopping place for stock companies and performers, such as Pasquale Vittore and Maria D'Amore, on their way to tour Cuba. In 1919 the opera *Evandro*, written by a local Italian, was performed by a touring company from New York.[94] "We had a theatre, a beautiful theatre," boasted the cigarmaker and opera aficionado Joe Maniscalco, whose favorite, of course, was *Carmen*. "We used to get the operetti from New York. The locals also formed a theatre to work with them."[95] One such group called itself the Garibaldini Players.[96] "They [Latin societies] had all the beautiful theatres," stated Mary Italiano. "I remember when we [Italians] got Angelo Musco to sing."⁹⁷ Italians also patronized the Spanish-language theaters at the other clubs, utilizing their bilingual talents.

In addition to providing a cultural center and place to socialize, L'Unione also served as a point of entry for newly-arriving immigrants who were able to obtain information about employment, housing, and the city bureaucracy. As a result, there is no evidence that a labor agency or *padroni* system ever existed in Ybor City. Newcomers gained access to these services through family connections or the Italian Club, which continued to welcome them even after the immigration restriction acts of the 1920s. Ledgers surviving from the 1920s and 1930s reveal a broadening membership as individuals born outside the Magazzolo valley migrated to Tampa, generally after extended stays elsewhere. During this period new members born in Cagliari, Casteltermini, Sambucca, Zabot, Alcamo, Catania, Burgio, Macarata, Pueblo (Colorado), Minneapolis, Key West, New York City, Buenos Aires, and Havana all joined the society. On April 5, 1924, Salvatore Buggica became a member of L'Unione, his file carefully recorded in a massive ledger. Buggica, who was born in Lercara Friddi and emigrated to Tampa in 1921, also enrolled his son Roberto, who in 1985 still visited the club each day.⁹⁸

These clubs gave the Anglo community a convenient and logical point of contact with Latin groups. They promoted activities that enabled Latins and Anglos to come together in amicable settings, thereby improving immigrant group identities in the wider city. Local politicians, for example, made the clubs regular stops on their campaign trails, routinely attending the major picnics, parades, and holiday celebrations of these organizations. It is a rare group photo of one of these events that does not include one or more members of the Anglo elite seated prominently in front, and only the tensest strike situations disturbed these patterns.

Club sporting teams—baseball, boxing, and track—also regularly participated in city leagues after 1900, thereby providing additional bridges with Anglo Tampa. Ethnic clubs even joined in Anglo Tampa's most cherished civic ritual, the Gasparilla Parade, a minor version of the New Orleans Mardi Gras, which celebrates the city's mythical buccaneer beginnings. Organizations entered floats and sent marchers to these functions. Unfortunate occurrences, such as the time in 1912 when a Cuban girl covered herself with gold paint to ride on a float and subsequently died of toxic poisoning, were rare.⁹⁹

From the Latin point of view these clubs served to maintain ethnic identity while seeking integration into city life for their members. By organizing ethnic variation in Ybor City and West Tampa the clubs furnished points of consolidation for each of the major ethnic groups. They confronted the very real needs of everyday life for Latins and provided a moral sense of community, an identity that drew upon the cultural heritage of each component. Over time they were perhaps the principal instruments of ethnic adaptation in the city, primarily due to their long lives and unusually high degree of community interaction and support.

Cooperative Medicine

Perhaps the most far-reaching and progressive accomplishment achieved by Ybor City's mutual aid societies occurred not in the theater or on the picnic grounds but in the field of cooperative medicine. If in the building of immigrant aid societies the groups committed greater resources than their contemporaries in New Orleans or Chicago, in terms of health care they anticipated the need for socialized medicine by a century. The clubs took care of their own in ways seldom duplicated by American standards today. One cannot appreciate the complexity of Ybor City's mutual aid societies in the absence of an examination of cooperative medicine, for without it the societies might not have flourished so vigorously.

Yellow fever served as midwife to the birth of cooperative medicine for Ybor City. In the early days "immigrants were dying like flies," remembered Fernando Pendás, president of El Centro Español.[100] Frank Adamo, a physician who practiced medicine in Ybor City in the 1920s, encountered diseases long eradicated in most American communities: typhoid, dengue fever, yellow fever, malaria, and tuberculosis.[101] Yet Ybor City shared its suffering with countless other industrial-immigrant communities that did not respond with the same outburst of collective energy. The very forces that voiced Ybor City's labor movement and leftist yearnings articulated responses toward medicine. The issue of collective medicine had long been a topic of debate in Spain, Cuba, and Italy; in Ybor City, leaders put this doctrine into action.

Spaniards and Cubans had participated in and carried to Tampa working models for cooperative medicine. In nineteenth-century Cuba a number of mutual aid societies had established medical programs and built hospitals for the benefit of their membership. The idea germinated in Ybor City in 1888 when Dr. Guillermo Machado, a Spanish physician, organized *La Igual* (The Equal). For fifty cents a week immigrant cigarmakers received free medical care at *La Igual*'s clinic. Cigar manufacturers, led by Enrique Pendás, quickly combined enlightened self-interest with benevolence, co-opting the idea of contract medicine and broadening it to include all workers. Named *El Porvenir* (The Future), the plan provided the services of a physician for a fee of one dollar and twenty-five cents a month. Faced with the alternative of American physicians who could neither speak Spanish nor understand many of the tropical ailments associated with Cuba and the cigar industry, cigarmakers flocked to the new programs. Like-minded societies spun off the conceptual idea of *El Porvenir*.[102]

The inauguration of El Centro Español moved organizational life onto a larger scale. With hundreds and potentially thousands of dues-paying young members, leaders realized that such collective strength could build not only elaborate clubhouses but perhaps large medical clinics, even hospitals. Those in charge debated the fiscal prudence of cooperative medicine, arguing not against the efficacy of health benefits but against the economic drains upon the society. In 1901, El Centro Español rejected proposals to build a private hospital, a decision that prompted the secession of several hundred Spaniards to organize El Centro Asturiano.

El Centro Asturiano proved visionary in its concept of cooperative medicine. In 1903 the young club had already recruited 1,000 members and embarked upon an ambitious and far-reaching medical program, leasing the old St. James Hotel on Tampa Street and converting it into a temporary hospital. The membership soon authorized construction of a modern hospital at the corner of Jackson and Ola streets. Dedicated in April 1905, El Centro Asturiano's *sanatorio* may have been the first such hospital constructed by an immigrant group in the United States. Built at a cost of $15,000, the facility ranked among the most modern and best-equipped in Florida. The complex included a pharmacy, an x-ray lab, a modern operating room, beds for sixty patients, and a pavilion. The society hired Dr. G. H. Altree to serve as full-time medical director, and he supervised a staff of seventeen Cuban and Spanish physicians, nurses, and aides.[103]

During the hospital's first decade the income from El Centro Asturiano's membership fees, canteen receipts, and social activities consistently exceeded expenses from the clubhouse and the hospital. Prior to 1939 an average of 250 members received hospitalization each year, costing about $18 per patient. Experts have estimated that such care at a private hospital would have cost $100 per patient, thus saving club members and the city of Tampa hundreds of thousands of dollars. For $1.50 per month members received full social and recreational benefits and complete medical coverage. *La Beneficencia Asturiana* permitted family members to enjoy the same benefits at a nominal fee.[104]

El Centro Español, spurred by its rival, unveiled its own equally impressive medical program in 1903. A committee led by President Vicente Guerra, a prominent cigar manufacturer, toured Cuba studying hospital designs and returned with blueprints and ideas. Cuban experts urged El Centro Español to locate its hospital away from Ybor City, preferrably on a salubrious site by the sea. So prepared, the committee selected a picturesque location on Bayshore Boulevard, overlooking Tampa Bay.[105]

In February 1906 El Centro Español dedicated a three-story *sanatorio* that rivaled the state's most modern facility. Described by the *Morning Tribune* as "conspicuously handsome," the brick structure featured a range of up-to-date facilities, including what was believed to be the first "electric ambulance" in Florida. Visitors at the dedication included Gabriel Ricardo Españo, editor of Havana's *Diario de la Marina*. In its first thirty years the hospital treated 7,959 patients, of which 1,623 required operations. *La Benefica Española* enabled members' families to receive the same cradle-to-grave protection for a small fee; members themselves paid $1.50 per month for social benefits and total medical protection.[106]

Dr. José Ramón Avellanal became the first director of El Sanatorio del Centro Español. Born in Gijón (Asturias) in 1869, he emigrated with his parents to Cuba, where he compiled a remarkable academic record that culminated with the receipt of medical and dental degrees from the University of Havana. In 1904 Dr. Avellanal moved to Tampa and almost from his arrival dedicated his life to ministering to Ybor City's working classes. Before assuming the directorship of the *sanatorio* he headed *El Porvenir*. During the frequent labor strikes many people recalled that Dr. Avellanal donated his services to the cigarworkers. The Cuban Club, in gratitude for his efforts, made him its first honorary member. His charitable work and proclivity toward collective medicine did not prevent him from pioneering a string of drugstores in Tampa, and he later became president of Liborio Cigar Company and vice-president of the Latin-American Bank. In 1923, with the crusading editor Victoriano Manteiga, he helped launch *La Gaceta*, a Spanish-language newspaper that survives to this day.[107]

El Centro Español and El Centro Asturiano offered members a generous medical plan reflective of their peculiar needs. Both societies, for instance, designed special funds for the care of tubercular patients, a disease of particular concern among cigarmakers and one requiring a lengthy convalescence. Members in need of a trip to Spain, Cuba, or Colorado for recuperation received $415 and transportation under El Centro Español's *Agrupación de Embarques*. Under El Centro Asturiano's protection plan, stricken members received a steamship ticket worth $60 and $25 a month compensation for a year and a half. If desired, Asturians could convalesce in a Havana sanatorium. El Centro Asturiano also established a propaganda department, the purpose being to raise funds for indigent members.[108]

The completion of club hospitals demonstrated the commitment by Ybor City's Latins to the collective welfare of thousands of families. To appreciate the nature of such an attachment, one must understand that after 1905 Ybor City's cigarmakers and their families could expect better health services than almost anyone in Tampa. When the Spanish societies completed their institutions in 1906, Tampa's municipal hospital consisted of a makeshift facility housed in an abandoned courthouse. In 1910 the city completed the two-story Gordon Keller Hospital, but the $24,000, thirty-two bed facility paled in comparison to the modern brick structures built by the Spaniards. Members of Tampa's black community rightfully dreaded a visit to the Clara Frye Hospital, a two-story frame building with room for only seventeen beds.[109]

The existence and increasing popularity of collective medicine among Ybor City's Latins angered Tampa's medical community. The Hillsborough County Medical Society (HCMS) battled the concept of contract medicine for a half-century, labeling it "socialistic," "un-American," and "radical," and in particular waged an incessant battle with physicians who wished to serve the Latin societies. The very first amendment of the HCMS's constitution prohibited its members from participating in contract-medicine programs. In 1902 the society passed a resolution stating, "Any doctor who continued to hold any already accepted contract organized to obtain a fee for less than regulation [was] guilty of unprofessional and unethical conduct." Shortly thereafter the organization broadened its condemnation, prohibiting its members from even "consulting" with these medical pariahs. The Committee on Illegal Practitioners published lists of the guilty doctors, later expanded to include nurses.[110] In addition the accused faced expulsion from the American Medical Association. Dr. Louis Sims Oppenheimer accepted a position with the Latin societies but after two years returned to private practice because, according to his biographer, "he could no longer stand the censure of his peers."[111] In 1938 the HCMS barred Dr. M. R. Winton from practicing at the city's municipal hospital because he served as medical director for El Centro Español. The HCMS added the names of thirteen others to the list in 1938.[112]

The verbal and legal salvos between the HCMS and the ethnic societies caught some physicians in the crossfire. Such was the case with Dr. Frank Adamo. Born in the heart of Ybor City's "Little Italy" in January 1893, Adamo's early life mirrored the Italian colony. His father, Giuseppe, a peasant, had joined *paesani* in 1889 laying rail track and working in the sugar fields of St. Cloud before migrating to Ybor City in the early 1890s. In 1904 Giuseppe returned to Santo Stefano with his wife, Maria Leto, and their son, Frank. They remained in Sicily for a year and a half before returning to Ybor City with three cousins. Frank received a modicum of education before apprenticing in the cigar factories. During the 1910 strike he accompanied a Cuban friend, José Pérez, to Key West, where they rolled cigars while waiting for good times to return to Tampa. Upon returning to Tampa, Frank decided to join friends who were departing for Chicago. "We left April 1, 1911," the nonagenarian remembered. In Chicago the trio worked at the Wingler-Mandel cigar factory by day and attended school at night. "It was in Chicago where I learned English," Adamo recalled. He used his newfound passion for education as a springboard to medical school. While interning he met a Scottish nurse whom he married.[113]

The couple moved to Ybor City in 1919. Adamo established a private practice along Seventh Avenue between Nineteenth and Twentieth streets, in the Italian district, and catered "mainly to Italians." "I did very well," the doctor admitted. He also confessed to the pressure applied by medical groups against entering any type of cooperative arrangement. "The medical society was against that type of practice," he reminisced. "I didn't think it was right, but. . . . We [doctors] couldn't even go to the hospitals [El Centro Español's and El Centro Asturiano's] then. . . . They said it was contract medicine." Adamo eventually moved his office from Ybor City, choosing private practice over group medicine.¹¹⁴

Despite decisions by physicians such as Adamo to practice elsewhere and the national popularity of private insurance companies, collective medicine gained strength, stature, and numbers following World War I. El Círculo Cubano and L'Unione Italiana, while agreeing with the virtues of cooperative medicine, debated the wisdom of building separate hospitals. In a move marking a new era of Latin interdependence and cooperation, El Centro Asturiano and El Centro Español permitted Cubans and Italians to join their medical programs. Although economic motivations undoubtedly played a role in opening access, the move allowed interethnic cooperation to function at social and economic levels unimaginable two decades earlier.

Collective medical efforts defined new parameters of mutual aid and dependence. The economic benefits generated by thousands of participants allowed existing hospitals to modernize facilities. In August 1928 El Centro Asturiano dedicated a new, $175,000 facility in Ybor City. These medical programs provided an invigorating stimulus to the entire structure of the clubs. Since the clubs were the mechanisms by which members gained entrée to medical services, they retained healthy membership rolls for remarkably long periods of time.¹¹⁵

For Italians alliance with other societies did not end the debate over cooperative medicine, nor did it mean L'Unione turned the problem over to Spanish hospitals. No single issue after 1920 consumed more energy than the perplexing problem of group health care. What in the 1890s had been an overwhelmingly youthful Italian colony had aged by the 1920s. The colony reflected the spectrum of the life cycle: older fathers and mothers who dreaded lingering illness; children who required vaccinations; cigarmakers who had contracted tuberculosis. L'Unione Italiana debated the exigencies of health care and boldly accepted responsibility, establishing its own medical clinic in the early 1920s. At the clinic, open six days and five nights a week, treatment ranged from tonsillectomies and dental work to routine medical services.¹¹⁶

Medical privileges accounted for the major reason why Ybor City's mutual aid societies retained their cohesiveness and strength even after World War II. At L'Unione Italiana male members aged fifteen to forty-seven required a medical examination before admission (curiously, only females aged twenty to forty were so examined). In the 1920s and 1930s members paid 65¢ a week for complete medical coverage at the Italian clinic and El Centro Asturiano's hospital (Spaniards paid only $1.50 a month for the same benefits at their respective clubs). In case of illness members received $2 a day in worker's compensation. L'Unione Italiana managed to operate efficiently through World War II. For example, in January 1933, at the very depth of the depression, the club's ledgers revealed a $2,362 balance for the previous year. The depression wrought an unsettling effect on the club, and in June 1932 the executive board responded to the plight of the unemployed by agreeing to allow members to retain medical and social privileges despite their inability to pay their dues.[117]

Summary

The mutual aid society embodied ethnic solidarity, generational change, and the evolving urban community. The genius of Ybor City's collective associations was their ability to adjust to the changing realities of ethnic group relations, the workplace, and new waves of immigrants. Immigrant collectives, which began as simple institutions dispensing death and accident benefits, grew into complex agencies of insurance, medical care, recreation, and culture. Beginning in the 1890s with a few hundred male immigrants, Cuban, Spanish, and Italian societies crested in power and influence in the immediate pre- and post-World War II era, boasting two modern hospitals, five pharmacies, five medical laboratories, seven clubhouses (including West Tampa), and a membership totaling over 20,000 persons.

In the comparative perspective of North America's "Little Italies," Ybor City's network of mutual aid stands out as extraordinarily complex and far-reaching. Studies of other locales most often depict similar Italian societies as being handicapped by small size, poorly financed and managed, restricted to immigrants from a single old-world village or region, and generally designed to provide aid to members and families troubled by death, sickness, and unemployment. At best these organizations recognized the necessity of mutual dependence in the face of shared peril; at worst they followed the fault lines of *campanilismo*, perpetuating a quarrelsome record of needless conflict and competition.

The Tampa experience diverged sharply from the North American organizational portraits sketched in the historical literature. L'Unione Italiana must be understood within the specific context of Ybor City's Latin mutual aid complex and in the wider spectrum of Latin American associational life. Borrowing from organizational models brought by Latin neighbors, L'Unione leaned heavily upon the pattern of broad-based societies characterizing places such as Buenos Aires and Havana.

Samuel Baily's studies of Argentina suggest that Italian immigrants in South America behaved differently from their North American *paesani*. Contrasted to New York, where the overwhelming majority of societies served 500 members or less, in Buenos Aires a small number of large societies (1,000 or more members) "dominated the movement and provided a distinct kind of leadership." Baily noted, "These societies had substantial assets in both buildings and capital reserves," providing members with "schools, medical clinics, hospital care, pharmacies, restaurants and in some cases, job placement services."[118]

Tampa's Italian community, drawing into its fold a concentration of Sicilian villagers, did not result in the predictable pattern of narrow-based organizations, such as that seen elsewhere. L'Unione Italiana helped preserve culture (funerals, language, courtship) and redefine individual/family/group obligations in a new urban-industrial environment. The club combined the functions of an immigrant receiving station, insurance agency, medical clinic, performing arts center, and political broker. Immigrants also used the society to adjust to the new order, facilitating processes whereby newcomers developed the knowledge and skills that allowed them to function effectively and competitively.

In sheer economic and physical terms, Tampa's Italians and other Latins invested their moral and financial capital into their societies, erecting magnificent structures. Club buildings on Seventh Avenue sponsored, in the *cantina*, theater, dance floor, and library, a wide range of activities justifying such commitment. Hospitals provided modern medical care at inexpensive prices: in 1946 El Centro Español charged members $1.50 per month for total society and medical benefits—the same fee charged in 1891.

L'Unione Italiana served as an agent of Italian ethnicity but also provided a matrix within which Italians further identified themselves as Latins. The presence of Spanish and Cuban societies profoundly shaped the form and direction of the Italian Club. Spaniards, Cubans, and Italians lived in a densely populated, geographically defined, one-industry setting. Ybor City's mutual aid societies could draw upon a membership with relative ease, in contrast to organizations in other urban centers with their heterogeneous ethnic groups, diverse economic bases, and widely dispersed ethnic residential settlements.

Ybor City's mutual aid societies exhibited a high degree of ethnic interaction, economic cooperation, and institutional sharing. A wide range of activities drew Cubans, Spaniards, and Italians together, ranging from Latin picnics to athletic leagues to shared facilities during moments of mutual distress. Nothing, however, demonstrated more clearly the extraordinary degree of ethnic interaction than the outpouring of collective energies involved in cooperative medicine. Latins responded to problems of medical care with a dignity and dedication rarely found in urban America. The interchange among Ybor City's immigrants that so powerfully shaped the mutual aid movement also affected the community's other institutions. Religion, for example, felt the impact of this phenomenon, though with very different outcomes.

NOTES

1. Greenfield, *Economics and Liberalism*, 122–23; Horowitz, *Italian Labor Movement*, 12, 14–17, 100; Carr, *Spain*, 417, 434, 455–57.
2. Long, "Immigrant Cooperative Medicine," 418–19; Westfall, "Immigrants in Society," 42.
3. *Tampa Journal*, January 6, 1890.
4. "Twenty-Five Years Ago," *Tampa Daily Times*, June 12, 1918.
5. FWP, assorted "Life Histories," 1936–41.
6. Muñiz, *Movimiento Obrero*, 10; FWP, "Life History of José García."
7. Lemos, "Early Days of Ybor City."
8. *Daily Tampa Tribune*, May 28, 1891.
9. FWP, "Life History of José García."
10. Muñiz, *Movimiento Obrero*, 13.
11. Florida State Board of Health, *Fifteenth Annual Report*, 39–40, quoted in Long, "Immigrant Cooperative Medicine," 422; *El Internacional*, July 15, 1916, April 20, 1917.
12. *El Internacional*, January 26, April 2, 1917, April 18, 19, 1918, July 21, 1922; Minutes, Tampa Board of Trade, January 31, 1906. Proper ventilation of the work area and scrupulous cleaning of spittoons were frequent demands made by cigarworkers to owners.
13. *El Internacional*, September 1, October 7, 1922 (dengue fever); *Tampa Morning Tribune*, July 7, 1911 (typhoid fever); minutes, Tampa Board of Trade, January 31, 1906 (yellow fever).
14. Harney, "Records of the Mutual Benefit Society," 1; Barton, "Eastern and Southern Europeans," 150–75.

15. Manteiga, *Centro Español;* FWP, "Centro Español."
16. FWP, "Life History of B. M. Balbontín."
17. FWP, "Life History of Enrique Pendás"; *Tampa Morning Tribune,* March 17, 1926.
18. *Reseña Historica,* 10; FWP, "Centro Español"; Norton, *Hand-Book of Havana and Cuba,* 116–17.
19. U.S. Congress, *Immigrants in Industries,* 228.
20. *Tampa Tribune,* June 15, 20, 23, August 12, 1892; FWP, "Life History of B. M. Balbontín"; FWP, "Centro Español."
21. FWP, "Centro Español"; interview with Frank Juan, in *Tampa Tribune* (Peninsular edition), October 20, 1983. Generalizations about the social composition of the membership derived from matching membership lists with newspaper reports, oral interviews, and other documentary sources. All paint a picture of an extremely varied body, including a wide spectrum of classes and viewpoints.
22. *Tampa Morning Tribune,* March 25, April 22, 1909; "The Society Is in Splendid Financial Condition," ibid., May 1, 1909; ibid., April 18, 1917, December 20, 1925.
23. Interview with Sara Wohl Juster, May 4, 1984; *Tampa Morning Tribune,* January 3, 1904; FWP, "Centro Español," 346.
24. "Shine On, Shine On, Latin Moon," *Tampa Morning Tribune* (Florida Accent), April 23, 1972.
25. FWP, "Members in the Centro Español."
26. *Tampa Morning Tribune,* April 8, 1902; FWP, "Centro Asturiano," 318.
27. Norton, *Hand-Book of Havana and Cuba,* 114–15.
28. FWP, "Centro Asturiano," 319.
29. *El Centro Asturiano en Tampa,* 11–13; *Tampa Morning Tribune,* January 23, 1909, September 9, 1911, October 9, 1912; *Tampa Daily Times,* June 16, 1912.
30. *El Centro Asturiano en Tampa,* 13–19; FWP, "Centro Asturiano," 322–24; *Tampa Daily Times,* August 28, 1914; *Tampa Morning Tribune,* May 15, 17, 1914.
31. *Tampa Morning Tribune,* May 15, 17, 1914; interviews with Tony Pascual (who manages the theater), October 4, 1983, August 6, 1984.
32. Interview with Anthony Muñiz, May 20, 1982; El Centro Asturiano Record Books, 1902–20.
33. *El Centro Asturiano en Tampa,* 20.
34. FWP, "Centro Asturiano," 326.
35. *Tampa Morning Tribune,* April 20, October 4, 1909, April 3, September 18, 23, 1911; see also ibid., October 4, 1907.
36. Mardis, "Federal Theatre in Florida," 167.
37. Ibid., 95, 154–56; *El Internacional,* March 22, 1918; *Tampa Morning Tribune,* January 14, 1917.
38. Mardis, "Federal Theatre in Florida," 154–203; interview with Mary Fontanills, March 5, 1982.
39. Yglesias, "Radical Latino," 5–6; Carmen Ramirez de Esperante Papers, Special Collections, USF.
40. Mardis, "Federal Theatre in Florida," 197; "Spanish Opera Company," *Tampa Tribune,* August 12, 1892; interviews with Tony Pascual, October 4, 1983, August 6, 1984; interviews with Nelson Palermo, March 23, 1979, March 6, 11, 1982; interview with Mary Fontanills, March 5, 1982; *Tampa Morning Tribune,* March 11, 1911.
41. Yglesias, "Radical Latino," 5.
42. FWP, "Centro Asturiano."
43. Ibid.

44. *Tampa Morning Tribune*, January 31, 1899; FWP, "Círculo Cubano"; FWP, "Members in the Círculo Cubano."
45. *Tampa Morning Tribune*, November 15, 1907, May 23, 1909; FWP, "Círculo Cubano"; *Tampa Morning Tribune*, April 7, 1911, November 17, 1916, May 19, 1917.
46. FWP, "Círculo Cubano." The first Círculo Cubano burned on April 30, 1916, to be replaced by an equally splendid structure. Both Spaniards and Italians put their club buildings at the disposal of Cubans until the new building was completed. Muñiz, *Cubanos*, 141.
47. Yglesias, "Radical Latino," 66.
48. FWP, "Círculo Cubano."
49. Muñiz, *Cubanos*, 122; Muñiz, "Letter to Editor," 314.
50. FWP, "Life History of José Ramón Sanfeliz."
51. *Tampa Morning Tribune*, January 31, 1899; Pérez, *Cuba Between the Empires*.
52. Woodward, *Strange Career of Jim Crow*, 67–110; Shofner, "Custom, Law and History," 277–99.
53. Interview with Alfonso Díaz, August 15, 1982.
54. Interview with Juan Mallea, August 15, 1982.
55. FWP, "Unión Martí-Maceo"; La Unión Martí-Maceo Manuscript Records, Special Collections, USF.
56. Ibid.; interview with José Díaz, May 3, 1980; *Tampa Morning Tribune*, January 2, 1906, September 24, October 4, 1908.
57. FWP, "Unión Martí-Maceo"; interview with Francisco Rodríguez, June 18, 1983; interview with Juan Mallea, August 15, 1982; interview with José Díaz, May 3, 1980; interview with Silvia Grinán, April 15, 1977.
58. Interview with José Díaz, May 3, 1980.
59. FWP, "Unión Martí-Maceo."
60. Interview with Juan Mallea, August 15, 1982; Greenbaum, "Afro-Cubans in Exile," 59–73.
61. Chapman, *Milocca*, 27.
62. L'Unione Italiana, *Statua della Unione Italiana, Società di Mutuo Soccorso Istruzione e Recreazione, Fondata il 4 Aprile 1894*, 1–5. The constitution also prohibited any "official religion."
63. Massari, *Comunità Italiana*, 749–52.
64. Interview with Annie Licata Lazzara, November 17, 1984; interview with Concetta Licata Nuccio, November 17, 1984. Mrs. Lazzara and Mrs. Nuccio are the surviving daughters of Mr. Licata. *History of Florida*, II, 190–91; Robinson, *History of Hillsborough County*, 302.
65. Interview with Annie Lazzara, November 17, 1984; interview with Concetta Nuccio, November 17, 1984. Filogamo did not come from the Magazzolo valley, but his holding of the first presidency of L'Unione can be explained by his unusual connections in the early community.
66. Ibid.; *History of Florida*, 191; *Tampa City Directory*, 1917, 35; *Tampa Morning Tribune*, July 27, 1931. The Merchant's Association that Licata headed included the Spaniards B. M. Balbontín and F. S. Sánchez as treasurer and secretary, respectively.
67. Interviews with Paul Longo, June 1, 1979, March 13, June 30, July 2, 1980. Mr. Longo has amassed club memorabilia which he graciously shared with us.
68. L'Unione Italiano, *Statuto della Unione Italiana*, chap. 3, art. 21.
69. Messina, *Caso Panepinto*, 149.
70. A variety of sources document the composition of L'Unione. See *Registro Soci Famigliari, L'Unione*, 5 vols., Special Collections, USF.

71. Interviews with Tony Pizzo, 1978–84.
72. *Libro Soci, Società Sicilia,* Special Collections, USF; *Tampa Morning Tribune,* April 28, 1929; *La Voce della Colonia,* July 22, 1911; *El Internacional,* March 31, 1916; manifesto, "Protest for Ettor and Giovanetti," September 28, 1912, PKY.
73. Interview with Domenico Giunta, May 18, 1984. Like the other Latin clubs L'Unione contained a broad membership. The anarchist Alfonso Coniglio belonged to the club (and was elected to the executive council in the 1920s), as did the socialist Giovanni Vaccaro and the international banker Angelo Massari. See L'Unione Italiana, membership records.
74. *Tampa Tribune,* October 13, 1893. Since undertakers did no cosmetic work then, the photos further served to retain pleasant memories.
75. Bryan, "Photographs on Tombstones."
76. Interview with César Medina, May 22, 1984.
77. *Tampa Morning Tribune,* November 28, 1911.
78. L'Unione Italiana, minutes, Board of Directors, January 24, 1928.
79. Interview with Paul Longo, June 30, 1980; "L'Unione Will Build Expensive Club House," *Tampa Morning Tribune,* June 18, 1910; ibid., March 26, 31, May 26, July 13, 1911, October 10, 1912; *Tampa Daily Times,* October 9, 1912.
80. *Tampa Morning Tribune,* April 4, 1915, April 18, 1917.
81. Interview with Mary Italiano, April 20, 1980.
82. Interview with Giovanni Rumore, October 8, 1984; FWP, "L'Unione."
83. Interview with Joe Maniscalco, April 3, 1980.
84. *Tampa Morning Tribune,* July 31, 1911.
85. Ibid., September 8, 1911.
86. *Tampa Daily Times,* August 19, 1912; interview with Manuel La Rosa, October 2, 1982.
87. *Tampa Daily Tribune,* May 13, 1924; see also ibid., September 27, 1909, February 24, May 10, 15, July 22, 1911, August 4, 1912.
88. Interview with Nina Ferlita, April 25, 1980.
89. L'Unione Italiana, minutes, September 29, 1932.
90. Interview with Alfonso López, April 24, 1980.
91. Pozzetta, "Immigrant Library," 10–12.
92. *Tampa Daily Times,* May 22, 1920.
93. *Tampa Morning Tribune,* August 29, 1908.
94. L'Unione Italiana Archives; *Tampa Morning Tribune,* March 10, 1919.
95. Interview with Joe Maniscalco, April 3, 1980.
96. *Tampa Morning Tribune,* July 25, 1906, January 24, October 4, 1908.
97. Interview with Mary Italiano, April 20, 1980.
98. *Registro dei Soci,* 5 vols., Special Collections, USF; interview with Roberto Buggica, September 15, 1984.
99. d'Ans, "Legend of Gasparilla."
100. *Tampa Daily Times,* June 8, 1965.
101. Interview with Frank Adamo, April 20, 1980.
102. Long, "Immigrant Cooperative Medicine," 417–34; *Tampa Daily Times,* May 24, 1901; Bryan, "Fifty Years of Group Medicine."
103. *Tampa Morning Tribune,* February 28, 1904, April 9, 1905; *El Centro Asturiano en Tampa,* 4–7. As the membership aged, El Centro Asturiano added a convalescent nursing home.
104. FWP, "Centro Asturiano Hospital"; *Tampa Morning Tribune,* December 12, 1926; *El Federal,* May 3, 1902.

105. FWP, "Centro Español."
106. *Tampa Morning Tribune*, February 4, 1906.
107. Avellanal Family Papers, Special Collections, USF. Dr. Avellanal performed the first craniotomy in Florida at El Centro Español's hospital.
108. FWP, "Welfare Aid, Centro Asturiano"; FWP, "Welfare Aid, Centro Español"; *Socidades Españolas*; Luening, "Cigar City Rises," 46.
109. Grismer, *Tampa*, 199.
110. Slusser, "Hillsborough County Medical Association," 47–60.
111. Ingram, "Louis Sims Oppenheimer," 20. See also *Tampa Morning Tribune*, August 25, 1907.
112. *Tampa Morning Tribune*, February 11, 1973.
113. Interview with Frank Adamo, April 20, 1980.
114. Ibid.
115. *Tampa Daily Times*, November 14, 1935; FWP "Centro Asturiano"; *Tampa Morning Tribune*, December 30, 1970.
116. L'Unione Italiana, minutes, 1925–41. Members suffering from tuberculosis received a travel indemnity of $120 and a monthly stipend of $30.
117. Ibid.; L'Unione Italiana, *Bollettino della Sezione Cultura* (July 1949, February 1949); *Il Conto Economico*, 1940–49.
118. Baily, "Adjustment of Italian Immigrants," 293. See also Scarzanella, *Italiani d'Argentina*.

7 The Religious Encounter

The people there [Ybor City] are nearly all Catholics, at least in name, though many of them do not practice, and have not gone to church or approached the sacraments for years.

Woodstock Letters, February 1890

Tampa was a celebrated, if unlikely, first chapter in the long history of the Catholic church in Florida. In 1549 the Dominican Fray Luis Cáncer de Barbastro celebrated the first recorded mass in North America, not far from the future Ybor City. The following day Tocobaga Indians clubbed the priest to death with their *macanas* (clubs). Subsequent Spanish efforts to Christianize the natives crumbled after the Indians of Tampa Bay suffered wholesale extinction.[1] Some 350 years later the Catholic church renewed its attempt to save Ybor City's residents; as before, it stumbled miserably.

While mutual aid societies, radical groups, and working-class labor unions attracted thousands of Ybor City immigrants to their ranks, organized religion did not. To outside observers the Roman Catholic church logically figured to become the key institution to broker between Spanish, Cuban, and Italian immigrants and to unify a diverse community. One minimally might have expected the church to play a pivotal institutionalizing role in the early immigrant community, a pattern exhibited in many other urban areas.[2] Ironically, Ybor City's immigrants did converge in their responses to religion but in ways not intended by church officials. The precise reasons why can be found primarily in the social and cultural fabric of Ybor City's immigrant world, not in decisions emanating from diocesan board rooms or Protestant mission headquarters.

The arrival of the Catholic church in Ybor City, like the inception of cooperative medicine, owed much to yellow fever, which ravaged the Tampa area in 1887–88. This deadly disease decimated the priestly ranks, killing three clerics and forcing Bhp. John Moore, head of the St. Augustine diocese, to search frantically for replacements. He wrote to Rev. John O'Shanahan, S.J., superior of the Jesuits of Louisiana, for assistance, which soon arrived in the form of Fr. Thomas de Carriere.[3] The latter's diligent work among the fever victims prompted Bishop Moore to request that the Jesuits assume responsibility for the spiritual health of all South Floridians, which they agreed to do. Rev. John B. Quinlan was sent in late 1889 to serve as pastor, assisted by the Spanish-speaking Father de Carriere. These two priests erected the first Catholic church in Ybor City, Our Lady of Mercy, in 1890 and began the first serious efforts to minister to a rapidly growing flock.[4]

Early in 1890 Father Quinlan wrote the bishop his assessment of the task he faced: "The Catholics of Tampa [meaning St. Louis parish in downtown Tampa] are fervent, attend church regularly, and approach the sacraments frequently. . . . Besides these, there are 2,500 Cubans in Ybor City, all professing the Catholic religion; but in general they are not practicing Catholics." In addition to the Cubans, Father Quinlan mentioned that Italian and Spanish Catholics resided in Ybor City and "already formed the nucleus of a congregation [that was] daily increasing."[5] Never again would a Catholic priest speak so optimistically of possibilities for the church in Ybor City.

The church had, in part, compromised its community position by accepting donations from wealthy Spanish factory owners for the erection of Our Lady of Mercy. This fact rankled the more patriotic Cubans, who viewed the Catholic church and the colonial Spanish government as twin oppressors of their homeland.[6] The Spanish upper classes soon came to dominate church affairs, founding sodalities, endowing additions to the church, and financing magnificent wedding ceremonies for their children.[7] From the beginning, therefore, Ybor City residents identified the church with the Spanish; and inevitably the institution became inextricably entwined in the network of divisions and rancors generated by the Cuban independence struggle.

More significant than revolutionary passions, however, were the deeply rooted sentiments emanating from Ybor City's working-class culture. The proletarian ideologies that found such favor in the cigar industry and so pervaded the wider community invariably regarded the church with hostility. For many leftists, organized religion, and particularly the Catholic church, was an even greater foe than capitalism. As the anarchist newspaper *L'Alba Sociale* observed, "Hypocrites and Jesuits . . . the clergy, the government, the system. . . . it is from these that we have the behavior that makes man become an animal, a wolf, a hyena."[8] If people are inherently good, argued the anarchists, then society's malaise must be blamed upon the corrupting institutions, none so evil as the Catholic church. For those who had vilified the church in the Old World, of course, there was no reason to accept it in the new. Freemasons, anarchists, and socialists continued to attack Catholicism as vehemently in Florida as they had in Sicily, Spain, and Cuba.[9] The Catholic church, roared the Cuban Nestor Carbonell, "stands as the enemy of scientific truth, justice, and liberty." Passions ran high. If one is to believe a report in the *St. Petersburg Times,* in 1901 an Ybor City Italian killed his wife because she insisted on attending church services.[10]

Condemnations such as Carbonell's struck responsive cords in the community. Parish priests, missionaries, and the Sisters of St. Joseph, who arrived in September 1891, battled a stream of anticlerical invective which filled the pages of leftist newspapers and frequently spilled over into street-corner rhetoric. Sister Mary Lourdes remembered walking down Seventh Avenue in the 1920s and being insulted, in Spanish, by people sitting on the porches. "People did not like the priests and brothers," she sighed.[11] In hushed tones the veteran cigarmaker José Vega Díaz explained the dominant attitude in a literary allegory he learned from the reader's platform: "You know what Victor Hugo say? In every town and every place they have a school teacher. . . . the school teacher is the light. And in every town there is someone who—wheeww—try to blow away the light—the preachers!"[12]

In 1892 an energetic young Jesuit priest, Fr. William Tyrrell, arrived in Ybor City to replace Father Quinlan. He threw himself into his work with a vigor that amazed even his detractors. Soon he earned the name "Tyrrell the Builder" for his successes in erecting churches, missions, and schools.[13] But these triumphs were not matched in the realm of building loyal congregations. While contemporary church almanacs and jubilees published by the parishes Father Tyrrell had founded paint a picture of steady growth and wide community participation, confidential documents in diocesan and parish archives, oral testimony, and county courthouse records portray a different situation.

As of the late 1890s, a few among the two dozen Sisters of St. Joseph and the parish priests in Ybor City spoke fluent Spanish or Italian. The nuns, moreover, were almost all Irish Americans who were shocked by the state of religious training they found among the children. Reflecting the perspective of their Irish American Catholicism, the Sisters believed the children to be "utterly ignorant of their religious duties, knowing little beyond the existence of God, and yet with a strange love for our Blessed Lady, St. Joseph and St. Anthony. . . . The men, with very few exceptions, have no faith."[14] Realizing that fluency in Spanish and Italian would facilitate effective work in Ybor City, Father Tyrrell made special efforts to secure clerics with the necessary language skills.

When Father Tyrrell acquired the services of two Italian-speaking priests, Fr. Archille Vasta (1896) and Fr. John A. DiPietro (1903), he believed real progress was possible. However, a lengthy letter from Father DiPietro to Bhp. William J. Kenny of St. Augustine in 1905 describes how little had been accomplished. After decrying the "slanders against the Catholic clergy and the Catholic Church" circulating in Ybor City, the priest continued: "Your Lordship might imagine that the Italians would resent such insults uttered against the religion of their fathers, but on the contrary they are only too glad to take hold of any argument that might possibly defend the neglect of religious matters in which they have fallen. The majority of them—I regret to state it, but it is the truth—are rank infidels. I could not bring myself to this conviction but after proofs that cannot be gainsaid. Just imagine, your Lordship! Every week about 70 copies of the most infidel, anarchical and lascivious paper published in Italy, are distributed among them. The name of the paper is 'L'Asino' [The Donkey] and is forwarded to them from Rome."[15]

Not much had changed by 1911. In a plaintive letter to the bishop, Father Tyrrell asked, "Can anything be done to save so many of the Cuban and Sicilian and Italian population[s] of this place, who are so indifferent about all religious practices? There have been devoted, good, and zealous priests and Sisters working here for years and yet it is hard to see the fruit of their labors." While clerics in other parts of the country agonized over whether to build national or territorial parishes, Father Tyrrell confronted the embarrassment of no parish at all. Yet the possibilities for success still tantalized him. "There are about 46 blocks here inhabited almost exclusively by Sicilians (not many Italians) counting 12 houses to a block and some blocks have 16 and 18 houses and allowing 10 people to each house (some of the houses have more than 20) we would have 4,520 souls. In the other sections the Cubans and Spaniards are more numerous, so we might say that there are about 10,000 souls here that should be faithful members of the true fold. And [they] have been baptized Catholics (the Census gives more)."[16]

The yearly parish reports demonstrate how few of these "10,000 souls" responded to the church's message. Father Tyrrell's summation for 1912, as a representative example, shows a meager 160 persons made their Easter duty; only nine marriages and eleven burials were recorded that year, and no confirmations at all appeared on the register.[17] Notaries, justices of the peace, and officials at the courthouse, not priests, were the individuals who charted Ybor City's Italians through life's rites of passage.[18] Financially the parish suffered repeated embarrassments in its attempts to be self-sufficient. In 1907 donations totaled only $489.67, a sum that missed covering necessary expenses by $454.58.[19] The fact that at the same time immigrants were building multistory marble and granite clubhouses costing tens of thousands of dollars was not lost on the clergy. Our Lady of Mercy's simple frame structure reflected as eloquently as any statistic the relative unimportance of the church in this community.

Father Tyrrell lived and worked among the people he described. His reports reveal a sure sense of the community's social fabric, as demonstrated in his careful use of the terms "Sicilian" and "Italian" to delineate the distinctive identities present in Ybor City and in his firsthand estimations of household numbers and sizes. His experience proved, however, that close contact and long-term personal service did not guarantee success.

By 1920 it was clear that almost nothing had changed, as Father Tyrrell lamented in a letter to the bishop. "As this mission has no defined limits," he bluntly explained, "and has a moving population of Cubans, Spaniards, Italians and Sicilians who never come to Church (not 3 percent of them) most of them have no respect for religion or priest, and many will not have their children baptized and many are married outside the Church, it is very hard to say how many are Catholic."[20] Sister Mary Norberta, ninety-eight years old and living at the St. Joseph's retirement convent in St. Augustine, reminisced in 1982 about her work among the Latins in early Ybor City. She remembered years spent ministering to the children of the community in a small parish school. With her coworker,

Sister Mary Edith Mallard, she recalled nothing of the tumultuous labor strikes that convulsed Ybor City or of the hurly-burly of Seventh Avenue in its heyday. Living a cloistered life by and large had shielded them from these realities. What they did remember with poignant clarity about their service in Ybor City was the fact that "the parents did not practice their religion. They were lax, very careless about their religion."[21]

As a new generation of Italians came of age during the 1920s, hope stirred that perhaps the futility of past efforts could be reversed. The bishop authorized the creation of an Italian parish (commonplace in other urban centers) and appointed an Italian-speaking pastor, Fr. Vincente M. Dente, to lead its fortunes.[22] Even before work began on an Italian church, however, the entire project nearly collapsed as a result of a vicious quarrel among the Bishop of St. Augustine, a handful of Italian Catholics in Ybor City, and the Bishop for Italian Emigrants in Rome. The immediate cause of the furor involved Father Dente's purchase of property for the proposed Italian church and day nursery. Driven by his zeal in working for Ybor City's Italians and, according to one supporter, his "despair of the situation" in the city, he acquired the land in his own name in order to expedite matters. His immediate superior in Tampa, Fr. S. Farrell, S.J., contacted Arch. Michael J. Curley of St. Augustine to demand that Father Dente be removed for violating his vow of poverty.[23]

Father Dente's supporters in Tampa wrote to Bhp. Michele Cerrati in Rome, beseeching his office to uphold the priest and intercede for his retention. They enclosed reports and newspaper clippings documenting the extensive work being done by Protestants among Italians in the city, claiming that the Catholics in the community desperately needed an Italian pastor and parish. Several especially bitter letters deplored the Irish influence in the Catholic church in Florida, claiming that much of the opposition to Father Dente stemmed from prejudicial attitudes against Italians. Some, in fact, believed that the entire affair was an attempt by the Irish hierarchy to discredit and destroy work among Italians so that church resources could be used elsewhere.[24]

After extensive correspondence the principals resolved their outward differences, although lingering bitterness remained on every side. Bishop Curley donated a sum of money toward the new parish, citing, as he had done earlier, the critical need for such an agency in light of "the constant activities of proselytizing agencies." Father Dente renewed his efforts to find the necessary funds to complete the church building project.[25]

The new parish, Most Holy Name, celebrated its first mass on Christmas Day 1922, perhaps hoping that the selection of Jesus' birthday would provide extra blessings. Ironically, the church stood within sight of its two great rivals, the Labor Temple and the Italian Club. To the consternation of its benefactors and the expectations of its critics, Most Holy Name never attracted more than a few hundred Italians and languished in persistent financial difficulty. A 1934 survey estimated that of 437 members on the parish rolls, only 115 were active, almost all of them women.[26]

For institutional and psychological support Italians looked to their mutual aid clubs, described by more than one immigrant as "working class cathedrals," and to their unions. The census of 1930 dramatically documents the contrast between club and religious participation (see Table 8). Membership figures for clubs covered the principal mutual aid societies in Ybor City and West Tampa and therefore almost certainly referred only to men. Except for Spaniards, who manifested high single-male ratios, many of these men headed households. Since families actively participated in club life, the figures alone do not accurately reflect club influence in the community. On the other hand, church attendance figures leaned heavily toward women, who were generally less successful in integrating the church into the wider dimensions of family life. Sundays, for families, usually centered around club excursions and programs, not church services.

Not only did clubs attract a far greater percentage of Latins than the Catholic church, but the societies allowed religion to play almost no role in their activities. Catholic priests may have blessed club cemeteries, but the organizations never required their members to practice any religion at all, or deceased members to have received the last rites, in order to be buried there. "The number that die without complying with the last religious rites is large," one observer found. "They are buried anyway,

TABLE 8 Club and Catholic Church Participation by Ethnic Population, 1930

Ethnic group	Population in Tampa	Club members	Percent	Church attendance	Percent
Cubans	12,372	4,596	37.1	100	0.8
Italians	8,477	2,500	29.5	400	4.7
Spaniards	8,386	4,606	54.9	1,000	11.9

SOURCE: Adapted from FWP, "Ybor City Sociological Study," 293, and based upon *Fifteenth Census*, 34–35. Tampa population figures include both first- and second-generation individuals.

without any censure." The rights of members to burial space overrode any religious requirements.[27]

The men defiantly resisted church appeals and continued old-world practices that rarely saw them set foot in churches. Some bitterly remembered well-fed priests amid the starving peasantry in Sicily. The Sicilian proverb *"Senza quattrini non se ne cantano messe"* (Without cash they don't sing the masses) caught the prevailing bitterness toward priests. Philip Spoto recalled the men of his father's immigrant generation: "They just didn't like those monks they had over there, and some of them used to abuse their authority, let's face it. They used to probably get the fat of the land, eat the best crops, and this and the other." Other immigrants simply accommodated to local mores. One churchgoer revealed the cost of not doing so: "When I was attending the Catholic Church, and practicing the Catholic religion, at the Club and other places where the religious insignia was seen on me, I was subjected to all sorts of ridicule because of my belief in the Catholic Church." Of those who were practicing Catholics in Ybor City, nearly all were women. Indeed, in the opinion of some Ybor City males, the church occupied a similar place for women as the clubs did for men. "You could practically count the men who went to church," claimed Mary Italiano, holding up one hand.[28]

In one respect, however, Italians continued to look to religion as mothers dutifully took their children to the church to be baptized (although the percentage of baptisms edged downward over time—see Table 9). The total number of baptisms during the period 1891–1934 (13,671) appears remarkably high given the trends already described, yet this figure must be placed in a broader context. When measured against data covering church and club participation (see Table 8) and the incidence of church and nonchurch marriages (see Table 10), the pattern becomes obvious.

Clearly, Latins showed a decided preference for civil marriages over church ceremonies. Throughout the period under review, Cubans and Spaniards consistently, and by a wide margin, selected justices of the peace, notaries, and county judges over Catholic priests or Protestant ministers. Italians manifested slightly different patterns during the earliest years of settlement, as they turned almost exclusively to the Catholic church for marriage; for example, 90 percent of Italian marriages in 1895 and 80 percent in 1900 took place in the church. Thereafter, Italians shifted to patterns paralleling their Latin neighbors: by 1915 only one of sixty-seven Italian marriages was performed by the Catholic

TABLE 9 Baptisms by Immigrant Population, Tampa, 1891–1934

Year	Cubans	Spaniards	Italians	Total
1891[a]	12 (0.9%)	10 (4.3%)	5 (8.9%)	27
1892	33	10	16	59
1893	31	19	23	73
1894	37	15	45	97
1895	59	27	26	112
1896	110	35	89	234
1897	118	43	51	212
1898	153	44	86	283
1899	96	64	75	235
1900	98 (2.7%)	81 (8.4%)	117 (8.8%)	296
1901	72	56	95	223
1902	108	92	162	362
1903	75	104	137	316
1904	112	117	135	364
1905	99	110	121	330
1906	107	164	186	457
1907	83	124	199	406
1908	82	110	218	410
1909	126	186	368	680
1910	103 (2.6%)	122 (5.2%)	209 (8.2%)	434
1911	100	118	157	375
1912	96	149	137	382
1913	118	121	121	360
1914	96	136	164	396
1915	81	128	121	350
1916	88	162	116	366
1917	117	152	90	359
1918	70	116	76	262
1919	127	142	75	344
1920	75 (2.1%)	84 (3.0%)	79 (2.8%)	238
1921	65	98	81	244
1922	102	128	88	318
1923	111	119	122	352
1924	113	106	103	322
1925	162	165	174	501
1926	160	158	169	487
1927	148	140	123	411
1928	107	131	135	373
1929	127	104	104	335
1930	87 (1.7%)	82 (2.3%)	113 (3.4%)	282
1931	72	86	91	249
1932	89	61	92	242
1933	73	105	143	321
1934	82	73	57	212
Total	4,180	4,397	4,994	13,671

SOURCE: Adapted from FWP, "Study of Churches," 280. Percentages relate the numbers of baptisms to the foreign-born population as a whole and supply evidence of change over time.

[a]Total foreign-born population figures for this entry are from the 1890 census.

TABLE 10 Status of Latin Marriages by Ethnicity, 1890–1935

Year	Endogamous Latin marriages		Percent Catholic	Percent Protestant	Percent civil
1890	Italian	0	0	0	0
	Hispanic	16	31.2	25.0	43.8
	TOTAL	16			
1895	Italian	10	90.0	0	10.0
	Hispanic	62	16.3	46.7	37.0
	TOTAL	72			
1900	Italian	25	80.0	0	20.0
	Hispanic	79	8.9	31.6	59.5
	TOTAL	104			
1905	Italian	59	28.9	10.1	60.1
	Hispanic	176	6.2	8.0	85.8
	TOTAL	235			
1910	Italian	67	20.9	1.5	77.6
	Hispanic	139	1.4	7.9	90.7
	TOTAL	206			
1915	Italian	67	1.5	1.5	97.0
	Hispanic	175	11.4	17.8	70.8
	TOTAL	242			
1920	Italian	35	0	0	100.0
	Hispanic	175	4.0	2.8	93.2
	TOTAL	210			
1925	Italian	102	2.9	0	97.1
	Hispanic	197	2.5	5.0	92.5
	TOTAL	299			
1930	Italian	51	15.6	5.8	78.6
	Hispanic	208	2.9	3.4	93.7
	TOTAL	259			
1935	Italian	64	50.0	6.2	43.8
	Hispanic	204	0	5.8	94.2
	TOTAL	268			

SOURCE: Marriage records, Hillsborough County, 1890–1935. Records include all persons in Ybor City, West Tampa, and Tampa proper. The term "Hispanic" refers to Cubans and Spaniards. The county has preserved the actual marriage licenses, listing marriage date, names of partners, their sponsors, and the conducting official, but these records defy interpretation by surname analysis; hence the use of "Hispanic."

church; in 1920 not a single Italian marriage received the church's blessing. This alteration reflected the growing immersion of Italians in the radical subculture of Ybor City and in the cigar industry, where leftist views enjoyed the widest popularity. That is, in their religious attitudes Italians more and more came to resemble their Latin coresidents. For Italians the pattern remained consistent until 1930, when the number of church marriages began to climb, from 15.6 percent in that year to 50 percent in 1935, suggesting a return to the church by third-generation ethnics and a decline of the Italian presence in the cigar factories. Cuban and Spaniards retained their strong prejudice against Catholic marriages until 1935.

The importance of baptisms in cementing Italians to a lifelong, or even short-term, commitment to the church appears to have been minimal. Except for a few individuals, adult immigrants—and their grown offspring—did not actively join congregations or use churches in their later lives. A willingness to baptize children may have had as much to do with the Old World as with the new. Near universal infant baptism, followed by adult indifference to formal church participation, characterized southern Italy and Sicily. In the early years Ybor City baptisms may have reflected the in-between mentality of individuals engaged in the process of migration. For those contemplating a return, baptisms in the New World assured a smooth reentry into the old-world village. Yellowing baptismal documents sent by sojourners and tucked into the parish records of Sicilian churches attest to these links. But whereas the Roman Catholic church exerted a profound socializing role in Sicilian villages, few immigrants looked to priests or parishes for support once they became acclimated to Ybor City's social world. And once begun these practices tended to carry over even to those who chose to remain, persisting into subsequent generations. The importance of the church's childhood rituals in Ybor City was captured in the comment of one resident who explained, "Although we went to the convent and we take communion and all that kind of monkey business, but after we grow up and in the factory especially, [we] didn't believe in that monkey business."[29]

In a 1935 letter to the Apostolic Delegate to America, an exasperated Bhp. Patrick Barry of St. Augustine assessed the work of the Tampa church. Responding to questions concerning the condition of Italians in this location he explained:

There are members who should belong to the Church of many nationalities in Tampa, who never attend services, never receive the Sacraments and whose lack of interest and support of church and school may be attributed to their membership in secret societies condemned by the Church.

Some of the more prosperous Italians in Tampa belong to condemned societies and they are never seen in our churches nor do they send their children to the Catholic schools. The poorer classes, who look up to these leaders amongst them, copy their example and follow them in absence from church and sacraments. This indifference to the desires of the church in their regard is not peculiar to the Italians alone. The Spaniards, Cubans, and other nationalities are equally at fault in this report, and no amount of zeal and effort on the part of Jesuits, Salesians and Redemptorists has been able to convert them to the practices of religion. For fifty years and more, zealous, unselfish priests and sisters have exhausted themselves in trying to save these people, and their reward must be sought in heaven for they receive no earthly one.[30]

Although the essential details of Bishop Barry's comments ring true, he failed to see the more subtle religious manifestations at work in Ybor City. The fact that the great majority of Ybor City's Italians broke with the Catholic church cannot be denied. Yet old religious practices survived in the community, although altered to fit the local context. An elderly cigarmaker, Angelina Comescone, clarified her personal view of the situation: "Frankly, in Ybor City there was no religion, maybe little old ladies or little old men, but nothing like today. The church wasn't strong because they [the immigrants] didn't have the time and they were going through so much. Everyone was poor, working hard. We were never church people, but I pray more than people who go to church. Others dress up pretty and sit in church—heavens knows what they are thinking! We were always believers in our own way."[31] Angelina Comescone's "own way" and that of her Italian neighbors were the end products of a process of selection and choice that accompanied the transfer of their religion from Sicily to Tampa.

Sicilian villages possessed a broad range of possible responses to the church, ranging from vigorous anticlerical hostility to scrupulous devotion. Immigrants therefore arrived in the New World already familiar with many different models of adjustment to religious institutions. Most of them made a rather clear distinction between religion and the church, and attitudes propelling individuals away from the church gained ascendancy in this immigrant community. For those who arrived already imbued with anticlerical beliefs, no encouragement was necessary. What changed for them was the fact that now their viewpoints enjoyed a level of acceptance that outdistanced anything in their old-world villages.

The elements of Catholicism surviving in Ybor City came from the folk religion of feast days and peasant traditions. Ybor City immigrants and their progeny stripped these practices away from church buildings and appointed ministers of God, secularizing them and placing them in the home and the neighborhood. Thus altars, statues, and candles graced the homes of many Italians, as women continued to make their "promises" and devotions to various saints. Anticlericalism did not translate into atheism. Public celebrations became social rituals virtually devoid of purely formal religious meaning, reflecting instead the popular piety and the internalized religious attitudes of the Italians. As one observer noted of the festivals, "It is very rare that there is a discussion on religious beliefs. The main reason . . . lies in a phrase now frequently used: 'God is very discredited.'"[32]

The feast of St. Joseph survived the voyage to Tampa, though not without alteration. Celebrated on March 19, St. Joseph's Day is the only religious function that can trace its history back to the earliest years of settlement. In large part the longevity and popularity of this feast day are functions of its important role in tying together the various Sicilian elements of the Ybor City community. "March 19th is a date that everybody knows," explained Angie Terrano. "It's just like Christmas. Everybody knows Christmas and everybody knows March 19th."[33] In Sicilian villages this was (and is) the day when sojourners returned home from scattered workplaces. Villagers in Santo Stefano, for example, began the day with mass at the central church, followed by a solemn procession during which communicants carried a statue of St. Joseph down the main thoroughfare. The statue came to rest in a community hall, encircled by tables laden with food and wine. A great feast honoring not only the saint but also the returned men of the village climaxed the day's events.[34]

In Tampa the celebration centered around food and community participation, guaranteeing its popularity. Italian women prepared foodstuffs from ingredients they begged from neighbors and friends, as nothing was to be purchased for this day honoring the patron of the poor. A specially cooked wheat accompanied the feast, along with *cardune,* a fibrous vegetable. Italians erected altars in their homes, surrounding them with tables filled with food, and then opened their homes to visitors. Friends, neighbors, and relatives circulated throughout the community, stopping for brief stays and sampling liberally from the prepared dishes. The celebration therefore served a social as well as a religious function in confirming the existence of a community identity and integrating its particulars. Significantly, in its new-world setting the Festa di San Giuseppe had lost its clerical but not its spiritual dimension.[35]

A much later addition to the religious festivals of Tampa reveals how the needs of the community had changed over time. On the surface the feast of La Madonna della Rocca (Our Lady of the Rock) has all the earmarks of a Sicilian *festa* transferred intact to Tampa by devoted Catholics.[36] Oral history confirms another interpretation. Domenico Giunta explained how the celebration came into existence: "In the early 1930s, an Italian grocer, a Mr. Benedetto, a religious man, went to Italy and brought back a likeness of La Madonna della Rocca. He gave the statue, which was about three feet tall, to the church and every year after that, people celebrated the anniversary." Taking place on the last Sunday in August, the *festa* featured a band concert in front of Most Holy Name Church, a display of fireworks, a procession with the statue at its head, and liberal supplies of sandwiches and cold drinks.[37] By the 1930s, however, the closely knit, cohesive community of thirty years earlier no longer existed. Italians were moving to the suburbs and to West Tampa, and the *festa* was more a nostalgic exercise for second- and third-generation ethnics seeking reattachment to the old community and its perceived customs. The fact that the feast of La Madonna della Rocca was not a traditional church celebration from the past bothered no one, since historical accuracy was beside the point.

The Protestant Crusade

Various Protestant denominations surveyed the wreckage of Catholic attempts to turn the hostile attitudes of Latins into true devotion and envisioned unmatched opportunities for gaining new converts. As a result, Baptists, Congregationalists, Presbyterians, Methodists, and Episcopalians directed a blizzard of proselytizing efforts toward this seemingly rich lode of lost souls. Protestant mission houses sprouted like nocturnal mushrooms in both Ybor City and West Tampa. Each attempted initially to convert Cubans; and then as the Italian presence increased, staff and mission facilities were added. To supplement religious conversion, all Protestant missions offered heavy doses of Americanization and indoctrination to their religious work, far outdoing their Catholic rivals in this respect.[38]

Just as Italians and Cubans had had very little exposure to Protestant evangelism, so too did the Protestant missionaries who labored in Tampa have minimal experience with Catholic immigrants. Despite a historic role in the settlement of Florida, the twentieth-century Catholic church ranked fifth in terms of membership in the state. Although small in number, the presence of Catholic foreigners worried southern Protestants. As both John Higham and Richard Hofstadter have noted, anti-Catholicism had long been a significant part of American nativism. Florida's 1916 gubernatorial campaign, which saw an obscure, itinerant Baptist preacher nicknamed the "Cracker Messiah," Sidney Catts, swept to power on a Catholic-baiting platform, confirmed the existence of anti-Catholicism in the Sunshine State.[39]

Tampa, which Catts carried in 1916, had already witnessed a flagrant example of anti-Catholicism when a large mob burned a Catholic schoolhouse in 1894. The church had shortly before purchased an old Methodist church building and, after renovation, converted the structure into a school for blacks, thereby challenging the city's emerging Jim Crow system. After destroying the building vigilantes warned, "In case another institution is operated in this vicinity, it too will meet the same or worse fate, and to persist . . . will certainly cause destruction of the Convent and your other churches."[40]

Recent scholarship has expanded our understanding of the motivations underlying Protestant mission work in general, identifying a complex of factors that went beyond a mere bigoted misunderstanding of Catholicism. Southern Protestantism manifested its own distinctive style. As John P. McDowell has pointed out, southern Protestants distrusted the ability of Catholics to conform to American ideas and values. In their minds the church's panoply of priests, bishops, and pope represented the antithesis of freedom and democracy and endangered American republican virtues. The South thereby stood in jeopardy of losing its moral will and of witnessing the destruction of its most cherished institutions.[41] In 1919 Tampa Bay Baptists preached that America remained threatened by "un-American" elements and evangelism was necessary for rescue. Embracing the two causes of Christianization and Americanization, southern Protestants set out to save immigrant souls and maintain the American way of life.[42]

In attempting to reach these goals the diverse Protestant missions adopted very similar strategies, typically revolving around the building of a mission center, the acquisition of staff members who could work with a polyglot population, the use of education as a missionary device, and, to a limited extent, the pursuit of charitable work among the immigrants. Funds to support these endeavors normally came from the home mission boards of the various Protestant denominations—at the state and/or national level—although some local contributions were in evidence. Catholic pastors frequently pointed to the sizable financial resources available to Protestant missions as they bemoaned their own impoverishment.[43]

Congregationalists were the first to enter the field of Protestant mission work in Ybor City. Sponsored by the American Home Mission Society, a chapel and Sunday school opened in 1893, and by the end of that first year missionaries claimed that some 210 Latins had attended their services (Sunday schools were the biggest attractions). Although the mission was generously funded the early success did not last.[44] Attendance figures dipped, and in September 1898, when a yellow fever outbreak in Cuba diverted a Red Cross ship laden with food and provisions to Tampa, a local civic committee decided to use the churches as distribution agencies for supplies. Linking church membership with free handouts, Latins began attending mission services in droves. The missions' own records relate what happened when the largess ran out: "During this period of loaves and fishes . . . the church increased with wonderful rapidity. No less than 87 were added, of whom 80 joined in profession of faith. The total membership, as reported in the Yearbook of 1899, was 103. Upon the giving out of the supplies almost the entire membership immediately vanished."[45] The Ybor City mission struggled on, increasingly troubled in the areas of staffing and finance. By 1904 its "Cuban School," which met intermittently, counted only twenty-three students, all of whom were Italian. One observer described the mission as a "dirty and unkept building inside and out." Later in the year the home mission board closed the mission amid a swirl of accusations involving fraudulent use of funds and mismanagement.[46]

Episcopalian missions enjoyed no greater longevity. Arriving in Ybor City in 1894, the Episcopalians added a center in West Tampa within a year and counted nearly 100 churchgoers on their rolls. The early successes were almost all attributable to the efforts of an energetic Cuban minister, Rev. Juan Baez. When he died, no one of equal capabilities was found to run the mission.[47] Church officials reported empty pews in Ybor City after 1897 and diminishing attendance in West Tampa. The Ybor City mission soon collapsed, and the West Tampa center survived only as a struggling congregation of Afro-Cubans.[48]

Baptist mission work also produced depressingly few gains. The

Home Mission Society began the Fort Clarke mission in 1902 after several earlier initiatives had failed completely. This mission center, with its small congregation, survived into the 1930s. As with other Protestant missions, generous outside funding proved necessary to provide essential services. Baptists directed part of their evangelizing efforts toward Italians, opening an Italian Baptist mission in Ybor City that was blessed with an Italian minister, a church building, and a school. Later they added a West Tampa mission, which attempted to open a day nursery for women working in the cigar factories. These programs were peripheral to the Baptists' main effort, however, which centered on the Cubans.[49]

Presbyterians started late, and their programs, even by the standards of Ybor City, paled. The Ybor City Presbyterian church began in 1908, offering services in three languages. As with other Protestant denominations, this church received generous assistance from outside the community. In 1910 Rev. P. H. Hensley, Jr., described the problems in Ybor City to the Presbyterian home mission committee: "Of the alien races that invade our shores, none affect the varied life of our Anglo-Saxon people more widely than those of Latin extraction." He spelled out the dangers that might be expected: "They spend lavishly of time, thought and money to gratify their love for pleasure, as their club life and numerous festive occasions abundantly testify. This greed for pleasure, coupled with American ingenuity in providing it, form a combination that is too often mutually seductive and demoralizing."[50] What worried the cleric and his co-workers more deeply was the influence Latins wielded on the religious and moral values of the city. "On Sundays are held their public picnics, processions, theatrical performances and moving picture entertainments, and the day of rest is regarded simply as a day of pleasure and leisure. Gambling is practiced in all its varied forms and in spite of law is widely prevalent." Reverend Hensley did recognize positive qualities in Latin immigrants and urged that work with them be continued, but the Presbyterian mission gathered only a small handful of converts to its doors. By the 1930s the mission counted a total congregation of forty.[51]

Of the five Protestant denominations active in Ybor City, the Methodist Episcopal Church, South (MECS), committed the greatest resources to mission efforts and made the most durable impression. In fact, throughout the South the organized home mission movement among MECS women produced a wide-ranging, vigorous campaign for social reform in the period 1886–1939. During more than fifty years of work these women saw themselves as "serving humanity, building character, and saving souls."[52] There existed an abundance of opportunities to do so in Tampa.

Schools formed the core of the Methodist program in Ybor City and West Tampa. As early as 1892 the Wolff Mission School, located in the heart of Ybor City, accepted students for instruction. Well financed by home mission board donations and staffed by Cuban ministers, the school attracted substantial numbers of Cubans. Soon thereafter two energetic women opened another school in West Tampa, boasting a total enrollment of nearly 200 by 1902. The arrival in 1905 of the Roman missionary Evaristo Ghidoni augured a new era. The conference board of missions confidently reported, "A large and promising field for missionary enterprise has opened in the Italian colony in Tampa." Ghidoni quickly erected a day school, which soon claimed an attendance of 100.[53]

Among adults the mission picture was considerably less bright. Perhaps because of more aggressive proselytizing, the Methodist mission attracted greater community hostility than other Protestant centers. Reports circulated among Italians that Ghidoni had been accused of adultery in Missouri and that he could not be trusted with women. No charge could be calculated to incur greater distrust among Italians. Ghidoni's public claim that in Italy the keeping of a "left-hand" wife was universally accepted produced the expected ribald humor and a blistering response from various Italian groups. When information surfaced that he was living out of wedlock with an Italian opera singer (who bore him two children), mission officials relieved him of his duties.[54]

As Methodist expectations continued to outstrip results, ministers groped for ways to explain their failure. One analysis generated hoots of derision. Since most of the older immigrants were cigarmakers, a Methodist source theorized, "it is said that in many cases the saturation of their bodies with nicotine has a decidedly adverse effect on their health and mentality. . . . that because of the nicotine 'in many cases we find it difficult to bring them to understand in fullest measure the meaning of Christianity.'" Although Methodists claimed the largest Protestant congregation in Ybor City, their membership rolls never totaled more than 400.[55]

In only one area did church programs, both Protestant and Catholic, find a willing, though only partial, acceptance in the Italian community. Despite the parables of Victor Hugo and the diatribes of anticlerics, Italians routinely sought out and utilized church-sponsored schools, day nurseries, and kindergartens. The denomination supporting the school appeared to have made little difference, since adults rarely, if ever, joined the congregation. They concluded, correctly as events worked out, that the family environment could erase whatever veneer of religious instruction and indoctrination children brought home with them. The determining factors were school location, flexible scheduling to allow for work and family responsibilities, and curriculum.[56]

The classrooms and nurseries of every church school included Italian children, who often elbowed out their Cuban and Spanish playmates by force of numbers. Domenico Giunta, who described his parents as devout Catholics, attended the Italian Methodist mission school along with his brothers and sisters. The attractive force for the Giunta family was a Mr. Rumore, who taught Italian at the school. By the time younger brother Frank Giunta arrived, the school had run out of money and closed, but older siblings had finished the program by then and taught the rest of the family to read and write Italian. Mr. Giunta recalled how elderly immigrants unable to grasp formal Italian asked him to read them Italian-language newspapers once a week.[57]

The attendance of children at church schools did not signal the willingness of adults to attend services or to participate in church programs. A consistent pattern of complaints to the contrary appears in the yearly reports of every denomination and attests to this fact, as did the testimony of the people involved. Just as Italians shrewdly used bits and pieces of scrap tobacco to learn cigarmaking skills, so too did they selectively utilize those aspects of religious institutions that would help them achieve their family goals.

Summary

The relationship between religion and ethnicity cannot be examined in a vacuum. The interactive immigrant world of Ybor City generated a response to organized religion that dovetailed with the diverse elements of the local community. It is at this level that one gains the clearest view of how religion affected the lives and mentalities of individuals.[58]

In the end churches in Ybor City were unable to assimilate or Americanize immigrants, the reasons being largely external to church policies. It is true that the ignorance shown by Irish clerics and Protestant proselytizers of the Latins' sociocultural backgrounds, and the political infighting within the Catholic church in Florida, influenced developments.

Indeed, these factors worked to make going to church a "foreign" experience in Ybor City. Yet in the last analysis the weakness of the Catholic church—and its Protestant rivals—in Ybor City was directly proportional to the strength of mutual aid societies, labor unions, and radical groups, and to the attendant ideological structure of these groups.

Neither Catholics nor Protestants succeeded in challenging the patterns of apathy and hostility toward organized religion existing in Ybor City. These attributes could be found in each of the principal ethnic groups, and as they circulated among them they gained added force from the process of sharing. Consequently, the ability of organized religion to structure immigrant life and lead newcomers toward Americanization and assimilation was frozen out by the immigrants themselves. Until well into the 1930s the evidence points to a continuance of folk-religious practices divorced from formal church connection, avoidance of church attendance by males, and a strong attachment to clubs that were opposed to church participation. Whatever minimal successes organized religion enjoyed occurred almost solely among immigrant women. The overwhelming number of immigrants and their second-generation offspring failed to respond to either evangelical or Catholic appeals for their loyalties.

NOTES

1. Gannon, *Cross in the Sand*, 9–14, contains the full story of Father Cáncer's efforts.
2. Mormino, *Immigrants on the Hill*, documents an Italian settlement in which the Catholic church was the central organizing institution for the community. For an examination of the church in the southern part of Florida see McNally, *Catholicism in South Florida*.
3. FWP, "Historical Records of the House and Church Society of Jesus," Book 1.
4. A Friend, *Jesuits in Florida*, 18; *Catholic Directory*, 91–103.
5. A Friend, *Jesuits in Florida*, 16–17.
6. Valdez, "Life History of Pedro Barrios," 5.
7. Quinn, "Nuns in Ybor City," 28–32.
8. FWP, "Church in Ybor City," 14–16; *L'Alba Sociale*, August 1, 1901. The June 15 issue of *L'Alba* reported that priests were worried that anarchists were planning to disrupt the *"festa del sacramento."*
9. For example, see also the anarchist newspaper *La Voce dello Schiavo*, January 26, 1901.
10. Carbonell is quoted in Steffy, "Cuban Immigrants," 19–20; *St. Petersburg Times*, August 10, 1991; *Tampa Tribune*, August 6, 1901.
11. Interview with Sister Mary Lourdes, September 13, 1982.
12. Interview with José Vega Díaz, May 3, 1980. During an interview with Arturo Camero, March 3, 1984, Mr. Camero said: "I remember my father telling me how evil the

Catholic Church in Spain was. . . . my parents never went to Church. A Justice of the Peace married them."

13. "Early History," in *Dedication Souvenir: Our Lady of Perpetual Help Church*, 6–10; "Sacred Heart Parish."

14. Sister Mary Alberta, "Study of the Schools," 19–20; D. Falconio to Rt. Rev. William J. Kenny, April 21, 1905, Archives, St. Augustine Diocese; Quinn, "Nuns in Ybor City," 28.

15. John A. DiPietro, S.J., to Rt. Rev. William J. Kenny, November 17, 1905, Archives, St. Augustine Diocese.

16. W. J. Tyrrell to Bishop Kenny, Annual Parish Report, *Notitiae*, 1911, Archives, St. Augustine Diocese.

17. W. J. Tyrrell to Bishop Curley, Annual Parish Report, *Notitiae*, 1912, Archives, St. Augustine Diocese.

18. The incidence of Italian notaries on city rolls increased steadily after the mid-1890s, as did the number of civil marriages performed by them. Available records and oral histories document no known case of an Ybor City Italian becoming a priest, nun, or minister during the period under review. Marriage records and notary lists for Hillsborough County for the period 1890–1935 were consulted.

19. John Navin, S.J., to Bishop Kenny, Annual Parish Report, *Notitiae*, 1907, Archives, St. Augustine Diocese.

20. W. J. Tyrrell to Bishop Kenny, appended to *Financial Statement*, January 1, 1920, Archives, St. Augustine Diocese.

21. Interview with Sister Mary Norberta, September 13, 1982; interview with Sister Mary Edith Mallard, September 13, 1982.

22. "A Final Mass for Old Church," *Tampa Tribune*, June 14, 1975; FWP, "Study of the Church," 253. Tomasi, *Piety and Power*, discusses the creation of Italian parishes in metropolitan New York.

23. *Posizione 406*, Archivio del Prelato per l'Emigrazione Italiana, microfilm, CMS. This file contains nearly 100 items of correspondence and/or documentation concerning the affair. The authors wish to thank Drs. Silvano and Lydio Tomasi for bringing this material to our attention.

24. Ibid., letter dated May 15, 1922, signed by Teresa.

25. Ibid.

26. FWP, "Study of the Church," 25. See Robert Harney's insightful discussion of the relationships commonly existing between the church and its rivals in "Religion in Ethnocultural Communities," 1–10.

27. FWP, "Study of the Church," 261.

28. Interview with Mary Italiano, April 20, 1980; interview with Philip Spoto, June 30, 1979; FWP, "Study of Religion," 288. One Spanish immigrant well into his eighties spoke for many of his peers when he claimed, "I have never been in a church since I left Spain."

29. Interview with Eugenio Rodríguez, July 6, 1984; FWP, "Study of the Church," 288, 292.

30. Bhp. Patrick J. Barry to Amleto Giovanni Gicognani, August 25, 1935, Archives, St. Augustine Diocese.

31. Interview with Angelina Comescone, July 18, 1979.

32. FWP, "Study of the Church," 291. See Vecoli's perceptive "Cult and Occult," 25–47, for an extended discussion of Italian *feste* and their role in immigrant life.

33. *Tampa Tribune*, March 20, 1983.

34. By chance, the authors arrived in Santo Stefano for their first research visit on March 19, during the St. Joseph's celebration. Actual participation in the event and subsequent discussions with villagers confirmed the details.

35. Interview with Nelson Palermo, March 6, 1982; interview with Anthony Antinori, March 6, 1982.

36. FWP, "Study of the Church," 27–28. Oral tradition tells that devotion to La Madonna della Rocca stems from an incident involving a very devout blind girl in Alessandria della Rocca. One day while the girl was praying, Our Lady appeared and told the girl to go to a certain mountainside nearby and say that the Virgin wanted a church built there. The little girl was told that when she reached the correct spot her sight would be restored, which it was. The first thing that the girl saw was an image of the Virgin engraved in the rock.

37. Interview with Domenico Giunta, May 18, 1984.

38. Observations on the nature of Protestant mission work in Ybor City have benefited from the insights contained in two seminar papers prepared at UFG: Smith, "Americanization and Christianization," and Mulholland, "Missionary Work among the Immigrants."

39. Flynt, *Cracker Messiah*; Hofstadter, *Paranoid Style of American Politics*, 19–20; Higham, *Strangers in the Land*, 5–6, 77–87.

40. *Tampa Daily Times*, October 19, 1894; O'Neill, "Sisters of the Holy Name."

41. McDowell, *Social Gospel in the South*, 67–68.

42. Tampa Bay Baptist Association of Florida, Reports, 1912–53, microcopy, PKY; Davis, *Immigrants, Baptists, and the Protestant Mind*, 97–130.

43. American Home Mission Society, *Incoming Correspondence, Florida*, 1832–93, microfilm, PKY.

44. "The Congregational Home Mission Scandal in Florida," 1904, ms. copy, box 74, PKY.

45. Ibid., 3.

46. Ibid., 10, quoted in Smith, "Americanization and Christianization," 6.

47. *Journal*, Convocation of the Episcopalian Church Missionary, Jurisdiction of Southern Florida, 1894–1917, PKY.

48. Ibid.; Cushman, *Sound of Bells*, 23–24.

49. *Memorial*, First Baptist Church of Tampa; Tampa Bay Baptist Association, Reports, 1930; *Tampa City Directory*, 1920, 3, 35; ibid., 1928, 28; *Tampa Morning Tribune*, March 11, 1911.

50. Hensley, "Our Spanish Work in Tampa," 35.

51. Ibid.

52. McDowell, *Social Gospel in the South*, 70. Also see Brooks, *Saddlebags to Satellites*, 231–32.

53. McDowell, *Social Gospel in the South*, 12; *Tampa Morning Tribune*, February 2, 1895; *Minutes*, Methodist Episcopal Church, South, 32–33.

54. The entire Ghidoni scandal can be followed in *Tampa Morning Tribune*, July 5, 6, 11, 13, 18, 20, 1907. In the end the court awarded custody of the two children to the Italian opera singer, and Ghidoni went off with another woman to Nashville.

55. Clark, *Latin Immigrant in the South*, 23, 26–27, 52. As of 1924 Clark reported, "One of the greatest difficulties faced by the Home Department is that of securing workers for the Italian field." He described the establishment of a training program for Italian volunteers, financed at $3,000 for its initial year.

56. This estimate is based upon an examination of the reports from all church programs in Ybor City and West Tampa. The pattern is also consistent with Italian immi-

grant behavior elsewhere. See, Seller, "Protestant Evangelism and Italian Immigrant Woman," in Caroli et al., *Italian Immigrant Woman,* 124–25, for a discussion of this point.

57. Interview with Domenico Giunta, May 18, 1984; interview with Frank Giunta, July 20, 1980.

58. Serious scholarship dealing with church history suffers from a dearth of local studies in favor of those featuring a national or regional orientation. Several studies, however, have begun to shift attention to local congregations, parishes, and personalities in an effort to relate religion to ethnicity. See Luebke, "Church History," 68; Greene, "For God and Country," 460; Rischin, "The New American Catholic History," 228.

8 Social Relations in a Latin Community

Ybor City was all one big family.

Angelina Comescone

"In the neighborhood," remembered Domenico Giunta of his childhood in Ybor City, "the word fear was never in our vocabulary. My mother went to work at 2:30 in the morning to start stripping. She had to leave in the dark, at times carrying two of us, with bottles of milk. No one ever bothered her, nor did we ever hear of someone being bothered." Giunta is not alone in his fond memories of the neighborhood and community. A wistful Angelina Comescone recalled, "If someone was sick, all the neighbors came with different remedies. . . . they were mixed, Spanish, Cuban, and Italians. In the evenings our parents would take us walking. We all loved one another. We would sing as loud as we could, Italian, Spanish and American songs. Other children would sing back at us while doing their housework. Nobody walks anymore. It was beautiful then. Nobody sings anymore."[1] While these statements might be dismissed as pure nostalgia, there is no doubt Ybor City's sense of community was deeply held and socially meaningful.

The crystallization of community identity resulted from simultaneous developments within and without the Ybor City environment. Housing and residential patterns, linguistic accommodations, migration strategies, and economic trends served as midwives to this birth. While such factors affected the contours of the interior community, the hostile climate awaiting immigrants outside of Ybor City turned Latins further inward to their mutually satisfying and dependent world. "As an American creation," observed Kathleen Neils Conzen, "ethnic culture could be nurtured only where a shared predicament and shared institutions supported the development of a community life."[2] Powerful Cuban, Spanish, and Italian cultures existed in Ybor City, but over time a distinctive Latin community evolved, supplying and nurturing dual identities among residents.

The Physical Dimension

Basic considerations of housing and shelter dominated Ybor City's early history. In a combination of enlightened self-interest and communal concern, Martínez Ybor and several other manufacturers reclaimed swampland, erected wooden sidewalks, and constructed an infrastructure for the new development. Realizing the profits to be reaped from real estate as well as the importance of domesticating a largely male work force, Martínez Ybor organized the Ybor City Land and Improvement Company in October 1886. Anticipating the needs of employees, he had already constructed over 200 cottages by July 1886.[3] Haya and others quickly followed his example.[4] These corporations built thousands of homes, leasing and selling them to workers.

The homes all bore the classic design of the shotgun style endlessly duplicated across working-class America. In Tampa the humidity, heat, and insects dictated that houses be built off the ground, supported by brick pillars. Florida pine furnished the inexpensive walls and floors, and carpenters topped off each house with cedar shingles. Later, they would autograph their products with gingerbread designs, but the early homes featured indistinguishable patterns and few luxuries other than a picket fence, window blinds, and an outside privy.[5]

Martínez Ybor and Haya soon demonstrated the profits that were to be amassed through real estate. By March 1889 the Ybor City Land and Improvement Company employed seven gangs of carpenters who were continuously at work. "The homes are invariably rented as soon as they are completed," noted the *Tampa Journal*. Bachelors paid $1.50 to $2.00 a week for a worker's cottage, though some preferred to stay at boardinghouses where, for a few dollars a week one could have a bed, three meals a day, and camaraderie. Lots in 1886 and 1887 sold for as little as $35, while homes cost $750, a very inexpensive investment considering that the average cigarmaker earned $673 a year in the early 1890s. Fernando Lemos and John Cacciatore remembered purchasing their first homes from Ybor's company for $750, at no interest and $5 a week.[6]

By clustering housing the cigar industry profoundly influenced the nature of social interactions taking place in Ybor City. The grouping of factories close by each other and the constellation of workers' homes about them resulted in a high degree of residential concentration (but relatively low density because of a virtual absence of multifamily units).[7] The generally low cost of housing and rentals, coupled with the frontierlike quality of surrounding areas, limited possibilities for wider dispersal. These factors tended to reduce opportunities for dense concentrations of kin or *paese* group settlement as housing choices in early years were limited by the few homes available. The mere grouping of houses did not in itself make for intergroup solidarity or contact as even close neighbors can be socially invisible. But as Cubans, Spaniards, and then Italians continued living next to each other, and as Spanish became the lingua franca, patterns of avoidance proved difficult to maintain. Individual and group contacts appear to have been frequent and fervent.[8]

The enclave's topography added its own flavor to the evolving immigrant community. The land was flat and few buildings stood more than one story in height, the major exceptions being factories and clubhouses. More significant than building heights was the closeness—people conversed with neighbors from window to window and family secrets had to be whispered lest everyone hear them. One resident revealed that a friend boiled and stirred hot water in the kitchen during hard times so that more affluent neighbors would think that stew was cooking. In pre-air-conditioning days doors and windows were left open; and Ybor City's streets were intersected by numerous alleys which people used as short cuts and byways. In this physical setting such social events as parades, picnics, and festivals almost invariably came to possess a broadly defined public dimension. Unlike residents of the canyons of New York's Lower East Side, few residents of Ybor City could avoid notice of their neighbors' public lives. As housing and shops filled the gaps between factories, a rich context for social interaction developed.[9]

Ybor City was constantly evolving. From its beginning a succession of immigrants, migrants, and exiles shifted between Cuba, Spain, Sicily, and Florida. City directories and census data clearly show that by the turn of the century thousands of individuals annually left and entered the enclave, scores of new enterprises opened and closed, and hundreds of residents changed houses within the city. There were differences between groups—Italians were always the most stable—but, considering such flux, Ybor City's ability to transmit and maintain a set of community symbols and images requires explanation.

The frequent shifting of people should not be seen as social disorder. There was order and continuity, and immigrant institutions provided the necessary cohesion. As immigrants moved from family to group to multi-ethnic focal points, they created an institutional network that fostered stability and coherence. This conglomeration of unions, mutual aid societies, newspapers, and radical groups stabilized the unsettled nature of Ybor City life and allowed immigrants to pass from smaller to larger social and organizational planes.

The nature of Ybor City vis-à-vis the prototypical immigrant ghetto bears examination. Immigrant neighborhoods across America provided shelter and social comity for millions of new arrivals. Recent scholarship has questioned whether such neighborhoods constituted the bedrock or the quicksand of immigrant concentration. Sam Bass Warner, Stephan Thernstrom, Howard Chudacoff, and David Ward challenge the conventional portrait of the ghetto as a protracted, concentrated pocket of homogeneous immigrants.[10] In reality, they argue, the ghetto served as a revolving door for groups of rapidly shifting first-generation immigrants. "The extent to which foreign-born immigrants typically huddled together in neighborhoods composed largely of their fellow countrymen has often been exaggerated, and even where there were highly segregated ethnic neighborhoods, there was little continuity of the individuals who composed them over time," concluded Thernstrom.[11]

The evolution of residential patterns over time provides evidence to test the ghetto thesis. Ybor City must be understood as a dynamic, ever-expanding enclave, pushing its boundaries outward from its inception in 1885 until the Second World War. Land was cheap and plentiful in the unincorporated areas, allowing individuals and groups relative freedom to choose residence. By 1900 Ybor City's boundaries were clearly defined: Nebraska Avenue to the west, Twenty-second Street to the east, Michigan Avenue [Columbus Drive] to the north, and Third Avenue to the south. Italians congregated in the less-developed eastern half of Ybor City, while Cubans and Spaniards generally resided in the western

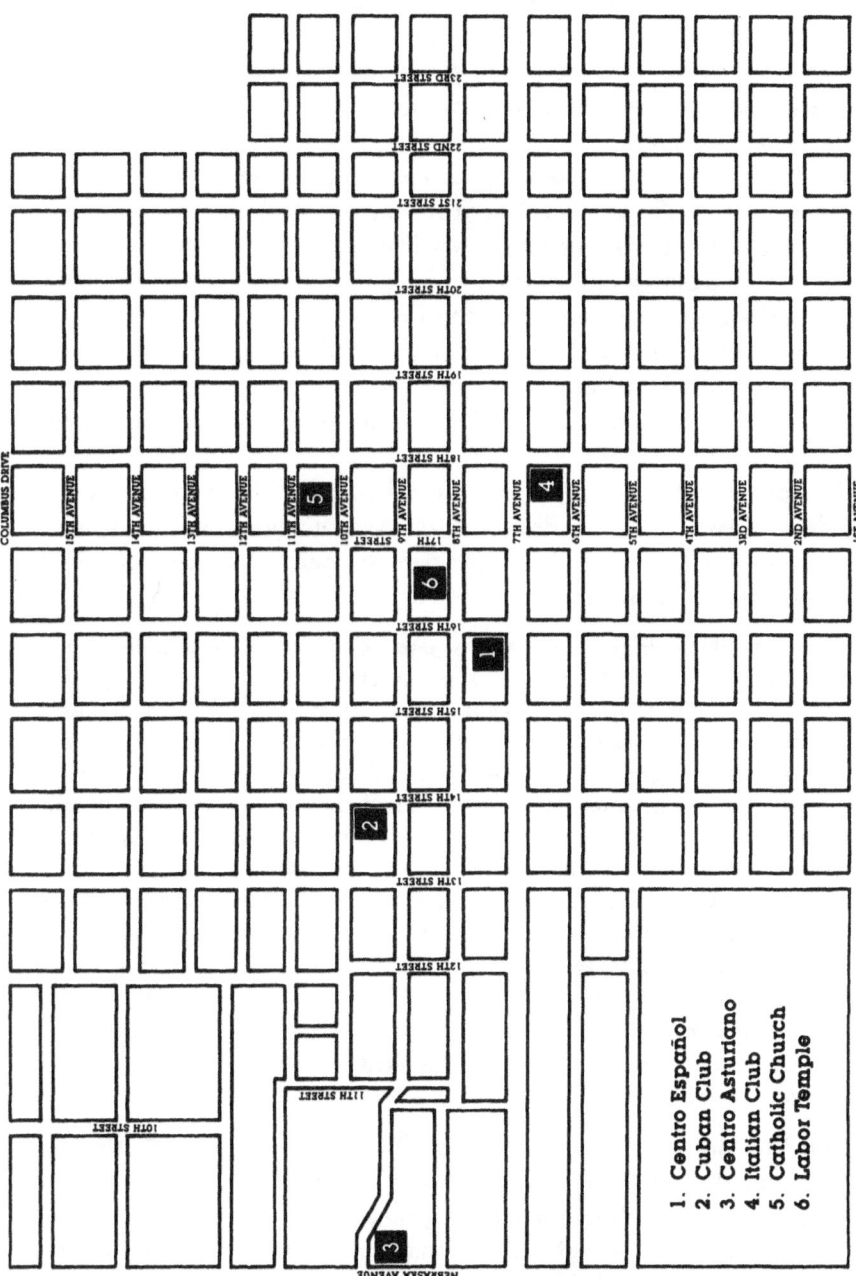

Map 3. Ybor City, 1920.

sections. In 1900 Italians typically clustered around a center already called "Little Italy," bordered by Nineteenth Street, Seventh Avenue, Seventeenth Street, and Ninth Avenue. At no time, however, did any ethnic group exclusively dominate any area, and rarely a single block. Remarkable for a city in the Deep South, Afro-Cubans resided in integrated neighborhoods.[12]

By 1920 Ybor City pressed its boundaries to the north and east. Nebraska Avenue buffered Afro-American settlements to the west, whereas McKay Bay halted expansion southward. Italians in particular expanded their colony, pushing eastward beyond Twenty-third Street. Rich farmlands and cheap dairy acreage to the east satisfied Italian land hunger while permitting them easy markets and ethnic attachments. Spaniards and Cubans followed this eastern drift, a phenomenon due in part to the tendency of Italians to acquire several small shotgun houses for rental purposes.

In spite of heterogeneity within neighborhoods, the mental maps of residents clearly regarded certain sections as ethnically marked. Alfonso López, born in Ybor City of Spanish parents, painted a vivid portrait of ethnocommunity boundaries.

Well, we got along alright. The Italians, most of the Italian neighborhoods ran from around 15th or 16th Street all the way up to 23rd Street, and between Eighth Avenue up, and all the way maybe to about 15th Street, in that area there, and then there was some that went on the other side in back of the Columbia restaurant over around Fifth Avenue and Sixth Avenue. . . . There was a little Italian village in through there. And then there was some on the other side of 22nd Street. . . . The Cuban people were from 16th over to I'd say around 12th [streets] and up in through there. And then the Spanish people, there was a few, there wasn't quite as many Spaniards in that area. There was some around in boardinghouses. In those days, they, guys used to come from Cuba to work in the cigar factories and they were single, so they all lived in boardinghouses around, around between I'd say 12th Avenue and I'd say between 16th and 18th and up in through there. . . . there was two or three factories, cigar factories in that area. But they were living, . . . a lot of them were living in boardinghouses at that time in that area.[13]

While Ybor City comprised pockets of Cubans, Spaniards, and Italians, the community contained an almost exclusively Latin population. Only a few hundred non-Latins, consisting primarily of Chinese (many from Cuba), Rumanian Jews (who spoke Spanish), and Afro-Americans (living on the fringe), resided in Ybor City. In the long run the character of immigrant relationships bears more significance than the composition of the community.

"I grew up in a neighborhood with Cubans, Italians, and Spanish," explained eighty-year-old Angelo García. "We used to have new families move into the neighborhood all the time. There was never any trouble."[14] Such contacts must be understood as part of a much larger process, however. One reason Cubans, Italians, and Spaniards began to think of themselves as Latins was because of the way Anglo Tampa reacted to them. "We Latins stuck together," remembered Domenico Giunta. "We had a common language, first of all. We called ourselves 'Latins.' Anglos called us that too, and sometimes a lot worse. . . . When fist fights broke out, you knew who your friends were."[15]

Anglo-Latin Relations

Throughout this period Latin and Anglo Tampa were separate, hostile worlds. "To grow up in Tampa during those days and having a Latin name was a tough undertaking," explained Cuban César Medina. "A Latin couldn't cross Twenty-second Street."[16] To ensure that social boundaries were absolutely clear, Anglos posted signs proclaiming "No Dogs or Latins Allowed" at various picnic and bathing spots. Many Latins today remember these with bitterness. Philip Spoto thundered, "They considered us worse than blacks. And a lot of places had signs 'No Dagoes'. . . . No, the Latins didn't battle too much against each other, but we did with the Anglo-Saxons." Joe Maniscalco shared similar feelings: "Many times we used to go to a dance . . . like at Sulphur Springs. They [Anglos] used to put signs there. They don't want no Latins. No Italians, no Spanish, no Cubans, nothing! But the Italian boys and the Cuban boys and Spanish boys used to go in there and fight."[17] Bruised sensibilities have yet to heal completely. "We were at the bottom of the list of persons allowed," remembered Honorato Domínguez, "and we built Tampa!"[18]

Anglo perceptions of the early Latin community crystallized around a number of enduring but not endearing images. Tampans generally saw Cuban, Spanish, and Italian workers as inherently good, albeit imbued with the "Latin race's proclivity toward excessive emotionalism, romantic violence and un-American values."[19] The great mass of working-class Latins, living in a foreign enclave within earshot of city hall, grated on the nerves of Tampa's native community in at least three critical ways: its mistrust of Catholicism, its concern over a racial imbalance of undesirable aliens, and its worries about foreign radicalism.[20] "The Indo-European group of humanity has a volcanic tendency that is well nigh universal," observed the *Tribune* in 1888.[21] "The Cubans and Spaniards are alike mercurial in temperament and quick to act," the paper declared four years later, "but they are not bad when no evil influences are working amongst them. . . . When subjected to the devilish influences of even one unprincipled socialist, communist or anarchist, they are transformed into little less than madmen."[22]

There were always elements within the Anglo community which perceived grave dangers in the social customs of Latins. The first moral firebell in the night rang just months after annexation in 1887, when temperance leaders threatened to impose their standards upon Ybor City. Prohibition seemed ludicrous to Cuban and Spanish immigrants who, Martínez Ybor explained, had enjoyed "light wines from childhood." Such a ban, he threatened, would result in a relocation of the cigar industry to "where people are not dictated to as how they are to dress and what they are to drink." Tampans narrowly defeated prohibition, reinforcing Macaulay's dictum that most citizens would rather be free than sober.[23]

Actual misuse of alcohol was not the issue; the crucial matter was social control. The decision to keep Tampa wet would not be the last morality crusade fought over regulation of Ybor City. For the next half century Anglos grappled with a tethered situation: the city's economic health depended almost solely upon Ybor City, whose Latin culture seemed to deviate from the host society's Anglo-Protestant-southern values. Latins imported such customs as *bolita* (numbers gambling), *riña de gallos* (cockfighting), and *omertà* (silence), and Anglo Tampa reacted sternly and disapprovingly. To them the Ybor City life-style was reminiscent of a Latin barrio, which of course it was. Explained financier Peter O. Knight in an 1897 interview with the *Morning Tribune*, "We [Tampans] have always had great difficulty to properly handle the foreign element that is in this city."[24]

Cubans in particular displeased many Tampans. For one thing they seemed to enjoy life far more than their economic resources dictated. In 1890 a number of Hyde Park residents complained of "Sunday circuses" and "Sunday amusements" being held in Cuban saloons and theaters, clearly a flaunting of the Sabbath. Editorialized the *Tribune*: "Even the most orthodox Christians of Tampa recognize the fact that the ideas and habits of the Cuban population in our midst are quite different from theirs. But at the same time, there is a limit to even these things, and on Sunday circuses the people of Tampa draw the line."[25] The very differences between the two communities evoked a hue and cry among natives. In 1896 the *Morning Tribune* called into question the morality of Ybor City's Cubans, who "seem to have very little decency in their composition. You can at any time of the day if you promenade along the streets of Ybor City or West Tampa see children from all ages one to seven years playing around in the garb which nature gave them with a little additional covering of dirt or cheesecloth, generally the former."[26] Cubans quickly became pariahs.

Italians generated their own brand of anxieties in native Tampa. The mafia specter appeared periodically, accompanied by lurid newspaper headlines and nativist charges. A shooting in 1899 (a jury later found Giuseppe Licata innocent of the deed) prompted the *Morning Tribune* to warn, "We want no Mafia in Tampa!"[27] Rare editorials in the early years of settlement branded Italians as "degraded laborers" and warned that they would undermine American wage levels. Yet these negative assessments were just as often balanced by positive rebuttals, and in general Anglo Tampa accepted Italians quite openly, at least during periods of prosperity.[28] The Spanish enjoyed favorable images in the eyes of native Tampa, only marred by the frequent involvement of Spanish cigarworkers in anarchist activities. These points of tension typically surfaced during periods of labor strife or national emergency, such as World War I.

No Anglo complaint engendered more spirited Latin responses than claims that Latins were not members of the "white race." Anglos seldom exercised great care in discriminating among the Ybor City population on this point. In the early years the English-language press occasionally referred to Italians as nonwhites, which never failed to draw protests from Italian residents.[29] If the native community infrequently made such charges about Italians, they rarely employed restraint with reference to Cubans. Natives may have been puzzled by color differences existing among Cubans, but they usually solved any dilemmas by simply referring to them as "niggers" or "Cuban niggers." "If the crackers really wanted to make us Latins mad," remembered Frank Urso, "they'd call us Cuban niggers."[30] Alfonso Noto captured the legacy of resentment left from these characterizations: "Let's face it, the Anglo-Saxons think that they're the only Americans. They're very prejudiced. Even today, they talk to us and they chew us, but they won't swallow us."[31]

During periods of crisis the gap separating Anglo and Latin Tampa became even wider. The vigilante practices so often resorted to by native Tampans dramatically reminded Latins of the composite identity they held in the eyes of the city's elites. Over time the most strongly held Anglo attitudes tended to oscillate in accordance with the fortunes of the cigar industry. But throughout, the prejudicial stereotypes held by natives, their propensity toward violence, and their reluctance to grant a full share of political and economic participation to immigrants tended to drive Latins together.[32] A community, observed Kenneth L. Kusmer, "does not only grow spontaneously from within; it can also be imposed from without."[33]

Intergroup Relations

To suggest that forces were at work causing Latins to draw together is not to imply that social relations within the Latin community were always harmonious. Ethnic division remained a significant fact of daily life. As Italians in greater numbers moved into the cigar industry starting in the late 1890s, for example, they increasingly clashed with Cubans. Indeed Italian movement into the cigar trades came primarily at the expense of Cubans. This competition was especially galling to Cubans in light of the assistance they had rendered to Italians in gaining their initial cigarmaking skills. Cuban cigarmaker Domingo Ginésta expressed the essence of this bitterness: "How are we paid today [1935] for the kindness we showed them [Italians] in those days? They consider us today a lower class. They practically control the politics and business in Tampa today."[34]

To charges of ingratitude Cubans added complaints based upon subjective views of group difference. They pointed to the country background of Italians and their propensity to keep rabbits, chickens, pigeons, and goats in their backyards. From the perspective of urbanized Cubans, Italians appeared to be hopeless bumpkins, *guarjiros* (peasants).[35] Italian parsimony, manifested by the raising of animals and the cultivating of small gardens, also struck Cubans as excessively rustic. They mocked Italians as "goats" for their propensity to eat vegetables and keep herd animals. Cubans claimed that Italians possessed the worst kind of miserliness, insisting that their obsessive hoarding actually retarded the development of Tampa. In the Cuban view, their own free-spending ways put money into the local economy, thereby stimulating consumer demand and business enterprise.[36]

Spaniards did not escape criticisms. The haughty, aloof, sometimes stubborn behavior of Spaniards contrasted sharply in Cuban eyes with their own outgoing manners. But Cuban conceptions of their contributions to Tampa did not rest solely on their spending habits or approachable personalities. Many believed that they possessed inherent—some even said "racial"—cigarmaking skills which made them the indispensable element in the fortunes of the cigar industry and of Tampa.[37]

Within the immigrant world of Ybor City, Cubans occupied the lowest rung of the social ladder. They were the least residentially stable of the groups and the most downwardly mobile during times of economic disruption. More important, both Italians and Spaniards derided Cubans for not sharing their values concerning hard work, thrift, responsibility, and seriousness of purpose. Perceptions of Cuban behavior crystallized around several themes. "The Cubans were fun-loving . . . ," banker Ray Grimaldi explained, ". . . a wild group, very happy. . . ."[38] "Cuban women had more freedom," added Domenico Giunta; "they dated without chaperones first."[39] Commenting on Cuban transiency and fickleness, Rosemary Craparo observed, "If they earned twenty dollars, they took a trip and spent it. They didn't believe in building a home."[40] Cubans were undesirable particularly in the eyes of Spanish factory owners and foremen, who branded them as lazy, fractious, and undependable. These Spaniards saw Cubans as the principal reasons for Tampa's turbulent strike history.

Spaniards initially perceived Italians as undesirable elements due largely to the New Orleans lynching incident. During the formative years of Ybor City, Italians appeared most often as street vendors, farmers, or common laborers, occupations that hardly created enviable images among Spanish elites. Italian accommodation to the Spanish language—a courtesy rarely reciprocated—engendered feelings that they had somehow compromised their pride and culture. However, as Italian enterprise resulted in more stable businesses and a heavier representation in the cigar industry, the mental boundaries within Ybor City shifted and Spaniards acquired more favorable impressions.[41]

From the Italian perspective Spaniards constituted one of the more attractive role models in Ybor City. To the extent that Spaniards shared similar work values, held high status, and enjoyed connections with the wider Anglo community, Italians endeavored to copy at least their successful approaches to Ybor City life. The Spanish model of mutual aid, ranging from the architectural designs of club buildings to social and medical benefits, received the sincerest form of flattery: imitation.

The interior history of Ybor City reveals ethnic variations. Italian sections of the city beheld distinctive sights and smells because of the proliferation of small garden plots, backyard animals, and outdoor brick ovens. "There were cows and goats at each [Italian] home in Ybor City," reminisced Joe Cacciatore, and "everyone made cheese, butter, and had their own ovens to make bread."[42] On baking day the family ovens, fashioned from brick, filled the areas surrounding Italian homes with delicious odors of freshly baked bread. The act of baking bread itself fulfilled social as well as physical needs. "Every Friday, that was the day to bake bread," remembered Mary Italiano. "So we'd all get together that day, then we'd bake bread . . . and we all ate together. Talk about a holiday! Well, my uncle and our Italian friends, well he had a table that would be from this end to over there and we'd eat there that day and the bread was really beautiful, oh, beautiful bread!"[43] For major family celebrations or important holidays the ovens cooked *capretto arosto* (roast goat) and a variety of Sicilian pastries.

Crops grown in family plots added further distinctiveness to Italian homes. Many of the foods raised came from Sicily, such as the *fico d'India* (prickly pear), *cardune* (thistle), *cuccuzza* (squash), and *escalore* (escarole). Family milk cows provided the ingredients for homemade ricotta and butter. "Easily forty percent of our diet was supplied by our garden," claimed Domenico Giunta.[44] The raising, processing, and cooking of these items assumed significance in outlining the ethnic identities of Italians, just as drinking cider and wearing the *boina* (beret) did for Spaniards, and planting guava and mango trees did for Cubans.

Formal socializing for Italians tended to take place at the Italian Club and picnic grounds, but familial patterns unfolded in Tampa much as they had in Sicilian villages. Relatives and *paesani* grouped for the Sunday meal. "We started with soup," recalled Mary Italiano, "then we had to have spaghetti, then we had to have meat, our salad, all kinds of dessert you can think about. Everybody brought something. . . . Sunday was a holiday."[45] The men played card games and drank wine, while the women knitted and discussed the events of the day.

Particular celebrations and holidays also worked to identify the limits of each group while often supplying the context for interaction. Perhaps nothing served to illustrate the emergence of a Latin culture more than the blending of social occasions. National holidays (such as Cuban Independence Day), religious observances (such as the feast of St. Joseph, for Italians), and secular celebrations (such as founder's day at El Centro Español) drew together huge numbers of people, cutting across immigrant and class lines yet still affording opportunities for ethnic particularism.

Old-world holidays tended to become panethnic festivals; witness the Fiesta de Noche Buena (literally the Good Night Festival). The celebration became an Ybor City tradition by the 1920s, one enjoyed by all groups. It consisted of a simple Christmas Eve family custom that had been broadened to include extended families, even neighborhoods. The centerpiece of the celebration was a roast pig, carefully marinated in a *mojo* sauce for days ahead of time and baked in a wrapping of palm fronds and guava leaves. Italians quickly adapted to Noche Buena, stylizing the affair to their own ethnic preferences, adding such touches as *cucidate* (fig cookies) to the holiday meal.[46]

The mutual sharing of ethnic customs often bred mutual regard. Manuel Alfonso, an Afro-Cuban born in Ybor City, elaborated on the meaning of respect. "We used to get along good," he reflected, remembering his youthful neighborhood. "When my grandmommy died [1923], she was buried on Noche Buena—Christmas eve—which in Cuban homes always had a big celebration. The only black family on that block was my family. And when she died, nobody celebrated Noche Buena on that block out of respect for her."[47]

As Ybor City matured Seventh Avenue (La Gran Séptima Avenida) evolved as the social magnet for Latins. Here one witnessed the boundaries between Ybor City's public and private cultures. The ritualized evening walk in the plaza of the Italian or Spanish village or the *paseo de Martí* of Havana transferred to Ybor City. For most families a promenade down Seventh Avenue became the crowning event of Saturday night. "*Everybody* would go to Seventh Avenue," remembered Angela Menéndez. "Oh, so many people going there."[48] A pattern of social behavior evolved that ultimately adopted something of a stylized format. "We would go down to Seventh Avenue," recalled Rosemary Craparo. "People were sitting in the streets, with chairs; as we went walking, everyone spoke and visited. People would join us. . . . on Seventh Avenue, everyone would be there, bumping on the streets."[49] Latins who experienced the lure of Seventh Avenue uniformly commented on the crush of people and the intensity of the social interaction. Nelson Palermo recalled "not being able to walk too fast because of so many people, you could hardly stand on the sidewalk." Similarly Nick Nuccio remarked, "You could not walk along the sidewalks. Promenaders would stop and talk with friends. It was very, very pleasant."[50]

Evening strollers were not the only ones to vie for space on Saturday nights. Carts and wagons of various vendors circulated the length of Seventh Avenue. The *chavateros*—always a Galician—invited housewives to bring their knives for sharpening; *mondongo* men sold cooked tripe and kidneys from their wagons; the *heladeros* sold fruit-flavored sherbets; and the *maniseros* found ready customers for their peanuts all along the thoroughfare.[51] For children the most avidly awaited arrival was that of the *pirulí* man. "He would have a white butcher apron," observed Sara Wohl Juster, "and he'd have a long stick, and on the stick, he would have the cone shaped lollipops made out of sugar and different colors for a penny apiece."[52] During the 1920s open-air movies made their appearance on the avenue as stores draped sheets over their second-story balconies and treated crowds to the latest films.

Young bachelors went to flirt—at a distance—and gaze at the local girls. Sara Wohl Juster remembered them standing at the corners, whispering in hushed tones as young ladies passed by, *"Que simpática!"* Ray Grimaldi outlined the importance of the walk from a young man's perspective: "We would walk down Seventh Avenue to 15th Street, across the street, cut back to 17th Street, cross and back, so we would get to see the girls constantly. . . . It happened all my life until the war broke out in 1941."[53] And always groups of men congregated in front of the mutual aid clubs to discuss philosophy and politics in the fresh air. Conversations halted when women, particularly attractive ones, walked by, to resume heatedly after they had passed.[54]

The vigorous street life of Ybor City played an important role in shaping community identity. By bringing individuals and families together in a myriad of public encounters, the interactions on Seventh Avenue assisted in supplying a collective sense to Ybor City's diverse elements. Tamara Hareven found the same processes at work in the street life of Manchester, New Hampshire, where "entertainment and leisure took on meaning as public and community events." In New Hampshire's great textile center "the continuity between public life and private life provided a sense of being part of a larger social context."[55] Unlike Manchester, however, organized sports in Ybor City became a significant vehicle for creating mutual ties and a community awareness.

Sport

In 1949 Ybor City's cigarmakers hired a translator to rebroadcast the World Series in Spanish from a radio feed.[56] The episode symbolized both the city's continuing interest in sport and its changing fashions. The *lector*, once a vital disseminator of news and values, had long been displaced, his position taken by the radio, just as the thriving cigar industry had been devastated by new technologies, altered tastes, and the Great Depression. Latin fascination with sport, however, was not a simple byproduct of the wireless; rather, athletics had always been an integral, though changing, feature of Ybor City.

Across America immigrant traditions of work and leisure split into separate spheres as newcomers confronted an urban-industrial environment. But for most Ybor City artisans who worked in the insulated cigar factories the work experience retained vestiges of preindustrial life. From the beginning Cubans considered the company baseball team and flexible work schedules to allow time for games to be rights, not privileges. They transferred their leisurely life-styles to Ybor City, which resulted in Italians and Spaniards acclimating to a new environment, one that included sport.

Among Cubans baseball quickly became a popular recreational pastime, easily adapted to the Florida climate. The sport first appeared in Ybor City in 1887, but Cubans had been playing the game for at least a quarter of a century before that. In 1878 Cuban promoters organized the world's second professional baseball league,[57] and by 1889 author Wenceslao Bálvez y Delmonte noted that the game threatened to replace cockfighting as the Cuban national sport.[58]

Not all immigrants saw baseball, or sport in general, as socially meaningful. Italians and most Spaniards who came directly from Spain wrestled with the issue of sons aspiring to the baseball diamond as opposed to the more immediate concerns of economic and familial primacy. Debate within various mutual aid societies revealed the generational tensions precipitated by the sport question. One observer recorded "hostility" from the older members of El Centro Asturiano who chided youths, telling them to pay for the hospital rather than spend money for a new gym. Yet the Asturians erected and supported a gymnasium, along with a billiard parlor and a bowling alley,[59] and athletic teams affiliated with the club won local league championships in the 1920s and 1930s. El Centro Español had turned down a 1905 proposal to build a gym, rebuking the younger members with the bromide, "Work hard all day and you'll need no exercise."[60] But it, too, ultimately succumbed to the lure of organized recreation.

Radicals were the most consistently antisport faction of the community. The anarchists especially saw in organized athletics a serious diversion from the proper goals of the working class. In their view sport served to defuse the energies of workers and to turn their attentions away from the crucial tasks of organization and agitation. Ultimately they believed sport depoliticized workers, making the working class more exploitable by capitalist owners. Anarchists saw company support of athletic teams as proof of their thesis.[61]

Baseball, popular only among Cubans in the 1880s, achieved community-wide acceptance by the 1920s. In part this was due to the influence of the cigar factories, which sponsored company teams. As the workplace came to include a full spectrum of ethnic peoples, so too did the ball teams. Moreover the *lector* always reserved part of his reading time for sporting news, initially at the insistence of Cuban workers but later because of widespread demand. The flexible schedules of cigarworkers also served to increase attendance at ball games and heighten interest. Baseball became a community focal point, as factory workers, club members, and the general citizenry watched and participated together. Alex Scaglione, born in Sicily at the turn of the century, quickly fell in love with America's game through his apprenticeship at the cigar bench. "In those days," he recalled, "the Italian Club, the Cuban Club, Centro Asturiano, Centro Español, they all used to have baseball clubs. You should have seen the crowds on Sundays. Oh Lord, have mercy. It was good I tell you, we enjoyed it."[62]

Conditions surrounding the earliest years of Italian entry into Ybor City mitigated against any role for athletics. Temporary migrants possessed neither the time nor the inclination to expend effort in formal recreational activities. They typically spent leisure time enjoying a glass of wine with friends, telling stories, and perhaps playing card games. However, more permanent settlement brought opportunities for participation in more organized forms of recreation. On an institutional level Italians appear to have supported the principle of such activities from a very early date—most likely in imitation of other Latin mutual aid club programs. Italian Club picnics, for example, featured athletic events such as long-distance races and boxing matches since the early 1900s. The first clubhouse, erected in 1914, contained a gymnasium with a bowling alley and billiard room.

The existence of such facilities must be viewed in the context of the values that dominated Italian immigrant life during these early years. Work and family commanded the energies of most early-arriving Italians, leaving little room for sport. Italian economic pursuits largely dictated attitudes toward recreation: whereas the vast majority of Cubans labored in the cigar industry, Italians initially gravitated to small shops, dairies, and farms. These enterprises consumed long hours and often required familial assistance. An examination of cigar factory baseball rosters for 1908 reveals not a single Italian name.[63]

Substantial Italian entry into the Ybor City sportsworld awaited the 1920s, when three socioeconomic factors converged. First, Italians had improved their economic status so that sons were freed from the most constrictive demands of the family economy. Second, the 1920s witnessed a rush of second-generation Latins, including Italians, into public schools, where organized athletics occupied an important niche. It was no coincidence that Italian American involvement in sport paralleled an increased interest in formal education. By the 1920s Italian parents had shifted familial strategies away from using children as producers at the earliest possible age to embrace the promise of education. Third, Italians were able to utilize what was by then an extensive community recreational network that provided structure and community sanction to sporting events. Thousands of youths and adults participated in multileague baseball and basketball competitions, boxing tournaments, and high school football games. Indeed many of these activities dovetailed with the programs of mutual aid clubs by the 1920s.

As these events expanded, so too did the range of social contacts among Italians and their Latin and Anglo neighbors. Not only did Italians mingle with a more diverse cross section of the community, but the context of these meetings changed also, moving from encounters in the marketplace and work site, usually as individuals or family members, to the realm of recreation and play, often as squad members or fans supporting a particular team. As sport occupied a more central place in Ybor City its role in shaping the outlooks of residents changed as well.

In earlier years Ybor City possessed a reputation as an intellectual center for radical thinkers, a training ground for union leaders, and a haven for patriotic revolutionaries. New heroes emerged in the 1920s based upon very different values. Dr. Ferdie Pacheco, who eventually left Ybor City to become boxing champion Muhammad Ali's physician, recalled of this era: "Our heroes . . . were the *bolita* barons, and athletes. They were heroes to us. . . . In an ill-defined way we were really doing socially acceptable combat with the Anglos from Plant High School. A football hero was on the same plane as a political guy who was winning and a gangster who was winning a bloody struggle. They were our heroes. The preoccupation of this immigrant society was those three things: who was winning at sports, who was politically oriented, and who was doing the *bolita* counting."[64]

Journalists such as Grantland Rice, Damon Runyon, and Heywood Hale Broun glamorized the emerging sport champions, and radio brought sporting events into the homes of millions by the 1930s. The American people, argued Ben Rader, sought "compensatory heroes" as they felt the pressures of increasing regimentation and bureaucratization. A public that revered Charles Lindberg also idolized Jack Dempsey, Bobby Jones, Babe Ruth, and Red Grange. Ybor City youth could readily identify with role models such as Cuban-born Adolfo Luque, a stellar pitcher during the Twenties, while Italians cheered Ernie Lombardi, Tony Lazzeri, and Joe DiMaggio.[65]

A new breed of Latin athlete served as both cause and effect of the local and national adoration given to sportsmen. The distinction of being Ybor City's first professional baseball player belongs to Alfonso Ramón López. Born in 1909, one of nine children of Spanish immigrant cigarmakers, López did not speak English until the fourth grade. He recalled his youthful encounter with sports on Thirteenth Avenue and Twentieth Street in the Spanish district: "We had all kinds of games. . . . But we played baseball mostly. I loved to play ball. We had a playground and used to play until it closed. . . . I got interested in baseball in the 1920 World Series, naturally all the kids were talking about the World Series."[66]

Al López attracted the attention of a sportswriter working for *La Traducción* who encouraged the sixteen-year-old catcher to turn professional. At the time López was working as a delivery boy for an Italian bakery owned by Angelo Ferlita, but he quit both his job and school to sign a minor league contract in 1924. His playing career began with the Tampa Tarpons of the Class D League, which then featured a number of

Cuban players. "I got paid $150 a month, which made me feel like I was stealing," admitted López. He quickly advanced to the Brooklyn Dodgers, assuring his mother that he was working, not playing.[67]

The career of Al López exemplified Ybor City's interest in baseball. Recalling the large crowds in Tampa as a player he reminisced, "Tampa was a good draw. It was mostly, and I'm not being prejudiced, mostly cigarmakers that used to get off early from the factory and come out and see the ball game. They were great baseball fans." Clearly he fostered a sense of pride among Latins who vicariously shared his success. "I didn't notice it at first," he explained. "I was just one of the local guys and I lived in the area. I played around the clubs, played dominoes with them. I never figured I was a hero, but I guess I was."[68] Tony Pizzo recalled how groups would greet López at the end of each season and parade him down Seventh Avenue. "Al López was a real hero to everyone from Ybor City. It didn't matter that you were Spanish, we all stuck together."[69]

Baseball may have been America's game, but in Ybor City boxing challenged its popularity, for boxing provided an alluring avenue of upward mobility for the second generation. Whereas baseball often required Latins to subordinate individual values to the interests of a team, boxing allowed participants to achieve material success *and* remain rooted in their culture and community. A surprising number of Ybor City boxers turned professional.[70]

Boxing was the quintessentially urban sport. A plethora of gyms dotted Ybor City, and the Cuban Club became the community's boxing mecca with the completion of a 2,000-seat boxing arena and training complex in 1925. "The club's gymnasium in those days was filled with talent," remembered boxer-turned-trainer Lou Viscusi. The Cuban Club hosted a fight every Monday night from the 1920s through the 1940s and, according to Viscusi, "used to sell out every week." He recalled young Italians and Cubans "coming in the gymnasium to see if they could pick up a bout for ten dollars. That's how they got started. Survivors kept going on." The "survivors" graduated to Benjamin Field, Tampa's larger facility, where fights were held every Friday. Promoters, keenly aware of marketing opportunities, often matched a Latin against an Anglo to boost sales. "A Latin against a Cracker," Viscusi smiled. "It made an interesting fight and drew well."[71]

The public school provided Latins with a socially approved context for athletic competition and at the same time accelerated upward mobility and the integration of Ybor City youths into mainstream Tampa. The presence of the Latin athlete accompanied the mass education of second-generation ethnics. The 1920 Hillsborough High School football team featured only two Latins, but by 1925 fourteen Latins started on offense and defense. The yearbook described Joseph ("Big Joe") Domingo as "one of the best fullbacks that Hillsborough has ever produced, perhaps All-state." Throughout the Thirties and Forties Latins comprised at least one-half the starting lineups for Hillsborough High. A handful of Latin athletes—Tommy Gómez, Chelo Huerta, Tony Cancela, Rick Casares, Nelson Italiano, Lou Piniella, and Tony LaRussa—entered the sport galaxy. "Our folk heroes," explained Ferdie Pacheco, "were the fellows who wore red-letter sweaters." Baseball produced similar results and proportional representation. The 1939 Hillsborough High baseball photographs included fourteen players, eleven of whom were Latin.[72]

Baseball, football, and boxing, while highlighting individual ethnic achievements, also introduced Latins to a wider Anglo world via the medium of athletics. Sporting competitions transported Latins away from the sheltered immigrant neighborhood and into rival arenas. Sport crested in popularity during the 1920s and 1930s, paralleling the demise of the radical left. Latin youths came to prefer the we-ness of athletic competition to the brotherhood of the doctrines espoused by the defeated left. In this sense the dangers that radicals saw in sport amply fulfilled their fears.

Sport promoted the idea of a Latin community by helping to break down antagonisms between ethnics. Team sport brought together diverse individuals and taught them the benefit of group effort. Even boxers, supreme individualists, remained fixed in their immigrant cultures and served as emblems of the wider group. When Latins fought against Anglos, feelings of "we" against "them" assumed an added dimension. Beginning in the 1920s athletic teams in Ybor City began to show a high level of ethnic intermixing. One elderly Spaniard recalled that in the early part of the decade Italians played on El Centro Asturiano's ball team and "Cuban fellows played for the Italian Club." By the 1930s it was a rare team of any sport that did not include representatives of each major Latin element.[73]

Sport played a somewhat conflicting, dual role in the formation of urban ethnic values. On the one hand it speeded acculturation, introducing Latins to the outside world, forcing individuals and groups to mingle with others in schools, gyms, and on the playing fields. Sport provided a public forum where Anglos and Latins participated vicariously and athletically. "A visit to the ball park," wrote Gunter Barth in *City People*, "provided man with a new perspective on life in the modern city. Watching a professional baseball game, as well as knowing its ins and outs, turned them [immigrants] into true spectators who not only saw the events on the field, but also could sense their significance for everyday life."[74] On the other hand, sport fostered ethnic and community identity through the competition of local teams and individuals, accentuating the Latin character of Ybor City. Taunts of "Cuban nigger" by opponents and rival fans tended to solidify group identity. Yet the cohesion of a community can exist on a number of levels, intersecting at the crucial junctures of family, class, ethnic group, and neighborhood. One way of judging the depth and breadth of community is to examine the phenomenon of intermarriage.

Intermarriage

If intermarriage poses the ultimate test of one group's acceptance of another, the statistics detailing Italian intermarriage in Ybor City suggest a low level of approval. The incidence of Latin intermarriages tended to increase over time, as groups experienced longer periods of contact with one another and with Anglo Tampa. This was particularly true after 1910, when intermarriages only totaled 5.2 percent of all Latin marriages; yet the percentage of intermarriages remained low, the high point being 1935 with 15.2 percent (see Table 11). This indicates that Latins were still marrying heavily within their own groups. When Italians out-married they most commonly chose a Latin partner. The overall number of Italian out-marriages is so small, however, that their reliability in outlining general patterns is doubtful.

Oral testimony supplies certain details that statistics cannot, evidence that reinforces the limited nature of intermarriage but suggests certain patterns. When first- and second-generation Italians married outside their group such liaisons most commonly involved Spaniards. Strongly entrenched prejudices against marriages with Cubans characterized the Italians. Angelina Comescone explained her family's point of view: "If you married a Cuban, your parents would disown you. A Spaniard? Possible."[75] Of course high Cuban transiency worked against intermarriage with a much more permanent Italian population. Italians and Cubans

TABLE 11 Latin Intermarriages, 1890–1935

Year	Total marriages involving Latins	Total Latin intermarriages no.	percent	Italian/Hispanic no.	percent	Italian/Anglo no.	percent	Hispanic/Anglo no.	percent
1890	16	0	0	0	0	0	0	0	0
1895	75	3	4.0	0	0	0	0	3	100
1900	128	12	9.3	6	50	0	0	6	50
1905	255	15	5.8	8	53	1	12.5	6	34.5
1910	230	12	5.2	6	50	0	0	6	50
1915	300	29	9.6	16	55	0	0	13	45
1920	278	34	12.2	13	38	0	0	21	62
1925	463	56	12.0	17	30	4	7.1	35	62.9
1930	349	45	12.8	10	22	8	17.7	27	60.3
1935	386	59	15.2	22	37	7	11.8	30	51.2

SOURCE: Marriage records, Hillsborough County, 1890–1935.

did, in fact, live next to each other for years, but the specific Cubans residing in neighborhoods changed often, thus reducing the chances for the highly personal interactions that could lead to marriage.

In addition to structural considerations there were strong pressures to marry within the group. "All our neighbors were Cubans and Spaniards," revealed Mary Italiano, "but when it came to marriage, they [the parents] wanted you to marry an Italian."[76] The *Morning Tribune* noted such proclivities in 1903: "It is well known that the Italians object most strenuously to the marriage of one of their race with another race."[77] Ray Grimaldi's family experienced the costs of out-marriage: "My mother is Spanish, and there was a tremendous amount of bitterness in my own family that my father would marry my mother with all the Italian girls [around]."[78] Alena Noto remembered a more vivid manifestation of opposition to out-marriage. In this particular instance an Italian girl married a Spaniard, and the Italian father "took her and . . . all the family came in and spit in her face. It's incredible, but it really happened."[79]

The evidence also suggests that a high percentage of Anglo/Latin marriages involved unions of Spanish factory owners or foremen and Anglo women. Notices of these ceremonies appeared frequently in newspapers, almost always the object of favorable comment by Anglos. Although not an exhaustive source, an examination of the *Morning Tribune*'s society page reveals precious few reports of Anglo marriages involving Italians or Cubans, even to the late 1930s.[80]

Just as Italians differed from their Latin neighbors in their propensity to in-marry, so too were their attitudes toward unmarried females in the household distinctive. "The home life of the different nationalities has changed considerably," remarked a 1934 report; "however, the old influence is still very strong, especially in the Italian families." The reporter added, "The young girls are still kept under close surveillance until the time of their marriage."[81] Of course factory employment worked against such scrutiny, but as long as immigration continued to bring new arrivals to Ybor City, traditional patterns of marriage selection remained strong. The frequency of arranged marriages, often between cousins, was high, as a look at the pre-1924 records quickly reveals. The year 1900, for example, documents two sets of Spotos entering into nuptials.[82]

By the later 1920s, however, old-world fathers in the new land began to discover that their daughters saw little romance or utility in Sicilian-style marriages. As restrictionist legislation diminished the numbers of newly arrived marriage partners, and as parents moved away from traditional attitudes, marriage patterns changed. The chaperone entered the scene.

Courtship in Ybor City followed a strict code of ethics. "Mother would take us walking up and down Seventh Avenue," smiled Angelina Spoto Comescone, "and all the boys would be standing on the curb and the mothers would look like little hens watching their chicks. So that nobody would look at us or touch us. . . . The boys would go wild trying to get a word with us."[83] Not everyone had positive memories of the practice. "But her mother had to go," remembered Joe Maniscalco. "If I didn't have the mother, I had the sister. They wouldn't let her [his wife] go alone!" Mary Italiano, who married at age fifteen, recalled similar scrutiny: "We had to have two or three to follow us, which was awful. If you even sat on the porch outside . . . somebody had to be there."[84] Rosemary Scaglione Craparo offered her insights into the institution: "Marriage was the only way, the only way to get from out, from under the skirts of the mother. . . . We thought that by getting married young— you see we couldn't see a fella, couldn't sit on the porch with the light on at night—so the first [male] to come along and smile at us, we would marry him. *And* there was not divorce."[85]

Chaperonage had a direct and obvious role in shaping marriage patterns. Although the rigor of old-world scrutiny slipped to allow a greater degree of contact and intimacy, there still existed relatively rigid control. Within such a system opportunities for more diffused marriages were limited. This meant that community identity could, and did, exist among

Italians, but when wider conceptions of Latin-ness reached the bedrock of acceptable marriage partners, the image constricted to a narrower set of individuals. Although Italians had broadened their social relations since arriving in Ybor City—moving to ever-widening bands of associations—they retained a tight grip on this essential feature of their personal existence.

Summary

The Ybor City experience suggests that there was not a simple community continuum at work, stretching from a less-unified, more-Balkanized, premodern cluster of groups to a more unified, "modern," Americanized existence. What happened was much more complex than that, with many smaller dramas acted out within the larger scenario. Yet the long-term trend, at least to 1940, suggests that in some important ways the reverse of the sketchy model posited above was true. That is, once nativist interventions from the outside diminished and groups followed divergent routes to social mobility and ethnic adjustment, they tended to become more distinct. During the early years groups possessed a set of common problems and enemies, and in some cases a set of integrative institutions that by 1940 had largely fallen away. Ybor City no longer contained such a heavy concentration of working-class immigrants. To be sure the second generations of each group formed friendships based on schools, sport, and social activities, and there were elements of a shared community life. Yet by the end of the period in question the groups differed, in some respects, more than when they had first come together. Ultimately the sense of community that resulted from the coming together of these disparate immigrant groups was not static. Rather, it changed significantly over time, shifting to meet the different combinations of group, class, and culture existing in Ybor City.

NOTES

1. Interview with Domenico Giunta, May 18, 1984; interview with Angelina Comescone, July 18, 1979.
2. Conzen, "Immigrants," 604.
3. Westfall, "Martínez Ybor," 68–70.
4. Sabe, "Early Days," 71.
5. *El Productor*, December 22, 1888, quoted in Poyo, "Cuban Émigré Communities." The *Tampa Morning Tribune*, April 17, 1911, noted that "brighter and more cheerful

colors are now in evidence as many small homes are painted." See also Wood, "Whetting, Setting and Laying Timbers," 3–8.

6. *Tampa Journal*, May 26, December 1, 1887, June 27, November 7, 1889; *Tampa Morning Tribune*, June 23, 1895; del Rió, *Yo Fui Uno de los Fundadores*, 46.

7. *Tampa City Directory*, 1899–1935, Hillsborough County Library and Special Collections, USF. The maps of the Sanborn Insurance Company, which show the clustering effect clearly, are available for Tampa beginning in 1884 (with some missing years) and are located in the Map Collection, UFG, and at USF.

8. Steffy, "Cuban Immigrants," 14–15; Westfall, "Martinéz Ybor," 82–85.

9. The Sanborn Insurance Company maps reveal clearly the physical growth of Ybor City, including not only the location of structures but the type and function of the buildings as well.

10. Ward, *Cities and Immigrants*; Warner, "Cultural Change and the Ghetto," 173–87; Chudacoff, *Mobile Americans*, 40; Thernstrom, *Other Bostonians*.

11. Thernstrom, *Other Bostonians*, 232.

12. Interview with Juan Mallea, August 15, 1982; interview with Francisco Rodríguez, June 18, 1983.

13. Interview with Alfonso López, April 24, 1980.

14. Interview with Angelo García, November 29, 1982.

15. Interview with Domenico Giunta, May 18, 1984.

16. Interview with César Medina, May 22, 1984.

17. Interview with Philip Spoto, June 30, 1979; interview with Joe Maniscalco, April 3, 1980.

18. Interview with Honorato Domínguez, September 12, 1980.

19. *Tampa Morning Tribune*, February 10, 1895, August 4, 11, 1896, July 4, 1897, among numerous other references.

20. See Higham, *Strangers in the Land*, for a wider discussion of these fears. Tampans were usually able to separate upper-class Spanish factory owners from these negative images.

21. *Tampa Tribune*, May 2, 1888.

22. Ibid., September 8, 1892.

23. *Tampa Morning Tribune*, June 10, November 10, 1907; *Tampa Journal*, January 19, September 15, 1887.

24. *Tampa Morning Tribune*, October 13, 1897.

25. *Tampa Tribune*, January 9, 1890. Tampa's businessmen complained of Sunday activities because Ybor City merchants remained open to sell to crowds. See *Tampa Morning Tribune*, July 25, 1911.

26. *Tampa Morning Tribune*, August 4, 1896.

27. Ibid., November 9, 10, 1899.

28. *Tampa Daily Times*, May 13, 16, 1901.

29. *Tampa Morning Tribune*, May 16, 1911. The evangelist Rev. Richard Stough openly questioned whether Latins were members of the Caucasian race during a 1916 Tampa revival.

30. Interview with Frank Urso, January 3, 1982.

31. Interview with Alfonso Noto, March 4, 1980; see also interview with Phillip A. Bondi, January 8, 1974.

32. Interview with Domenico Giunta, May 18, 1984.

33. Kusmer, "Concept of 'Community'," 385.

34. FWP, "Life History of Domingo Ginésta," 4. The intergroup relations of Ybor City are discussed in Middleton, "Ethnicity in Tampa," 281–306.

35. Jahoda, *River of the Golden Ibis*, 226. For further discussion see Pozzetta and Mormino, "Concord and Discord," and the accompanying comments by Richard Juliani and Luciano J. Iorizzo.
36. Lemos, "Early Days of Ybor City," 5.
37. *El Internacional*, May 10, 1904.
38. Interview with Ray Grimaldi, November 9, 1978.
39. Interview with Domenico Giunta, May 18, 1984.
40. Interview with Rosemary Craparo, July 18, 1979.
41. Interview with Ray Grimaldi, November 9, 1978; interview with Eugenio Rodríguez, July 6, 1984.
42. Interview with Joe Cacciatore, March 5, 1982; also see interview with Philip Spoto, June 30, 1979.
43. Interview with Mary Italiano, April 20, 1980; interview with Helen Spoto, April 30, 1979.
44. Interview with Domenico Giunta, May 18, 1984.
45. Interview with Mary Italiano, April 20, 1980; interview with Josephine Scaglione, April 2, 1980.
46. Interview with Rosalia Ferlita, May 18, 1980.
47. Interview with Manuel Alfonso, July 21, 1984.
48. Interview with Angela Menéndez, February 5, 1979.
49. Interview with Rosemary Craparo, July 18, 1979.
50. Interview with Nick Nuccio, June 10, 1979; interview with Nelson Palermo, March 23, 1979.
51. *Tampa Morning Tribune*, February 9, 1954; interview with Philip Spoto, June 30, 1979.
52. Interview with Sara Juster, May 4, 1984.
53. Interview with Ray Grimaldi, November 9, 1978.
54. Interview with Sara Juster, May 17, 1984.
55. Hareven, *Family Time*, 381.
56. *Tampa Morning Tribune*, October 6, 1949.
57. Wagner, "Baseball in Cuba," 115; Fimrite, "Viva el Grand Old Game," 68–80.
58. Quoted in Compton and Díaz, "Latins on the Diamond," 11.
59. FWP, "Recreational Activities, Centro Asturiano," 3.
60. FWP, "Recreational Activities, Centro Español."
61. *La Federación*, December 8, 1899; *El Internacional*, March 24, 1911, October 6, 1916.
62. Interview with Alex Scaglione, April 2, 1980.
63. *Tampa Morning Tribune*, April 28, 1908.
64. Interview with Ferdie Pacheco, June 12, 1984.
65. Riess, *Touching Base*, 188–92; Roberts, *Jack Dempsey*; Rader, "Compensatory Sport Heroes," 11–23.
66. Interview with Alfonso López, April 24, 1980.
67. Ibid. See also Brandmeyer, "Baseball and the American Dream," 48–74.
68. Ibid.
69. Interview with Anthony Pizzo, February 23, 1974.
70. Interview with Arturo Camero, March 3, 1984. A scrapbook owned by Mr. Camero, a former prizefighter, lists more than fifty Latin boxers who turned professional in the 1920s and 1930s; approximately 30 percent of them were Italian. Also see *Tampa Morning Tribune*, June 6, 1927; *Tampa Daily Times*, April 13, 1944, for details of the

Ybor City boxing world. The Cuban Club opened its boxing ring in May 1924 with a match featuring Kid Camero and Willie Santana. *Tampa Daily Times*, May 9, 1924.

71. Interview with Lou Viscusi, February 12, 1980; FWP, "Círculo Cubano." Asked why he boxed, seventy-four-year-old Cuban Arturo Camero replied, "Hunger. Lots of hungry fighters!"

72. *The Hillsborean*, 1914–46; interview with Ferdie Pacheco, June 12, 1984.

73. Interview with Alfonso López, April 24, 1980; interview with Conrad Castillo, January 19, 1985; interview with Joe Maniscalco, April 3, 1980; interview with Carmelo Rocca, July 30, 1983; interview with Paul Longo, June 30, 1980. See *Tampa Daily Times*, September 8, 1934. The Municipal Baseball League championship team for 1915, the Italian Club, featured a roster that was half filled by Cubans and Spaniards. See also *Tampa Morning Tribune*, November 10, 1915.

74. Barth, *City People*, 149.

75. Interview with Angelina Comescone, July 18, 1979; interview with Frances Scaglione Paraja, March 11, 1980.

76. Interview with Mary Italiano, April 20, 1980.

77. *Tampa Morning Tribune*, February 21, 1903.

78. Interview with Ray Grimaldi, November 9, 1978.

79. Interview with Alena Noto, March 4, 1980.

80. Examination of *Tampa Morning Tribune* for 1893–1940.

81. FWP, "Family Life in Ybor City," 96.

82. Marriage Records, 1891–1940, HCC.

83. Interview with Angelina Comescone, July 18, 1979.

84. Interview with Joe Maniscalco, April 3, 1980; interview with Mary Italiano, April 20, 1980.

85. Interview with Rosemary Craparo, July 18, 1979; see also interview with Joe Maniscalco, April 3, 1980.

9 Economic Adjustments

> Italians practically control the politics and business of Tampa today, a position they reached by their economics and thriftness, while we [Cubans] always spent our money freely.
>
> Domingo Ginésta, "A History of Ybor City"

Italians from the Magazzolo valley arrived ill suited for America's rapidly urbanizing-industrializing economy. The majority had toiled as unskilled rural laborers, a background that poorly prepared them for newworld cities. Large families and meager schooling posed further handicaps. When compared to Cubans and Spaniards, established groups in Ybor City, Italians were clearly at a disadvantage in the search for economic security. Hispanic immigrants not only imported blueprints for the cigar industry to Tampa, but they also controlled access to jobs. During the early years of Ybor City, Spaniards filled cigar factories with foremen, managers, and skilled workers.[1]

The social and economic base of the Cuban and Spanish advantage—the omnipresent cigar industry—ultimately became a critical weakness; and the initial stumbling block for Italians—an unfamiliarity with cigarmaking and cigarmakers—ultimately became a strength. In time Italians solved the mystery of cigarmaking, but they never were married to the industry. They filtered into many sectors of Tampa's economic structure, achieving a breadth of integration that eluded their Latin neighbors.

Cigarmaking, once mastered, offered skilled workers an envied flexibility and mobility. Cuban and, to a lesser extent, Spanish cigarworkers plied their trade between Tampa, Key West, Havana, and New York, depending upon seasonal demand, ethnic holidays, political unrest, and industrial turbulence. The ease whereby cigarmakers transferred their skills and the illusion that wages, which between 1890 and 1920 rewarded workers handsomely, would continue to increase combined to place Cubans and Spaniards on a single, smoke-filled, economic track.

To understand the mobility process one must realize the perceptions and reality of the alternatives. The structure of the workplace defined which options were open to which laborers. On the whole the factory system consisted of a hierarchy through which upwardly mobile workers might rise step-by-step. The cigar industry fit this economic profile. Italians perceived and defined their relationships to the factory setting differently from Cubans and Spaniards. They correctly saw that Hispanics dominated the industry's upper echelons and therefore many ambitiously risked opening small businesses; energetic Cuban and Spanish cigarmakers did not.[2]

Italian men never saw the cigar bench as a lifetime position but rather as a springboard to other careers. The transition from factory to nonindustrial trades, stores, or other small businesses took anywhere from a few months to decades. "I was a good cigarmaker," boasted Paul Longo, who rolled cigars for two decades (1904–24) before he quit to sell insurance.[3] Cigarmaking skills often acted as a safety net, enabling former factory workers to return in case of personal crisis. In 1910 Giusseppe Cagnina worked as a farm laborer while his children, Salvatore and Giuseppina, labored at making cigars. In 1919 the elder Cagnina had temporarily given up farming in return for a stint at the cigarmaker's bench, but by 1921 Cagnina was back on the soil, listing "gardner" as his occupation.[4]

The occupational structure of Ybor City's Italian community was always more varied than its Spanish and Cuban counterparts. A 1900 random sample of 235 Italian adult males in Ybor City revealed an occupational pattern already diversified. Slightly less than half of these men worked at cigar trades; the majority spread themselves throughout Ybor City's working class, employed as laborers, barbers, bricklayers, carpenters, bakers, bartenders, farmers, shepherds, and peddlers. A singular absence of professional and managerial occupations characterized the 1900 occupational profile of Italian immigrants.[5]

The Ybor City economy, stimulated by scores of new cigar factories and thousands of new immigrants, expanded briskly between 1900 and 1920. Throughout this period Cubans and Spaniards reaffirmed their economic allegiance to the industry which brought them to Tampa, but Italians followed their own pathways. The 1910 census revealed 45 percent of Italian males employed in the cigar industry,[6] compared to 78 percent of the Spanish males and 82 percent of the Cuban males.[7] In 1924 a sample of 500 Italian adult males found 40 percent still laboring at various positions related to cigarwork, whereas two-thirds of Cubans and Spaniards continued in such employment (see Table 12).[8] Clearly the future for Italians, especially as it related to the second-generation, pointed toward careers in trades and stores, not factories. "The average Cuban youngster looked forward to being a cigarworker," observed Sam Ferlita, an Italian American born in Ybor City in 1918. "I wouldn't say I considered cigarwork inferior, but I thought along the line of business and getting ahead much faster than a cigarmaker." Phil LoCicero concurred, remembering his father's advice: "Don't go to work in a cigar factory! You must educate yourself."[9]

As already indicated, Italian families did not envision factory jobs as permanent employment. Women often stayed in the industry for long periods, but men pursued different options. Normally, males took work in the factories for a brief time, accumulating a nest egg that could be used for investment in property or business. Women and/or children frequently remained in cigarwork to supply the extra margin of income that permitted these initiatives to survive and grow.

Before 1925 Cubans and Spaniards retained a near monopoly of the elite positions in the cigar industry. In addition they dominated certain crafts and trades. Scissor and knife sharpening, a lucrative practice, traditionally belonged to Galicians. Cubans and Spaniards also controlled the coffee-roasting business; in 1920 they operated all seven Ybor City emporiums and by 1935 still controlled the city's roasting ovens. Italians managed to operate some small coffee shops, but here too Cubans and Spaniards outnumbered them.[10]

Italians aggressively pursued an expanding number of service-related jobs as the city grew. Peddling, shoemaking, butchering, and baking attracted an increasingly important share of the Italian working class. By employing all his children and using savings accumulated through cigarwork, a peddler or cobbler could improve his status by opening a permanent stand or shoe shop.

An Italian business-commercial class evolved to serve the immigrant

TABLE 12 Occupational Distribution of Latin Males, 1910–35

Year	Ethnicity	Number	Cigarwork (%)	Non-cigarwork (%)
1910	Cuban	500	82	18
	Italian	500	45	55
	Spanish	500	78	22
1924	Hispanic[a]	600	60	40
	Italian	500	40	60
1935	Hispanic[a]	600	40	60
	Italian	400	19	81

SOURCES: *Thirteenth Census;* random sample of male heads of household and boarders; *Polk's Tampa City Directory,* 1924, 1935.

[a] After 1910 the term "Hispanic" is used since directories do not distinguish between Cubans and Spaniards. Surname analysis was used to separate Italians.

clientele. Barbershops, bakeries, fish markets, shoe repair stores, and groceries flourished. By 1920 Italians operated thirty barbershops, eight bakeries, eight butcher shops, eight fish markets, two dry goods stores, six soft drink emporiums, and twenty shoemaking establishments, far outstripping their Latin neighbors.[11]

It was the mom-and-pop grocery store that epitomized Italian mobility. These corner stores proliferated throughout Ybor City, and then Tampa, during the first two decades of the new century. Tampa's Italians operated 58 groceries in 1920, a figure that nearly doubled to 103 a decade later.[12] From the beginning Italian groceries served the ethnic needs of fellow immigrants, but these shopkeepers also demonstrated a willingness to accommodate the demands of Cuban and Spanish customers. When the sheer number of grocery stores saturated Ybor City, Italians opened stores beyond the enclave's borders. In particular they found opportunities in Tampa's black neighborhoods, where they faced sparse competition. Possessing few racial animosities against blacks, they moved swiftly into these vacuums.

The Scaglione and Parrino families are representative of Italian business movement into black neighborhoods. Alex and Josephine Scaglione rolled cigars for over a decade before opening the Sunset Grocery in 1934, located in the Scrub. Josephine continued to work in the factory while Alex tended the store. "We only had black customers," he said. "It was a poor neighborhood. We used to sell one onion, one egg." The couple emphasized their determination to build a nest egg so their son could attend college.[13] Antonio and Laura Parrino began the Red Front Grocery Market in another black neighborhood during the 1930s. "We opened with fifty dollars of merchandise," remembered Sam Parrino. "We treated blacks fairly, and they treated us right."[14]

The 1910 census reveals a dearth of white-collar, professional positions among Italians: fewer than 1 percent of the Italian male immigrant population in Ybor City had achieved such status.[15] The 1920 city directory lists two physicians but no lawyers, while in 1930 a total of seven lawyers, one physician, and two dentists are included.[16] The initial Italian failure to penetrate the elite classes of Ybor City paralleled immigrant patterns sketched elsewhere. Italians did not think in terms of "careers" or "professions" but rather emphasized practical trades or pursuits, jobs that would complement the family economy, not reward individual talent.[17]

Two salient features characterized the adjustment of Ybor City Italians: the unusually high percentage of Italian women employed for wages and the scarcity of Italian men clustered on the lowest rungs of the occupational ladder. These two conditions must be seen as part of the same phenomenon. A remarkably high percentage of Ybor City's Italian women had entered the cigar industry by 1900, in part a response to structural changes in that industry. As Italian men envisioned cigarwork as a path to other enterprises, Italian women perceived the stripping table as a means of upward mobility to more skilled cigarwork and, more important, as a stabilizing element in the family drive for advancement. Italian wives and daughters walked each morning to the cigar factories in far greater numbers and proportions than their Hispanic counterparts. In 1900, 60 percent of the foreign-born women employed in the cigar industry were Italians; by 1910 the Immigration Commission observed the continuing Italian dominance, noting that Italian married women still outnumbered all other groups. In 1910 an extraordinary 85 percent of Italian women over the age of twenty who were employed in cigarwork were married; only 20 percent of Cuban women in the factories were married. The work choices made by Italian women must be understood in the light of family strategies, for Italian men seeking careers outside the cigar factory stood on the shoulders of their women.[18]

Tampa's Italians explored nearly every sector of the local economy. Immigrants dug ditches, hauled dirt, laid rail, and swept warehouses during the brief transitional period from the late 1800s to 1900. By the turn of the century 47 percent of Italian males labored in the cigar factories, many filling the lower levels of the industry. In 1910 only 11 percent of the male work force sampled listed their occupation as "laborer," with 45 percent classified as "cigarmaker." By this juncture the composition of the Italian work force deviated from employment patterns of Italian immigrants elsewhere, which tilted sharply to unskilled work. A total of 58 percent of the 1910 work force occupied "skilled" or semiskilled positions, such as cigarmaker, shoemaker, barber, baker, bricklayer, jeweler, carpenter, mechanic, tailor, and plumber. The pervasive impact of the cigar industry shaped the statistics, since only a small proportion of non-cigarwork positions offered opportunities for skilled employment. Occupations such as carpenters, masons, and plumbers were rarely found among Tampa's Italians; such positions remained largely under the control of Tampa's Anglo-dominated unions.[19]

The relative lack of unskilled and semiskilled laborers among Ybor City's Italian work force requires further explanation. Tampa, unlike most northern and midwestern cities prior to World War I, contained a large Afro-American population. Blacks had traditionally labored at the lowest occupational levels, a pattern they continued throughout the twentieth century. In 1920 Afro-American males aged twenty-one years and older comprised one-quarter of Tampa's adult male work force.[20] Blacks were overwhelmingly represented in unskilled labor sectors, dominating, for instance, the stevedore trade. Such labor in the North and East generally went to southern and eastern Europeans. Yet cigar factories remained virtually off-limits to Afro-Americans prior to the 1940s. In 1940 Tampa's cigar factories employed 2,413 white males and only 58 blacks. At the same time 1,166 Afro-Americans worked as construction laborers, railroad employees, and longshoremen, whereas only 164 whites worked at such jobs.[21] Thus Italians were cut off from jobs often controlled by them in the North but were offered cigarwork in exchange.

Potentially high wages in cigarwork initially appealed to Italian immigrants. In few American industries could they have leapt the chasm between unskilled laborer and skilled craftsman in such quick fashion. National data on the earning power of southern and eastern European immigrants permit a comparative examination (see Table 13). In 1910 southern Italian immigrant males ranked nationally near the bottom in yearly income, earning an average of only $396 per year; in contrast German immigrants earned $579 per year and Finns $683 per year. The Immigration Commission reported, however, that the typical male Italian immigrant in Tampa earned $723 per year, compared to Cuban earnings of $782 and Spanish incomes of $957.[22]

When one considers the cigar factories' impressive wages, the obvious

TABLE 13 Ybor City vs. National Yearly Earnings of Adult Immigrant Males, 1910

Area/ethnicity	Average earnings
Ybor City:	
Cuban	$782
Italian	723
Spaniard	957
United States:	
Croatian	$410
English	673
Finnish	683
German	579
Greek	300
Italian, South	396
Pole	428
Swede	722
Slovak	442

SOURCE: U.S. Congress, *Immigrants in Industries*, pt. 23: "Summary Reports on Immigrants in Manufacturing and Mining," Table 35; pt. 14: "Cigar and Tobacco Manufacturing," Table 147.

question arises: Why was so much of the history of Tampa's Italians centered around individuals trying to leave this high-paying industry? To understand this seeming contradiction one must examine differing immigrant strategies and the opportunities open to immigrants upon arrival.

Immigrant Strategies

Italian values preached the paramount importance of family security and stability. The remunerative but uncertain world of cigars troubled Italians. Francesco Pupello Settecasi arrived at this crossroad in 1920. A disciple of Lorenzo Panepinto in Sicily, he carried to Ybor City the romantic dream of a working-class utopia, only to discover that the reassuring environment of the radical cigarmaker was soon to end. Settecasi, like most newly arrived Italians of his time, obtained a job at a local cigar factory through friends, only to confront a bitter ten-month strike. "Every five minutes a strike," he grumbled as he sat under his beloved fig tree. "I came here to work, not strike. The cigarmakers were too crazy." Settecasi traded his cigar *chaveta* for a carpenter's hammer. A Cuban questioned his wisdom, asking why anyone would choose to toil under Florida's brutal sun. "I told him it was a lot hotter in Sicily. I want to be my own boss."[23]

The evidence does not suggest that Cubans and Spaniards worked less hard or embraced their families with less fervor than Italians but rather that their economic goals drew upon different values, producing contrasting results. For Cubans, their island country served as a dream world, dual home, and safety valve. "We lived in quite a few places," recollected eighty-year-old Arturo Camero. "I guess we moved about once a year. My parents used to go frequently to Cuba. We had lots of kinfolk there. When my mother was ill, she and I returned to Cuba for a year."[24] Alfonso Díaz, an Afro-Cuban, observed, "Cubans always went back and forth. There was an exodus every December."[25] Such intermittent traffic, while allowing Cubans freedom of movement, worked against the accumulation of property in Tampa.

The distinctive ways in which Ybor City Latins responded to labor turmoil revealed striking examples of immigrant social and economic attitudes at work. Italians responded to labor crises or economic downturns by finding other outlets of employment in the region. During the 1894 depression hundreds of Ybor City Italians worked as migrant laborers, cutting sugarcane at St. Cloud.[26] In the midst of the 1904 recession the *Morning Tribune* reported a large contingent of Italians leaving the city for work in Jacksonville.[27] The 1910 strike saw more than 400 Italians mining phosphate in nearby Polk County, and others worked the Citrus County mines.[28] Italians such as Joe Maniscalco returned to the mines at three dollars a day during the 1920 strike. "Had to work," sighed the elderly cigarmaker. "Got families. We came home on weekends."[29] Rosemary Craparo remembered her father's ordeal during one strike: "He had to go to work in the woods, cutting trees. He came home one day all bitten up, some kind of fly or insect. He was pitiful."[30] Cubans, in their rush to leave Tampa, frequently sold their possessions to the more permanent Italians.[31] By utilizing all employment possibilities in the local area, Italians built upon their gains obtained in Ybor City, emerging with much deeper roots than their Latin neighbors.

Ybor City's labor struggles served as midwife for many new careers. Francesco Di Maria, a sulphur miner from Cianciana, immigrated to Tampa in 1904. He and his wife, Maria Castellano, began their American work experiences at the Sidello Cigar Factory. During the 1920 imbroglio Di Maria mined phosphate, enabling him to open a grocery store near the county courthouse with accumulated savings from his labors.[32] The 1920 strike so disillusioned Paul Longo that he soon left cigarwork to sell insurance.[33]

The preservation of family meant different things to different groups. A 1910 survey examined the conjugal condition of foreign-born employees of the cigar industry and documented the varying patterns existing among Ybor City's immigrant groups (see Table 14). A high male/female imbalance characterized both Cuban and Spanish cohorts, while the Italian sample was nearly balanced. Although 43 percent of all Spanish-born immigrants residing in Ybor City were married, the extremely low number of Spanish women present spoke to the fact that most Spanish men lived apart from their spouses.[34]

Cubans and Spaniards changed residence with amazing regularity. To test geographic mobility 500 Spanish and Cuban adult male immigrants living in Ybor City were extracted from the 1910 census. Nearly 80 percent of the Cubans and 70 percent of the Spanish could not be found months later in the listing of the 1910–11 city directory; and only 10 percent of these Spaniards and 12 percent of the Cubans could be traced a decade later. Among Italians selected by the same procedure 68 percent could be traced to 1920. Another test, using Tampa city directories for 1921 and 1930, produced similar results. Only 38 percent of 500 Hispanics sampled could be traced between 1921 and 1930, whereas 54 percent of Italians persisted a decade later. Almost half of the Italian sample found in 1930 (49 percent) resided in the same house. Significantly, less than 2 percent of the Hispanic or Italian sample who remained had moved out of Ybor City or West Tampa, attesting to the resilience of the Latin enclaves.[35]

Cuban American life-styles mitigated against the accumulation of savings or property. "Italians and Spaniards liked to save a penny," reflected Aleida Huerta Camero, a Cuban American. "The Cubans, live today, forget tomorrow."[36] In 1912 Rev. J. D. Lewis, a missionary at the Cuban mission, observed, "It is principally among the Cubans that these conditions [poverty] are found. The Italians protect themselves better. They prepare for lean times, but the great numbers of Cuban cigarmakers do not."[37] The *Morning Tribune* concurred with this judgment, observing during the 1920 strike that Italians "usually have more money saved than the Cubans have."[38]

Italian gains came swiftly. Oral testimony agrees that Italians out-

TABLE 14 Conjugal Status of Foreign-born Employees in Tampa Cigar Industry, 1910

Ethnicity and sex	Total	Percent		
		Single	Married	Widowed
Cuban:	3,117	29.6	63.7	6.8
Male	2,742	29.6	65.8	4.6
Female	375	29.1	48.0	22.9
Italian:	1,220	18.8	77.9	3.4
Male	658	26.7	71.7	1.5
Female	562	9.4	85.1	5.5
Spanish:	1,708	45.5	49.2	5.3
Male	1,618	45.8	49.2	5.0
Female	90	40.0	48.9	11.1

SOURCE: Adapted from U.S. Congress, *Immigrants in Industries*, 427–28. Figures are for individuals twenty years of age and older.

stripped Cubans and Spaniards in property ownership. "Italians were more interested in building something," explained Nick Chillura Nuccio, who through his capacities as notary public, insurance agent, city alderman, county commissioner, and mayor of Tampa, knew Ybor City between 1910 and 1950 as well as anyone. "The Spanish and Cuban people at that time, they came here to make a little money and go back to Spain and Cuba. The Italian people knew they were going to live here for the rest of their lives, raise a family. I lived in the same house [in Ybor City] for thirty-five years."[39]

César Medina, Jr., an eighty-five-year-old Cuban immigrant, offered this overview: "Italians were concerned about the future. They would buy one little house and then they'd buy another house and another so the first thing you know, every Italian had three or four houses. In those days [1910] you could buy a house for five or six hundred dollars. My job was to inspect, cause I used to work at a bank and I had to inspect the houses. Italians were hard workers."[40] Eugenio Rodríguez, born in Havana in 1899, recollected, "In those days [1910–30], the only people who used to own houses were Italians."[41] Observed Alfonso Díaz, an Afro-Cuban: "All Italians owned their own homes. Today ninety-nine percent of Ybor City is owned by Italians."[42]

Despite this unanimity of opinion, documenting the Italian passion for property ownership is difficult because official records are scarce. Since Tampa was not a major urban center prior to the 1950s the U.S. Census

Bureau did not collect precise statistics on ethnic group behavior as it did for large metropolitan areas. There exists, however, scattered evidence to confirm oral recollections of Italian property accumulation.

In 1892 an Italian consul described the embryonic settlement in Ybor City and concluded, "The [Italian] colony in general is prosperous but does not own property or land."[43] The 1900 manuscript census reveals the astonishing gains made during a period of national depression and local unrest. An examination of all Italian households for that year indicates an overall 8-percent owner occupancy. Italian cigarmakers had a lower homeownership rate (4 percent) than non-cigarworkers (11 percent), reinforcing dual notions that cigar factories tended to be an entry point rather than a career goal for Italians, and that many immigrant cigarmakers had only recently arrived and were unable to purchase property.[44]

An examination of tax records between 1900 and 1930 confirms the Italian proclivity for acquiring property. Beginning with modest parcels of property in 1900—the mean value of Italian assets was only $200—Italians far outpaced their more numerous Hispanic neighbors. By 1920 hundreds of Italians had become holders of property throughout Tampa.[45]

Three principal characteristics underscored the Italian quest for property. First, Italians willingly began their property mobility with modest purchases. Second, when renting they paid the cheapest rates possible; in 1910 Italians spent an average of $7.80 per month, compared to $11.70 for Cubans and Spaniards.[46] Third, in order to finance such transactions Italians practiced what was often seen as a cruel economizing life-style. "The strictest economy is practiced in the purchase of food and clothing," observed an outsider. "Everything is subordinated to the end [property] in view." The official added: "Italian cigarmakers are not content until they own their own homes. The moment enough money is saved, the home is purchased. Often there are other houses to be bought, farms to be acquired, or stores and fruit stands to be opened. . . . The tendency to save and acquire property is very slight among Cuban cigarmakers. In the point of economy and the ability to save, there is no comparison between that race and the Italians."[47]

Tampa's low cost of living also enabled Italians to advance rapidly in homeownership. Few places in urban America afforded immigrants such accessibility to housing as did Tampa. In 1930 the median monthly house rental for foreign-born whites in Tampa was $22.81, lower than in any city of over 100,000 residents save Tacoma, Washington; the median value of a home owned by a foreign-born white was $2,882. In no other large American city could immigrants purchase less-expensive homes: for example, in Chicago the median value of such housing was $7,720; in San Francisco, $6,214; in Boston $5,508; and in Jacksonville, Florida, $4,962.[48]

Even in this market property ownership was not easy. Since Italian males occupied the bottom strata in the cigar factories, pooling family resources was a necessity. In 1910 Ybor City's Italian cigarmakers earned $2.00 per day, compared to $2.34 for Cubans and $2.56 for Spaniards. This statistic is misleading, however, for Italians maximized their collective earning power. Italian family incomes for 1910 averaged $943 per year compared to $881 for Cubans and $1,099 for Spaniards.[49] The Italian immigrant work experience therefore must be placed within the dynamics of the family economy.

Family Economy

Basic to understanding the Sicilian family is the knowledge of its function as a collective producer, a common pool of familial resources. In Sicily, in the presence of corruption and chaos, only the family could be trusted. Sicilians denigrated and denied individualism for the greater family good. Parents regarded children as economic assets whose incomes helped stave off disaster and added to family prestige.

Ybor City, initially a male-dominated outpost of sojourners, was in a state of flux. Women and children rarely participated in early migratory travels. Factory owner Enrique Pendás recalled the first years of settlement: "There were no women in Tampa in those days. I would go [to the street] and stand there hour after hour, but could not see a single woman."[50]

Unsettled conditions generated by the Cuban independence struggle retarded large-scale movement of their families, and Spanish migration patterns also featured a heavy incidence of male sojourning. The Tampa Board of Trade complained about Cuban workers in 1901, claiming they were "single men who have no family ties here, whose object is simply to earn money enough so in case they became dissatisfied, they can leave at a moment's notice."[51] Boardinghouses continued to be common fixtures of the Ybor City landscape until well into the 1970s, especially among the Spanish.[52]

While Cubans and Spaniards only gradually brought women and families to Ybor City, Italians experienced a very short period of predominantly male settlement. In May 1892 the Italian consul of New Orleans reported nearly 300 Italians in Tampa, of whom approximately one-third were women.[53] The 1900 manuscript census provides a more in-depth portrait of an emerging Italian community and an expanding female presence: the fraction of women in 1900 remained at one-third, but the overall colony numbers had increased to more than 1,300. The typical Italian female in early Tampa was sixteen years old, reflecting the youthful character of the community. A scant number of Italian women—only 2 percent in 1900—were aged fifty or older. Husbands, on average, were five years older than their wives.[54] Thus by the early years of the twentieth century Italian men had reconstituted their families, with women composing roughly half of the Italian population in Ybor City.[55]

Not only were there more immigrant Italian families residing in Ybor City relative to Cubans and Spaniards in the formative years, both proportionately and in absolute numbers, but the individuals comprising these families were more rooted to the Florida scene. In comparison to Italians elsewhere, who were among the most likely of all immigrants to make repeated return trips to the homeland, Ybor City's Italians manifested return rates far below their immigrant neighbors in the local community and their conationals in other locations (see Table 15).[56]

The Italian family economy drew upon the resources of its women and children. The U.S. Immigration Commission, although expressing admiration of Italian thrift, disapproved of what it perceived to be the exploitation of women and children. "Children of 6, 7, and 8 years are taught the trade [cigars] and the product of their labor is added to the family fund. . . . When girls and boys are earning in many instances between

TABLE 15 Trips Abroad by Foreign-Born Employees of the Cigar Industry, 1910

Ethnic group	Total	Percent			
		No trips	1 trip	2 trips	3 or more trips
Cuban	3,391	50.2	22.0	15.0	12.8
Italian	1,578	92.8	5.3	1.3	.06
Spanish	1,900	77.1	14.4	6.0	2.5

SOURCE: Adapted from U.S. Congress, *Immigrants in Industries*, Table 106. Although these figures missed two sets of individuals, those who had returned to villages earlier and remained and those who might have been absent from Tampa during the survey period but intended to return, they still portray a remarkably stable Italian population.

$20 and $25 per week, it is not surprising that parents would rather have their children learn so lucrative an occupation at an early age than have them lose precious time by going to school."[57] "I never saw my paycheck until I got married," admitted Louis Spoto, who worked in a cigar factory to help bolster his family.[58]

Not all children worked in cigar factories, however. "I used to shine shoes when I was a kid," remembered Joe Maniscalco. "I used to walk downtown to the old courthouse. About 5:30 or 6:00 in the morning and come back 11:30 or 12:00 at night. Making four or five dollars shining shoes and the money I make, I take it home, so it could take care of the family."[59] While the shoeshine stand underwrote Maniscalco's contribution to the family economy, for many other Italians the products of mother nature supplied avenues to material progress.

Fruits, Vegetables, and Dairies

The *Atlanta Journal* warned its readers in 1901 that a horde of 40,000 Italians was poised in Naples. "There is but one way to stop the flood of spaghetti emigration," the paper editorialized, "and that is to prohibit sidewalk fruitstands."[60] The Italian fruit vendor became an enduring stereotype in America's late-nineteenth-century urban economy. When asked why they or their fathers staked out careers in Tampa's produce trade, few interviewees could offer reasons other than the fact that Sicilians were farmers. Careful examinations of life histories reveal a complex interweaving of old-world skills, new-world economies, local/ regional opportunities, ethnic attitudes, and societal expectations.

Immigrants bring cultural resources with them which act as social and economic rudders, helping to select the first jobs taken and to determine the group's initial relationship with the host society. Previous work experiences did not rigidly predetermine new-world occupations. Millions of southern or eastern European immigrants had worked the soil, but few sought agricultural pursuits in America. A grid of possibilities shaped occupational selections. Immigrant networks figured heavily in sorting out employment patterns. The nature of early migration streams and the time of arrival were critical in this process. Immigrants clustered in certain occupations, often the result of premigration bonds of kinship and job skills. Chain migration frequently linked kinfolk in certain industries: Croatians in the oil refineries, Poles in steel mills, Jews in the garment trades, and Cubans and Spaniards in cigar factories.[61]

Italian timing proved propitious in seeking opportunities in a broader local and regional economy. When the first Italians settled in Ybor City in the late 1880s, Tampa Bay's economy was underdeveloped. Unlike Italians in Boston and other urban areas, who faced major obstacles because of entrenched social classes and limited industrial possibilities, Tampa's settlers accompanied, and in some cases accelerated, the area's growth.

The Ybor City ecology perfectly suited Italian capacities. East of the Italian enclave lay thousands of undeveloped acres of rich, mucky soil and grazing lands. Moreover the land could be purchased very inexpensively, much of it for a few dollars an acre in 1900. Eastern Hillsborough and Manatee counties, destined to become America's winter vegetable garden, awaited development. Italian immigrants in the Northeast and Midwest generally settled in densely populated urban centers where available land lay far away and/or was prohibitively costly.

By the early twentieth century newspaper reports of Italian agricultural successes were commonplace. Vincenzo San Pedro, "an Italian farmer on 22nd Street," told the *Morning Tribune* he expected to make $1,200 a year (1907) from his nine-acre truck garden of celery, beets, and cabbage.[62] Even more noteworthy, claimed the paper, was a "wealthy Italian" who farmed at the old city dump at Fort Brooke. The 1910 census found sixteen Italian immigrants who listed "garden farm" or "home farm" as an occupation. The real numbers were assuredly much higher, since Italians typically ventured into farming in gradual steps, making cigars, taking odd jobs, selling vegetables, and purchasing parcels of land over long periods of time. Salvatore Giunta sold produce for a living from his truck garden on Twenty-fourth Street between 1910 and 1930, yet the city directory, when it identified him at all, listed "laborer" as his occupation.[63]

Italian farms, ranging from backyard plots to large tracts, yielded massive amounts of produce; virtually every Italian home boasted a garden. A consuming passion for saving, combined with a genuine affection for the earth, made gardening an essential part of the Ybor City economy. Joe Caltagirone recalled his father shaking his head when passing fashionable neighborhoods, never understanding how anyone could waste space planting ornamental shrubs and grass.[64]

Italians, far more than Cubans or Spaniards, utilized the garden as a means of self-sufficiency. The product of economic necessity and cultural creativity, the Italian diet leaned heavily upon greens and fruits, both of which grew abundantly in Florida. Many Italian families maintained near meatless diets, complementing pasta with broccoli, fennel, escarole, beans, and tomatoes. Elderly Italians, when discussing the lowly *lenticchia* (lentil), describe it in almost mystical terms. Lentils with pasta became a Monday evening staple at Italian homes. "Mothers served it to cleanse our bodies," explained Sam Costa. "I'm telling you, lentils are wonderful for your body. Italian doctors in Ybor City—I'm not kidding—prescribed lentils as medicine."[65] The Italian diet followed a rhythmic pattern: Tuesdays—minestrone or pasta with escarole; Wednesdays—pasta with tomatoes; Fridays—fish or pasta Milanese (fennel or fish); Sundays—pasta *con sugo* (with sauce). "With a case of spaghetti and an Italian garden," boasted Nelson Palermo, "you could feed your family for a month."[66]

The most visible manifestation of the fruit and vegetable business was the ubiquitous Italian peddler. The Italian presence at fruit stalls and street corners ironically benefited from group stereotyping. Tampans believed that Italians possessed special talents at handling, arranging, and selling these products. Ascribed skills therefore reinforced economic patterns. Italians gravitated to the produce trades soon after arriving in Tampa, as no centralized market or previously established ethnic group controlled fruits and vegetables. Reports of Italian fruit vendors circulated in Tampa as early as 1895.[67] "Italian fruit dealers," noted the *Morning Tribune* in 1897, seemed "to monopolize the local trade in green stuff and persist in keeping their tempting stands open, often in front of a roasting fire of peanuts."[68] The proliferation of picturesque pushcarts soon posed a problem for city officials. In 1905 the sheriff ordered overzealous Italian vendors to halt trafficking produce on Sundays after 1:00 A.M. "Da Fruita Stand Shutta da Door," mimicked the *Morning Tribune*.[69] The sheriff arrested ten Italian peddlers in 1910 who persisted in hawking their greenery on Sunday.[70]

Despite these intrusions Italians launched an assortment of careers in the fruit and vegetable trade. The 1910 Immigration Commission graphically illustrated how quickly they came to dominate. The commission studied the now unavailable License Bureau permits, which in 1910 were issued to fifty-two Italians to peddle fruits and vegetables; not a single Cuban, Spaniard, or Anglo acquired such a license. In fact Italians stood out in all kinds of peddling. "One hundred and two licenses were issued in October of 1910 for a term of one year to Italian peddlers," observed the Immigration Commission.[71] Just as enterprising

Italians learned the Spanish language and the secrets of roasting coffee Cuban style, so too did they market Caribbean foodstuffs such as guavas, mangoes, tamarinds, and sapodillas.

The incomes derived from pushcarts supported scores of Italian families. While the business listings of the city directory recorded only two fruit and produce peddlers, a 1910 census sample of 500 Italian families found this to be the fourth most prevalent occupation, following cigarmakers (45 percent), laborers (11 percent), and grocers (9 percent). Fully 7 percent of all Italian males peddled fruit, vegetables, ice, or fish.[72]

Peddling appealed to Italian immigrants because of its ease of entry. "We must remember," observed a turn-of-the-century commentator, "that many general laborers, miners, and others are tempted to enter 'bisnesse' and that they can do so by learning fifty words of English and buying a fruit stand. . . ."[73] Peddling also offered ambitious immigrants in Tampa an enterprise without entrenched competitors. The relatively few Jews in Tampa had already established themselves in the dry goods business; by 1910, fifteen Jewish-owned shops operated in Ybor City.[74] The produce trade held little allure for Spaniards or Cubans, although a few sold deviled crabs and candies from carts. The Cuban peripatetic life-style worked against the daily routine of the pushcart vendor, who relied upon established routes and acquired reputations for quality merchandise.

Italians, by circumstance and dogged determination, controlled the fresh produce markets. Ybor City, with its myriad corner groceries and backyard gardens, could sustain only a limited number of pushcart vendors, thereby forcing Italians to deal with Latins, Anglos, and Afro-Americans on a commercial basis. Case histories reveal the roads traveled. Stefano Vicari, a Stefanesi, emigrated to Tampa around 1900. In familiar fashion he obtained his first job in a cigar factory. The 1920 strike disillusioned Vicari, as it had others, so he rented a horse and wagon, purchased a cartload of watermelons from local farmers, and peddled them through Tampa's black neighborhoods. His quick success induced him to buy a grocery store in West Tampa. His wife persisted at rolling cigars, acting as a safety net should the produce venture fail.[75] The Vicaris, with their tale of modest gains, typified the Italian experience. But a small number of individuals enjoyed fabulous successes in the fruit and vegetable trades, and their stories amplify other aspects of the Tampa urban economy.

Giuseppe Valenti, another Stefanesi, sailed for Ybor City in 1894. After a brief stint at cigarwork he took to the streets. His son, Joe ("Blue Eyes") Valenti, explained: "My father got started with a basket on his arm selling fruits. He had a bell and a regular route. The housewives used to come out and buy vegetables. Our family used to eat off the rejects on the wagon."[76] The elder Valenti died in 1920. "I quit school in the fourth grade," his son reminisced. "After my father passed away we had to go to work." The younger Valenti cleaned latrines at the Geraci Fruit Company for $1.50 a week, "which I took right home and gave it to my mother." Promoted to unloading carts of produce, Valenti had to get up at 2:00 A.M., yet the young man was eager to acquire experience. Recalling later days as a vendor, he said: "I used to push a wagon. I would go to the first Farmer's Market on 7th Avenue. The farmers used to bring in peppers, tomatoes. I went with my wagon, full of peppers, eggplant, and a small compartment of tomatoes. I went through Ybor City."[77] Tomatoes sold briskly, prompting Valenti to search for a dependable source. "I borrowed a truck, went to a place near Palmetto, where I saw the prettiest tomatoes I ever saw," he explained. "The Anglos were getting ready to throw them to the cows. I asked what he would take for them. He said, 'Three Cuban sandwiches and a gallon of wine.' I earned $600 with those tomatoes, pushing a homemade, four-wheel wagon. Then I bought a truck."[78] "Blue Eyes" Valenti thereafter specialized in tomatoes, eventually becoming the largest wholesaler of this product in the United States.

If the pushcart characterized the early beginnings of Italian peddlers, the Tampa Wholesale Produce Market symbolized Italian mastery of the produce sector. Prior to the 1930s wholesalers operated from the cramped quarters of the John Napoli Market at Seventh Avenue and Forty-seventh Street. In the early 1930s a group of predominantly Italian investors purchased twenty acres of land on a sparsely settled section along Hillsborough Avenue. The July 1934 minutes of the "Organizational Meeting of the Subscribers of the Tampa Wholesale Produce Market, Inc.," are revealing. Italians comprised fifty-two of the original sixty-five stockholders in what would become the leading wholesale produce market in the United States.[79] Only one Spaniard belonged to the powerful organization and no Cubans appeared among the directors. In an economic world where handshakes consummated deals, the Tampa Wholesale Produce Market proved the immigrant proverb, "It is worth more to have friends in the marketplace than money in the bank."

The careers of Vincenzo Ippolito and Nicolò Geraci also demonstrate the changing nature of the marketplace. Born in Santo Stefano in 1888, the son of a shepherd, Ippolito came to Tampa, where he exercised a familiar route of mobility: work on the railroad, time at the cigar bench, followed by a moderately successful ice business. His wife, Rosalia, rolled cigars. When he helped found the Wholesale Exchange in 1934 he had no experience in the fruit and vegetable trade.[80] But the industry had changed since the days of hawking pushcart vendors, and by the 1930s managerial expertise and knowledge of the Ruskin tomato crop mattered more than familiarity with the streets.

Nicolò Geraci exemplified the traditional hand-over-hand mobility from peddler to wholesaler. A native of Contessa Entellina, Geraci pursued the calling many *paesani* followed in New Orleans. Beginning his career with a horse and wagon, selling produce in Hyde Park, he saved enough money to open a small store on Seventh Avenue and Twenty-third Street. By 1921 he had expanded his business, dealing increasingly on a wholesale basis and erecting one of the largest cold-storage plants in Florida. By the 1920s Geraci could process fifty carloads of fruit and produce. In addition to harvesting Florida's bountiful orchards and fields, the Geraci family helped inaugurate international trade in commodities such as bananas. The family incorporated the American Fruit and Steamship Company for this purpose.[81]

Whereas Italians peddled fruit in virtually every corner of America, relatively few herded cows or operated dairies. Immigrants from the Magazzolo valley came to Tampa with experience as shepherds, an occupational skill in small demand in most urban centers. Dairying, like truck farming, appealed to the Italian penchant for property ownership, and Tampa offered inexpensive grazing lands within reach of a growing urban market.

In 1894 Castrenze Ferlita and Salvatore Reina, two veterans of the St. Cloud experiment, established a pioneering dairy. Other Italians followed their success, and by 1902 accounts describing dairies, goat herds, and milk routes were commonplace.[82] The 1910 Immigration Commission recorded twenty-six Italian, three Spanish, and no Cuban milk vendors. A study of the 1910 census found forty-four Italians classified as "dairymen"; however, the real figure was much higher because of blurred distinctions between farming and dairy pursuits.[83] Many laborers and cigarmakers herded cows and sold milk and cheese on the side.

Volumes of newspaper files reporting the activities of Italian dairy farmers indicate the pastoral economy's importance. Italians extensively utilized the pasturelands surrounding Ybor City, often prompting encounters over grazing rights. In 1899 a gunfight occurred between Giuseppe Licata and a Pasco County cattle rancher over the disputed ownership of a cow.[84] In 1904 the city of Tampa, agitated over "a large number of idle cattle" roaming throughout east Ybor City, dispatched Arthur Scheleman, its dog catcher, to impound the cows. Scheleman rounded up the herd and began his cattle drive when, according to the *Morning Tribune*, "he was set upon by an army of Italians," a crowd estimated at 500. One man even attempted to saw off Scheleman's wooden leg. "If people had not intervened," noted the paper, "Scheleman would have been killed."[85] Back on the job Scheleman later attempted to impose order on Ybor City's open range. This time he succeeded in seizing a sizable number of cattle. The *Morning Tribune* reported: "It was cows, cows, cows, in court . . . of the Italian Dairiano class—cows which run at large in the eastern section of the city."[86] A more serious complication involved Italian disregard for bureaucratic regulations. Scores of Italian dairy farmers faced arrest for failure to pasteurize milk or submit to other municipal restrictions. They disapproved of both the product (pasteurized milk) and the process (additional expense), preferring to cut costs and maximize profits.[87]

The dairy business reflected trends of regulation, rationalization, and economy of scale. During the 1930s small, independent dairies faced difficult times competing against larger, more modern establishments. The day of the small dairy, with a few cows and a diversified product, was rapidly ending. During the depression, Tampa's city council outlawed the keeping of cows in residential areas, further consolidating the larger dairies.[88]

Case histories illuminate the Santo Stefano–Tampa dairy connection. Born in Santo Stefano in 1870, Giuseppe Guagliardo herded sheep before coming to Tampa in 1904. Giuseppe, his wife, Vincenzina, and an older son worked in the cigar factories before the disruptive 1920 strike, at which time the family purchased a dairy cow and began home deliveries, the first inventory totaling eight quarts of milk. They steadily invested in more cows and more land, and in 1934 Giuseppe and his four sons incorporated the Florida Dairy, one of the largest enterprises in the state.[89]

The Buggica family founded the East Tampa Dairy. Salvatore Buggica purchased several cows after arriving from Sicily; he also tended a large garden to support his family. His wife, Lucia, and five sons continued to roll cigars while Salvatore increased his dairy business and truck garden. In 1932 the family purchased eighteen acres of land in Brandon for $1,800, moving their eighty cows east.[90]

The produce and dairy businesses reflected the adaptive capacities of Italian immigrants. Locally the traffic in vegetables and milk fit hand-in-glove with the cigar economy. Italians soon realized that the trade they helped pioneer was changing; indeed, in many ways they forced such change by founding wholesale cooperatives and exchanges. By the 1930s cold-storage facilities, modern milking machines, and new accounting procedures had replaced the individual milk peddler with horse and wagon. The fruit and vegetable business, however, resisted the severe consolidating tendencies affecting dairies. In both instances Italians who were forced out of the market often fared well because they had purchased inexpensive land which had increased immensely in value.

The local experience in truck farming, produce vending, and dairying calls into question conclusions reached recently by historian Dino Cinel. Northern Italians succeeded in California farming, Cinel has argued, because agriculture "required cooperation and marketing skills the individualistic Southerners were unlikely to possess."[91] This thesis, dangerous in its overgeneralization, fails to account for extraordinarily diverse Italian social and economic patterns. Southern Italians of agrarian backgrounds founded agricultural institutions in Tampa that were noteworthy for their adaptability, cooperation, and success. Collaborative endeavors extended into fields of enterprise which required even greater risk taking but permitted rich dividends—namely, organized crime.

Organized Crime

Scholars such as Mark Haller and Daniel Bell have pointed out that each ethnic group adjusted to crime in American society in its own distinctive fashion.[92] Such involvement should not be interpreted as inexorable cultural behavior but rather explained as a social-economic response to local, regional, and international factors. Enterprising individuals supplied consumers with services and products that were in demand, filling niches in the urban economy. Ethnic culture, with its panoply of moral codes and shared experiences, helped direct, but did not predetermine, individual and group responses to organized crime.

One of the ironies of the Ybor City experience is that Anglos and Latins came into perhaps their closest contact in the realm of crime. They shared illicit profits and the political power that came from this wealth. Crime also brought the various elements of Ybor City's immigrant world into new realms of interaction and cooperation. Although Italians initially specialized in bootlegging, while Spaniards and Cubans trafficked the much more profitable *bolita* (numbers), before long the dynamics of Ybor City brought the groups into a functioning network of alliances and deals. The unfolding of these arrangements reveals additional ways in which culture and local conditions combined to create specific outcomes.

Historians have contended that immigrants arriving in Chicago and New York during the late nineteenth century did not originate organized crime but rather followed previously arrived groups in a line of ethnic succession.[93] In Tampa, a place without deep urban traditions, such a sequence was not possible. The frontier qualities of early Ybor City gave birth to a variety of illicit activities. Prostitutes catered to the male work force, and clandestine cockfighting proved immensely popular.[94] Sunday liquor sales among Latins, anathema to Anglo Tampa, continued with protestations but little interference. The city's authorities reluctantly looked the other way, their morality assuaged by a prosperity built upon cigars. Ybor City richly deserved its reputation as a wide-open district. By 1900, however, one vice overshadowed all others—*bolita*.

Manuel Súarez, a Spaniard known as "El Gallego," is credited with having introduced *bolita* (literally little ball) to Ybor City in the late 1880s.[95] Whereas in Cuba the Loteria Nacional Cubana functioned under the aegis of the national government, *bolita* flourished in Tampa's free-enterprise economy at the hands of private entrepreneurs and with the unofficial blessing of politicians. "In Ybor City," complained the *Morning Tribune* in 1896, "those slick scoundrels [*bolita* peddlers] found a fat field. Cubans and Spaniards are naturally of a speculative turn of mind."[96] Once established, the history of *bolita* can be largely explained as a series of attempts by various civic, political, and ethnic factions to rationalize, regulate, and control an enormously profitable enterprise.

The evolution of *bolita* accompanied the rapid growth of Ybor City. In the beginning *bolita* functioned as a sideline of the saloon trade. By 1900 Ybor City supported more saloons than all of Tampa.[97] Patrons casually purchased a nickel ticket along with their wine or beer. "The foreign saloon element is composed largely of Spaniards," stated Sheriff Ed Hobbs in 1908. "They want to sell liquor and gamble all the time. . . . I am reliably informed that every Spanish saloon in Hillsborough County operates bolita. . . ."[98] Quickly *bolita* peddlers expanded operations, selling chances with eighty-to-one payoffs in grocery stores and clubhouses.

As the popularity and profitability of numbers increased, operations fell into the hands of a small number of Cuban and Spanish *boliteros*, men who organized the numbers syndicate shortly after the turn of the century and maintained a strong presence until the 1930s. The erection of lavish gambling emporiums epitomized the power associated with *bolita*. The El Dorado Club, run by Spaniard Rafael Reina, fit this grand style. Tony Pizzo, reminiscing about his boyhood in the 1920s, recalled the refined elegance of the El Dorado, with its roulette wheel, the sound of patrons playing dice, and policemen casually strolling among customers. The *bolita* throw climaxed the evening, remembered Pizzo:

A man all dressed up—black tie and tails—would stand up on a stage and beside him, all polished white and shining, would be one hundred solid ivory balls, each with a different number. Slowly he'd drop each of the balls into a velvet bag, mixing them as it filled. Then when the last ball would be inside it, he'd tie the drawstring and hand the bag to a member of the audience who'd mix it again, pass it on to another bettor who'd mix it once more and pass it on. . . . A man in tails would walk up with a big silk red ribbon. He'd give the bag a final shake and usually choose a woman to select a single ball by feeling through the bag without opening it. Then he'd tie the ribbon tightly around the spherical bulge and walk to the center of the stage where he'd pick up a pair of shiny scissors. Then with great flourish, he'd cut the bag, just above the ribbon. Then slowly, he'd untie the knot and drop the sacred ball into his palm. Holding the ball aloft he'd call the winning number.[99]

Bolita became part of Ybor City's Latin culture, as Cubans, Spaniards, and ultimately Italians came to regard it as an accepted fixture. On paydays at the cigar factories workers routinely paid *el cafetero, el lector*, and *el bolitero*. A cottage industry surrounded *bolita*, supporting hundreds of individuals ranging from sellers, bankers, and merchants dispensing chances and paraphernalia. Department stores, for instance, carried specially designed charts which instructed players how to bet last night's dream.[100] "Oh yes," remembered seventy-nine-year-old Anita Fuentes García, who proudly recalled how in 1930 she won *el pajarito* (literally little bird, a variant of *bolita*). "If you dreamed of a horse, you bet one; cat—four; elephant—nine; cow—ten; lady of the night—twelve; wildcat—fourteen; bull—fifteen; . . ."[101]

Gamblers also capitalized on the American market. Isidro Stassi, who worked *bolita* during the 1930s and 1940s recollected, "The choice sales districts were Hyde Park and downtown—they had the elite. Rather than playing nickels and dimes, they were playing with dollars!"[102] Black neighborhoods also generated feverish *bolita* traffic. César Medina, Jr., a Cuban immigrant who owned a string of bakeries, recalled plummeting sales in black neighborhoods on certain days. He finally connected sales to *bolita:* the day the number was thrown, residents did not buy bread.[103]

Bolita, with its Latin and American consumers, soon became a fixture of the Tampa scene. It existed because the public wanted it but also because certain Anglo civic leaders permitted it and because the industry funneled massive amounts of money into the pockets of politicians and police. The mechanisms necessary to manage and control this gambling empire flowed from the organizational skills of Charlie Wall.[104]

Sources confirm that Wall exercised absolute control over *bolita* until the late 1930s. "Charlie Wall was the Big Boss," recollected an elderly cigarmaker. "He used to run the city of Tampa."[105] Ciro Vaccaro added, "Charlie Wall had connections. You see, he was an *americano*. The Latin had nothing. What power did we have?"[106] Wall became a force in the state capital by dint of his ability to raise and contribute large sums of money. Since the governor of Florida possessed power to remove county sheriffs, prosecutors, and state's attorneys, Wall's payoffs ensured that local officials would continue to look favorably upon *bolita*.

Arrests appeared to have had no impact on the growing power of Tampa's underworld economy. Police "roundups" actually strengthened the *bolita* syndicate by "shaking down" the independents who could not afford payoffs. One individual claimed the police apprehended selected individuals to appear as if they controlled affairs. "You see," explained Isidro Stassi, "police would come in to make an example and list a 'John Doe' as arrested and take a $100 cash fine, forfeited to the court. They'd make a fictitious arrest to show they'd been making arrests. I paid many a $100 fine, but have no arrest record."[107] Hampton Dunn, a reporter for the *Daily Times* in the 1930s, recalled a grand jury indictment of the owners of twenty-two *bolita* shops. One week later, Dunn noted, the shops were again doing a brisk trade.[108]

The *bolita* business generated staggering profits. A Latin respondent, whose father ran a gambling den east of Ybor City in the 1930s, which included a *bolita* stall, slot machines, dice tables, and a tavern, recalled, "We'd take in $7,000 on a good night."[109] Fifty percent of proceeds went directly to Wall and his associates, who used the revenues to pay off police and other officials. *Bolita* bankers maintained "stalls" while controlling collectors and peddlers. A percentage went to the winning ticketholders; payoffs ranged from eighty- to ninety-to-one.

Reformers—and they were rare—occasionally brought pressure upon city hall to clean up *bolita*, but numbers continued unabated until the 1950s. Judge Horace C. Gordon, in a 1910 speech before the Civic Reform League, stated that "Tampa is more wicked than Gay Paris," urging the group to consider a bonus of fifty dollars "for the arrest and conviction of every white gambler in Tampa."[110]

By the 1920s reformers added Italian bootleggers to their list of undesirables. Cubans and Spaniards specialized in *bolita*, while bootlegging served as a conduit for attaining Italian goals. It allowed Italians an entry into Tampa's underworld economy, which some used as a springboard to later careers in organized crime, especially *bolita*.

Prohibition provided Italian immigrants, among others, with unforeseen opportunities to capitalize upon the American public's disdain for the Volstead Act. For Italians, singularly left out of the *bolita* bonanza, the prohibition era enabled them to carve a niche in organized crime. The timing was propitious. By 1920 Italians had gained a familiarity with the urban economy and its marketplaces. The potentially large profits to be made, the nearly unlimited demand for and acceptance of the illegal sale of alcohol by the public, and the Italian talent at manufacturing, supplying, and marketing moonshine brought together economic opportunity and immigrant resolution.

Philosophically and culturally Latins abhorred the puritanical restraints imposed by the Volstead Act. To them the neighborhood *cantina* served as a social refuge, a place where workers gathered at night to enjoy themselves. Taverns served as working-class social centers, in addition to representing a popular means of upward mobility for immigrant businessmen.[111]

Italian mastery of the field of bootlegging can perhaps best be explained in light of their economic experience in Ybor City. Italians initially followed paths of least resistance, entering fields in which neither Cubans nor Spaniards competed. Since Cubans and Spaniards initially controlled *bolita*, bootlegging permitted Italians an opportunity to establish themselves in a new enterprise with vast potential. Furthermore,

Italians had shown an ability to interact with Latins, Anglos, and Afro-Americans along economic lines, linkages that would prove important in bootlegging. "Italians dominated bootlegging," admitted an insider. "There were few Cubans."[112]

Bootleggers relied upon several sources to acquire the necessary amounts of whiskey, rum, gin, and wine. The easiest and safest system involved the home still. Every home was a potential factory. Some Italians erected stills in the rural expanses of Hillsborough County, where ample supplies of spring water and timber awaited distillers. Individuals who wished to eliminate the bothersome task of manufacture found it easy to smuggle rum from the Caribbean. Frequently, casks of rum came ensconced in specially hollowed-out cedar logs, which arrived in shipments of timber used to fashion cigar boxes.

Distribution involved an elaborate network of individual transactions. After 1920 many saloons had become cafés and so served as one medium of distribution. By 1928 Ybor City supported more than 100 restaurants and cafés, many of which sold liquor as a profitable sideline.[113] "Restaurants served whiskey in demitasse cups," remembered one individual. "You'd think they were drinking coffee!" Isidro Stassi explained how he delivered moonshine for his Sicilian-born father: "I was in high school and had this LaSalle with no rear seat. I used to fit twenty-two, five-gallon jugs of moonshine in the back. I'd deliver—primarily to the Rialto theatre on South Franklin Street. This would be at 3:30 in broad daylight, even as policemen inside would be drinking a cup of coffee."[114] "Alky" cooking and selling became a cottage industry for Tampa's Italians, a phenomenon repeated in other urban areas. When asked how many local families participated in the moonshine business, most interviewees estimated between 25 and 50 percent.

Bootlegging bolstered Italian incomes during the 1920s and 1930s. Some families were content simply to utilize homemade wine and moonshine as a supplemental income, while others, sensing the huge gains to be reaped, entered the business full-time. Many interviewees explained that Italians had become so adept at making high-grade whiskey that their product competed successfully with accepted brand names when Prohibition ended in 1933. The Stassi family, for example, continued—indeed expanded—its operations after Prohibition. Isidro Stassi explained: "In 1936, we brought an engineer from Chicago to help us set up a modern moonshine still—whiskey. We buried two, fifteen-hundred gallon stainless steel tanks. . . . He saw to it that the fumes were pumped into the city sewer system. The place was on 19th Street and 12th Avenue and was never raided."[115]

Bootlegging was part of a much larger process affecting not only organized crime but the urban economy in the 1920s and 1930s. A process of rationalization and regulation evolved to prevent ruinous competition, as witnessed by the quasi cartels formed by certain operatives in the early 1930s. Gamblers and bootleggers became legitimate businessmen upon whose successes depended hundreds of employees. "Part of their adjustment to American values," observed Humbert Nelli, "became an effort to apply certain big business practices—such as efficiency, specialization, monopoly through elimination of competitors—to the conduct of criminal activities."[116] Italians, bolstered by bootlegging profits, branched into *bolita* in the 1930s and within a decade supplanted the Charlie Wall–Cuban–Spanish hegemony. There is a distance measured in time between the Ybor City of 1900, symbolized by the pushcart peddler, cigarworker, and nickel *bolitero*, and the ethnic colony on the eve of World War II, represented by diesel trucks, white-collar trades, and commercial syndicates. Such changes also reflected a distance in attitudes. Few things dramatized change more than the shift in outlooks regarding the proper role of education in the family.

Education

"A father with many children is like a king with many vassals," is a popular Sicilian proverb. The educational legacy of Italian Americans bears the stigma of all-embracing family values that usurped the schooling of children for the greater collective good. This image, while essentially accurate for the first generation, fails to account for the capacity to change. The educational history of Italians in Tampa must be studied as a series of responses to an evolving society and viewed in the context of Italian conceptions of mobility.

During the period 1890–1920 the immediate demands of settlement, economic adjustment, and trade unionism surrendered little time to formal education. Compared to Cubans and Spaniards, Italians demonstrated little commitment to the educational process. In 1910 barely half of Ybor City's Italian population over the age of ten could read and write in their native language, compared to 97 percent of Cubans and Spaniards.[117]

The frontier nature of early Ybor City precluded a highly organized educational system. Poorly financed and ill equipped, Tampa's instructional facilities, even for Anglos, reflected the Deep South's poverty. Educational opportunities for blacks and immigrants were even worse. Mission schools and club-sponsored classes, which stressed the teaching of Italian and Spanish language and culture, attempted to fill the vacuum. Still, the socialist Lorenzo Panepinto, in his visit to Ybor City in 1907, criticized Italians for failing to meet the educational needs of their children.[118] The Italian School, organized in 1905, had enrolled 125 children by the following year. "Only a few months ago," noted the *Morning Tribune*, "these little street waifs were running wild, unkempt, and learning the vices of alleys and highways."[119]

In 1908 the county erected the V. M. Ybor School, called in the local vernacular the "Freeschoola." Public schools in general gave little attention to problems of linguistic and ethnic adjustment. Most Ybor City students before the 1930s spoke little or no English prior to formal schooling. Few teachers were Latins and fewer still spoke Spanish or Italian. Sam Marotta, a student at West Tampa's Cuesta School, remembered, "It was sink or swim. We struggled, but we managed."[120]

State law required students to remain in school until age sixteen, but Latins routinely circumvented this stipulation. In 1907 a labor leader complained that at least 1,000 children under the age of twelve labored in Tampa factories. "When you're hungry," philosophized J. C. Valenti, "you don't need permits."[121] The 1900 and 1910 censuses reveal hundreds of Italian youths, aged ten to sixteen, whose occupation and status (one could generally expect "student") remained blank.

The major educational hurdle to overcome was not teacher training or building needs but rather Italian immigrant attitudes. Parents had to believe that the reduction of earnings resulting from children attending school rather than working would be offset by higher dividends. Before the 1920s immigrant fortunes were too tenuous to permit such risk taking, and parents thus remained unconvinced. The labor press served to reinforce Latin parents' skepticism toward public education. "Our school systems and our textbooks are teaching human beings how to become valuable slaves, faithful serfs, and efficient employees," complained *El Internacional* in 1910.[122]

Italian culture stressed the primacy of the family. An individual's identity assumed importance only as it added to the family's well-being. Tampa's Italians, like Irish immigrants in Newburyport and French Canadians in Manchester, ranked owning a home higher than completion of schooling for their children.[123] These parents directed their children's career paths to occupations which, prior to the 1920s, required little schooling. Few Latins entered high school in these years. For example, in 1914 and 1915 Hillsborough High School, the magnet school for Ybor City, graduated only 2 Latins out of a total of 145 students; in 1919 there were only 2 Italian graduates out of a class of 92 students.[124]

Miriam Cohen's insightful study of immigrant education has suggested that during the period 1890–1920 the negative attitudes of Italians toward education represented logical and effective responses to their environment. Skepticism over the benefits of schooling thus was more than a simple legacy of Italy; it was a pragmatic recognition of the handicaps Italians labored under and the limited possibilities they faced.[125] From the perspective of most immigrant Italians childhood schooling represented a dangerous waste of familial resources. During the prosperous years of the cigar industry it made little sense to educate sons or daughters in schools.[126] Education, moreover, potentially undermined the supremacy of the family, breeding disobedience and foolish expectations. "I learned how to make cigars at age thirteen," recalled Joe Maniscalco. "All I got is sixth grade in school. I ain't got much education. But they had to take me out to support the family. My father say, 'You don't go to school for nothing. I gonna take you out to make cigars.' And I went to a buckeye and spent two weeks. Then my brother took me to be an apprentice. After two months I was making two dollars a week. Later I made fifteen to twenty dollars."[127]

If high school remained beyond the expectations of most Italian and other Latin males before the 1920s, females faced even greater odds. "Education was out of the question for a single girl," remembered Mary Italiano. "Not that they [parents] didn't want to send their kids to school, they had no money."[128] Philip Spoto recalled: "One time I was walking with my mother and an old Italian lady stopped my mother. My sister had just graduated from junior high school, and this woman says, 'Well, are you going to send her to work in the cigar factory now?' My mother says, 'She's going to high school.' 'High School!' the woman says. 'What for? When she comes out . . . she'll get married and she won't bring in no income.'"[129]

The 1920s brought profound change to Italian immigrant approaches to education. Families faced new economic realities which permitted different educational strategies. Children, once seen as workers, emerged as students whose educational investment promised future rewards and career advancement.

The Tampa Bay economy and most particularly the cigar industry underwent fundamental alterations in the 1920s. Increasingly machines replaced craftsmen. Cigarmaking tended to be more a function of women and machines and less the domain of men and skill. Large numbers of Italian women remained with the cigar factories in the 1920s, providing an economic hedge for family businesses, but men moved swiftly away. The Great Depression further transformed the cigar industry as many of American consumers switched to cheaper cigarettes instead of handrolled Tampa cigars. Economic calamity also caused greater enforcement of child labor laws, thus pushing Italian youngsters, including daughters, to stay in school.

The result was a reduction in the size of Ybor City's cigarmaker work force. The foreign-born Afro-Cuban population fell between 1930 and 1940 from 631 to 311. Cubans also departed for New York City and Cuba, their numbers diminishing by 35 percent during the decade of the Thirties, from 5,112 to 3,317. The Spanish foreign-born population fell by 26 percent. Italians suffered the least decline, losing only 18 percent of their immigrant population.[130]

Ironically, as the cigar industry changed during the 1920s and then deteriorated in the 1930s, the Tampa Bay area experienced dramatic growth. Hillsborough County grew from 36,613 persons in 1900 to 153,519 residents in 1930. The county's economic base broadened as new industries, such as shipbuilding, canning, and foundries, displaced cigarmaking as the central economic core. The greatest area of expansion occurred in the service economy, a sign of a national shift as well as a dynamic of local change.

The 1935 graduating class of Hillsborough High School graphically illustrated the impact of these changes on Latin families. Latins comprised 26 percent of the graduating class (82 out of 315 students) that year. Two-thirds of Italian graduates indicated plans for college, as compared to one-half of the Hispanic students. When Tony Pizzo graduated from high school in 1932 and enrolled at the University of Florida, he joined Sigma Iota fraternity, composed of 50 Latins (mostly Italian) from Ybor City. By 1936 Latins totaled one-third of the student body at Hillsborough High School, indicating an upward spiral of school attendance.[131]

An examination of class rosters at Jesuit High School points to another trend originating in the 1930s. Increasing numbers of Latin parents sent their children to private Catholic, college-oriented schools. Latins numbered nearly one-third of the school's enrollment during the 1930s.[132]

Italian attitudes toward education changed along with shifts in the economy, amply demonstrated by the surge of Italian students at the secondary level. "So what parents stressed in us mainly was education," remembered Nelson Palermo, a second-generation produce salesman. "The proudest moment of a parent's life was when they have their children well-educated and they come up in the world."[133] Rosalia Campisi, a produce wholesaler, stated with resolve, "I always prayed to God to give me schooling for my sons. I never wanted for myself an education or dance, just schooling for my boys."[134] Cuban-born César Medina captured the new perceptions regarding schooling: "Italians were, in my opinion, hard workers, very concerned about the future. . . . They were very concerned about their children's education, even if they didn't know how to read or write. The less educated of all the people here at the beginning was the Italian. Very few knew how to read or write, but they cared about their children."[135]

The Giunta family exemplified the social and economic directions of the second generation. Salvatore Giunta, an activist in Santo Stefano's *fasci*, left Sicily in 1906, settling in Ybor City. Giunta and his wife, Vittoria, worked in the cigar factories for several years. Salvatore also farmed for a Dr. Douglas and in the early 1920s purchased land in eastern Ybor City on Twenty-fourth Street. He became a truck farmer while Vittoria continued to work in the cigar factories. Their daughters, Gasparina and Teresa, also helped support the family by working in the cigar factories. The Giuntas taught their sons to expect more than cigarwork, however, and all the boys finished school. Frank became a banker, Dominic graduated from college and taught school, while Jimmy and Angelo became plumbers.[136]

Ybor City in 1935 stood at several crossroads. Figuratively speaking it had one foot entrenched in the nineteenth century and the other striding toward the future. Cigar factories, once the guarantor of prosperity, suffered grievously during the depression. In 1935 one official noted 3,000 unemployed cigarworkers looking for work and thousands who had already left the city.[137] As late as 1940 more than 700 unemployed cigarmakers continued to walk the streets.[138] A residue of elderly Cubans and Spaniards and a sprinkling of Italians still made hand-rolled cigars, a craft appreciated by diminishing numbers of consumers and manufacturers. The radio now supplied news to workers, symbolizing the new technologies which in time would replace virtually all cigarmakers.

Interest in education addressed the economic realities of the 1930s. A survey of 1,000 Latin households in 1935 revealed the new directions. Where thirty-five years earlier nearly one in two Italian males drew their pay from the cigar factories, in 1935 fewer than one in five labored at cigar trades. In 1900 four of five Cubans and Spaniards worked at cigar factories; by 1935 only two of five did so.[139]

Summary

The Italian work force of 1935 bore little resemblance to the 1900 profile. Relatively few Italians still plied fruit and vegetables by pushcart; that once flourishing trade had been institutionalized, as immigrants and their children presided over hundreds of groceries and shops. The greatest occupational shift occurred in the white-collar–professional category, as large numbers of Italians worked in sales and as clerks, managers, bookkeepers, and accountants. Society's demand for these new positions and the Italian family's educational flexibility accounted for this shift. Italians had not yet entered the medical profession in large numbers, although scores of physicians and dentists would graduate in the 1940s. A handful of Italians owed their jobs to politicians, with the city worker emerging as a new breed in Ybor City in the 1930s.[140] Overall, progress for Italians was a function of time; it was also a matter of timing, local conditions, and ethnic-economic strategies.

By dint of their initial exclusion from cigarwork Italians pressed into unskilled labor positions, farming, and street trades. Here they secured a foundation leading into the lower echelons of cigarwork. They eventually mastered the secrets of cigarmaking, but that trade never emerged for the group as the ultimate employment choice. Rather, Italians used total familial resources to structure an overall economic strategy that saw them concentrate on small businesses and professions, using cigarwork as a means to this end. Italian successes in dairying and the vegetable trades exemplified old-world skills and new-world opportunities. The fact that Italians were more anchored to Ybor City than Cubans or Spaniards and that they more often lived in family units gave them decided advantages.

By 1935 cigars no longer supplied economic prosperity to Ybor City, yet the Latins who had been drawn there by the cigar industry remained loyal to the community, infusing a vitality to the barrio. Nothing illustrated the tenacious grip Ybor City held upon Cubans, Spaniards, and Italians more than the fact that over the years few residents had left the old neighborhood. A random examination of 1,000 Latin names listed in the 1935 city directory reveals virtually no migration to Anglo neighborhoods. Fully 97 percent of Tampa's Latins resided in Ybor City or West Tampa. Further examination of selected streets in Hyde Park and Seminole Heights shows no Latin intrusion into those residential areas.[141] The great diaspora awaited the years following World War II. Ybor City may have been slightly tattered, its cigar factories disappearing, and its housing aged, but it still retained the heartbeat of a community.

NOTES

1. U.S. Congress, *Immigrants in Industries*, Tables 172–74.
2. For an elaboration of this thesis, see Crews, "Definitions of Modernity," 51–74.
3. Interview with Paul Longo, June 1, 1979.
4. *Polk's Tampa City Directory*, 1910–21.
5. 1900 Manuscript Census, Hillsborough County, microfilm, PKY.
6. 1910 Manuscript Census, Hillsborough County, microfilm, PKY. A random sample of 500 Italian adult males residing in Ybor City provided the base.
7. Ibid.
8. Ibid. A sample of 500 Italian, Cuban, and Spanish heads of households from the 1924 *Tampa City Directory* was compiled by extracting occupations from family names. The directory does not distinguish between Cuban and Spanish heritage, hence a collective "Hispanic" profile was compiled.
9. Interview with Sam Ferlita, April 3, 1985; LoCicero, quoted in *La Gaceta*, April 11, 1986.
10. *Tampa City Directory*, 1910–35.
11. Ibid.
12. *Tampa City Directory* and *Italian Business Directory*, 1909–10. See S. Hays, "Changing Political Structure"; Kessner, *Golden Door*, 108; Yans-McLaughlin, *Family and Community*, 46.
13. Interview with Alex and Josephine Scaglione, April 2, 1980.
14. Interview with Sam Parrino, December 20, 1984; see also "A Neighborhood of Contrasts," *Tampa Tribune*, November 25, 1984.
15. 1910 Manuscript Census, Hillsborough County, microfilm, PKY.
16. *Tampa City Directory*, 1920, 1930.
17. Kessner, *Golden Door*; Barton, *Peasants and Strangers*; Bodnar, *Immigration and Industrialization*; Yans-McLaughlin, *Family and Community*; Thernstrom, *Other Bostonians*.
18. Mormino and Pozzetta, "Immigrant Women in Tampa"; U.S. Congress, *Immigrants in Industries*, Table 150; Department of Commerce, *Historical Statistics*; 1910 Manuscript Census, Hillsborough County, microfilm, PKY. Fully 23 percent of Cuban

women employed in the cigar industries were widows, contrasted to only 5 percent of Italian women, indicating that cigar work was a last resort or safety net for some persons.

19. 1910 Manuscript Census, Hillsborough County, microfilm, PKY.
20. *Fourteenth Census*, Table 10, p. 195.
21. Kessner, *Golden Door*, 56–57; *Sixteenth Census*, III, Table 13.
22. U.S. Congress, *Immigrants in Industries*, pt. 23: "Summary Reports on Immigrants in Manufacturing and Mining," Tables 34, 38; ibid., pt. 14: "Cigar and Tobacco Manufacturing," Table 147.
23. Interview with Frank Settecasi, June 1, 1979.
24. Interview with Arturo Camero, March 3, 1984.
25. Interview with Alfonso Díaz, August 15, 1982.
26. *Kissimmee Valley*, November 11, 25, 1896.
27. *Tampa Morning Tribune*, June 15, 1904.
28. Ibid., April 1, 1908; Moroni, "Gli Italiani in Florida," 13.
29. Interview with Joe Maniscalco, April 3, 1980.
30. Interview with Rosemary Craparo, July 18, 1979.
31. *Tampa Morning Tribune*, December 15, 1910, September 7, 1919.
32. Interview with Alfonso Di Maria, July 30, 1983.
33. Interview with Paul Longo, June 1, 1979.
34. U.S. Congress, *Immigrants in Industries*, Tables 175–79.
35. *Tampa City Directory*, 1910, 1920, 1921, 1930; *Thirteenth Census*. Mobility studies in Tampa are fraught with pitfalls. Varied name spellings create major problems in census and city directory listings. Anglo census takers persistently misspelled Latin names, and Cuban and Spanish enumerators often Hispanicized Italian names: Cacciatore became Cachadore; Ippolito became Hippolito; Giuseppe became José, and so on.
36. Interview with Aleida Camero, March 3, 1984.
37. *Tampa Morning Tribune*, January 19, 1912.
38. Ibid., August 25, 1920.
39. Interview with Nick Nuccio, June 10, 1979.
40. Interview with César Medina, May 22, 1984.
41. Interview with Eugenio Rodríguez, July 6, 1984.
42. Interview with Alfonso Díaz, August 15, 1982.
43. Motta, "Nuova Orleans," 464.
44. 1900 Manuscript Census, Hillsborough County, microfilm, PKY. Since established immigrants tended to move away from cigar work, their homeowner rates tended to be higher than for cigarmakers.
45. Property Assessor's Office, Tax Rolls, 1900–1930, microfilm, HCC.
46. U.S. Congress, *Immigrants in Industries*, Table 159.
47. Ibid., 263–64.
48. Ibid., Table 158; *Fifteenth Census*, VI, Tables 67, 68.
49. U.S. Congress, *Immigrants in Industries*, Tables 76, 149.
50. FWP, "Interview with Enrique Pendás."
51. Tampa Board of Trade, minutes, December 10, 1901.
52. Weltz, "Boarders in Tampa." Statistics for the 1910 Manuscript Census, Hillsborough County, microfilm, PKY, showed 810 Spaniards, 352 Cubans, and only 45 Italians in boardinghouses.
53. Motta, "Nuova Orleans," 464.
54. 1900 Manuscript Census, Hillsborough County, microfilm, PKY.
55. 1910 Manuscript Census, Hillsborough County, microfilm, PKY.

56. See Cinel, *From Italy to San Francisco;* Yans-McLaughlin, *Family and Community* (for Buffalo); Caroli, *Italian Repatriation.*
57. U.S. Congress, *Immigrants in Industries,* 264.
58. Interview with Louis Spoto, May 2, 1980.
59. Interview with Joe Maniscalco, April 3, 1980.
60. *Atlanta Journal,* quoted in *Tampa Daily Times,* May 13, 1901.
61. Bodnar, "Immigration, Kinship, and Working-Class Realism," 48.
62. *Tampa Morning Tribune,* August 11, 1907. See also Pizzo, "Italian Heritage of Tampa," 123–41.
63. *Tampa Morning Tribune,* June 21, 1903, December 10, 1908; interview with Domenico Giunta, May 18, 1984; *Tampa City Directory,* 1910–35.
64. Interview with Joe Caltagirone, April 23, 1985.
65. Interview with Sam Costa, April 3, 1985.
66. Interview with Nelson Palermo, March 6, 1982.
67. *Tampa Morning Tribune,* February 10, 1895.
68. Ibid., July 4, 1897.
69. Ibid., May 2, 1905.
70. Ibid., March 28, 1910.
71. U.S. Congress, *Immigrants in Industries,* Table 137.
72. *City Directory,* 1910; *Thirteenth Census.*
73. Quoted in Kessner, *Golden Door,* 108.
74. *City Directory,* 1910.
75. Interview with Anthony Vicari, July 30, 1983.
76. Interview with Joe Valenti, April 18, 1980; *Tampa Daily Times,* January 13, 1982; *La Gaceta,* January 4, 1985; *Tampa Tribune,* March 13, 1985.
77. Interview with Joe Valenti, April 18, 1980.
78. Ibid.
79. Minutes, organizational meeting of the subscribers of the Tampa Wholesale Produce Market, Inc., July 11, 1934. Papers located at the Produce Market office, Tampa.
80. Interview with John and Anthony Ippolito, March 30, 1985. See also *Tampa Tribune,* August 16, 1982; Oscar Aguayo, "Silhouettes: Tony Ippolito," *La Gaceta,* November 15, 1985.
81. Pizzo, "Nick Geraci."
82. See Pizzo, "Italian Heritage of Tampa"; *Tampa Daily Times,* August 19, 1921.
83. U.S. Congress, *Immigrants in Industries,* Table 137; 1910 Manuscript Census, Hillsborough County, microfilm, PKY.
84. *Tampa Morning Tribune,* November 9, 10, 1899.
85. Ibid., August 1, 1904. See also ibid., September 26, 1908.
86. Ibid., March 5, 1905.
87. Ibid., December 23, 1900, April 13, May 28, July 3, 1911, November 6, 8, December 4, 1915, November 15, 1916, April 19, 1917; *Tampa Daily Times,* June 6, 1901.
88. Mistretta, "Sicilian Dairies in Tampa"; interview with Robert Buggica, September 15, 1984; interview with Josephine Militello, September 7, 1982.
89. *Tampa Morning Tribune,* December 14, 1947; *Tampa Tribune,* October 28, 1955; Massari, *Comunità Italiana,* 800.
90. Interviews with Robert Buggica, July 30, 1983, September 15, 1984.
91. Cinel, *From Italy to San Francisco,* 151.
92. Haller, "Organized Crime in Urban Society," 210–34; Bell, *End of Ideology.*

93. Haller, "Organized Crime in Urban Society," 210–18; Nelli, *Business of Crime*; Homer, *Guns and Garlic*, 1–46.
94. D. B. McKay, "Pioneer Florida," *Tampa Sunday Tribune*, May 6, 1951.
95. Interview with John Pizzo, October 2, 1982. Kennedy, *Palmetto Country*, 315, asserts that a Cuban named Francisco Gonzales brought *bolita* to Key West in 1885.
96. *Tampa Morning Tribune*, June 30, 1896.
97. *Sholes' Tampa City Directory, 1901.*
98. *Tampa Morning Tribune*, September 9, 1908.
99. Interview with Anthony Pizzo, February 23, 1974.
100. Kennedy, *Palmetto Country*, 315–16.
101. Interview with Anita Fuentes García, January 19, 1985.
102. Interview with Isidro Stassi, January 26, 1985. Stassi is a pseudonym for a confidential source.
103. Interview with César Medina, May 22, 1984.
104. Harris Mullen, "Florida Close Ups," *Jacksonville Dixie*, June 27, 1912.
105. Interview with Joe Maniscalco, April 3, 1980.
106. Interview with Ciro Vaccaro, March 9, 1985.
107. Interview with Isidro Stassi, January 26, 1985. The newspapers are filled with notices of hundreds of *bolita* arrests. For a sampling see: *Tampa Morning Tribune*, September 10, 1905, March 10, August 13, 14, 1907, March 12, May 28, August 27, 1911, February 10, 1912, April 12, 29, 1917, July 18, 1925, June 14, 18, 1927, August 15, 1928, November 15, 1935. Based on newspaper accounts, no Italians were arrested for selling *bolita* prior to 1925.
108. Interview with Hampton Dunn, July 20, 1980.
109. Interview with Isidro Stassi, January 26, 1985.
110. *Tampa Morning Tribune*, February 28, 1910.
111. Kingsdale, "Poor Man's Club," 472–92.
112. Interview with Isidro Stassi, January 26, 1985.
113. *Polk's Tampa City Directory, 1928.*
114. Interview with Isidro Stassi, January 26, 1985.
115. Ibid.
116. Nelli, *Business of Crime*, 139.
117. U.S. Congress, *Immigrants in Industries*, Table 172.
118. *Daily Tampa Tribune*, December 17, 1891; Messina, *Caso Panepinto*, 141–47; *Tampa Morning Tribune*, August 22, 1897.
119. *Tampa Morning Tribune*, February 3, 1906; see also ibid., September 25, 28, 1908.
120. "Cuesta School," *Tampa Tribune*, March 19, 1983.
121. Interview with Joe Valenti, April 18, 1980; *Tampa Morning Tribune*, November 9–10, 1907; Florida Code of Statutes, 1892, Article 6, p. 2773, 1906, Article 1124.
122. *El Internacional*, November 4, 1910.
123. Thernstrom, *Poverty and Progress*; Hareven, *Family Time*, 360.
124. *Hillsborean*, 1914, 1915, 1919.
125. Cohen, "Changing Educational Strategies," 443–66.
126. Bodnar, in "Materialism and Morality," 5, sees the same patterns at work among Slavic immigrants.
127. Interview with Joe Maniscalco, April 3, 1980.
128. Interview with Mary Italiano, April 20, 1980.
129. Interview with Philip Spoto, June 30, 1979.
130. Greenbaum, "Afro-Cubans in Exile," 11.

131. *Hillsborean*, 1935; interview with Anthony Pizzo, February 23, 1974.
132. Tampa College, *High School Catalogue*, 1930–31.
133. Interview with Nelson Palermo, March 23, 1979.
134. Interview with Rosalia Campisi, March 30, 1985.
135. Interview with César Medina, May 22, 1984.
136. Interview with Domenico Giunta, May 18, 1984; interview with Frank Giunta, July 20, 1980; *City Directory*, 1910–35.
137. FWP, "Seeing Tampa," 67.
138. *Sixteenth Census: Population*, III, Table 13.
139. Information based upon random samples of 600 Italian males and 800 Hispanic males in the 1935 *Polk's Tampa City Directory*.
140. Ibid.
141. Ibid.

10 World War II and Beyond

I guess we're the last of the Mohicans.

Nelson Palermo

In 1982, Perfecto-García locked its doors for the last time. While the closing of a seventy-year-old cigar factory scarcely diminished Tampa's bid to become the brightest jewel in the Florida Sunbelt, its demise reduced by one the handful of factories still operating in what used to be hailed as the Cigar City. The building's enormous windows remind one of a largely forgotten generation that needed the sunlight to discern various grades of tobacco leaf and welcomed the sea breezes to cool them at their workbenches. Eighty-six-year-old César Medina, Jr., confessed that he cannot walk by the abandoned cigar factories without hearing the sonorous voice of his father, *un lector*, rhapsodizing the tales of Don Quixote or Jean Valjean.

The day Perfecto-García closed its doors Antonio Muñiz paid a respectful last visit. As he descended the steps, hat in hand, he paused and asked, "You know what they used to call this factory? *El Paraíso*," explaining that once a tree of paradise grew nearby. Such trees no longer grace Ybor City. Nor do labor strikes like the one that began on August 4, 1927, when the reader at Perfecto-García urged workers to walk off their jobs to protest the fate of Sacco and Vanzetti. Fifteen thousand cigarmakers followed Perfecto-García's lead.[1]

A walk through Ybor City still takes one by the proud mutual aid society buildings, but the clubs and hospitals too have been transformed. The post–World War II era saw a slow but steady deterioration of such activity, for by the late 1940s the world of the cigarmaker was bleak. Once the elite of a skilled work force, cigarmakers became merely workers. The tribunes of the *lectores* had long since disappeared.

Ybor City residents now rely on their corporations, private insurance companies, and the government for health and death benefits. Television, radio, and American culture provide entertainment for this generation, not the domino tables or club dances. The very dreams that led immigrants to cross oceans now threaten their cherished institutions. "I guess we're the last of the Mohicans," mused Paul Longo and Nelson Palermo, former presidents of L'Unione Italiana.[2] Longo, who headed the club in the late 1940s, and Palermo, whose brother served as president during the Second World War, acknowledge what has disappeared, but they do so with sadness.

World War II served as the great watershed for Italian Americans everywhere, and Tampa was no exception. The war severed the umbilical cord to the old country, forged new relationships between individuals/ groups and the federal government, and upset the equilibrium of the ethnic neighborhood. For Italians in Tampa the experience of Mussolini had disillusioned many as to Italy's present and future promise. Antifascist clubs had kept up a steady barrage of criticism against Il Duce. When war broke out few shed tears publicly for Italy. Ybor City's youth and men volunteered in droves for the American cause, and for the first time in the colony's history large numbers of second-generation ethnics left the old neighborhood.[3]

Above all the war meant mobility and disruption. Mobilization regenerated Tampa Bay's slumbering economy: shipbuilding facilities, industrial plants, and military bases attracted tens of thousands of migrants. Ybor City, which chose to ignore the First World War's strident demands of 100 percent Americanism, caught the contagious spirit of this war. Wives and daughters sought defense work and sons and fathers left for military service. Everyone bought war bonds. War-induced prosperity and accumulated savings permitted many Italian Americans to purchase property outside Ybor City.[4]

The humiliation and embarrassment of Mussolini's fascist Italy accelerated the considerable distance already present between Italian Americans and the Old World. As increasing numbers of the first generation died after World War II, intimate relationships between Italian and American families grew fainter. Italy's relationship with the western alliance held little fascination for the next generation of Italian Americans—as opposed to the captivation of Israel for American Jews or the eastern bloc satellites for Slavic Americans. New immigration policies ensured that few Italians would enter the United States, reinforcing the orientation toward the future rather than the past.[5]

A number of far-reaching changes bearing profound consequences for the inner city in general and the Italian enclave in particular took place in Tampa during the immediate months following V-J Day, 1945. No single element of postwar American life played a more dramatic role in the lives of ethnic Americans than the federal government. Put simply, Washington now framed new relationships with ethnic America. During the period 1890–1930s the government practiced a policy of benign neglect, broadly defining economic and foreign policies but exercising little role in the private lives of citizens. The depression and a second war created a hydra-headed bureaucracy that would grow massively in influence after 1945.

With the war ended, an activist government resolved to rebuild cities and subsidize suburbia, policies that redefined the ethnic-urban neighborhood. Immigrant communities became pawns in the redevelopment of American cities, as urban renewal undermined the physical and social foundations of countless ethnic neighborhoods. Ybor City was one such community. The impetus for urban rebirth sprang from within and without the ethnic community. To understand the local example, one must examine a broad complex of conditions and images affecting the Tampa area.

Cuban, Spanish, and Italian servicemen returned to Ybor City in 1945, eager to resume the familiar patterns of their domestic lives. For most this proved impossible. While the community still retained its institutional infrastructure, profound change had occurred. Ybor City's housing stock was crumbling even before the war. Ray Grimaldi, a Ybor City banker, remembered how the neighborhood had transformed during the war years: "The area had deteriorated tremendously and people started moving out . . . like we moved out in 1950. . . . All the young kids who had gone in the service and to college . . . were leaving Ybor City."[6] Many veterans might have chosen to return to the old neighborhood, but a combination of the GI Bill (the closest public university was

130 miles away), the Veterans Administration (government-subsidized loans applied only to *new* homes), and urban ecology (Afro-Americans had begun to encroach upon Ybor City, further reducing a housing stock already insufficient for servicemen and their families) forced hundreds of families to relocate away from Ybor City. As the neighborhood felt the deteriorating effects of this population loss, pressures for urban renewal intensified.

The disintegration of ethnic neighborhoods, observed Rudolph Vecoli, "did not entail a breakup and dispersal of the ethnic community."[7] In Tampa, as in Chicago and other places, urban and suburban settlements became extensions of the old ethnic neighborhoods. West Tampa became Ybor City's halfway house to suburbia, offering residents decent housing, room for expansion, and a Latin infrastructure of stores, clubhouses, and ambience.

The migration from Ybor City to West Tampa intensified following V-J Day. Rev. Walter Passiglia explained: "When they [young veterans] came back, they had traveled across the country. Europe and the Pacific and their vision of life had been enlarged. It then became important for them to educate themselves in college. And along with the opportunities education gave them came the common American desire to move to the suburbs. The young Latins and their families had become Americanized to a point, but they still had this strong feeling of heritage and community. The only place in town that offered them a chance to buy good property in a suburban environment *and* still hold onto some of their culture and language was West Tampa. It could have been West Tampa, which was deeply rooted in the Latin ways, didn't hold the prejudice the other parts of town had...."[8]

West Tampa's population doubled between 1945 and 1955. "It was like a mass migration from the inner city to the suburbs of West Tampa," observed Jorge García. "It was the thing to do among members of my generation." Reverend Passiglia explained that his mission in Ybor City was losing members, so he established St. John's Presbyterian Church in West Tampa in 1958. "All 130 people from the mission transferred over here," he explained. By 1970 so many Latins had moved to West Tampa that they were able to elect Elvin Martínez to the state legislature.[9]

Economically cigars no longer controlled the city's destiny; more important, many leading downtown businessmen felt that the public linkage between cigars and Tampa hindered urban development. Cigars symbolized not only Ybor City but the Latin ethos and life-style. In 1949 city officials reprimanded the Chamber of Commerce when it presented a visiting dignitary with a box of Tampa-made cigars. Tampa's business community was searching for a new and more attractive image.

"Practically every tourist of any sense by-passes Tampa now," editorialized the *Morning Tribune* in 1961, "because they think of Tampa as a grimy factory town and shotgun-killing city."[10] A leading men's magazine branded Tampa in the 1950s as the "Hellhole for the Gulf Coast." Such epithets were the result of a quarter of a century of political and criminal excesses, and many Tampa leaders stigmatized Ybor City as the fountainhead of corruption.

The struggle for *bolita* profits had escalated in the 1930s as a result of the Italian entry into organized gambling. Gangland violence ensued, claiming the lives of scores of participants. Gang warfare clearly provided the most sensational aspect of organized crime, yet it was the political repercussions that changed the nature of Tampa.

The records show almost no direct Latin involvement in municipal politics before the 1930s. Voting laws posed a major hurdle to Latin immigrants, and the great majority of early immigrants perceived citizenship and its privileges as irrelevant. Cubans, and to a lesser extent Spaniards, saw little reason to file naturalization papers as they migrated between Cuba and Florida with regularity. In addition, Florida law, with its poll tax and residency requirements, dissuaded immigrants from voting.[11] By 1910 fewer than 10 percent of the city's adult Cubans and Spaniards had become citizens. Italians were even less inclined to pursue citizenship; in 1910, for example, only 3 percent of Italian adult males had been naturalized.[12] As late as 1930 fewer than one in four of Tampa's foreign-born adults had acquired citizenship, ranking Tampa at the bottom of American cities with populations of over 100,000. In comparison, 58 percent of New York City's immigrants, 67 percent of Jacksonville's foreign-born, and 71 percent of Atlanta's immigrants had received naturalization papers by 1930.[13]

Bolita galvanized Latin voters in the 1930s and in the process brought about a quarter of a century of machine politics. Gambling factions expended tremendous sums of energy and money to ensure the election of accommodating officeholders. Many political observers feel that corruption was so pervasive that it is unlikely an honest election transpired in the 1930s or 1940s. "I came to Tampa in February 1935 to take a job as a courthouse reporter for the *Tampa Tribune*," reminisced James Clendenin, who eventually became the chief editorial writer for the paper.

"This *was* the hellhole of the Gulf coast. It had open houses of prostitution, open gambling houses, almost every election was stolen!"[14]

The source of corruption is neatly revealed by informant José Fernández, who served as aide-de-camp for Mayor Curtis Hixon in the 1940s. "I was a police lieutenant, but my function was principally public relations and organizing money raising for the Mayor," Fernández explained. Hixon employed the officer to serve as "bag man" for his administration. "During those days," recollected Fernández, "the *bolita* bankers would give you a sizable amount. Then they wouldn't be arrested or prosecuted or persecuted. They'd give twenty, fifty, to $100,000. Mayor Hixon told me several times that there was nothing wrong with this as long as there was no greed or killings or no scandals."[15] In addition to bribes, much of the monies were spent paying Latins to vote early and often. J. A. Murray, a *Morning Tribune* reporter, aptly summarized the political scene in the late 1940s: "Gamblers hold the balance of power in Tampa today. . . . organized politics are run by the rackets in this county."[16]

In December 1950 the Kefauver investigation publicized Tampa's state of affairs to a shocked nation, and the national smear prompted Tampans finally to clean up their city. The motivation stemmed primarily from a new business class that felt *bolita* and cigars were relics of an old Tampa and by cleaning up the political mess the city would appeal to tourists and investors.[17] *Bolita* faded from the scene with scarcely a whimper in the 1950s.

The hurly-burly world of urban politics produced a number of local politicians who ministered to the needs of their Latin constituents. "The Ybor City politician took a great deal of pride in the power to fix things," remembered Dr. Ferdie Pacheco, whose family was politically active. "I can fix anything. What do you want—a driver's license? I'll take your mother—I know the guy who gives the test. It's like the guy in *Li'l Abner*—Available Jones. What do you want? You need to get out of the draft—I got a guy who'll talk to the board."[18]

The political career of Nick Chillura Nuccio exemplified the enduring tensions between Tampa's Latin and Anglo communities—both the maintenance of machine politics during the 1950s and 1960s and the emergence of Italians into the upper levels of political power. Nuccio was a transitional figure, moving Italians from peripheral participation in municipal politics in the 1930s to a successful integration into politics in the 1960s. The son of Sicilian immigrants, Nuccio became the first Latin to wrestle power away from the predominant Anglo establishment. He lived the life of a professional politician, his entire career consisting of the pursuit and use of political office. Elected as a city alderman from Ybor City in 1929, he succeeded to the county commission in 1936, a position he held for twenty years. The New Deal taught him the lessons of political patronage, which he mastered thoroughly. "There were more than 2,000 WPA jobs in my district," Nuccio recollected.[19]

In 1955 Nuccio challenged the popular incumbent mayor, Curtis Hixon. A fiscal conservative, Hixon profited heavily from a 1954 extension of the city limits that added 91,000 persons—mostly white Anglos who knew little of Nuccio except his Latin surname—to the voting list. Aided by a vicious Drew Pearson story linking Nuccio to the mafia, Hixon easily defeated his opponent by 9,000 votes. The loss failed to dampen Nuccio's spirit, however, and when Hixon died the following year he made a second run for the city's top post.[20]

Nuccio again met formidable opposition, chiefly from the influential *Tampa Tribune*. "Newspapers didn't like my name," he recalled, "didn't like where I lived in Ybor City. They said, 'It's a disgrace for a Mayor to live in Ybor City.'" Despite his difficulties with the press Nuccio scored an upset victory, defeating the weak interim mayor, J. L. Young, by a mere 125 votes. Nuccio scored heavily in the Latin precincts: 3,021 to 440 in West Tampa and Ybor City. The campaign "made everyone in the city with a Latin name, no matter where he lived, realize he was Latin and had a stake in the election," remembered one elderly resident.[21]

The man who later conquered Nick Nuccio and moved the Italian community to a new level in modern Tampa politics was Dick Greco, Jr. Greco became a force in Tampa and Florida politics because of an irresistible combination of personal and professional qualities. Like his adversary he was the son of Sicilian immigrants. At thirty-four he became the youngest mayor of any major city in the United States, solidly defeating Nuccio in the 1967 mayoral race, 34,011 to 25,169, and again four years later by an even wider margin.[22] Trilingual, Greco could play dominoes at El Centro Español or talk business with corporate executives. Well-tailored, handsome, and articulate, he was identified as the ambassador for the new Tampa. Significantly, Greco appealed to the voters who harbored few labor ties and had no awareness of or interest in past politics. His timing proved keen, for less than half of Tampa's 250,000 citizens in 1968 were Florida natives.[23]

The elections of Nuccio and Greco represented the coming of age of Italian, and wider Latin, political power. Ironically both men failed to ensure the salvation of Ybor City; indeed, urban renewal claimed large sections of the beleaguered ethnic colony during their administrations. In reality the fears of Latin control expressed by the *Tribune* and downtown spokesmen proved unfounded, signifying clashes over style, not content. Nuccio operated in office as a businessman, albeit one with an accent and a cigar. Stylistically Greco proved to be an Italian American who could win the approval and backing of a diverse electorate. Both men saw urban renewal as part of a regenerative process that would enhance Tampa's image, create jobs, increase property values, and stabilize old neighborhoods. They represented the aspirations of an ethnic group that was increasingly middle class in income and status. Like the road to hell, the path to the new Ybor City was paved with good intentions. The decisions to demolish the old Ybor City were neither conspiratorial nor narrowly conceived but represented a mainstream, consensual process.

By the 1960s large numbers of second- and third-generation Latins had graduated from universities, entered the corridors of power, and moved away from Ybor City. In general they supported and helped articulate the credo that "growth" was good for Tampa. Many genuinely believed that Ybor City could be transformed into a tourist mecca. From a superficial economic perspective Ybor City in 1960 was backward: elderly Latins still supported hundreds of mom-and-pop groceries and small retail shops, but the economic barometer was falling, not rising. One also cannot dismiss the element of human greed in the Ybor City denouement: many Italian American and Latin landowners and businessmen hoped to reap rich dividends from a revitalized and renewed community. Early in the colony's history Italians had become aggressive purchasers of property, a trend magnified in the 1950s. Finally, most Ybor City residents in 1960 trusted the government. The era of Watergate, Vietnam, and such notions as the credibility gap awaited the future. These residents, who had vigorously supported the New Deal and World War II, sincerely believed that urban renewal would mean a civic renaissance, that the architects' sketches of promenades and courtyards, of low-income housing and paved sidewalks, would become realities.

A comparative examination of postwar "Little Italies" that escaped the wrecking ball reveals one salient point: communities that survived were generally able to compress local energies and factions through an established institution (the church) or a newly created civic club (Saul Alinsky prototypes). Sadly, Ybor City, once an institutional hothouse, suffered atrophy by the 1950s. The Catholic church, although immeasurably stronger and more respected after World War II than before, was still weak and not widely supported by the generation that stayed behind. That sons and daughters who moved away often embraced the church with a fervency never seen in Ybor City suggests that accommodation to religion was a function of economic success, residential mobility, and social and class distance.

If the postwar church exercised more influence in comparison to an earlier era, such was not true of the mutal aid societies. Once the institutional linchpin of Ybor City, L'Unione Italiana and its Latin counterparts felt the whiplash of postwar change and new priorities. In large part the hard times were a function of demographics. In 1910 Ybor City was an enclave inhabited almost entirely by individuals under the age of forty; grandparents as a rule stayed behind. Consequently these mutual aid societies collectively built magnificent edifices, even modern hospitals. But aging occurred, and by 1960 every society faced an alarming fact: club coffers were being depleted by massive outlays in medical expenses and death benefits. Lack of planning spelled fiscal calamity.[24]

Young Italian Americans saw little reason to join or support the clubs that so satisfied their fathers and grandfathers. While these clubs still exercised considerable influence—in 1960 the combined membership counted over 16,000 persons, and Latin hospitals ministered to thousands—they failed to coalesce on the issue of urban renewal. Thus the most potentially powerful voice for the Italian and Latin communities fell silent in the 1960s.

The impulses of urban renewal flowed initially from the veins of a highly changed federal government. In the early 1950s the Eisenhower administration approved funds to improve inner cities, perpetuating the ideas of the New Deal and the Fair Deal on the national level. The Interstate Highway Act, also passed during the 1950s, augured profound changes for many ethnic communities. The Kennedy and Johnson administrations followed by supplying vast new sums for urban expenditures.

Florida first approved urban renewal legislation in 1959. Concern for downstate urban problems coincided with court-ordered reapportionment of the Florida legislature, thus shifting power to Hillsborough (Tampa) and Dade (Miami) counties.[25] A number of talented Tampa politicians succeeded to positions of leadership because of this, among them Louis de la Parte (president of the state senate), Emiliano Salcines and Paul Antinori (state's attorneys), Elvin Martínez and Guy Spicola (state legislators), Sam Rampello, Bob Bondi, James Greco, Al Chiaramonte, and Raul Palomino (school board members), and Rudy Rodríguez, Roy Cotarelo, and Bob Bondi (county commissioners).

In 1962 Tampa unveiled the state's first urban renewal agency. The charter spoke of hopes to "rehabilitate, clear and redevelop slum areas" and "preserve and strengthen the distinctive qualities . . . of Tampa's Latin heritage and present-day Latin community." One person's slum, of course, was another's community. Bulldozers began to tear down Ybor City in 1965. "Several years from now, you will be boastful about it," declared Mayor Nuccio. Ray Ragsdale of the urban renewal office predicted that the new Ybor City would become "a tourist attraction second to none in the U.S." A total of $9.6 million was earmarked for the project, and ultimately 660 structures housing 1,100 families were removed. The allure of low-cost family housing reverberated in many minds. Interstate Highway 4 displaced an additional 100 or more families, cutting a huge swath across the northern section of Ybor City.[26]

What remained of Ybor City fell victim to a self-fulfilling prophecy. The notion that the neighborhood would become a black ghetto was amplified by the media and compounded by misinformation. Ultimately racism doomed Ybor City, for once its image as a black ghetto became fixed, the economic underpinning and public acceptance of urban renewal collapsed. In June 1967 a Tampa policeman killed a black youth, and as Afro-Americans took to the streets Tampans confronted the reality of a riot. Although Ybor City was not the scene of the protests, the effect was cataclysmic. Tampa newspapers noted that rioting had damaged property in several neighborhoods, among them Ybor City, "a bad part of town." The linkage was immediate and dramatic.[27]

Racial demographics helped to determine Ybor City's destiny. Between 1950 and 1980 the area's Afro-American population increased 38 percent. Historically the Scrub, Tampa's largest black ghetto, had served as a buffer between Ybor City and downtown Tampa. Now urban renewal displaced thousands of black families, some of whom spilled over to the vacant housing in Ybor City.[28] Tampa's 1967 racial outburst, coinciding with a national backlash following riots in Detroit and Los Angeles, prompted a programmatic reassessment of the Great Society in general and Ybor City in particular. Naysayers challenged the efficacy of urban renewal while the business community questioned investments in the Latin quarter. Financial institutions red-lined Ybor City. "I *lost* insurance companies at the times," remembered Eddie Valdez of the Valdez Insurance Company, "because they said my 'book' of business was not desirable—because it was located in Ybor City. . . . [Then] when Urban Renewal came in and began tearing down buildings, the insurance companies [national] didn't want to touch anything—and I mean *nothing*." The American Reserve Insurance Company, for instance, mailed Valdez a map outlining Ybor City in its entirety and flatly stated that American Reserve would not underwrite the district because it was "too hot to handle."[29]

"I was the executive director and was responsible for the entire Urban Renewal operation," admitted Tim Fox, "but those things occurred many years ago and I don't recall the facts."[30] Others recall them only too well. Marshall Tison, the assistant director of the operation, explained: "We just cleared the land. We did a bang-up job on acquisition and clearance. We just didn't do a good job at all on keeping the program going." Nearly 70 acres of land—over 100 acres counting the interstate—had been razed. Armando Valdes, a jeweler, reflected, "People were moved out. Then homes were destroyed. But who came back? Where are the people?"[31]

Local bureaucrats blame Washington, specifically President Richard Nixon's attempts to dismantle the Great Society. Latins cursed the Department of Housing and Urban Development for needlessly complicating attempts to rebuild structures. Aside from Hacienda de Ybor, a small public housing complex for elderly Latins, in which few Italians elected to live, nothing replaced the businesses, homes, and institutions taken away. In fact former residents refer to the area as "Hiroshima," so completely were these blocks erased. "They raped the area," scowled Nelson Palermo, president of L'Unione Italiana. "When I say raped, I want to broaden that to the extent that when this place was cleaned out, it was said they were going to rebuild. Now, sixteen years later? Nothing." Nationally known artist and Tampa resident Mário Sanchez recalled his experience with urban renewal: "They threw us out. They treated us like Indians; they sent us to the mountains."[32]

Ethnic Revival

Urban renewal physically removed nearly all remnants of the Italian population that had begun leaving Ybor City in large numbers following World War II. What was left behind amounted to empty lots and some retail stores, restaurants, and mutual aid societies. While urban renewal intensified the plight of the mutual aid societies, stripping the clubs of their neighborhood constituencies, they nonetheless have demonstrated resilience, resisting demographic realities and social change. The mutual aid society, once the keystone of immigrant social life, remains the identifiable monument to Tampa's ethnic heritage.

Physically and socially the 1970s and 1980s stand as decades of drift but not death. Ethnic institutions responded to the challenges of urban renewal with varying degrees of success. The Sons of Italy, for instance, lost its building to the bulldozer but relocated in West Tampa, following the migration of membership. In fact much of the movement to the suburbs and other sections of Tampa has not been a random process. Clusters of settlements have appeared, both among upwardly mobile, middle-class Latins and working-class, former residents of Ybor City. These divisions have been replicated in the organizational structure existing among Italian Americans in the area. In West Tampa the Sons of Italy operates two societies, La Nuova Sicilia, with 800 members, and Unità, with 200 members. The societies actively promote various causes, such as spina bifida research, and also help preserve Italian culture by reconstituting various celebrations.[33] La Società Italia, another mutual aid society, also lost its building to urban renewal. But unlike the Sons of Italy, La Società Italia is in a state of suspended animation—legally alive but nonfunctional.

L'Unione Italiana, which once towered over a densely populated Italian quarter, today overlooks blocks of desolation. Across the street Cuervos Café, where Nick Nuccio held court each morning, is now an empty lot. A block away Ferlita's Bakery serves as a museum. City/state officials recently dedicated a former Italian block turned farmer's market and a row of restored cigarmakers' homes. Ybor City's future increasingly relies upon massive government subsidies for such projects. In 1986 the Florida legislature appropriated $250,000 to save the Cuban Club.

L'Unione Italiana endures mainly because the organization continues to represent the elderly, working-class, first- and second-generation types who stayed in the Ybor City environs. Membership continues to fall, however; in May 1986 it stood at 863, which included 375 persons still holding medical and death benefits (the club no longer provides such benefits to new members). Those who tour the club's lavish interior marvel at the ornate facilities, but few relate their needs to the society's future. Presently scores of old-timers return to the *cantina* daily, playing dominoes and cards. But who will take their place? Building maintenance and renovation require tremendous sums of money: in 1981 repairs to the roof cost nearly as much as it did to build the club in 1918.[34]

Only El Centro Asturiano, among all the societies, has managed to maintain a modern, well-equipped facility (a clubhouse *and* a hospital) and retain a wide following (half its membership is under the age of sixty-five). The club has benefited from an enlightened membership, numbering 3,400, strong programming, and the attraction of a modern hospital. The membership lists of the Spanish clubs include hundreds of Italians who seek camaraderie with their Hispanic counterparts but also medical protection.[35] Currently leaders are negotiating a merger with the moribund El Centro Español.

Italian American institutional life in the 1980s reflects the growing class and demographic differentiation between the generations. Some of the older institutions, such as the Sons of Italy, have refocused programs to relate to the changing needs of their constituents. The *Sons of Italy Newsletter*, for instance, features regular reports on the homeland but also includes dietary hints for senior citizens (eat whole-grain pasta!). The group attracts members through promotions such as an "Italian Luau" and Italian scholarship dinners. El Centro Asturiano attempts to attract professional members by emphasizing its gymnasium and its proximity to downtown. The Columbus Association, founded in 1958, appeals to a diverse clientele of Spanish and Italian elements, featuring dinner dances, the crowning of "Queen Isabella," and Columbus Day festivities. The Ybor City Rotary Club, founded in 1948, has also responded to the changing barrio.

New institutions reflect the needs of Tampa's suburban Italian Americans. In 1981 residents organized Italians United in America, headquartered in nearby Brandon. The club features a mixture of Tampa Italian Americans and migrants from New York and New Jersey, called "Yankee Italians." Behavior by younger and more affluent Italian Americans confirms Rudolph Vecoli's observation that "upward mobility . . . generates a need to identify more rather than less strongly with their ethnic group."[36]

Italian Americans recently resurrected the Feast of the Madonna, a rite not practiced in many decades. In August 1985 some 500 Italian Americans participated in the *festa*, held at the Italian Club. In 1980 and again in 1981 thousands of Italian Americans crowded the hallowed auditorium of L'Unione Italiana to celebrate ethnic heritage festivals. Several new organizations have formed that stress the historical importance of Ybor City. An Italian dance troupe performs locally. Area and state foundations have generously supported academic and popular activities centered in Ybor City, and sport has become a popular vehicle to trumpet ethnic virility: witness the successes of Al Lopez, Tony LaRussa, Lou Piniella, and Tino Martínez. Beginning in 1980 a coalition of urban professionals inaugurated the Italian American Golf Tournament, an annual fundraising fete which brings to Tampa celebrities such as Joe Garagiola, Tommy LaSorda, and Joe DiMaggio. Funds have been earmarked for restoration of the Italian Club.

Slippage in language has accompanied and accelerated the demise of the old Latin clubs. Ybor City in its heyday underscored the social primacy of language. Interviews with scores of Latins over the age of fifty reveal that virtually anyone reared in Ybor City became fluent in Spanish, while Italians mastered Italian, Spanish, and English. Few Latins spoke English before they entered the first grade. Historically the commonality of the Sicilian dialect and transethnic discourse in Spanish maintained a powerful medium of ethnic identity.

Mobility and urban renewal have affected language. Once families left Ybor City—where grandmothers generally tended the children, reinforcing the lingua franca—the retention of Spanish and Italian declined. "A lot moved out of their own homes at an earlier age and only come back on special occasions," commented César Medina. "A lot aren't getting the exposure to their elders that we had. They grew up in the American way of life. . . ." Jorge García, an educational psychologist for Hillsborough County and a student of the Latin family, observed that Italian, Cuban, and Spanish American youths frequently experience an "identity crisis" when peers hear them speaking a foreign language. "They're immediately ostracized," stated García. "They don't want to be different. So, as a defense mechanism, they drop the language. . . . [At home] the children hear Spanish and think there is something to be ashamed of."[37]

The struggling mutual aid society, the decline in Italian-speaking youths, and the abandonment of the old neighborhood must not be viewed as a destruction of ethnic bonds and a sign of total assimilation. The processes of assimilation are complex; Ybor City may have been physically abandoned and disfigured, but in its ruins the former immigrant colony has served as a powerful symbol and a source of ethnicity. If ethnicity is defined in one sphere as a commonly shared personal perception of allegiance supplying coherence and meaning at a group level, many Ybor City Italian Americans still draw from that cultural wellspring.

Trend watchers identified a "revolt of the ethnics" in the late 1960s. Alex Haley's *Roots* fired the flames of the movement. Haley, of course, had not really caused the phenomenon, but he did provide an endearing vehicle for its popularization. Ethnic pride appealed to a white America ridiculed by media caricatures. Demographically the movement was predictable. Marcus Hansen once remarked that what the second generation wishes to forget the third generation wants to remember. Third-generation ethnics whose families had left the old neighborhood could now indulge in the symbolic trappings of ethnicity without actually belonging to an ethnic group in the traditional sense. Retailers quickly capitalized on the market, offering T-shirts (KISS ME I'M ITALIAN), "roots tours" to Sicily (including the *Godfather*-inspired pilgrimage to Corleone), and frozen *fica d'India* (prickly pears). For some the resurgence remained merely symbolic—they returned to Ybor City only on weekends to participate in an ethnic celebration or to shop in the surviving import stores, but they didn't move permanently to the old neighborhood. Yet this sort of activity has not been inconsiderable and has generated a momentum of its own.

Resurgent ethnicity coincided with growing Italian and Latin anger at urban renewal and the accompanying migration of Afro-Americans into the area. Hence contemporary Italian ethnicity contains a vigorous political character. Sociologists Richard Juliani, Eugene Erickson, and William Yancey have explored the theoretical foundations of this issue, probing the question, "What social forces promote the crystallization and development of ethnic solidarity and identification?" They contend that new forms of dynamic ethnicity cannot be explained by traditional pluralistic answers which emphasize the cultural bases of ethnic groups: "Ethnic groups have been produced by structural conditions which are intimately linked to the changing technology of industrial production and transportation." Ethnic groups become interest groups, whose persistence is more attributable to salient economic and political issues than merely to quaint symbols of the past.[38]

Politics continues to function as an ethnic hothouse, resurrecting factions and memories. Individual successes by Latins in real estate and the professions have thrust scores of Spanish, Cuban, and Italian Americans into the public and political eye. Observers at the Hermitage Research Institute, a Tampa political foundation, report that Latin candidates record a high correlation of approval from Latin voters regardless of Italian, Spanish, or Cuban heritage. By contrast staffers assert that many newcomers to Tampa disapprove of what they interpret as "the good old boy network," which in many instances are old cliques of Latin lawyers and businessmen.

The 1984 race for Hillsborough County state's attorney featured some of the bitterest campaigning in recent history. Emiliano Salcines held that job for sixteen years, personifying the Latin political style: double-fisted handshake, fulsome embrace, trilingual salutations, and evocative memories of the old days. His opponent, Bill James, attacked Salcines on a personal and professional level, charging that corruption had consumed legal justice. The news media exacerbated the Latin-Anglo confrontation: one television station secretly filmed a Salcines campaign rally, releasing nightly snippets of film showing Salcines embracing friends and supporters who, the reporters gleefully pointed out, had Latin names and criminal records. Latins, in turn, flooded newspapers with letters to the editor that further inflamed the issue. Large numbers of Latins rallied to the defense of Salcines, raising the bloodied ethnic shirt of solidarity. On election day Salcines carried the city, soundly winning the Latin vote, but fared badly in the county and thus lost the contest. "The Sun Belt beat E. J. Salcines," explained one paper, suggesting that the old Latin style of politics was an anachronism in an area with so many new voters.[39]

Many political pundits believe that the ethnic dimension of Tampa politics will change, reflective of urban, economic, and demographic factors. "Most of the money you need for a campaign is still in the city," points out Tampa Mayor Bob Martínez. However Latins, and especially Italian Americans, are continuing to move to the county, a shift that will undoubtedly benefit the emerging Republican party as individuals become more successful. Mayor Martínez anticipated such changes when he switched to the Republican party in 1983, a change that suited his already announced 1986 run for governor and, more fundamentally, the shifting class structure of Tampa's Latins. "Make sure you haven't narrowed your field of influence," cautioned Martínez.[40]

In 1985, some 100 years after the inception of the community, Ybor City stands again on the threshold of change. In reality there are two Ybor cities: the celebrated strip of ethnic restaurants, shops, and clubs along Seventh Avenue; and the residential area the public prefers to ignore. The former is prosperous: property values along Seventh Avenue have risen 300 percent since 1980, reflective of the economic boom affecting downtown Tampa. Lunchtime crowds throng the cafés, disguising the malaise of the other Ybor City,[41] where 2,229 persons resided in

1980, 1,829 of whom were Afro-Americans. The collective profile is not encouraging for the revitalization of the new Ybor City. Nearly half of the district's residents live below the poverty level; fully one-third of the area's residents in 1970 have since vacated the premises; property values range among the city's lowest, averaging $10,000 per home; the police department rates Ybor City as one of the highest crime areas in Tampa. There remains only a remnant of the former Latin population—in 1980 less than 12 percent of the residents claimed Latin heritage.[42]

Yet ethnicity persists among Italian Americans in Tampa. Few second- and third-generation members would describe their heritage as a "life-organizing force," to use Richard Alba's phrase, but that is not to deny the remarkably resilient qualities of ethnicity in various aspects of Tampa's social and political life. In spite of the increasingly stratified community individuals utilize Italian ethnicity in various ways. A respect for family and deference toward the elderly, for instance, stands out as a salient characteristic of Italian American life. Few elderly Italians have migrated to the ever-popular housing complexes for senior citizens. Individual attitudes toward busing, sex, diet, and work reveal distinctive Italian American attitudes.

Intermittent ethnic outbursts appear dependent not only upon structural conditions but also cultural issues. Politics has served as an arena of ethnic identity in Tampa. To be sure political debates have centered around urban power—who governs—but they also pivot around noneconomic issues such as group identity. Ethnic tension generated by political debates in Tampa reflect symbolic issues (ethnic pride, group integrity) as well as functional behavior (the act of voting, contributing to a campaign). What is lacking in Tampa is the inner-city physical confrontation. As Italian Americans move to the county politics will increasingly be fought over good roads, not ethnic banners. Yet today ethnicity continues to play a powerful role.

Italians, in spite of the proverbial Latin bloc vote, are now more different from their Latin neighbors than ever. In part this reflects the vibrant economic growth that has dynamized Florida's west coast. Social scientists might well address the issue of emergent ethnicity and its functions in the Sunbelt as contrasted to the Frostbelt. In Tampa, groups with the most access to power have advanced the quickest and farthest, that is, Italians rather than Spaniards, Cubans, or blacks. Moreover Italians in Tampa were able to avoid protracted struggles over turf because of the absence of established groups, such as the Irish, Jews, or Germans. In such a dynamic area, where so many newcomers fight for political and economic power, the Latin connection forged in Ybor City and through intermarriage has served as a fulcrum of power for Italians.

The post–World War II era has witnessed dramatic gains by Italian Americans. Growing numbers have entered the professional classes, succeeding to political and corporate offices. Such success has meant that the Italian American social and occupational profile has become highly stratified. Whereas in 1900 almost all Italian immigrants in Tampa shared the common bonds of working-class status and residence in an ethnic enclave, today's Italian American population reflects growing class and residential differentiations.

Ethnicity has survived the passage to suburbia, proving to be a remarkably adaptive phenomenon. Its contours have helped shape Tampa's residential, political, and economic maps. New groups, comprised of business and professional classes, and old groups, composed of elderly, working-class residents, feel various needs to incorporate aspects of Italian American culture into their lives. The essential point is that a diverse number of individuals still stress the necessity of defining their identities around some aspect of Italian American life and of being with their own. In this sense there exists a continuous connection with the pioneers who first arrived in Ybor City during the 1880s. Ybor City lives.

NOTES

(Another version of this chapter was presented at the Societies in Transition conference in Philadelphia on October 12, 1985, and will appear in the conference proceedings, to be published by the Italian government.)

1. *Tampa Morning Tribune*, August 4, 1927.
2. Interview with Paul Longo, June 30, 1980; interview with Nelson Palermo, March 11, 1982.
3. Manifesto, "Anti-Fascists Alliance," April 27, 1923, PKY; interview with Carmelo Rocca, July 30, 1982; *El Internacional*, July 1, 1927; Massari, *Wonderful Life*, 230–33; Diggins, *Mussolini and Fascism*; *Tampa Morning Tribune*, July 31, September 9, 1943, April 17, 1944.
4. Polenberg, *One Nation Divisible*, 47–50.
5. Ibid., 47–57.
6. Interview with Ray Grimaldi, November 9, 1978.
7. Vecoli, "Coming of Age," 126.
8. Passiglia, quoted in Dietz, "West Tampa."
9. Ibid.
10. *Tampa Morning Tribune*, July 3, 1961.
11. *Tampa Journal*, February 23, 1888, August 22, 1889; *Tampa Morning Tribune*,

June 23, 1895; *New Charter of the City of Tampa*; Burdick, "Italian, Cuban, and Spanish Immigrants"; Gardner, "Tampa Political Change."

12. U.S. Congress, *Immigrants in Industries*, pt. 14, Table 185; *Thirteenth Census: Population*, II, Table 1; *Fourteenth Census: Population*, Table 9; *Tampa Morning Tribune*, October 29, 1915. See Minutes, Board of County Commissioners, June 7, 1900. Few registered voters bore Latin names. See also *Tampa Morning Tribune*, May 10, September 24, 1907; *Tampa Evening News*, July 25, 1907.

13. *Fifteenth Census: Population*, II, Table 21; *Tampa Morning Tribune*, February 8, 1912.

14. Interview with James Clendenin, April 21, 1980. The 1934 senatorial primary revealed dramatically the presence of machine politics. In that election Claude Pepper challenged the incumbent, Park Trammell, only to lose the race because of massive vote fraud in Ybor City and West Tampa. Kerber, "Park Trammell," 138–39.

15. Interview with José Fernández, July 16, 1982. See also "Political Careers Rested on Votes—Tied to Gamblers," *Tampa Tribune*, May 9, 1978.

16. J. A. Murray, "Gambling Interests Rated Number One Power in Tampa's Politics," *Tampa Morning Tribune*, October 6, 1947. "During the last registration drive, gamblers registered hundreds of voters utilizing 300 autos on election day," wrote Murray. Tom Inglis, "Guns of Tampa," *Tampa Daily Times*, July 1–30, 1971.

17. Kefauver, *Crime in America*; see also *Tampa Morning Tribune*, December 30, 1950, which reported, "The Kefauver Senate Committee turned back the bloody pages of Tampa Crime history in a sensation-packed public hearing."

18. Interview with Ferdie Pacheco, June 12, 1984.

19. Interview with Nick Nuccio, June 10, 1979; Tampa newspapers, 1956–65; *Tampa Morning Tribune*, June 10, 1979.

20. *Tampa Times*, October 9, 1955.

21. Ibid., September 23, 1959; *Tampa Morning Tribune*, September 22, 26, 1956; interview with Nick Nuccio, June 10, 1979.

22. Interview with Dick Greco, Jr., September 14, 1980; O'Conner, "Dick Greco."

23. Mormino, "From Hell Hole to the Good Life," 145–46.

24. Bagley, "Latin Clubs of Tampa"; various Tampa club records.

25. Dauer, "Florida," 92–165; Harvard, *Politics of Mis-Representation*.

26. Interview with José Díaz, May 3, 1980; *Tampa Morning Tribune*, June 2, 1965.

27. Dunlap, "Riot and Red Tape," and "Blacks Gain, Lose in Ybor."

28. Ibid.; Lawson, "From Sit-In to Race Riot," 257–81.

29. Valdez quoted in Dunlap, "Riot and Red Tape"; interview with Ray Grimaldi, November 9, 1978; interview with Nelson Palermo, March 6, 1982; interview with Dick Greco, September 14, 1980; interview with Philip Spoto, June 30, 1979.

30. Quoted in Dunlap, "Riot and Red Tape."

31. Quoted in ibid.; Dunlap, "Blacks Gain, Lose in Ybor," and "HCC's 51 Acres to Remain Barren."

32. Interview with Nelson Palermo, March 11, 1982; Sanchez, quoted in *La Gaceta*, May 9, 1986.

33. Interview with Ann LeMoine; interview with Grace Campisi, August 6, 1985.

34. Interview with Nelson Palermo, March 11, 1982; interview with Joe Caltagirone, November 30, 1984; interview with Vince Pardo, March 27, 1983; interviews with club officials; L'Unione Italiana *News*, May 1986. See also De Loache, "Ybor City Ethnic Clubs Decline."

35. Interview with Jack Fernández, April 15, 1985; Dunlap, "Only One Ybor Club."

36. Vecoli, "Coming of Age," 133.

37. García quoted in Dietz, "Latins Say"; interview with César Medina, May 22, 1984.
38. Yancey et al., "Emergent Ethnicity."
39. Quoted in Mary Jo Melone, "Growth," *St. Petersburg Times*, November 18, 1984.
40. Ibid.
41. "Tampa's Neglected Latin Quarter on a Roll with Renovations," *Orlando Sentinel*, October 14, 1985; "Tampa's Neighborhoods: Ybor City," *Tampa Tribune*, October 20, 1985.
42. Ibid.; *1980 Census of Population and Housing*.

Conclusion
Class, Culture, and Community

> The Ybor City community should be remembered for having proved those values which were held up so religiously by the immigrants who came here.
>
> Domenico Giunta

Like numerous urban centers across the United States, Ybor City nurtured a plethora of factions, classes, and cultures. Different immigrant groups lived together, each attempting to recreate familiar societies amid the challenges imposed by a rapidly industrializing city. Yet from this mixture emerged a community held together by the commonality of shared residence, institutions, and adversity. Ybor City, in fact, tolerated extraordinarily diverse elements within its borders. Radicals and cigar manufacturers belonged to the same mutual aid societies; ethnic groups—black and white—lived, worked, and played side-by-side; residents debated a full spectrum of ideas on street corners and in club rooms. How these various ingredients fit together, and changed over time, speaks to a wider immigrant experience, one of old-world peoples coming together in scores of North American cities to create new-world communities.

The study of communities has become something of a growth industry. In its historic and present forms the chameleon-like term encompasses everything from the shtetl to the New England commons to immigrant enclaves. While scholars disagree over the precise definition of community, and hence what must be studied, there exists a core of agreement as to its characteristics.

Communities share a number of traits. "Community," suggests Harold R. Kaufman, "is a social unit of which space is an integral part; community is a place, a relatively small one. . . . community indicates a configuration as to ways of life, both as to how people do things and what they want—their institutions and collective goals. A third notion is that of collective action. Persons in a community should not only be able to, but frequently do act together in the common concerns of life."[1] At the most elemental level communities evoke a sense of togetherness or weness. Thomas Bender has noted that "communities must be studied from their perspective as a network of social relationships marked by mutuality and emotional bonds."[2] Primary and secondary relationships follow from such interconnections, guided by families, schools, unions, youth groups, and mutual aid societies. Much recent literature has focused on the connective links that tie communities together and in the process has perhaps overendowed these connections with romantic qualities. This often sentimental tendency overlooks other considerations: heterogeneous communities typically contained important fault lines of race, class, and ethnicity.

While the contemporary urge is to paint communities in rosy hues, observers once derided immigrant enclaves as breeding grounds for social disorder. This older view is also inaccurate in its simplicity. The immigrant community played important roles in structuring lives, being, as it was, the primary world in which newcomers sorted out new arrangements. Ethnicity, for example, required a critical mass only brought about by high-level immigrant clustering. In Milton Gordon's terminology ethnicity serves as "the commonly shared personal perception of ultimate allegiance that supplies coherence and community on a group level." Furthermore, ethnicity suggests a "network of organizations and informal social relationships which permits and encourages the members of the ethnic group to remain within the confines of the group for all their primary and some of their secondary relationships in all stages of the life cycle."[3] These relationships, however, are never static; rather they respond to the shifting needs of group members as they deal with varying internal and external situations.

Ybor City's frontier beginnings bonded immigrants together in immediate and close contact. The conditions at hand forced them to come to grips with the physical problems of living and working in this outpost, even though many in these years intended only a short stay. Although privation is not necessarily a handmaiden to harmony, almost from the beginning outside intrusions from the host society—ranging from uncomplimentary stereotypes to vigilante violence—added important centripetal forces to the emerging community. These factors worked against what were powerful centrifugal pressures that threatened to erode any thread of community consensus.

In time a common identity evolved, resulting largely from cross-group sharing and cooperation. This proved particularly true of the institutions Latins created to organize and humanize their new world. Community life unfolded in the saloons, groceries, club halls, union rooms, and debating forums that gave Ybor City its distinctive culture. But Ybor City was always more than wrought iron and granite cornices. As Philip Spoto explained, "You see, it's not the physical buildings itself [sic] that existed here. . . . It was a close knit community. I mean, everybody knew each other, they were all workers. . . . The doors were kept open, and everybody was welcome."[4]

America's urban and industrial transformations created alarming new uncertainties for immigrants who knew too well the old-world fears of disease and famine but now faced fresh threats from the new industrial order. Factory accidents, industrial violence, and nativist hostility generated novel solutions, defensive modes of adaptation. Immigrants demonstrated remarkable powers of adaptability in forming collectives to resist these new intrusions. The organization of broad-based mutual aid societies, trade unions, and family/group cooperative's represented such responses.

The merging of Ybor City's population in working relationships did not in itself guarantee the creation and perpetuation of a working-class unity. Fundamental areas of difference separated the immigrant groupings. Traditional values and folk cultures propelled them along their own trajectories even as they experienced areas of overlap and commonality. Cubans, Spaniards, and Italians ultimately all structured diverse work experiences in Ybor City, distinctions that involved divergent conceptions of group behavior, career orientation, and upward mobility. These disparities also meant that the community produced enduring internal sources of ethnic variation.

In this sense Ybor City tied itself into wider patterns of national development. Unity amid diversity emerges as a principal theme of this community's experience, as indeed it does for America generally. More than a single working-class culture operated among Latins even at the height of the popularity of class-based unions and leftist rhetoric. Class and ethnicity therefore emerge more as reflections of the accommodations people fashioned to cope with the insecurities that came with social change rather than ends in themselves. Union policies, for example, appealed to most Italians by promising to deliver rewards they anxiously sought—better wages, property ownership, and a secure family base. In the end the blend between unity and diversity depended upon how work, ideologies, ethnic interactions, and culture combined over time.

The Great Depression, which in other communities often induced a strong working-class identity, had the opposite effect in Ybor City. During the 1930s the community's vigorous institutional base fell into serious decline, eroding the bonds that connected the Latin population. Divergent mobility patterns begun earlier now accelerated, and the general trend was toward a higher degree of individualism and privatization. This presaged the much greater fragmentation and disaggregation that followed in the post–World War II era. The result was a telling paradox: class issues in this community, which earned a deserved reputation for working-class activism, became less rather than more important during the depression.

The Ybor City experience suggests caution in accepting overarching generalizations about immigrant life. Conceptions of ethnic group development neatly depicting immigrants moving steadily through expanding bands of associations, from family and kin to regional clusters to ethnic group and finally to a wider set of American affiliations, appear too simplistic. To be sure the social relationships of immigrants became increasingly formalized and institutionalized after arrival. In the context of Ybor City's local history, however, there was not a linear development but rather a series of measured steps that could go as easily backward on this continuum as forward. Ybor City's Italians very early experimented with formal organizations and networks that went beyond kin and ethnic group in their memberships and aims. By the 1930s these associations had largely disintegrated, giving way to more narrow, and at times individualized, approaches to family and group goals. A different notion of group development is thus in order, one that can provide for varying arrangements over time and that depends largely on how class, culture, and community consciousness intersected.

To the extent that multiethnic settings typified most American urban centers, it is instructive to examine more generally how Ybor City's immigrants accommodated the presence of other groups. By looking to the broader contours of this experience one sees that immigrants responded to a variety of contexts, conditions, and outcomes. Over time a pattern of interethnic adaptation developed that included a measure of sharing and rivalry, of cooperation and conflict, of intimate contact and social distancing.

Timing helped mold immigrant relationships. Those groups reaching Ybor City first claimed key resources and garnered a variety of entrées and status labels that proved difficult for later arrivals to acquire. This was particularly true of the residential and occupational environments created by the cigar industry, seminal factors in determing the contact between groups. Moreover the nature of the early migrant streams assisted in defining immigrant encounters. The different composition of each cluster, the distinctive causes for leaving, and, most important, the diverse goals shaping each immigrant group's experience were crucial elements.

The degree to which immigrant cultures shared values guided the patterns of development. In some instances a high degree of commonality existed and mutually satisfying cooperation ensued. In other situations disparities produced clashes, minimizing the chances for harmony.

Interaction was a constantly evolving phenomenon. As the structure of Ybor City and wider Tampa changed, and as groups followed dissimilar paths of mobility, relationships changed. Outside forces occasionally intruded into Ybor City, influencing the way immigrants reacted to one another. None was more significant than Anglo Tampa itself. Its consistent efforts to control Latins induced a closing of the ranks, producing strongly held feelings of "we" against "them." In this context the intensity of internal differences diminished and the ties binding groups together strengthened.

The chances for more diffused and intensive group contact lessened as Italians increasingly pulled away from the cigar industry and became more residentially mobile. The bases of their Latin identity—and the interaction that gave it meaning—shifted further when situations that had first held groups together eroded. By the 1930s each segment of the Ybor City world had carved out its own niche, responsive to its own specific needs and cultural imperatives. The conditions then underpinning a sense of Latin solidarity differed from those characterizing earlier periods. The range of interactions had moved from the highly personal relationships of union hall, radical group, consumer cooperative, and cigarworker's bench to the more secondary associations of sporting teams, public schools, mutual aid picnics, and neighborhood rituals. Hence the largely working-class identity that had distinguished Ybor City's earlier years gave way to new formulations.

These developments did not mean that a sense of community failed to exist but rather that it had been redefined. Like so many other aspects of the Italian experience community consciousness and Latin identity were malleable realities. They operated in certain well-defined spheres of life and varied to conform to the specific conditions existing at particular historical moments.

The Italian encounter with Ybor City addresses the issue of continuity and change in the immigrant experience. Recent scholarship has debated the relative importance of old-world cultures and new-world structures. What has emerged is a view that posits a blending of these two alternatives and a recognition of the ambivalence and contradiction inherent in the human condition. As Dino Cinel discovered in his study of San Francisco's Italians, "the drive for material success put a premium on change; the attachment to tradition made them resist it."[5] Ybor City reveals the existence of layers of experimentation and change. Italians willingly embraced the economic structure they found, molding traditional outlooks to allow them to work with other immigrants and to join diverse organizations. Yet they did not abandon their familial goals of security and stability, their kinship networks, or the cultural imperatives that gave their private lives meaning. Old-world values could survive for long periods of time but not without taking on the distinguishing characteristics of the local environment. Ultimately inquiries of this sort are best guided by the specific experiences of immigrant groups in identifiable locations over precise periods of time, not by the framing of generalized models.

As has been suggested, class, culture, and community intersected in Ybor City in different ways, changing to meet new realities. Communities must be studied as dynamic phenomena. Like countless other immigrant communities across America, Ybor City was a mosaic of different groups, not the homogeneous entity described by outsiders. An analysis of how the various elements of this small world operated to produce a unique cultural landscape therefore has relevance to a more general immigrant experience. Since these processes were instrumental in shaping parts of urban America's human dimension, a comprehension of them can help to unravel some of the complexities of our multifaceted American character.

NOTES

1. Quoted in Rutman, "Social Web," 60. See also Rutman, "Community Study," 29–37, for further discussion of the approaches to community study.
2. Bender, *Community and Social Change*, 7. See also di Leonardo, *Varieties of Ethnic Experience*, for a perceptive discussion of the "Myth of the Ethnic Community."
3. Gordon, *Assimilation in American Life*, 25–30.
4. Interview with Philip Spoto, June 30, 1979.
5. Cinel, *From Italy to San Francisco*, 261.

Bibliography

1. Oral Interviews

In her masterful studies of textile workers in Manchester, New Hampshire, Tamara Hareven observed that former employees expressed puzzlement why anyone should wish to interview them. So too did present and former cigarmakers, fruit venders, and *bolita* bankers voice initial reluctance to share their memories, asking why we had chosen them. A series of photo exhibitions and conferences drew attention to Tampa's Latin heritage and helped build bridges to the immigrant community. In May 1980 over 1,000 Tampans crowded into L'Unione Italiana to participate in an exploration of Ybor City's Italian immigrant experience. Nothing, however, stimulated dialogue more than our persistent efforts to talk with community residents on their ground.

Our interviewing procedure followed several general rules. We attempted to pursue as far as possible the full life histories of our respondents. We were able to find a surprisingly large number of immigrants to interview, most of them over eighty years of age. From these people we connected ourselves with old-world villages and neighborhoods in ways that would have been impossible otherwise. Most of our interviewees, however, were the children of immigrants, individuals who were mainly in their sixties and seventies. Questions about their parents and kin enabled us to make contact with that generation.

We also structured a standard questionnaire very early in our interviewing process. This common set of questions provided focus and gave us the ability to compare events and personalities systematically. A number of "trigger questions" soon came to the fore as especially effective devices to probe the texture of Ybor City's world. "Who was your favorite reader?" for example, was often the key that unlocked commentary on the workplace, radical ideologies, and strikes. Despite the fact that our questioning was controlled, we never attempted to impose a rigid model or theoretical straitjacket on the process. Each interview contained open-ended portions so as to allow respondents the opportunity to add their own perspectives on their lives.

It was evident very soon after we began interviewing these people that they indeed had their own visions of what they had done and were doing. They had created a cultural landscape uniquely their own, one that had survived in the face of rather formidable odds. Our task was to probe this in all its complexity. Once people accepted our inquiries as sincere the interviewing process flowed smoothly. Indeed individuals began contacting us, asking if we had approached personalities they believed deserved taping. Like Hareven we found prospective candidates most commonly through primary networks such as families, mutual aid societies, and cigar factories. Like her we made special efforts to interview a wide range of individuals so as to ensure that our sources were representative of the broader community.

The following persons generously gave us their time, trust, and, most important, parts of their own personal histories. Unless otherwise noted all interviews were conducted by the authors in Tampa. Tapes transcribed by the University of Florida Oral History Program are designated OHP.

Dr. Frank Adamo, April 20, 1980, OHP
Manuel Alfonso, July 21, 1984
Rosalia Ferlita Anello, October 25, 1984
Anthony P. Antinori, March 6, 1982
Hipólito Arenas, November 1, 1982
Pedro Blanco, February 5, 1979 (by Rita M. Hammond)
Philip A. Bondi, January 8, 1974 (by Nelson Malavenda), OHP
Robert Loria Buggica, July 30, 1983, September 15, 1984
Joseph Cacciatore, March 5, 1982
Alfonso Caltagirone, November 30, 1984
Joseph Caltagirone, November 30, 1984, April 23, 1985
Arturo and Aleida Huerta Camero, March 3, 1984
Rosalia Campisi, March 30, 1985
Giuseppe Capitano, October 15, 1984
Alberto Capodici, March 18, 1981, in Santo Stefano
Giovanni Capodici, March 15, 1981, in Santo Stefano
Dottoressa Serafina Castellano, March 20, 1981, in Alessandria della Rocca
Conrad Castillo, January 19, 1985, OHP
Francesco Centinaro, May 6, 1981, in Santo Stefano
James Clendenin, April 21, 1980, OHP
Angelina Spoto Comescone, July 18, 1979, OHP
Sirio Bruno Coniglio, May 2, 1976, OHP
Sam Costa, April 3, 1985
Rosemary Scaglione Craparo, July 18, 1979, OHP
José de la Cruz, ca. 1978 (by Louis A. Perez)
Julio Cuevas, September 1, 1978, July 29, 1983
Alfonso Díaz, August 15, 1982, OHP
José Vega Díaz, May 3, 1980, OHP

Victor DiMaio, September 26, 1984
Alfonso DiMaria, July 30, 1983
Mark Demmi, March 30, 1980
Honorato Henry Domínguez, September 12, 1980
Hampton Dunn, July 20, 1979, OHP
Aldino Felicani, ca. 1954 (by Columbia University Oral History Project), in New York
Antonio Ferlita, May 6, 1981, in Alessandria della Rocca
Nina Ferlita, April 25, 1980, OHP
Rosalia Cannella Ferlita, May 18, 1980, OHP
Sam Ferlita, April 3, 1985
Aurora Fernández, April 24, 1980, OHP
Jack Fernández, April 15, 1985
José Fernández, July 16, 1982
Mary Aparicio Fontanills, March 5, 1982, OHP
Giovanni Frisco, March 18, 1981, in Santo Stefano
Angelo García, November 29, 1982
Anita Fuentes García, January 19, 1985, OHP
Charles García, February 10, 1979 (by John C. Rupertus)
Manuel Michael García, July 27, 1979, OHP
Julio L. Gavilla, May 25, 1985
Domenico Giunta, May 18, 1984, OHP
Frank Giunta, July 20, 1980, OHP
Angelo Greco, July 30, 1983, September 15, 1984
Dick Greco, Jr., September 14, 1980
John (Ray) Grimaldi, November 9, 1978, OHP
Silvia Grinán, April 15, 1977
John and Anthony Ippolito, March 30, 1985
Mary Pitisci Italiano, April 20, 1980, OHP
Nelson Italiano, February 7, 1980
Sara Wohl Juster, May 4, December 17, 1984, OHP
Annie Licata Lazzara, November 17, 1984
Paul Longo, June 1, 1979, March 13, June 30, July 2, 1980, OHP
Alfonso López, April 24, 1980, OHP
Armando López, February 10, 1979, April 14, 1980, OHP
Sister Mary Lourdes, September 13, 1982, in St. Augustine, Fla.
Sister Mary Edith Mallard, September 13, 1982, in St. Augustine, Fl;
Juan Mallea, August 15, 1982
Joe Maniscalco, April 3, 1980, OHP
Victoriano Manteiga, September 2, 1978
Angelo Martino, February 23, 1985
John Massaro, August 1, 1983

César Marcos Medina, May 22, 1984, OHP
Angela Menéndez, February 5, 1979
Josephine Militello, September 7, 1982
Anthony Muñiz, May 20, 1982
Irene Myrick, September 17, 1982
Sister Mary Norberta, September 13, 1982, in St. Augustine, Fla.
Alena, Alfonso, and Lora Noto, March 4, 1980, OHP
Concetta Licata Nuccio, November 17, 1984
Nick C. Nuccio, June 10, 1979, OHP
María Ordieres, June 11, 1981
Ferdie Pacheco, June 12, 1984, OHP
Nelson Palermo, March 23, 1979, March 6, 11, 1982, OHP
Raoul Palomino, July 26, 1984
Frances Scaglione Paraja, March 4, 1980
Alberto Pardo, October 12, 1982
Vincent Pardo, March 27, 1985
Sam Parrino, December 20, 1984
Tony Pascual, October 4, 1983, August 6, 1984
Mario Paula, June 15, 1980
Anthony Pizzo, February 23, 1974, 1978–84 (numerous conversations), OHP
John Pizzo, October 2, 1982, February 25, 1984
Alfredo Prende, September 12, 1979
Tina Assunta Provenzano, March 13, 1982
Mario Puig, August 1, 1980
Carmelo Rocca, March 6, October 2, 1982, July 30, 1983, February 25, September 15, 1984
Eugenio Rodríguez, July 6, 1984, OHP
Francisco Rodríguez, June 18, 1983, OHP
Wilfredo Rodríguez, April 1, 1982, OHP
Emmanuel La Rosa, October 2, 1982
Giovanni Rumore, October 21, 1982, October 8, 1984
Zoila Salas, February 25, 1974 (by Nelson Malavenda), OHP
Alex and Josephine Scaglione, April 2, 1980, OHP
Emilio Settecasi, March 16, 1981, in Alessandria della Rocca
Frank Settecasi, May 18, June 1, 1979, October 8, 1984
Carlo Spicola, September 22, 1984
Francis and Angelina Spicola, February 4, 1974 (by Nelson Malavenda), OHP
Frank Castellano Spoto, October 2, 1982, September 15, 1984
Helen Martínez Spoto, April 30, 1979, OHP
Louis Spoto, May 2, 1980
Philip Spoto, June 30, 1979, OHP
Isidro Stassi, January 26, 1985

Francesca Adamo Tagliarini, May 22, 1982, OHP
John L. Traina, October 23, 1984
Frank Urso, January 3, 1982
Ciro Vaccaro, March 9, 1985
Frank Vaccaro, February 25, 1984
Joe Valenti, March 27, April 18, 1980, OHP
Anthony Vicari, July 30, 1983
Louis Viscusi, February 12, 1980

2. Federal Writers' Project

Ybor City benefited from an unusually rich collection of Federal Writers' Project (FWP) studies and interviews. Unfortunately the sources are scattered in a number of locations throughout Florida, often surviving only in unedited first drafts and barely legible carbon copies. Yet the extant material provided an extremely useful base of information to guide our own oral interviews and other investigations. Among the most helpful were:

Bryan, Lindsay. "A Study of the Latin Press in Ybor City, Tampa, Florida" (1939; in *Newspapers in Tampa*)
———. "Photographs on Tombstones: A Latin Custom" (1936)
Cannella, Felix. "Tampa and Its Latin Colonies" (1936)
"Centro Asturiano Hospital" (n.d.)
"Cruize [*sic*] on the Minnehaha" (diary, November 27, 1891; Historical Records Survey, 1937, Special Collections, USF)
"Cuban Family in Ybor City" (1936)
"Family Life in Ybor City" (n.d.)
García, José. "History of Ybor City" (1936)
Ginésta, Domingo. "A History of Ybor City" (1936)
Historical Records of the House and Church Society of Jesus, Tampa (1938)
"Interview with Enrique Pendás" (1934)
"Interview with Pedro and Estrella" (1939)
Lemos, Fernando. "Early Days of Ybor City" (1936)
"Life History of B. M. Balbontín" (1939)
"Life History of Domingo Ginésta" (n.d.)
"Life History of Enrique Pendás" (1936)
"Life History of Fermín Suoto" (1935)
"Life History of Fernando Lemos" (1935)
"Life History of José García" (n.d.)
"Life History of José Ramón Sanfeliz" (n.d.)
"Life History of Mr. John Cacciatore" (1939)
Marrerro, Manuel. "Story of the Cuban Family in Ybor City" (1936)

"Members in the Centro Español" (n.d.)
"Members in the Círculo Cubano" (n.d.)
"Recreational Activities, Centro Asturiano" (n.d.)
"Recreational Activities, Centro Español" (n.d.)
Sabe, Quien. "Early Days of Ybor City and the Beginnings of the Cigar Industry" (1939)
"Seeing Tampa" (1935)
"Social Life, Ybor City" (1936)
"Study of La Unión Martí-Maceo, Cuban Club for the Colored Race" (n.d.)
"Study of the Centro Asturiano in Ybor City" (n.d.)
"Study of the Centro Español" (n.d.)
"Study of the Círculo Cubano" (n.d.)
"Study of the Church in Ybor City" (1934)
Suoto, Fermín. "History of Ybor City" (n.d.)
"Trade Jargon of the Cigar Industry in Tampa" (n.d.; typewritten, bound copy in PKY)
"L'Unione Italiana" (n.d.)
Valdez, F. "Life History of Pedro Barrios" (1939)
"Welfare Aid, Centro Asturiano" (n.d.)
"Welfare Aid, Centro Español" (n.d.)
"Ybor City Historical Data" (1934)

3. Newspapers

L'Alba Sociale (Tampa)
L'Aurora (Tampa)
Boletín Obrero (Tampa)
El Comercio (Tampa)
La Cronaca Sovversiva (Barre, Vt.; Lynn, Mass.)
Daily Tampa Tribune
La Defensa (Tampa)
El Despertar (Tampa)
La Federacíon (Tampa)
El Federal (Tampa)
La Fiaccola (Buffalo, N.Y.)
The Florida Peninsular (Tampa)
La Gaceta (Tampa)
El Internacional (Tampa)
Jacksonville Dixie
Jacksonville Times Union
Kissimmee Valley
Il Martello (New York)

Il Martire (Tampa)
El Obrero Industriale (Tampa)
Ocala Banner
L'Ora (Palermo)
L'Organizzatore (Tampa)
La Parola dei Socialisti (Chicago)
Il Progresso Italo-Americano (New York)
Il Proletario (New York)
La Protesta Umana (Chicago)
La Riscossa (Tampa)
St. Petersburg Times
Tampa Citizen
Tampa Daily Times
Tampa Evening News
Tampa Guardian
Tampa Journal
Tampa Morning Tribune
Tampa Sunland Tribune
Tampa Tribune
Tampa Weekly Tribune
United States Tobacco Journal (New York)
La Voce della Colonia (Tampa, 1911)
La Voce della Colonia (Tampa, 1929)
La Voce dello Schiavo (Tampa)

4. Government Documents

Archivio Comunale, Santo Stefano, Provincia di Agrigento.
Bureau of Immigration and Naturalization, Record Group 85. National Archives, Washington, D.C.
"Casellario Politico Centrale," *Archivio Centrale dello Stato*, Rome.
Department of Commerce, Bureau of Census. *Historical Statistics of the United States: Colonial Times to 1970*, I. Washington, D.C.: Government Printing Office, 1975.
———. Industries Study Section. *The Tobacco Study*. Tobacco Unit, Division of Review. Washington, D.C.: Government Printing Office, 1936.
Department of Justice. Investigative Case Files of the Bureau of Investigation, 1908–22, National Archives, Washington, D.C.
———. "Strike File—Cigarmakers, 1911," Record Group 60. National Archives, Washington, D.C.
Department of Labor, Women's Bureau. *Women in Florida Industries*. Washington, D.C.: Government Printing Office, 1930.

Department of State. State Decimal File, 1910–29, "Tampa Lynching Incident." National Archives, Washington, D.C. .
Florida, Board of Health. *Fifteenth Annual Report, 1904.* Jacksonville: Drew Press, 1905.
Florida Code of Statutes, 1892, 1906. Tallahassee.
Ministero di Agricoltura, Industria e Commercio-Direzione Generale della Statistica. *Statistica della Emigrazione Italiana.* Rome: Instituto Centrale di Statistica, 1894.
Muncipal Council Meetings, 1891–92, Communal Archives, Santo Stefano Quisquina.
Passenger and Crew Lists of Vessels Arriving at New York, 1897–1942, VIII, March 13, 1905. National Archives, Washington, D.C.
Rose, R. E. "The Disston Sugar Plantation," in *Twelfth Biennial Report of the Department of Agriculture of the State of Florida.* Tallahassee: T. J. Appleyard, State Printer, 1912, pp. 85–88.
Sumner, Helen L. *Women and Children Earners in the United States,* 19 vols. IX: "History of Women in Industry in the United States," 61st Cong., 2d sess., Sen. doc. 645. Washington, D.C., 1910.
U.S. Census Bureau. Manuscript Census Schedules, Hillsborough County, Fla., 1900, microfilm, PKY.
———. *Ninth Census of the United States, 1870: The Statistics of the Population of the United States.* Washington, D.C.: Government Printing Office, 1872.
———. *Tenth Census of the United States, 1880: The Statistics of the Population of the United States.* Washington, D.C.: Government Printing Office, 1883.
———. *Eleventh Census, 1890: Report of Population of United States.* Washington, D.C.: Government Printing Office, 1895.
———. *Twelfth Census of the United States, 1900: Population.* Washington, D.C.: Government Printing Office, 1902.
———. *Thirteenth Census of the United States, 1910: Population.* Washington, D.C.: Government Printing Office, 1913.
———. *Fourteenth Census of the United States, 1920: Population.* Washington, D.C.: Government Printing Office, 1922.
———. *Fifteenth Census of the United States, 1930: Population.* Washington, D.C.: Government Printing Office, 1932.
———. *Sixteenth Census of the United States, 1940: Population.* Washington, D.C.: Government Printing Office, 1942.
U.S. Congress. *Proceedings* of the Cuba and Florida Immigration Investigation, Senate Committee on Immigration, Senate Committee on Epidemic Disease, and House Committee on Immigration and Naturalization, December 28–31, 1892, pp. 65–98.
U.S. Congress (Senate). Immigration Commission Report. *Immigrants in Industries,* XIV: "Cigar and Tobacco Manufacturing"; XXIII: "Summary Reports

on Immigrants in Manufacturing and Mining." Washington, D.C.: Government Printing Office, 1911.

The War of the Rebellion: A Compilation of the Official Records of the Union and Confederate Armies. 51 vols. Washington, D.C.: Government Printing Office, 1891.

5. Local Public Documents

Hillsborough County

Marriage Records, 1890–1940
Minutes, Board of County Commissioners, 1885–1900
Petitions to the County Commission, 1886–1916
Tax Rolls, Property Assessor's Office, 1900–1930
Voter Statistics, Bureau of Elections, 1935–45

City of Tampa

The Gate-to-the-Gulf Tampa City Directory (Tampa: J. O. D. Clark Publishers, 1893)
Minutes, City Council, 1886–1920
New Charter of the City of Tampa (Tampa: Tribune Printing Company, 1903)
Petitions, City Council, 1910–12
R. L. Polk's City Directory of Tampa (Columbus, Ohio: R. L. Polk, 1899–)
Records, Board of Trade, 1885–1910
Records, Chamber of Commerce, 1910–40
Sholes' Directory of the City of Tampa (Savannah: Morning News Printer, 1899–1901)

6. Institutional Records and Private Papers

American Federation of Labor Records, CMIU *Constitutions and Proceedings*
Avellanal Family Papers, Special Collections, USF
Carmen Ramirez de Esperante Papers, Special Collections, USF
Cigar Makers International Union (CMIU), *Cigar Makers Official Journal,* Washington, D.C.
———, Papers, "National and Internationals File," AFL-CIO Headquarters, Washington, D.C.
La Società Sicilia Collection, Special Collections, USF
Tony Pizzo Papers, Special Collections, USF
La Unión Martí-Maceo Collection, Special Collections, USF
L'Unione Italiana Collection, Special Collections, USF
V. Martínez Ybor Collection, THS

Church Records

Archives, La Madre della Chiesa, Santo Stefano Quisquina
Archives, St. Augustine Diocese, St. Augustine, Fla.
Incoming Correspondence, Florida, 1832–93, American Home Mission Society
Marriage Registers, 1923–35, Church of the Most Holy Name, Tampa
———, 1891–1935, Our Lady of Perpetual Help, Tampa
———, 1895–1935, Sacred Heart, Tampa
Minutes of the Journal of the Florida Annual Conference, 1894–1917, Methodist Episcopal Church, South
Parish Reports, *Notitiae*, 1895–1935, Archives, St. Augustine, Fla.
Reports, 1912–53, Tampa Bay Baptist Association of Florida

Ethnic Club Records

These include minutes of monthly and yearly meetings, membership lists, medical records, library accounts, and various related documents.
El Centro Asturiano
El Centro Español
El Círculo Cubano
L'Unione Italiana
L'Unión Martí-Maceo

7. Unpublished Works

Alberta, Sister Mary. "A Study of the Schools Conducted by the Sisters of St. Joseph in Florida." M.A. thesis, University of Florida, 1940.
Bagley, Salatha. "The Latin Clubs of Tampa, Florida." M.A. thesis, Duke University, 1948.
Barker, Eirlys M. "Seasons of Pestilence: Tampa and Yellow Fever, 1824–1905." M.A. thesis, University of South Florida, 1984.
Bayless, Cathy. "The Invisible Pioneers: Mid-Nineteenth Century Slaves in Hillsborough County." Unpublished ms., University of South Florida, 1981.
Burdick, Jennifer. "The Role of Italian, Cuban, and Spanish Immigrants in Tampa Politics." Unpublished ms., University of Florida, 1984.
Chamberlin, Donald. "Fort Brooke, A History." M.A. thesis, Florida State University, 1968.
Cooper, Patricia Ann. "From Hand Craft to Mass Production: Men, Women and Work Culture in American Cigar Factories, 1900–1919." Ph.D. dissertation, University of Maryland, 1981.
Cordero, Enrique A. "The Afro-American Community in Tampa Florida." Unpublished ms., University of South Florida, 1982.

Davis, Gayle Everette. "Riot in Tampa." M.A. thesis, University of South Florida, 1976.
Ellis, Gary D. "A Late-Nineteenth Century Historical Site in Ybor City Historical District in Tampa, Florida." M.A. thesis, University of South Florida, 1977.
Gardner, Larry. "Tampa Political Change, 1910–27." Unpublished ms., University of South Florida, 1982.
Green, George N. "Florida Politics and Socialism at the Crossroads of the Progressive Era." M.A. thesis, Florida State University, 1962.
Hendry, Earl R. "A Revisionist View of the Italian Immigrants of Ybor City in 1900." Seminar paper, University of Florida, 1982.
Johnson, Barbara Ruth. "Origin of the Partido Revolucionario Cubano in Tampa: Martí and the Tobacco Workers." M.A. thesis, University of Florida, 1968.
Kerber, Steven. "Park Trammell: A Political Biography." Ph.D. dissertation, University of Florida, 1979.
Leon, Joseph M. "The Cigar Industry and Cigar Leaf Tobacco in Florida." M.A. thesis, Florida State University, 1962.
McFarlin, Roby Hull. "Diary: Tampa, Florida, January 1, 1887 to April 1888. Unpublished ms., Special Collections, University of South Florida.
Mackle, Elliott James, Jr. "The Eden of the South: Florida's Image in American Travel Literature and Painting, 1865–1900." Ph.D. dissertation, Emory University, 1977.
Mardis, Robert Frances. "Federal Theatre in Florida." Ph.D. dissertation, University of Florida, 1972.
Mistretta, Mike. "A History of Sicilian Dairies in Tampa." Unpublished ms., University of South Florida, 1982.
Mulholland, Kevin. "Missionary Work among the Immigrants of Tampa." Seminar paper, University of Florida, 1982.
O'Neill, Sister Mary Roselina. "History of the Contribution of the Sisters of the Holy Name of Jesus and Mary to the Cause of Education in Florida." M.A. thesis, Fordham University, 1930.
Parrish, Charles James, "Minority Politics in a Southern City: Tampa, Florida, 1950–60." M.A. thesis, University of Florida, 1960.
Poyo, Gerald E. "The Anarchist Challenge to the Cuban Independence Movement, 1885–90." Research paper, University of Texas, 1982.
———. "Cuban Émigré Communities in the United States and the Independence of Their Homeland, 1852–95." Ph.D. dissertation, University of Florida, 1983.
Puglisi, Josephine. "Ybor City: A Study of an Hispanic Heritage." M.A. thesis, Florida State University, 1952.

Rickenbach, Richard B. "A History of Filibustering from Florida to Cuba, 1895–98." M.A. thesis, University of Florida, 1948.
Robbins, Ray F. "The Socialist Party in Florida." M.A. thesis, Samford University, 1971.
Scaglione, Peter. "The Cigar Industry of Florida." M.A. thesis, University of Florida, 1933.
Schellings, John William. "Tampa, Florida: Its Role in the Spanish American War, 1898." M.A. thesis, University of Miami, 1954.
Slusser, Catherine Bayless. "A Professional Opinion: A History of the Hillsborough County Medical Association, 1895–1970." M.A. thesis, University of South Florida, 1982.
Smith, Helen. "Americanization and Christianization: Protestant Home Missions in Tampa, 1890–1920." Seminar paper, University of Florida, 1983.
———. "Immigrant Women in Tampa's Cigar Industry." Seminar paper, University of Florida, 1982.
Steffy, Joan M. "Cuban Immigrants of Tampa, Florida (1886–98)." M.A. thesis, University of South Florida, 1975.
True, Marshall MacDonald. "Revolutionaries in Exile: The Cuban Revolutionary Party, 1891–98." Ph.D. dissertation, University of Virginia, 1965.
Weltz, Karen. "Boarders in Tampa, 1900 and 1910." Unpublished ms., University of South Florida, 1983.
Westfall, L. Glenn. "Don Vicente Martínez Ybor, The Man and His Empire: Development of the Clear Havana Industry in Cuba and Florida in the 19th Century." Ph.D. dissertation, University of Florida, 1977.
Westmeyer, Paul D. "Tampa, Florida: A Geographical Interpretation of Its Development." M.A. thesis, University of Florida, 1953.
Wilson, Jon. "Hard Times and Long Faces: Early Reconstruction in Tampa." Unpublished ms., University of South Florida, 1981.

8. Articles and Book Chapters

Appel, John C. "The Unionization of Florida Cigarmakers and the Coming of the War with Spain," *Hispanic American Historical Review* 36 (February 1956), 38–49.
Baily, Samuel L. "The Adjustment of Italian Immigrants in Buenos Aires and New York, 1870–1914," *American Historical Review* 88 (April 1983), 281–306.
Barton, Josef. "Eastern and Southern Europeans," in *Ethnic Leadership in America*, ed. John Higham. Baltimore: Johns Hopkins University Press, 1978, 150–75.
Bodnar, John. "Immigration, Kinship and the Rise of Working-Class Realism in Industrial America," *Journal of Social History* 12 (Fall 1980), 45–65.

———. "Materialism and Morality: Slavic-American Immigrants and Education, 1890–1940," *Journal of Ethnic Studies* (Winter 1976), 1–19.
Bodnar, John, Michael Weber, and Roger Simon. "Migration, Kinship, and Urban Adjustment: Blacks and Poles in Pittsburgh, 1900–1930," *Journal of American History* 66 (December 1979), 548–65.
Boggs, Ralph S. "Spanish Folklore from Tampa, Florida," *Southern Folklore Quarterly* (June 1938), 46–52.
Boyte, Harry. "Populism and the Left," *Democracy* 1 (April 1981), 58–61.
Brandmeyer, Gerard A. "Baseball and the American Dream: A Conversation with Al Lopez," *Tampa Bay History* 3 (Spring/Summer 1981), 48–74.
Breton, Raymond. "Institutional Completeness of Ethnic Communities," *American Journal of Sociology* 70 (1964), 193–205.
Broquet, Paul. "The Geology of the Madonie Mountains of Sicily," trans. Jacques Marie, in *Geology and History of Sicily*, ed. Walter Alvarez and Klaus Gohrbardt. Veeto: Petroleum Exploration Society of Libya, 1970, 201–30.
Bugea, Alfonso. "Santo Stefano di Quisquina: Un Paese Che non Cresce," *Giornale di Sicilia*, October 8, 1982.
Buker, George E. "Tampa's Muncipal Wharves," *Tampa Bay History* 5 (1983), 37–47.
Canfield, D. L. "Tampa Spanish: Three Characters in Search of a Pronunciation," *Hispania* 35 (January 1951), 95–98.
Carey, George W. "The Vessel, the Deed, and the Idea: Anarchists in Paterson, 1895–1908," *Antipode* 10/11 (1979), 51–56.
Carpi, Leone. "Condizioni delle Donne," in *Delle Colonie e Dell' Emigrazione Italiana all' Estero*. 4 vols. Milan: Tipografica Editrice Lombardia, 1874.
Cassels, Alan. "Fascism for Export," *American Historical Review* 69 (April 1967), 707–12.
Cerrito, Gino. "Sull' Emigrazione Anarchica Italiana negli Stati Uniti d'America," *Volontà* 4 (July–August 1967), 269–76.
Cohen, Miriam. "Changing Education Strategies among Immigrant Generations: New York Italians in Comparative Perspective," *Journal of Social History* 11 (Spring 1982), 443–66.
Compton, George, and Adolfo Solórzano Díaz. "Latins on the Diamond," *Américas* 3 (June 1951), 9–11, 40–41.
Conzen, Kathleen Neils. "Immigrants, Immigrant Neighborhoods, and Ethnic Identity: Historical Issues," *Journal of American History* 66 (December 1979), 603–15.
Corbitt, Duvon C. "Immigration in Cuba," *Hispanic American Historical Review* 22 (May 1942), 280–308.
Covington, James. "The Armed Occupation Act of 1842," *Florida Historical Quarterly* 60 (July 1961), 41–53.

———. "Life at Fort Brooke, 1824–36," *Florida Historical Quarterly* 36 (1958), 319–30.

———. "The Tampa Bay Hotel," *Tequesta* 26 (1966), 3–20.

Crews, David. "Definitions of Modernity: Social Mobility in a German Town, 1880–1901," *Journal of Social History* 7 (Fall 1973), 51–74.

d'Ans, André-Marcel. "The Legend of Gasparilla: Myth and History on Florida's West Coast," *Tampa Bay History* 2 (1980), 5–30.

Dauer, Manning. "Florida: The Different State," in *The Changing Politics of the South*, ed. William Havard. Baton Rouge: Louisiana State University Press, 1962.

Day, Allen Willey. "Cuban Settlers in America," *The Chautauquan* 27 (July 1898), 346–48.

De Loache, Frank. "In Changing Times, Ybor City Ethnic Clubs Decline," *St. Petersburg Times*, September 6, 1983.

Dietz, Ed. "Latins Say When Language Slipped, So Did Family," *Tampa Tribune*, September 17, 1977.

———. "West Tampa Became Boom Town after World War Two," *Tampa Tribune*, September 17, 1977.

Dodson, Pat. "Hamilton Disston's St. Cloud Sugar Plantation, 1887–1901," *Florida Historical Quarterly* 49 (1971), 356–70.

Dovell, J. E. "The Railroads and the Public Lands of Florida, 1879–1905," *Florida Historical Quarterly* 34 (January 1956), 236–58.

Dumoulin, John. "El Movimiento Obrero en Cruces, 1902–25," *Islas* 62 (January–April 1979), 96.

Dunlap, Jeff. "Blacks Gain, Lose in Ybor." *Tampa Tribune*, May 16, 1979.

———. "HCC's 51 Acres to Remain Barren," *Tampa Tribune*, May 15, 1979.

———. "Only One Ybor Club Continues to Thrive," *Tampa Tribune*, May 15, 1979.

———. "Riot and Red Tape Snarled Ybor Revival," *Tampa Tribune*, May 14, 1979.

"Emigración," in *Gran Enciclopedia Asturiana*, 17 vols. Gijon: n.p., 1981.

Estrade, Paul. "Las Huelgas de 1890 en Cuba," *Revista de la Biblioteca Nacional de José Martí* 21 (January–April 1979), 27–51.

Fara, Forni, "Gli Italiani di Nuova Orleans (Stati Uniti)," *Bolletino dell' Emigrazione* 17 (1905), 3–17.

———. "Gli Italiani nel Distretto Consolare di Nuova Orleans," *Emigrazione e Colonie* (Roma, 1909), 217–18.

Fernández, Frank. "Los Anarquistas Cubanos (1865–98)," *Guangara Libertaria* 5 (1981), 4–5.

Fimrite, Ron. "In Cuba, It's Viva el Grand Old Game," *Sports Illustrated* 46 (June 1977), 68–80.

Furio, Columbia. "The Cultural Background of the Italian Immigrant Woman and Its Impact on Her Unionization in the New York City Garment Industry," in *Pane e Lavoro*, ed. G. E. Pozzetta. Toronto: Multicultural History Society of Ontario, 1980, 81–98.

Gabaccia, Donna. "Migration and Peasant Militance: Western Sicily, 1880–1910," *Social Science History* 9 (Winter 1984), 67–80.

———. "Neither Padrone Slaves nor Primitive Rebels: Sicilians on Two Continents," in *Struggle a Hard Battle*, ed. Dirk Hoerder. DeKalb: Northern Illinois University Press, 1985.

———. "Sicilians in Space: Environmental Change and Family Geography," *Journal of Social History* 16 (1982), 53–66.

Gallo, Gaspar. "El Tabaquero en el Trayectoria Revolucionaria de Cuba," *Revista Bimestre Cubana* 22 (1936), 100–121.

Gómez, R. A. "Spanish Immigrants in the United States," *The Americas* 19 (July 1962), 59–77.

Greenbaum, Susan. "Afro-Cubans in Exile: Tampa, Florida, 1886–1984," *Cuban Studies* 15 (Winter 1985), 59–73.

Greene, Victor R. "For God and Country: The Origins of Slavic Self-Consciousness in America," *Church History* 35 (1966), 446–61.

Grele, Ronald J. "Movement Without Aim: Methodological and Theoretical Problems in Oral History," in *Envelopes of Sound: Six Practitioners Discuss the Method, Theory and Practice of Oral History and Oral Testimony*, ed. Ronald Grele. Chicago: Precedent Publishing, 1975, 127–54.

Gutman, Herbert. "Work, Culture, and Society in Industrial America, 1815–1919," *American Historical Review* 78 (June 1973), 531–87.

Haller, Mark. "Organized Crime in Urban Society: Chicago in the Twentieth Century," *Journal of Social History* 4 (Winter 1971), 210–34.

Handlin, Oscar. "The Immigrant and American Politics," in *Foreign Influences in American Life: Essays and Critical Bibliography*, ed. David F. Bowers. Princeton: Princeton University Press, 1944.

Hareven, Tamara K. "The Search for Generation Memory: Tribal Rites in Industrial Society," *Daedalus* 107 (Fall 1978), 137–49.

Harney, Robert F. "Ambiente and Social Class in North American Little Italies," *Canadian Review of Studies in Nationalism* 2 (Spring 1975), 208–24.

———. "Boarding and Belonging: Thoughts on Sojourning Institutions," *Urban History Review* 2 (October 1978), 8–37.

———. "Chiaroscuro: Italians in Toronto, 1885–1915," *Italian Americana* 1 (Spring 1975), 142–67.

———. "The Ethnic Press in Ontario," *Polyphony* 4 (Spring/Summer 1982), 3–14.

———. "Introduction to Records of the Mutual Benefit Society," *Polyphony* 2 (Winter 1979), 1–3.

———. "Religion in Ethnocultural Communities," *Polyphony* 1 (Summer 1978), 1–10.

Hauptman, O. E. "Spanish Folklore from Tampa, Fla.: Superstitions," *Southern Folklore Quarterly* (March 1938), 90–105.

Hays, Francis C. "Anglo-Spanish Speech in Tampa," *Hispania* 32 (February 1949), 48–52.

Hays, Samuel P. "The Changing Political Structure of the City in Industrial America," *Journal of Urban History* 1 (November 1974), 6–38.

Hensley, Rev. P. H., Jr. "Our Spanish Work in Tampa, Florida," *The Home Mission Herald* 3 (February 1910), 35–36.

Higham, John. "Hanging Together: Divergent Unities in America," *Journal of American History* 61 (June 1974), 5–28.

Ingalls, Robert P. "General Joseph B. Wall and Lynch Law in Tampa," *Florida Historical Quarterly* 62 (July 1984), 51–71.

———. "Radicals and Vigilantes: The 1931 Strike of Tampa Cigarworkers," in *Southern Workers and Their Unions, 1880–1975*, eds. Gary Fink and Merl Reed. Westport, Conn.: Greenwood Press, 1981, 44–57.

Ingram, James M. "Dr. Louis Sims Oppenheimer—Culture among the Sandspurs," *The Sunland Tribune* 3 (1977), 18–24.

Isaac, Rhys. "Ethnographic Method in History: An Action Approach," *Historical Methods* 13 (1980), 43–58.

Johnson, Dudley S. "Henry Bradley Plant and Florida," *Florida Historical Quarterly* 45 (October 1966), 118–32.

Juliani, Richard, and Mark Hutter. "Research Problems in the Study of Italian and Jewish Interactions in Community Settings," in *The Interaction of Italians and Jews in America*, ed. Jean A. Scarpaci. New York: American Italian Historical Association, 1975.

Keene, Jesse L. "Gavino Gutiérrez and His Contributions to Tampa," *Florida Historical Quarterly* 36 (July 1957), 33–42.

King, Russell. "Geographical Perspectives on the Sicilian Mafia," *Tijdschrift Voor Economische en Sociale Geografie* 1(1973), 21–34.

Kingsdale, John M. "The Poor Man's Club: Social Functions of the Urban Working-Class Saloon," *American Quarterly* 25 (October 1973), 472–92.

Krause, Corrine Azen. "Urbanization with Breakdown," *Journal of Urban History* 4 (May 1978), 291–305.

Kusmer, Kenneth L. "The Concept of 'Community' in American History," *Reviews in American History* 7 (Spring 1977), 385.

Lawson, Steven F. "From Sit-in to Race Riot: Businessmen, Blacks, and the Pursuit of Moderation in Tampa, 1960–67," in *Southern Businessmen and Desegregation*, eds. Elizabeth Jacoway and David Colburn. Baton Rouge: Louisiana State University Press, 1982.

"The Life and Times of Sacred Heart Parish," *Souvenir Program for Sacred Heart Parish.* Tampa: Catholic Publishers, 1960.

Long, Durward. "An Immigrant Cooperative Medicine Program in the South, 1887–1963," *Journal of Southern History* 31 (November 1965), 417–34.

———. "Labor Relations in the Tampa Cigar Industry, 1885–1911," *Labor History* 8 (Fall 1971), 551–59.

———. "*La Resistencia:* Tampa's Immigrant Labor Union," *Labor History* 6 (Fall 1965), 193–214.

———. "The Making of Modern Tampa," *Florida Historical Quarterly* 49 (April 1971), 333–45.

———. The Open-Closed Shop Battle in Tampa's Cigar Industry, 1919–21," *Florida Historical Quarterly* 47 (October 1968), 101–21.

Luening, William. "Cigar City Rises from the Ashes," *Historic Preservation* 34 (July/August 1982), 46–51.

MacDonald, John S. "Agricultural Organization and Labour Militancy in Rural Italy," *Economic History Review* 16 (August 1963), 61–75.

———. "Italy's Rural Social Structure and Emigration," *Occidente* 12 (1956), 437–56.

MacDonald, John S., and Leatrice D. MacDonald. "Chain Migration, Ethnic Neighborhood Formation and Social Networks," *Milbank Memorial Fund Quarterly* 17 (1964), 113–18.

Melone, Mary Jo. "Along with Growth in Hillsborough County Comes Politics," *St. Petersburg Times*, November 18, 1984.

Middleton, DeWight. "The Organization of Ethnicity in Tampa," *Ethnic Groups* 3 (1981), 281–306.

Mormino, Gary. "Tampa: From Hell Hole to the Good Life," in *Sunbelt Cities: Metropolitan Growth and Political Change Since World War Two*, eds. Richard Bernard and Bradley Rice. Austin: University of Texas Press, 1983.

———. "Tampa and the New Urban South," *Florida Historical Quarterly* 60 (January 1982), 337–56.

Mormino, Gary, and George E. Pozzetta. "Concord and Discord: Italians and Ethnic Interactions in Tampa, Florida," in *Italian Americans: New Perspective in Italian Immigration and Ethnicity*, ed. Lydio Tomasi. New York: Center for Migration Studies, 1985, 341–57 (with comments by Luciano Iorizzo and Richard Juliani).

———. "The Cradle of Mutual Aid: Immigrant Cooperative Societies in Ybor City," *Tampa Bay History* 7 (Fall/Winter 1985), 36–58.

———. "Immigrant Women in Tampa: The Italian Experience, 1890–1930," *Florida Historical Quarterly* 61 (January 1983), 296–312.

Moroni, G. "L'Emigrazione Italiana in Florida," *Bolletino dell'Emigrazione* 1 (1915), 40.

Motta, Ricardo. "Nuova Orleans, Rapporti del R. Consolare," *Emigrazione e Colonie, Rapporti di Agenti Diplomatici e Consolari,* May 14, 1892 (Roma, 1893).
Mullen, Harris H. "Florida Close Ups: Charlie Wall," *Florida Trend* 8 (March 1966), 20–22.
Muñiz, José Rivero. "La Lectura en las Tabaquerías," *Hoy* (May 1, 1948), 78.
———. "La Lectura en las Tabaquerías," *Revista de la Biblioteca Nacional* 2 (October–December 1951), 190–272.
———. "Letter to Editor," *Florida Historical Quarterly* 40 (1962), 314.
———. "El Tabaquero en la Historia de Cuba," *Islas* 5 (July 1963), 293–312.
———. "Tampa at the Close of the 19th Century," trans. Charles J. Kolinski, *Florida Historical Quarterly* 41 (April 1963), 332–42.
Munroe, Kirk. "A Gulf Coast City," *The Christian Union* 25 (January 19, 1982).
Murray, J. A. "Gambling Interests Rated Number One in Tampa's Politics," *Tampa Morning Tribune,* October 6, 1947.
Nahirny, Vladamir C., and Joshua A. Fishmann. "America Immigrant Groups," *Sociological Review* 13 (1965), 311–26.
"Nuova Orleans, Rapporti del R. Console cav. avv. Riccardo Motta," *Emigrazione e Colonie, Rapporti di Agenti Diplomatici e Consolari,* May 14, 1982 (Rome, 1893), 462–65.
O'Connor, Rory. "The Rise and Fall of Dick Greco," *Tampa Magazine* 2 (October 1982), 32–40.
Orovio, V. Consuelo Naranjo. "Analisis Histórico de la Emigracion Española a Cuba, 1900–1959," *Revista de Indias* 44, no. 174 (1984), 505–27.
Otto, John Solomon. "Florida's Cattle Ranching Frontier: Hillsborough County (1860)," *Florida Historical Quarterly* 63 (July 1984), 71–84.
Pérez, Louis A., Jr. "Cubans in Tampa: From Exiles to Immigrants, 1892–1901," *Florida Historical Quarterly* 57 (October 1978), 129–41.
———. "Reminiscences of a *Lector:* Cuban Cigar Workers in Tampa," *Florida Historical Quarterly* 53 (April 1975), 443–49.
———. "Ybor City Remembered," *Tampa Bay History* 7 (Fall/Winter 1985), 171–73.
Pizzo, Anthony. "Gutiérrez Descrube a Tampa," *Tropico* (March 1955).
———. "The Italian Heritage in Tampa," in *Little Italies in North America,* eds. Robert Harney and Vincenza Scarpaci. Toronto: Multicultural History Society of Ontario, 1981.
Pizzo, Tony. "James McKay, I, the Scottish Chief of Tampa Bay," *Sunland Tribune* (Journal of the Tampa Historical Society) 7 (1982), 6–19.
———. "Nick Geraci: Tampa's First Italian Produce King," *Eighth Annual Italian Invitational Golf Tournament Program.* Tampa: n.p., 1985.
Pozzetta, George E. "An Immigrant Library: The Tampa Italian Club Collection," *Ex Libris* 1 (1978), 10–12.

———. "Italians and the Tampa General Strike of 1910," in *Pane e Lavoro: The Italian American Working Class*, ed. George E. Pozzetta. Toronto: Multicultural History Society of Ontario, 1980, 29–46.
Poyo, Gerald E. "Key West and the Cuban Ten Years War," *Florida Historical Quarterly* 57 (January 1979), 289–307.
———. "Cuban Patriots in Key West, 1878–86: Guardians at the Separatist Ideal," *Florida Historical Quaterly* 61 (July 1982), 20–36.
Quinn, Jane. "Nuns in Ybor City: The Sisters of St. Joseph and the Immigrant Community," *Tampa Bay History* 5 (Spring/Summer 1983), 24–43.
Rachaels, Nancy J. "Peter O. Knight: Pioneer and Spokesman for Florida," *Sunland Tribune* (Journal of the Tampa Historical Society) 5 (1972), 2–6.
Rader, Benjamin G. "Compensatory Sport Heroes: Ruth, Grange, and Dempsey," *Journal of Popular Culture* 16 (Spring 1983), 11–23.
Rischin, Moses. "The New American Catholic History," *Church History* 41 (1972), 228.
Rutman, Darrett B. "Community Study," *Historical Methods* 13 (Winter 1980), 29–41.
———. "The Social Web: A Prospectus for the Study of the Early American Community," in *Insights and Parallels: Problems and Issues of American Special History*, ed. William L. O'Neill. Minneapolis: University of Minnesota Press, 1973, 57–89.
Schellings, William. "Florida and the Cuban Revolution, 1895–98," *Florida Historical Quarterly* 30 (1961), 175–86.
Scherberger, Tom. "Tampa's Neglected Latin Quarter," *Orlando Sentinel*, October 14, 1985.
Shaw, Renata V. "19th Century Tobacco Label Art," *The Quarterly Journal of the Library of Congress* 28 (April 1971), 76–102.
Shofner, Jerrell H. "Custom, Law, and History: The Enduring Influence of Florida's 'Black Code,'" *Florida Historical Quarterly* 45 (January 1977), 277–98.
———. "Smuggling Along the Gulf Coast of Florida During Reconstruction," *Sunland Tribune* (Journal of the Tampa Historical Society) 5 (November 1979), 14–18.
Simon, Roger T. "Housing and Services in an Immigrant Neighborhood," *Journal of Urban History* 2 (August 1976), 435–59.
Smith, Timothy L. "Immigrant Social Aspirations and American Education, 1880–1930," *American Quarterly* 21 (Fall 1969), 523–43.
Stelzner, H. G., and Damio Bazo. "Oracle of the Tobacco Bench," *Southern Speech Journal* 31 (1965), 124–31.
Thistlethwaite, Frank. "The Atlantic Migration of the Pottery Industry," *Economic History Review* 11, 2d ser. (1958), 264–78.
———. "Migration from Europe Overseas in the Nineteenth and Twentieth

Centuries," in *Population Movements in Modern European History*, ed. Herbert Moller. New York: Macmillan, 1964, 73–92.

Tilly, Louise. "Migration in Modern European History," in *Human Migration: Patterns of Policies*, ed. William McNeill. Bloomington: University of Indiana Press, 1978.

Toca, Evelro Tellerias. "Los Tabaqueros Cubanos y sus Luchas en Cayo Hueso y Tampa," *Bohemia* (April 28, 1967), 13–23.

Varbero, Richard. "Philadelphia's South Italians and the Irish Church: A History of Cultural Conflict," in *The Religious Experience of Italian Americans*, ed. S. Tomasi. New York: AIHA, 1975, 33–54.

Vecoli, Rudolph J. "The Coming of Age of the Italian-Americans," *Ethnicity* 5 (June 1978), 119–47.

———. "*Contadini* in Chicago: A Critique of *The Uprooted*," *Journal of American History* 51 (1964), 404–17.

———. "Cult and Occult in Italian American Culture: The Persistence of a Religious Heritage," in *Immigrants and Religion in Urban America*, ed. Randall Miller and Thomas Marzik. Philadelphia: Temple University Press, 1977, 25–47.

———. "The Formation of Chicago's 'Little Italies,'" *Journal of American Ethnic History* 2 (Spring 1983), 5–20.

———. "Italian American Workers, 1880–1920: Padrone Slaves or Primitive Rebels?" in *Perspectives in Italian Immigration and Ethnicity*, ed. Silvano Tomasi. New York: Center for Migration Studies, 1977, 25–50.

———. "The I'alian Immigrants in the United States Labor Movement from 1880 to 1929," in *Gli Italiani Fuori d'Italia: Gli Emigrati Italiani nel Movimenti Operai dei Paesi d'Adozione 1880–1940*, ed. B. Bezza. Milano: Franco Angeli Editore, 1983, 257–306.

———. "Pane e Giustizia," *La Parola del Popolo* 68 (September–October 1976), 55–61.

———. "Peasants and Prelates: Italian Immigrants and the Catholic Church," *Journal of Social History* 2 (Spring 1969), 217–68.

Wagner, Eric A. "Baseball in Cuba," *Journal of Popular Culture* 18 (Summer 1984), 113–20.

Warner, Sam. "Cultural Change and the Ghetto," *Journal of Contemporary History* 4 (1969), 173–87.

Weber, Eugen. "Gymnastics and Sports in Fin-de-Siecle France: Opium of the Classes," *American Historical Review* 76 (February 1971), 70–98.

Westfall, L. Glenn. "Hugh Macfarlane: West Tampa Pioneer," *Sunland Tribune* (Journal of the Tampa Historical Society) 5 (1979), 20–24.

———. "Immigrants in Society," *Americas* 34 (July–August 1982), 41–46.

Will, Lawrence. "King of the Crackers," *Tequesta* 26 (1966), 31–39.

Wonk, Dale. "Sons of Centessa Entellina," *Times Picayune* (Dixie Magazine), October 16, 1983, 11–15.
Wood, Peter H. "Whetting, Setting and Laying Timbers: Black Builders in the Early South," *Southern Exposure* 8 (Spring 1980), 3–8.
Yglesias, José. "The Radical Latino in the Deep South," *Nuestro* 1 (August 1977), 5–6.
Zucchi, John. "The Italian Immigrants of St. Johns Ward, 1875–1915: Patterns of Settlement and Neighborhood Formation," in *Occasional Papers in Ethnic and Immigration Studies*. Toronto: Multicultural History Society of Ontario, 1981.

9. Books

A Friend. *The Jesuits in Florida: Fifty Golden Years*. Tampa: Salesian Press, 1939.
Akerman, Joe A. *Florida Cowman: A History of Florida Cattle Raising*. Kissimmee: Florida Cattlemen's Association, 1976.
Alba, Richard. *Italian Americans: Into the Twilight of Ethnicity*. Englewood Cliffs, N.J.: Prentice Hall, 1985.
Angiolini, Alfredo. *Socialismo e Socialisti in Italia*. Firenze: Nerbini, 1903.
The Atlantic and Gulf Coast Canal and Okeechobee Land Company. Philadelphia: William F. Murphy's Sons, 1885.
Avrich, Paul. *The Modern School Movement*. Princeton: Princeton University Press, 1980.
———. *The Russian Anarchists*. Princeton: Princeton University Press, 1967.
Aya, Roderick. *The Missed Revolution: The Fate of Rural Rebels in Sicily and Southern Spain, 1840–1950*. Amsterdam: University of Amsterdam, 1975.
Baer, Willis N. *The Economic Development of the Cigar Industry in the U.S.* Lancaster, Pa.: Arts Printing Co., 1933.
Bailey, David E. *A Study of Hillsborough County's History, Legend and Folklore*. Gainesville: University of Florida Press, 1949.
Bailey, George Ryland. *Tampa Boy*. Chicago: Dartnell Press, 1945.
Baliño, Carlos. *Documentos y Artículos*. Havana: Biblioteca Nacional José Martí, 1976.
Balletta, Francesco. *Le Banco di Napoli e le Rimesse degli Emigranti (1914–25)*. Napoli: Edizioni Scientifiche Italiane, 1972.
Barbagallo, Francesco. *Lavoro ed Esodo nel Sud 1861–1971*. Naples: Guida Editori, 1973.
Barth, Gunter. *City People*. New York: Oxford University Press, 1980.
Barton, Josef F. *Peasants and Strangers: Italians, Rumanians, and Slovaks in an American City, 1890–1950*. Cambridge: Harvard University Press, 1975.

Bayor, Ronald. *Neighbors in Conflict: The Irish, Germans, Jews, and Italians in New York City, 1929–41.* Baltimore: Johns Hopkins University Press, 1978.
Bell, Daniel. *The End of Ideology.* New York: Free Press, 1960.
Bender, Thomas. *Community and Social Change.* New Brunswick: Rutgers University Press, 1978.
Bernard, Richard M. *The Melting Pot and the Altar: Marital Assimilation in Early Twentieth-Century Wisconsin.* Minneapolis: University of Minnesota Press, 1980.
Blok, Anton. *The Mafia of a Sicilian Village, 1860–1960: A Study of Violent Peasant Entrepeneurs.* Oxford: Basil Blackwell, 1974.
Bodnar, John. *Immigration and Industrialization: Ethnicity in an American Mill Town, 1870–1940.* Pittsburgh: University of Pittsburgh Press, 1977.
———. *Workers' World: Kinship, Community, and Protest in an Industrial Society, 1900–1940.* Baltimore: Johns Hopkins University Press, 1982.
Bodnar, John, Roger Simon, and Michael P. Weber. *Lives of Their Own: Blacks, Italians, and Poles in Pittsburgh, 1900–1960.* Urbana: University of Illinois Press, 1981.
Bookchin, Murray. *The Spanish Anarchists: The Heroic Years, 1886–1936.* New York: Free Life Editions, 1977.
Braudel, Fernand. *The Mediterranean and the Mediterranean World in the Age of Philip II.* 2 vols. New York: Harper and Row, 1972.
Brenan, Gerald. *The Spanish Labyrinth: An Account of the Social and Political Background of the Civil War.* Cambridge: Cambridge University Press, 1964.
Briggs, John W. *An Italian Passage: Immigrants to Three American Cities, 1890–1930.* New Haven: Yale University Press, 1978.
Brody, David. *Workers in Industrial America: Essays on the 20th Century Struggle.* New York: Oxford University Press, 1980.
Brooks, William E., ed. *From Saddlebags to Satellites: A History of Florida Methodism.* Nashville, Tenn.: Parthenon Press, 1969.
Buder, Stanley. *Pullman: An Experiment in Industrial Order and Community Planning, 1880–1930.* New York: Oxford University Press, 1967.
Buechler, Hans, and Judith-Maria Buechler, eds. *Carmen: The Autobiography of a Spanish Galician Woman.* Cambridge, Mass.: Schenkman, 1981.
Builders of Florida. Mount Vernon, N.Y.: Building Trade Publications, n.d.
Campbell, Archer Stuart, and W. Porter McLendon. *The Cigar Industry of Tampa, Florida.* Gainesville: University of Florida Press, 1939.
Cantor, Milton. *The Divided Left American Radicalism, 1900–1975.* New York: Hill and Wang, 1978.
Carocci, Giampiero. *Storia d'Italia dall' Unità ad Oggi.* Torino: Einaudi, 1975.
Caroli, Betty Boyd. *Italian Repatriation from the United States, 1900–1914.* New York: Center for Migration Studies, 1974.

Caroli, Betty B., Lydio Tomasi, and Robert Harney. *The Italian Immigrant Woman in North America*. Toronto: Multicultural History Society of Ontario, 1978.

Carpi, Leone. *Delle Colonie e dell' Emigrazione d'Italiani all' Estero sotto l'Aspetto dell' Industria, Commercio, Agricoltura e con Trattazione d'Importante Questioni Sociali*. 4 vols. Milan: Tipographica Ed. Lombarda, 1874.

Carr, Raymond. *Spain, 1808–1939*. London: Oxford University Press, 1966.

Casasus, Juan J. E. *La Emigracion Cubana y la Independencia de la Patria*. Havana: Talleres Tipografiros de "Editorial Lex," 1953.

Catholic Directory. Tampa: Mary Help of Christians School, 1939.

El Centro Asturiano en Tampa Inauguracion del Edificio Social 15 de Mayo de 1914. Tampa: n.p., 1914.

Cerase, Francesco. *L'Emigrazione di Ritorno: Innovazione o Reazione*. Rome: Carucci, 1971.

Cerrito, Gino. *Radicalismo e Socialismo in Sicilia (1860–82)*. Messina-Firenze: Casa Editrice G. D'Anna, 1958.

Chandler, Lester V. *Inflation in the United States*. New York: Harper, 1951.

Chapman, Charlotte Gower. *Milocca: A Sicilian Village*. Cambridge, Mass.: Schenkman, 1971.

Chudacoff, Howard. *Mobile Americans*. New York: Oxford University Press, 1972.

Cinel, Dino. *From Italy to San Francisco: The Immigrant Experience*. Stanford: Stanford University Press, 1982.

Clark, Elmer T. *The Latin Immigrant in the South*. Nashville: Cokesbury Press, 1924.

Cooper, Patricia. *Once a Cigar Maker: Men, Women, and Work Culture in American Cigar Factories, 1900–1919*. Urbana: University of Illinois Press, 1987.

Covello, Leonard. *The Social Background of the Italo-American School Child*. Leiden: E. J. Brill, 1967.

Covington, James W. *The Billy Bowlegs War, 1855–58*. Chulota, Fla.: Mickler House, 1982.

Cushman, Joseph D., Jr. *The Sound of the Bells: The Episcopal Church in South Florida, 1892–1969*. Gainesville: University of Florida Press, 1976.

Davidoff, Zino. *The Connoisseur's Book of the Cigar*. New York: McGraw-Hill, 1976.

Davie, Richard. *Cuba: Past and Present*. New York: Charles Scribner's Sons, 1898.

Davis, Lawrence B. *Immigrants, Baptists, and the Protestant Mind in America*. Urbana: University of Illinois Press, 1973.

Davis, William Watson. *The Civil War and Reconstruction in Florida*. New York: Columbia University Press, 1913.

Dean, Susie Kelly. *The Tampa of My Childhood, 1897–1907*. Tampa: Sylvia Dean Harbert, 1966.
Dedication Souvenir: Our Lady of Perpetual Help Church. Ybor City: Rinaldi Printing, 1937.
del Rió, Emilio. *Yo Fui Uno de los Fundadores de Ybor City*. Tampa: n.p., 1950.
de Madariaga, Salvador. *Spain: A Modern History*. New York: Praeger, 1958.
des Planches, E. Mayor. *Attraverso gli Stati Uniti: Per l'Emigrazione Italiana*. Torino: Editrice Torinese, 1913.
de Stefano, Francesco, and Francesco Luigi Oddio. *Storia della Sicilia dal 1860 al 1910*. Bari: Laterza, 1963.
de Vita, Guiseppe. *Dizionario Geografico dei Comuni della Sicilia*. Palermo: F. Pravata, 1906.
Diggins, John P. *Mussolini and Fascism: The View from America*. Princeton: Princeton University Press, 1972.
di Leonardo, Micaela. *The Varieties of Ethnic Experience: Kinship, Class, and Gender among California Italian-Americans*. Ithaca: Cornell University Press, 1984.
Dubofsky, Melvyn. *We Shall Be All: A History of the Industrial Workers of the World*. Chicago: Quadrangle Books, 1969.
———. *When Workers Organize: New York City in the Progressive Era*. Amherst: University of Massachusetts Press, 1968.
Dollo, Corrado, Letterio Briguglio, Innocenzo Cervelli, and Rosario Spampinato. *I Fasci Siciliani: La Crin Italiana di fine Secolo*. Bari: DeDonato, 1976.
Dumoulin, John. *El Movimiento Obrero en Crucese, 1902–25: Corrientes Ideologicas y Formas de Organizacion en la Industria Azucarera*. Havana: Editorial de Ciencias Sociales, 1982.
Elazar, Daniel J. *American Federalism: A View from the States*. 2d ed. New York: Crowell, 1972.
Esteve, Pedro. *La Legge*. Ybor City, Fla.: Poliglota Press, 1911.
Fainsod, Merle. *International Socialism and the World War*. New York: Octagon Books, 1966.
Fenton, Edwin. *Immigrants and Unions, A Case Study: Italians and American Labor, 1870–1920*. New York: Arno Press, 1975.
Fernández, Eustasio, and Henry Beltran. *The Ybor City Story, 1885–1954* (translation of *Los Cubanos en Tampa* by José Rivero Muñiz). Tampa: n.p., 1977.
Fink, Leon. *Workingmen's Democracy: The Knights of Labor and American Politics*. Urbana: University of Illinois Press, 1983.
Florencio, Rafael Núnez. *El Terrorismo Anarquista, 1888–1909*. Madrid: Siglo 21, 1983.
Flynn, Elizabeth Gurley. *The Rebel Girl: An Autobiography, My First Life (1906–26)*. New York: International Publishers, 1955.

Flynt, Wayne. *Cracker Messiah: Governor Sidney J. Catts of Florida.* Baton Rouge: Louisiana State University Press, 1977.
Foerster, Robert. *The Italian Emigration of Our Times.* Cambridge: Harvard University Press, 1919.
Foner, Philips. *Antonio Maceo.* New York: Monthly Review Press, 1977.
Franchetti, Leopold, and Sidney Sonnino. *Inchiesta in Sicilia nel 1876.* 2 vols. Florence: G. Capponi, 1877.
Gabaccia, Donna. *From Sicily to Elizabeth Street: Housing and Social Change among Italian Immigrants.* Albany: State University of New York Press, 1984.
Gambino, Richard. *Vendetta: A True Story of the Worst Lynching in America.* New York: Doubleday, 1977.
Gannon, Michael V. *The Cross in the Sand.* 2d ed. Gainesville: University of Florida Press, 1983.
Garcia Gallò, Gaspar M. Jorgé. *Biografià del Tabaco Habano.* Santa Clara: Universidad Central di Las Villas, 1959.
Giarrizzo, Guiseppe, and Gastone Manacorda. *I Fasci Siciliani.* 2 vols. Bari: De Donato Editore, 1975.
Gilmore, Al-Tony. *Bad Nigger: The National Impact of Jack Johnson.* Port Washington, N.Y.: Greenwood Press, 1974.
Goldfield, David R. *Cotton Fields and Skyscrapers: Southern City and Region, 1607–1980.* Baton Rouge: Louisiana State University Press, 1982.
Goldfield, David R., and Blaine A. Brownell. *Urban America: From Downtown to No Town.* Boston: Houghton Mifflin, 1979.
Goldman, Emma. *Living My Life.* 2 vols. New York: Dover, 1970.
Gordon, Milton. *Assimilation in American Life: The Role of Race, Religion, and National Origins.* New York: Oxford University Press, 1964.
Grantham, Dewey W. *Southern Progressivism: The Reconciliation of Progress and Tradition.* Knoxville: University of Tennessee Press, 1983.
Green, James R. *Grass-Roots Socialism: Radical Movements in the Southwest, 1895–1943.* Baton Rouge: Louisiana State University Press, 1978.
Greene, Victor R. *The Slavic Community on Strike: Immigrant Labor in Pennsylvania Anthracite.* Notre Dame: University of Notre Dame Press, 1968.
Greenfield, Ken. *Economics and Liberalism in the Risorgimento: A Study of Nationalism in Lombardy.* Baltimore: Johns Hopkins University Press, 1965.
Grismer, Karl. *Tampa: A History of the City of Tampa and the Tampa Bay Region of Florida.* St. Petersburg: St. Petersburg Printing Company, 1950.
Guerra y Sánchez, Ramiro. *Historia de la Nación Cubana.* Havana: Editorial Historia de la Nación Cubana, 1952.
Gutman, Herbert G. *Work, Culture and Society in Industrializing America: Essays in American Working Class and Social History.* New York: Oxford University Press, 1977.

Hareven, Tamara K. *Family Time and Industrial Time: The Relationship Between the Family and Work in a New England Industrial Community.* Cambridge: Cambridge University Press, 1982.

Hareven, Tamara K., and Randolph Langenbach. *Amoskeag: Life and Work in an American Factory City.* New York: Pantheon Books, 1978.

Harner, Charles E. *A Pictorial History of Ybor City.* Tampa: Trevel Publishers, 1975.

Havard, William. *The Politics of Mis-Representation: Rural-Urban Conflict in the Florida Legislature.* Baton Rouge: Louisiana State University Press, 1972.

Herr, Richard. *Spain.* Englewood Cliffs, N.J.: Prentice-Hall, 1971.

Hidalgo, Ariel. *Orígines del Movimiento Obrero y del Pensamiento Socialista en Cuba.* Havana: Editorial Arte y Literatura, 1976.

Higham, John. *Strangers in the Land: Patterns of American Nativism.* New York: Atheneum, 1954.

———, ed. *Ethnic Leadership in America.* Baltimore: Johns Hopkins University Press, 1978.

The Hillsborean. Tampa: n.p., 1914–46.

History of Florida, Past and Present. 3 vols. Chicago: Lewis Publishing Company, 1923.

A History of Port Tampa, 1888–1961. Tampa: Port Tampa City Women's Club, 1972.

Hobsbawm, Eric J. *Primitive Rebels: Studies in Archaic Forms of Social Movement in the 19th and 20th Centuries.* New York: Praeger, 1959.

Hofstadter, Richard. *The Paranoid Style of American Politics.* New York: Knopf, 1964.

Homer, Fredrick D. *Guns and Garlic: Myths and Realities of Organized Crime.* West Lafayette: Purdue University Studies, 1974.

Horowitz, Daniel. *The Italian Labor Movement.* Cambridge: Harvard University Press, 1963.

Iorizzo, Luciano, and Salvatore Mondello. *The Italian-Americans.* Boston: Twayne Publishers, 1971.

Istituto Centrale di Statistica. *Comuni e loro Popolazione ai Censimenti dal 1861 al 1951.* Rome: Azienda Beneventana Tipografica Editoriale, 1960.

Italian Business Directory, 1907–12. New York: Italian Publishers, 1907–12.

Jacini, S. *I Risultati della Inchiesta Agraria (1884).* Torino: Giulio Einaudi, 1976.

Jahoda, Gloria. *River of the Golden Ibis.* New York: Holt, Rinehart and Winston, 1973.

Joll, James. *The Anarchists.* Cambridge: Cambridge University Press, 1980.

Junco, José Alvarez. *La Ideología Política del Anarquism Español (1868–1910).* Madrid: Siglo Veintiuno de Espana Editores, 1976.

Kaplan, Temma. *The Anarchists of Andalusia*. Princeton: Princeton University Press, 1978.
Kefauver, Estes. *Crime in America*. Garden City, N.Y.: Doubleday, 1951.
Kennedy, Stetson. *Palmetto Country*. New York: Duell, Sloan and Pearce, 1942.
Kern, Robert. *Red Years/Black Years: A Political History of Spanish Anarchism, 1911–37*. Philadelphia: Institute for the Study of Human Issues, 1978.
Kessner, Thomas. *The Golden Door: Italian and Jewish Immigrant Mobility in New York City, 1880–1915*. New York: Oxford University Press, 1977.
Laumer, Frank. *Massacre*. Gainesville: University of Florida Press, 1968.
Leitner, Maria. *Eine Frau reist durch die Welt*. Berlin: Agis-Verlas, 1932.
Leuchtenberg, William. *Perils of Prosperity, 1914–32*. Chicago: University of Chicago Press, 1958.
Mack Smith, Denis. *A History of Sicily: Medieval Sicily, 800-1713*. London: Chatto and Windus, 1968.
———. *A History of Sicily: Modern Sicily after 1713*. London: Chatto and Windus, 1968.
———. *Italy: A Modern History*. Ann Arbor: University of Michigan Press, 1969.
Madariaga, Salvador de. *Spain: A Modern History*. 2d ed. New York: Praeger, 1958.
Maggiore-Perni, Francesco. *La Popolazione di Sicilia e di Palermo, dal X al XVIII Secolo*. Palermo: Stabilimento Tipografico Virzi, 1892.
Mahon, John K. *History of the Second Seminole War, 1835–42*. Gainesville: University of Florida Press, 1967.
Manteiga, Victoriano. *Centro Español de Tampa Bodas de Oro, 1891–1941 Resena Historica de Cincuenta Anos*. Tampa: n.p., 1941.
Marino, Guiseppe Carlo. *Movimento Contadinio e Blocco Agrario Nella Sicilia Giolittina*. Palermo: S. F. Flaccovio, 1979.
Martellone, Anna Maria. *I Siciliani fuori dalla Sicilia: L'Emigrazione Transoceanica al 1925*. Firenze: G. Capponi, 1979.
Martí, José. *Obras Completas*. ed. M. Isidro Mendez. 2 vols. Havana: Editorial Lex, 1953.
Massari, Angelo. *La Comunità Italiana di Tampa*. New York: Europe America Press, 1964.
———. *The Wonderful Life of Angelo Massari*. trans. Arthur D. Massolo. New York: Exposition Press, 1965.
Mayor des Planches, E. *Attraverso gli Stati Uniti: Per l'Emigrazione Italiana*. Torino: Unione Tipographico Editrice Torinese, 1913.
Mays, Benjamin Elijah. *Born to Rebel: An Autobiography*. New York: Scribner, 1971.
McCall, George Archibald. *Letters from the Frontiers*. Philadelphia: Lippincott, 1868.

McDowell, John Patrick. *The Social Gospel in the South: The Woman's Home Mission Movement in the Methodist Episcopal Church, South, 1886–1939.* Baton Rouge: Louisiana State University Press, 1982.
McKay, Donald Brenham. *Pioneer Florida.* 3 vols. Tampa: Southern Publishing Co., 1959.
McNally, Michael J. *Catholicism in South Florida, 1868–1968.* Gainesville: University of Florida Press, 1982.
Messina, Calogero. *Il Caso Panepinto.* Palermo: Herbita, 1977.
———. *La Ricerca Municipale per il Progresso: La Comarca di Luigi Tirrito.* Palermo: Edizioni Leopardi, 1982.
———. *S. Stefano Quisquina. Studio Storico-Critico.* Palermo: U. Manfredi, 1976.
Michener, James A. *Iberia: Spanish Travels and Reflecting.* New York: Random House, 1968.
Miller, Randall, and Thomas Marzik, eds. *Immigrants and Religion in Urban America.* Philadelphia: Temple University Press, 1977.
Miller, Sally. *The Radical Immigrant.* New York: Twayne Publishers, 1974.
Mohl, Raymond. *The New City: Urban America in the Industrial Age, 1860–1920.* Arlington Heights, Ill.: Harlan Davidson, 1985.
Mormino, Gary Ross. *Immigrants on the Hill: Italian-Americans in St. Louis, 1882–1982.* Urbana: University of Illinois Press, 1986.
Muñiz, José Rivero. *Los Cubanos en Tampa.* Habana: Revista Bimestre, 1958.
———. *El Movimiento Obrero Durante la Primera Intervencíon.* Santa Clara: Universidad de las Villas, 1961.
———. *The Ybor City Story, 1885–1954.* trans. Eustasio Fernández and Henry Beltram. Tampa: n.p., 1976.
Murray, Robert K. *Red Scare: A Study in National Hysteria, 1919–20.* New York: McGraw Hill, 1955.
Nelli, Humbert. *The Business of Crime: Italians and Syndicate Crime in the United States.* New York: Oxford University Press, 1976.
———. *The Italians of Chicago.* New York: Oxford University Press, 1970.
Nicotri, Gaspare. *Storia della Sicilia nelle Rivoluzioni e Rivolte.* New York: Italian Publishers, 1934.
Ninetieth Anniversary of the Contessa Entellina Society, 1886–1976. New Orleans: n.p., 1976.
Norton, Albert. *Norton's Complete Hand-Book of Havana and Cuba.* Chicago: Rand, McNally and Co., 1900.
Nuñez Florencio, Rafael. *El Terrorismo Anarquista 1888–1909.* Madrid: El Siglo, 1983.
Odencrantz, Louise C. *Italian Women in Industry.* New York: Russell Sage, 1919.

Ortiz, Fernando. *Cuban Counterpoint: Tobacco and Sugar.* New York: A. A. Knopf, 1947.
Panteleone, Michele. *The Mafia and Politics.* New York: Coward, 1966.
Pérez, Louis A., Jr. *Cuba Between the Empires, 1878–1902.* Pittsburgh: University of Pittsburgh Press, 1983.
Pescatello, Ann M. *Power and Pawn: The Female in Iberian Societies and Cultures.* Westport, Conn: Greenwood Press, 1976.
Pettengill, George Warren. *The Story of the Florida Railroads, 1834–1903.* Boston: Railway and Locomotive Historical Society, 1952.
Pizzo, Anthony. *Tampa Town, 1824–86: The Cracker Village with a Latin Accent.* Tampa: Trend House, 1968.
Polenberg, Richard. *One Nation Divisible: Class, Race, and Ethnicity in the U.S. since 1938.* New York: Viking Press, 1980.
Powell, Evanell. *Tampa That Was.* Boynton Beach, Fla.: Star Publishing Co., 1973.
Pozzetta, George E., ed. *Pane e Lavoro: The Italian American Working Class.* Toronto: Multicultural History Society of Ontario, 1980.
Prince, Richard E. *The Atlantic Coast Line Railroad.* Green River: Wheelwright Litho Co., 1966.
Rabinowitz, Howard N. *Race Relations in the Urban South.* New York: Oxford University Press, 1978.
Raper, Arthur. *A Study of Negro Life in Tampa.* Tampa: n.p., 1927.
Renda, Francesco. *Socialisti e Cattolici in Sicilia, 1900–1904.* Caltanissetta-Roma: Sciascia, 1972.
———. *L'Emigrazione in Sicilia.* Palermo: Edizione "Sicilia al Lavoro," 1963.
———. *I Fasci Siciliani, 1882–94.* Turin: Guilio Einaudi, 1977.
Rerick, Rowland. *Memoirs of Florida.* 2 vols. Athens, Ga.: Southern Historical Association, 1902.
Reseña Histórica de Cincuenta Años. Tampa: Tribune Press, 1941.
Riess, Steven A. *Touching Base: Professional Baseball and American Culture in the Progressive Era.* Westport, Conn.: Greenwood Press, 1980.
Roberts, Randy. *Jack Dempsey, the Manassa Mauler.* Baton Rouge: Louisiana State University Press, 1979.
Robinson, E. L. *History of Hillsborough County, Fla.* St. Augustine: Record Co., 1928.
Rolle, Andrew. *The Immigrant Upraised.* Norman: University of Oklahoma Press, 1968.
Salomone-Marino, Salvatore. *Customs and Habits of the Sicilian Peasants.* trans. from *Costumi e Usanze dei Contadini di Sicilia* by Rosalie N. Norris. Rutherford: Fairleigh Dickinson University Press, 1981.
Saltam, Richard B. *The Social and Political Thought of Michael Bakunin.* Westport, Conn.: Greenwood Press, 1983.

Salvemini, Gaetano. *Italian Fascist Activities in the United States.* New York: Center for Migration Studies, 1977.

———. *The Origins of Fascism in Italy.* New York: Harper and Row, 1973.

Sanchez, Ramiro Guerra. *Historia de la Nación Cubana, "Antecedentes del Movimiento Obrero."* Havana: Editorial Historia de la Nación Cubana, 1952.

Santillán, Diego Abad de (pseud., de Sinesio García Delgado). *Contribucion a la Historia del Movimiento Obrero Español: Desde sus Orígenes Hasta 1905.* 2 vols. Puebla: Ediciones Cajica, 1965.

Savatar, Fernando. *Para la Anarquía.* Barcelona: Tusquets, 1977.

Scarzanella, Eugenia. *Italiani d'Argentina: Storie di Contadini, Industriali e Missionari Italiani in Argentina, 1850–1912.* Venice: Marsilio Editori, 1983.

Schneider, Jane, and Peter Schneider. *Culture and Political Economy in Western Sicily.* New York: Academic Press, 1976.

Sciascia, Leonard. *Mafia Vendetta.* New York: Knopf, 1964.

Scott, Joan, and Louise Tilly. *Women, Work, and Family.* New York: Holt, Rinehart and Winston 1978.

Sereni, Emilio. *Il Capitalismo nelle Campagne, 1860–1900.* Turin: Einaudi, 1968.

Seventh Annual Observance Homecoming and 130th Anniversary Tribute, St. Paul African Methodist Episcopal Church. Tampa: n.p., 1983.

Shannon, David A. *The Socialist Party of America.* Chicago: Quadrangle, 1967.

Shofner, Jerrell H. *Nor Is It Over Yet: Florida in the Era of Reconstruction.* Gainesville: University of Florida Press, 1974.

Sicily (Region) Presidenza. *Le Elezioni in Sicilia: Dati e Grafici dal 1946 al 1956.* Milano: A. Giuffè, 1956.

Sitterson, J. Caryle. *Sugar Country: The Cane Sugar Industry in the South, 1753–1950.* Lexington: University of Kentucky Press, 1953.

Smyth, G. Hutchinson. *The Life of Henry Bradley Plant.* New York: G. P. Putnam's Sons, 1898.

Socidades Españolas, 1931. Tampa: Tribune Press, 1931.

Sonnino, Sidney. *I Contadini in Sicilia.* Florence: Vallecchi Editore, 1925.

Spicola, Rose F. *The Spicola Story: The Life of Charlie Spicola.* Tampa: Axelrod Publishing, 1985.

Stearns, Peter N. *European Society in Upheaval: Social History since 1800.* New York: Macmillan, 1967.

Storia di Alessandria della Rocca. typescript copy, n.p.

Suárez, Enrique Álvarez. *Asturias.* Gijon: n.p., 1924.

Tampa College, *High School Yearbook.* Tampa: n.p., 1930–31.

Tebeau, Charlton. *A History of Florida.* Coral Gables: University of Miami Press, 1971.

Terkel, Studs. *Hard Times.* New York: Pantheon Books, 1970.

Thernstrom, Stephan. *Poverty and Progress: Social Mobility in a Nineteenth Century City*. New York: Atheneum, 1973.
Thomas, Hugh. *Cuba: The Pursuit of Freedom*. New York: Harper and Row, 1971.
Thompson, E. P. *The Making of the English Working Class*. New York: Random House, 1963.
Tomasi, Silvano. *Perspectives in Italian Immigration and Ethnicity*. New York: Center for Migration Studies, 1977.
―――. *Piety and Power: The Role of Italian Parishes in the New York Metropolitan Area*. New York: Center for Migration Studies, 1975.
Tricarico, Donald. *The Italians of Greenwich Village*. New York: Center for Migration Studies, 1984.
Ward, David. *Cities and Immigrants. A Geography of Change in Nineteenth-Century America*. New York: Oxford University Press, 1971.
Ward, G. H. B. *The Truth about Spain*. London: Cassell and Co., 1911.
Warner, W. Lloyd, and Leo Srole. *The Social System of American Ethnic Groups*. New Haven: Yale University Press, 1945.
Webb, Wanton S. *Wanton S. Webb's Jacksonville and Consolidated Directory of the Representative Cities of East and South Florida, 1886*. Poughkeepsie: Haight and Dudley, 1886.
Weber, Eugen. *Peasants into Frenchmen: The Modernization of Rural France, 1870–1914*. Stanford: Stanford University Press, 1976.
Weinstein, James. *The Decline of Socialism in America, 1912–25*. New York: Random House, 1967 (reprinted by Vantage Books, 1969).
Wiebe, Robert. *The Search for Order, 1877–1920*. New York: Hill and Wang, 1967.
Williamson, Edward C. *Florida Politics in the Gilded Age, 1877–93*. Gainesville: University of Florida Press, 1976.
Woodcock, George. *Anarchism: A History of Libertarian Ideas and Movements*. Cleveland: Meridan Books, 1962.
Woodward, C. Vann. *The Strange Career of Jim Crow*. New York: Oxford University Press, 1966.
Wolf, Eric. *Peasants*. Englewood Cliffs, N.J.: Prentice-Hall, 1966.
Yans-McLaughlin, Virginia. *Family and Community: Italian Immigrants in Buffalo, 1880–1930*. Ithaca: Cornell University Press, 1977.
Yglesias, José. *The Truth about Them*. New York: World Publishing, 1971.

Index

Adamo, Dr. Frank, 197, 201–2
Adamo, Giuseppe, 201
Adamo, Maria Leto, 201
L'Africa Italiana (Panepinto), 25, 212
Afro-Americans, 56, 130, 153, 200, 238, 263–64, 265, 276, 283, 306, 312–13. *See also* Blacks
Afro-Cubans: arrival of, in Ybor City, 78–79; in cigar factories, 101; and the depression, 289; discrimination against, 152–53; missions for, 225; and mutual aid clubs, 185–88; residence patterns of, 186, 245
Agrigento (Girgenti), 16, 17, 23, 24, 84
Alba, Richard, 313
L'Alba Sociale, 116, 117, 145, 165
Alcamo, 196
Alessandria della Rocca, 18, 20, 33, 35, 84, 104, 116, 124, 173, 190
Alfonso, Manuel, 245
Alonzo, Francisco, 161
"Altagracia," 136
Altree, Dr. G. H., 198
American Cigar Co., 116
American Federation of Labor (AFL): and blacks, 153; and dual unionism, 116; locals in Tampa, 114; policies during strikes, 118, 160
American Fruit and Steamship Co., 278
American Home Mission Society, 225
American Medical Association (AMA), 201
"American Plan," 140, 160, 173
Americani, 16, 35, 84
Anarchists, 143, 146; Anglo images of, 112, 115, 151, 156, 240; and athletics, 248; in Cuba, 77–78; and groups, 144–45, 147, 151; ideologies of, 144, 149–50; and Italians, 116; and labor unions, 112, 118, 119; newspapers of, 165; and race relations, 152–53; and religion, 144, 212, 220, 229, 240; in Spain, 77; and socialism, 150; and World War I, 154–56; in Ybor City, 80–81, 144, 146,
151–52, 154. *See also* Cubans; Italians; Spaniards
Anarcho-syndicalism, 113
Antifascism, 162, 298–99
Anti-Fascist Alliance of North America, 162
Anti-Fascist Federation for the Freedom of Italy, 162
Antinori, Paul, 305
Antinori, Vincente, 145, 161, 174
Antorcha, 150, 171
Antuono, F. M., 194
Antuono, Val, 136, 155, 164
Aparicio, Manuel, 103, 182–83
Arenas, Hipólito, 79
Argentina, 196, 204
L'Asino, 23, 213
Asociación de beneficiencia, 175
Asturias, 70–72, 175, 180
Atlantic Coast Line Railroad Co., 49
Avellanal, Dr. José Ramón, 199–200, 209
Avrich, Paul, 151
L'Aurora, 166, 167, 174
L'Avanti (Mussolini), 162

Baez, Juan, 225
Bagheria (Palermo), 106
Baily, Samuel, 204
Bakunin, Mikhail, 71, 102, 145, 195
Balbín Brothers Cigar Co., 120
Balbontín, B. M., 207
Baliño, Carlos, 80
Bálvez y Delmonte Wenceslao, 247
Baptist Home Mission Board, 223–26
Baptists, 225–26
Barbato, Nicolò, 29, 40
Barcelona, 5, 77, 102, 150
Barre, Vt., 148, 173
Barry, Bhp. Patrick, 220–21
Barth, Gunter, 253
Bartlett, Charles W., 177
Baseball, 187, 190, 194, 196, 247–53, 259

357

Bassetti, Luigi, 106
Bejucal, 77, 78
Bell, Daniel, 280
Bellanca, Frank, 173
Belmonte, 17, 25
La Beneficencia Asturiana, 199
La Benefica Española, 199
Benites, Santo, 112
Benjamin Field, 251
Bertelli, Guiseppe, 123, 149
Biblioteca Popolare Educativa, 145
Biblioteca Socialista-Anarchica, 145
Billy Bowlegs War, 44
Bivona, 18, 29, 33, 35
Blacks (Afro-Americans): and Anglos, 58; in cigar factories, 101, 130; and Jim Crow, 57–59; and radicals, 153; and slavery, 44; in Tampa, 56–58; in Ybor City, 153
Blok, Anton, 22, 39
Bloxham, William B., 46
Boardinghouse, 75, 178, 271
Bodnar, John, 9, 295
Bolita, 4; origins of, 281; commentary on, 240, 250; demise of, 302; operations, 281–84, 295, 301–2; payoffs, 283–84; and politics, 43, 53, 283–84
Bolletino dell'Emigrazione, 108
Bolshevism, 127, 158
Bondi, Bob, 306
Bootlegging, 281, 284–86
Borghi, Armando, 163
Boxing, 196, 249, 251–53, 259
Boycotts, 157
Boyte, Harry, 133
Braccianti, 22
Brandon, Fla., 280, 309
Braudel, Fernand, 20
Briggs, Asa, 7
Briggs, John, 7
Brody, David, 140
Buenos Aires, 196, 204
Buggica, Lucia, 279
Buggica, Roberto: and the Italian Club, 196; as dairy owner, 279–80
Buggica, Salvatore, 196, 279–80
Bureau of Investigation, 154, 156
Burgio, 196
Burke, Frank, 158
Bustillo and Diaz Co., 97, 98

Cabrera, Antonio, 120
Cacciatore, Angelo, 34
Cacciatore, Antonio, 34
Cacciatore, Giovanni, 66
Cacciatore, John, 33, 235
Cacciatore, Salvatore, 34

Cagnina, Guiseppe, 261
Cagnina, Giuseppina, 261
Cagnina, Salvatore, 261
Calcagno, Pietro, 165, 174
Caltagirone, Giovanni di, 17
Caltagirone, Joe, 274
Caltagirone family, 186
Caltanisetta, 24
Camero, Aleida Huerta, 268
Camero, Arturo, 229–30, 258, 267
Caminata, Ludovica, 150
Campanilismo, 18, 88
Camparito, Ignazio, 86
Campisi, Rosalia, 290
Camporeali, 88
Cancela, Tony, 252
Cándamo, 74
Cannella, Salvatore, 84
Cannella family, 24, 84
Cantina, 183, 184, 194, 204, 308
Cantor, Milton, 152
Capello, Salvatore, 194
Capitano, Nicolò, 82
Carbonell, Elegio, 79
Carbonell, Nestor, 79, 212
Cardenas, 77
Carocci, Giampiero, 27
Caroti, Arturo, 149
Cartabón, 115, 134
Caruso, Enrico, 183
Casares, Rick, 252
El Casino Español. *See* El Centro Español
Castellammare del Golfo, 87, 88, 189
Castellano, Maria, 267
Casteltermini, 196
Catania, 196
Catholic church: baptisms in, 217–18; in Florida, 210–11; and Latins, 210–23; marriages in, 217, 219–20; parishes, 214, 215, 216; and radicals, 211, 212, 213; in Sicily, 23, 212, 213, 220, 221; and women, 216, 217; in Ybor City, 210–23, 304–5
Catts, Sidney, 156, 224
Cefalù, 18
Cemetery, 192–93, 208, 216
Central Trades and Labor Assembly of Tampa, 173
El Centro Asturiano de Habana: founding of, 175; description of, 180–81
El Centro Asturiano de Tampa: clubhouse, 181–82; hospital and medical programs of, 198–203, 208, 305, 309; membership of, 181–82; recreation at, 182, 195, 247–48, 252, 305, 309; social life at, 305, 309; theater in, 182–83, 195–96
Centro de Propaganda Obrera, 80

El Centro Español: clubhouse, 179–80; formation of, 177–78; hospital and medical programs of, 197, 198–203, 305, 309; leadership of, 188–89; membership of, 178–80, 181; organization of, 190; recreation at, 182, 195, 248; social life at, 303, 305, 309; theater in, 182–83, 195–96; in West Tampa, 179
El Centro Español de Recreo e Instruccion de Tampa. *See* El Centro Español
El Centro Español Hospital, 197, 198–203, 305, 309
Cerrati, Bhp. Michele, 215
"El Cerro," 67
Chain migration, 84, 89
Chapin, C. W., 50
Chapman, Charlotte Gower, 188
Chavatero, 101, 246
Chiaramonte, Al, 306
Chinchal(es), 105, 113
Chinese, 72
Chudacoff, Howard, 236
Cianciana, 17, 18, 23, 27, 267
Ciarrocca, Guido, 174
Cigar industry: ambience of, 99–102; apprentices in, 101, 107, 108, 135; in Cuba, 77–78; daily schedule of, 101; decline of, 187, 300–301; ethos of, 100–102, 113, 264–66; growth of, 68–69; and hand-rolled process, 100; and *el lector*, 97, 98, 102–3, 131; and tobacco stripping, 107; and strikes, 110, 111, 112
Cigar Makers International Union (CMIU), 129, 130; and Italians, 123, 124, 125, 127, 161, 162; and the IWW, 126; locals in Tampa, 118, 124, 127, 129, 161, 162; origins in Tampa, 114; and radicals, 118, 125, 126, 129, 162; and socialists, 119, 129, 162; support during strikes, 118, 120, 128, 129, 141
Cigar Makers' Trade Union, 77
Cigar Manufacturing Association, 127, 128
Cinel, Dino, 7, 280, 322
Circolo Agricolo-Operaio di Mutuo Soccorso (Agricultural Workers Circle of Mutual Aid), 24
Circolo Socialista Bivonese, 41
Circolo di Studi Sociali, 145, 166
El Círculo Cubano (Cuban Club): clubhouse, 184–85, 207, 251, 252, 309; membership of, 185; origins in Tampa, 184, 186; programs of, 184–85, 199, 248, 251, 252, 309
Citrus County, 267
Citizens committee(s): 1901 strike, 117; 1910 strike, 121; 1920 strike, 128; 1931 strike, 131

Citizenship, 301
Civic Reform League of Tampa, 178, 284
Civil War, 44, 45
Clara Frye Hospital, 200
Clear Havana Cigar Manufacturers Association (the "Trust"), 116, 119, 127, 128
Clendenin, James, 301
Club Ignacio Agramonte, 79
Club Nacional Cubano, 184, 186
Cocinas económicas, 117
Cohen, Miriam, 288
Colajanni, Napoleone, 11
Columbus Association, 309
Columbus Day, 309
Comescone, Angelina, 132, 221, 233, 253, 255
Committee on Illegal Practitioners, 201
Communist party, 131, 240
Communists, 143, 170
Compagnía de Opera Creatore, 183
Compagnía Zarate, 183
Confederacy, 44, 45
Congregationalists, 225
Congreso Obrero, 78
Coniglio, Alfonso: and anarchism, 116, 129, 145, 148, 169; and antifascism, 164; and the CMIU, 125–26; government surveillance of, 129, 159; and the 1901 strike, 116; and the 1910 strike, 122, 125; and radicals, 161; and Sacco and Vanzetti, 116; in Sicily, 116
Coniglio, Bruno, 125, 145
Coniglio, Francesco, 84
Consumer boycott, 127
Consumer cooperatives, 151, 152, 157–59, 170
Contadini, 18, 22, 23, 25, 28
Contessa Entellina, 83, 95, 191, 278
La Contienda, 79
Conzen, Kathleen, 234
Cooper, Patricia, 137
Cooperative medicine: and the AMA, 201; attitudes of Anglos toward, 200–202; and hospital programs, 197–203; old-world backgrounds, 197; origins of, in Ybor City, 197–203
Corbitt, Duvon, 72
Corleone, 20, 35
Coruña Cigar Factory, 104
Costa, Sam, 275
Cotarelo, Roy, 306
Covadonga, 70, 175
Craparo, Rosemary, 243, 245, 255, 267
Crispi, Francesco, 26
Cuba: connections with Florida, 66, 73, 76, 243; and migration, 5, 76–77; and the labor

Cuba (continued)
  movement, 77-78; social conditions in, 72, 77, 175, 184, 186, 197, 225, 247, 267, 281, 289; and Spanish rule, 72; War of Independence, 72-73, 79, 211, 212
Cuban Federation of Trade Unions, 112
Cuban Revolution, 72-73, 79, 80. See also Cuba
Cubans: and anarchists, 77-78, 80-81, 112, 113, 137, 212, 240; arrival of, in Ybor City, 66, 73, 76, 111-12, 117-18, 197, 235, 267, 272, 273; and the Catholic church, 211, 217-19, 221; and the cigar industry, 111-12, 136-37, 177, 178, 185, 207, 260-62, 264-65, 289; and the cigar unions, 111, 113; economic patterns of, 260-62, 264, 266, 268-69, 270-71, 281-82, 284; and education, 286-91; ethnic revival of, 307-14; and housing, 256-57, 270-71; marriage patterns of, 253-56; and migration process, 76-77; and mutual aid societies, 175-76, 184-88, 248-49, 305, 308; and newspapers, 200, 212, 287; origins of, 72, 77, 177, 184, 186, 197, 273; and politics, 300-301; as Protestants, 223-28; and radical groups, 185-89, 200, 241; and revolution, 79-81; settlement patterns of, 76, 235-36, 238-39, 267, 298, 300; and socialists, 77-78, 112, 137; social/racial relations of, 177-78, 184, 186, 195, 196, 233, 240-41, 254
Cuesta, Angel La Madrid, 74
Cuesta School, 287
Cuevas, Julio, 4, 14, 71
Curley, Bhp. Michael J., 215
Cusumano, Vincenzo, 157

Dairies, 273, 278-80
D'Amore, Maria, 195
Dawley, Alan, 7
De Barbastro, Luis Cáncer, 210
Debs, Eugene, 123
De Carriere, Thomas, 211
De Cervantes, Miguel, 102
De la Campa, José, 121, 122, 124, 125
De la Cruz, José, 77
De la Parte, Louis, 305
Del Pino brothers, 67
Demens, Peter, 82
De Mincies, Ivo, 162
Democratic party, 52, 147
Dente, Rev. Vincente M., 214, 215
De Soto Park, 194
El Despertar (Key West), 102, 148
Di Maggio, Joe, 250, 310

Diario de la Marina (Havana), 199
Díaz, Alfonso, 102, 186, 267, 269
Díaz, Blanca, 4
Díaz, José Vega, 4, 14, 77, 149, 187, 212
Díaz, Luis, 141
Diggins, John, 162, 173
Di Maio, John, 174
Di Maria, Francesco, 267-68
DiPietro, Rev. John A., 213
Disston, Hamilton, 46, 82
Domingo, Joseph ("Big Joe"), 252
Domínguez, Henry, 103, 239
El Dorado Club, 282
Dumas, Alexander, 102
Dunn, Hampton, 283

Easterling, James, 138
East Tampa Dairy, 279
Education, 225, 226, 227, 251-52, 286-91
Elazar, Daniel, 51
Episcopalians, 223, 225
Erickson, Eugene, 311
Escogedores, 80, 99, 100
Españo, Gabriel Ricardo, 199
Esposito, José, 161
Esteve, Pedro, 80, 140, 145, 149, 150, 167, 169
Ethnic revival, 307-14
Ettor and Giovannitti defense fund, 171

Farmer's Market (Ybor City), 277
Farrell, Rev. S. J., 215
Fasci dei lavoratori, 16, 24, 25, 26, 27, 28, 30, 31, 83, 114, 116, 165
Feast of La Madonna della Rocca, 223, 309
La Federación, 137
El Federal (Tampa), 134
Federal Theatre Project, 182-83
Felicani, Aldino, 165, 174
Fenton, Edwin, 123
Ferlita, Angelo, 250
Ferlita, Castrenze, 32, 83, 90, 106, 278
Ferlita, Gaetano, 82, 90
Ferlita, Nina Tagliarini, 85, 194-95
Ferlita, Rosalia Cannella, 84
Ferlita, Sam, 262
Ferlita's Bakery, 250, 308
Fernandez, José, 302
Ferrera de los Gavitos, 74
Ferrol de Galicia, 74
Festa di San Giuseppe, 223, 231, 245
Fiesta de Noche Buena, 245
Figuerado, Fernando, 79
Filogamo, Bartolomeo, 87, 188-89, 207
Fink, Leon, 133

Fitts, J. L., 169
La Flor de Sánchez y Haya, 66
Florida Central and Peninsular Railroad Co., 61
Florida Dairy, 279
Flynn, Elizabeth Gurley, 126
Fondaci, 20, 35
Food, 222, 244–45, 275
Football, 250
Fox, Tim, 307
Francisco Ferrer School, 151
French, A. V., 154, 158, 159
Fruit stands and vending, 273–80
Fuller, Alvan T., 161
Funciones, 182
Funerals, 192–93

Gabaccia, Donna, 28, 41, 139
Gabelloti, 21
La Gaceta, 4, 200
Galicia, 70–71, 246, 262
Galleani, Luigi, 149
Galli-Curci, Amelita, 183
García, Angelo, 239
García, Anita Fuentes, 282
García, José, 66, 177
Gargol, Bernardino, 63
Garibaldini Players, 195
Gasparilla Parade, 196
"Geg Gegs," 83
General Strike, 113, 116, 161
Geraci, Nicolò, 278
Geraci Fruit Co., 278
Ghidoni, Evaristo, 227, 231
GI Bill, 299–300
Los Gigantes Cubanos, 187
Giglia, Pietro, 106
Gijón (Asturias), 199
Gillett, M. E., 158, 159
Ginésta, Domingo, 105, 242, 260
Giolitti, Giovanni, 26
Giornalieri, 22
Giovannitti, Arturo, 140
Giro di propaganda, 149, 150, 163
Giunta, Angelo, 290
Giunta, Domenico, 35, 192, 223, 228, 231, 239, 243, 244, 290
Giunta, Frank, 29–30, 103, 132, 228, 290
Giunta, Gasparina, 290
Giunta, Jimmy, 290
Giunta, Salvatore, 274, 290
Glowgowski, Herman, 53
Goldfield, David, 55
Goldman, Emma, 71
Gómez, Tommy, 252

Gompers, Samuel, 117, 138
Gonzales, Francisco, 295
Gordon, Horace C., 284
Gordon Keller Hospital, 200
Great Depression: and Afro-Cubans, 187, 289; and the cigar industry, 131, 132, 289–91; and Cubans, 289, 291; effect of, 320; and Spaniards, 291; and unemployment, 289–90
Great Society, 4, 305, 307
Greco, Dick, Jr., 303–4
Greco, James, 306
Greco, Salvatore, 90
Grimaldi, Giovanni, 89, 189, 191
Grimaldi, John, 124
Grimaldi, Ray, 243, 246, 254, 299
El grito de guerra, 80
Grupo La Luz, 152
Gruppo Lorenzo Panepinto, 41, 146, 152, 174
Gruppo Antifascista di Tampa, 162
Gruppo Risveglio, 152
Gruppo Volontà, 145, 169
Guagliardo, Giuseppe, 279
Guagliardo, Vincenzina, 279
Guastella, José, 157
Guerra, Vicente, 74, 199
Guerrero, doña Maria, 183
Gutiérrez, Gavino, 64–65, 74
Gutman, Herbert, 99

Hacienda de Ybor, 4, 307
Haller, Mark, 280
Hansen, Marcus, 311
Hareven, Tamara, 15, 246, 326
Harney, Robert, 7, 41, 86, 230
Havana, 5, 73, 74, 75, 77, 78, 79, 101, 150, 156, 175, 178, 180, 181, 186, 187, 188, 196, 199, 204, 245, 261, 269
Hava-Tampa Cigar Co., 129
Haya, Ignacio, 64–67, 74, 178, 234
Haywood, William ("Big Bill"), 119, 126
Henseley, Rev. P. H., Jr., 226
Hermitage Research Institute, 311
Higham, John, 125, 224
Hillsborough County, 44, 56, 146, 274, 285, 289, 305, 312–13
Hillsborough County Medical Society (HCMS), 200–202
Hillsborough High School, 252, 288–89
Hixon, Curtis, 302
Hobbs, Ed, 281
Hofstadter, Richard, 224
Home Mission Board, 225–26
Honduras, 117, 158
Hooker, William, 44

Housing, 234–39, 270–71, 299–300, 306
Huerta, Victoriano, 154
Huerto, Chelo, 252
Hugo, Victor, 102, 195, 212, 227
Hyde Park, 51, 53, 240, 278, 283, 292

La Igual, 198
L'Inchiesta Agraria sulle Condizioni dei Contadini, 20, 22
Los Independientes, 79
Industrial Workers of the World (IWW), 118, 119, 126, 127, 144, 152
Infiesto, 74
Inghilleri, Calcedonio, 16
Internal Improvement Fund, 46
El Internacional, 118, 155, 287
Ippolito, Vincenzo, 278
Irish, 213
Italian-American Golf Tournament, 310
Italian Chamber of Labor (New York), 140
Italian Communist party, 42
"Italian locals," 146
Italiano, Mary, 14, 67, 120, 193, 195–96, 217, 244, 254, 255, 288
Italiano, Nelson, 252
Italians: and anarchists, 116, 129, 144, 145, 148, 174, 213; and antifascism, 162–64, 173; arrival of, in Ybor City, 82, 83, 85–88, 91, 213–14, 272, 273; and bootlegging, 284–86; and the Catholic church, 213–14, 217–19, 221; in the cigar industry, 104–11, 116, 118, 122–25, 127, 130, 132, 135, 138, 260–62, 264–69, 272, 289; in the cigar unions, 116–18; and crime, 241, 243, 284–86, 301–3; economic patterns of, 86, 104, 106, 107–11, 260–86; and education, 286–91; and ethnic revival, 307–14; first contacts of, with Florida, 32–34, 38, 47, 81; and housing, 270–71; marriage patterns of, 253–56; and migration process, 31, 35–36, 81–89, 263–64, 299; and mutual aid clubs, 188–97, 248–49, 259, 305; and newspapers, 155, 213; political activity of, 146–48, 301–5, 312–14; and Protestants, 223–29; and radical groups, 144–45, 220, 306; and Sacco and Vanzetti, 297–98; settlement patterns of, 82, 86–87, 176, 235–36, 238–39, 300; and socialists, 173, 222–23; social/racial relations of, 186, 189, 195, 196, 215, 233, 241–47, 263–64; and sports, 248–53; and strikes, 116–18, 138, 139; women and work, 107–11; and World War I, 155; and World War II, 297–99
Italian Socialist Federation, 123
Italian Socialist Federation of Tampa, 156

Jacksonville, Fla., 47, 301
Jacksonville, Tampa, and Key West Railroad, 47
James, Bill, 312
Jesuit High School, 289–90
Jews, 179, 238, 273, 276, 299, 313
Jim Crow legislation, 57, 153, 224
John Napoli Market, 277
Johnson, Lyndon, 305, 307
Joint Advisory Board (JAB), 121, 125
Jones, Charles E., 54
Juan, Frank, 179
Juliani, Richard, 14, 311
Junta Central de Artesanos de la Habana, 77
Juster, Sara Wohl, 179, 246

Kaplan, Temma, 71
Kefauver Commission, 302, 315
Kenny, Bhp. William J., 213
Key West, 46, 64, 72, 73, 76, 77, 80, 118, 176, 187, 196, 261, 295
Kissimmee, Fla., 32, 47
Knight, Peter O., 51, 52, 61, 240
Knights of Labor, 112, 114, 119, 133
Knights of Pythias, 190
Kropotkin, Peter, 102, 145, 195
Ku Klux Klan, 131
Kusmer, Kenneth L., 242

Labor Temple, 98, 121, 131, 145, 161, 168, 179, 216
La Rosa, Manuel, 194
LaRussa, Tony, 252
Latifondi, 18, 21
Lazzara, Pasquale, 193
Lazzaro, Virgilio, 183
Lazzeri, Tony, 253
Lecca, 88
Lector, 4, 11, 97, 98, 152, 247, 297; background of, in Cuba, 102; demise of, 131; duties of, 102–3; memories of, 325; and newspapers, 165; and radicalism, 102–3; readings by, 103; and red scare, 155; skills of, 103
Lega di Miglioramento fra i Contadini, 29, 31, 36
Lehti, Frank, 173
Lemos, Fernando, 66, 176–77, 235
L'Engle, Claude, 54
Lercara Friddi, 35, 88, 196
Lesley, John T., 65
Leto, Angelo, 148, 167, 174
Leto, Guiseppe, 194
Leto, Maria, 201
Lewis, J. D., 268
Liberty Bond Fund, 172

Liborio Cigar Co., 200
Libreria Sociologica, 145
Licata, Antonio, 189
Licata, Filippo F., 189–90, 195, 207
Licata, Giuseppe, 87, 241, 279
Licata, Providenzia, 189
Liceo Cubano, 117
Llumas, José, 77
LoCicero, Philip, 262
Lodato, Domenica, 156
Lodato, Nicholas, 148
Lodato, Salvatore, 148
Longo, Paul, 6, 14, 20, 35, 104, 106, 190; and the Italian Club, 193, 298; work of, 261, 268
Longo, Pietro, 84
López, Alfonso Ramón, 75; and baseball, 250–51; at dances, 195; neighborhood of, 238
López, Modesto, 75
Lorenzoni Report, 20
Lotta di Classe, 162
Lotteria Nacional Cubana, 281
Louisiana, 81, 82, 84, 85, 86, 89, 90, 95, 96
Lourdes, Sister Mary, 212
Lozano, Pendas and Co., 178
Luque, Adolfo, 250
Lykes, Howell T., 44, 53
Lynching, 57, 82, 120, 130

Macarata, 196
MacDonald, John S., 27
McDowell, John P., 224
Maceo, Antonio, 81, 185, 186, 187
Macfarlane, Hugh Campbell, 67
Machado, Dr. Guillermo, 198
El Machete (Key West), 102
Macinato, 39
McKay, David Brenham, 53, 124, 172
McKay, James, 44, 53
La Madonna della Rocca, 223, 231
Madrid, 150
Mafia, 22, 23, 36, 82, 86, 105, 241, 243, 303
Magazzolo valley, 17, 26–28, 31, 81, 86, 91, 188, 191, 196, 260; and cultivation, 20; emigration from, 34, 35; trade patterns of, 18
Malatesta, Errico, 102, 145, 149, 150
Mallard, Sister Mary Edith, 214
Mallea, Juan, 186, 187
Manatee County, 274
Maniscalco, Joe, 6, 14, 103, 108, 121; and club life, 194; and courtship, 255; and education, 288; and ethnic relations, 239; and opera, 195; work of, 267, 273
Manrara, Eduardo, 4, 14, 103, 134, 200
Marotta, Sam, 287

Marriage, 253–56, 268
Il Martello (New York), 148
Martí, José, 79, 80, 103, 185, 187
Martí-Maceo Club. *See* La Unión Martí-Maceo
Martinez, Bob, 312
Martínez, Elvin, 300, 305
Martínez Ybor, Vicente, 64–65, 66, 67, 73, 74, 80, 81, 111, 115, 234, 235, 240
Martínez Ybor cigar factory, 66, 80, 111, 112, 114, 115
Martino family, 186
Il Martire, 41, 123, 139
Marx, Karl, 71, 102
Massari, Angelo, 10, 16, 23, 34, 35, 83, 106, 144, 149, 150, 163, 166, 208
Massaro, John, 124
Massolo, Arturo, 150, 163, 166, 174
Matteotti, Giacomo, 162
May Day, 160
Medical clinics. *See* Cooperative medicine
Medina, César, 193, 239, 269, 290, 297, 310
Méndez, Félix, 138
Menéndez, Angela, 245
Menocal, Mario, 185
Methodist Episcopal Church, South (MECS), 226–27
Methodists, 223–24
Mezzadria, 21, 26
Milián, Francisco, 98, 134
Mitchell, L., 74
Moore, Bhp. John, 211
Moroni, Gaetano, 120
Morrison, Frank, 126
Most Holy Name Parish, 216, 223
Moutras, 74
Muñiz, Antonio, 297
Muñiz, José Rivero, 77, 112, 185–86
Munroe, Kirk, 45
Murray, J. A., 302
Murray, Robert K., 157
Musco, Angelo, 195–96
Mussolini, Benito, 37, 162, 163, 164, 173, 298–99

Nativism, 239–42, 257
Naturalization, 301
Nelli, Humbert, 286
New Deal, 303, 304, 305
New Haven Steamboat Co., 47
New Orleans, 31, 34, 35, 80, 83, 84, 85, 95, 156, 163, 164, 188, 189, 197, 243, 272, 278
New York City, 32, 33, 35, 41, 76, 110, 148, 188, 196, 204, 261, 289, 301
Nixon, Richard, 307
Norberta, Sister Mary, 214

Noto, Alfonso, 241
Noto, Lena, 254
Noto, Luigi, 148
Nuccio, Concetta, 207
Nuccio, Nick Chillura, 246, 269, 302–4, 306, 308
Numero Unico, 164
La Nuova Sicilia, 308
La Nuova Vita, 157
Il Nuovo Mondo, 163, 173

El Obrero Industriale, 126, 129
Ocala Banner, 47
Ocala Mail and Express, 57
O'Halloran Cigar Co., 137
O'Hare, Kate Richards, 146, 169
Olivette (ship), 77
Opera, 179, 183, 195–96
Oppenheimer, Dr. Louis Sims, 201
Oral history, 13–14, 268–69, 325–26
Orange Belt Railroad, 82
Ordieres, María, 74
O'Shanahan, Rev. John, 211
Our Lady of Mercy Parish, 211, 214
Owen, Charles, 57

Pacheco, Dr. Ferdie, 103, 250, 252, 302, 310
Palazzo Adriana, 88
Palermo, E., 164
Palermo, Nelson, 134, 246, 275, 290, 297, 298, 307
Palermo, Onofrio, 134
Palermo, 5, 16, 20, 24, 35
Palma Ceia (Tampa), 51
Palomino, Raul, 306
Panepinto, Giuseppe, 25
Panepinto, Lorenzo Nicolò, 123, 143; death of, 29; *fasci* leadership of, 25–30; philosophy of, 40–41; political activities of, 29; in Sicily, 25
Papini, Carlo, 156
La Parola dei Socialisti (Chicago), 149, 170, 171
Parrino, Antonio, 263–64
Parrino, Laura, 263–64
Parrino, Sam, 263–64
Partido Revolucionario Cubano, 79–80
Passiglia, Rev. Walter, 300
Paterson, N.J., 148, 150
Patricio, Carlo, 20
Pearson, Drew, 303
Peddling, 261, 262, 263, 273–78
Pedroso, Paulina, 79, 185
Pedroso, Ruperto, 79, 185
Pendás, Enrique, 74, 178, 188, 271
Pendás, Fernando, 197

Pepper, Claude, 315
Perdomo Empresa, 195
Péres, José, 201
Pérez-Galdós, Benito, 102
Perfecto-García cigar factory, 297–98
Perkins, George, 118, 119, 126, 138
"Piccola Posta," 170
Pinar del Río, 77
Pinellas County, 56
Piniella, Lou, 252
Pintueles, 74
Pirulí man, 4, 246
Pizzo, Antonio, 84
Pizzo, Giuseppe, 84
Pizzo, Tony, 251, 282, 289
Pizzolato, Pietro, 83
Plant, Henry B., 47
Plant High School, 250
Plant Investment Co., 47, 49
Plant Railroad System, 47
La Poliglota Press, 145, 167
Populists, 133
Port Tampa, 47, 49, 69
El Porvenir, 198
Poyo, José Delores, 79
Prende, Alfredo, 67
Presbyterians, 223, 226
El presidente de la lectura, 98, 103
El Príncipe de Gales, 66, 73
Prizzi, 88
El Productor (Cuba), 77, 150, 171
Prohibition, 240, 284–86
Il Proletario, 148, 162
Pro-Prisoner Committee, 161
Prostitution, 281
Protestantism, 215, 223–28
Provenzano, Tina, 103, 114
Pueblo, Colo., 196

La Questione Sociale, 150
Quinlan, Rev. John B., 211, 212

Radical Education Series, 145
Radicals. See Anarchists; Socialists; Ybor City
Ragsdale, Ray, 306
Ramirez de Esperante, Carmine, 183
Rampello, Sam, 306
Reconstruction, 45
Red scare, 129, 157, 160
Reina, Rafael, 282
Reina, Salvatore, 278
La Resistencia, 116–18, 125
Rey, Peregrino, 74
Rey, Roberta, 183
Rezagadores, 99, 100
Rice, Grantland, 250

Riña de gallos, 240
La Riscossa, 163
Risveglio, 145
Il Risveglio, 174
Rivera, Manuel, 137
Rivero y Rivero, Ramón, 79
Rocca, Carmelo, 103, 122, 124, 129
Rodríguez, Alfredo Rubio (a.k.a. Jack Rubio), 171
Rodríguez, Eugenio, 269
Rodríguez, José ("El Mejicano"), 103
Rodríguez, Rudy, 306
Rodríguez, Wilfredo, 102
Roïg, Bruno, 79, 187
Roïg San Martin, Enrique, 77
Roman Catholic church. *See* Catholic church
Romería, 179
Rossi, Adolfo, 24
Rossi, Giuseppe, 22
Rubiera, Ramón, 111
Rubio, Jack, 171
Rumore, Giovanni (John), 90
Rumore, Guiseppe, 89, 90, 194
Rumore family, 228
Runyon, Damon, 250
Ruskin, Fla., 146, 278

Sacco and Vanzetti, 160–62, 297–98
St. Cloud, Fla., 32–34, 38, 47, 81, 82, 87, 90, 201, 267
St. Cloud and Sugar Belt Railroad, 33
St. John's Presbyterian Church, 300
St. Joseph's Day. *See* Festa di San Giuseppe
St. Louis Parish (Tampa), 211
St. Petersburg, Fla., 146
St. Petersburg Times, 212
Salcines, Emiliano, 305, 312
Salvemini, Gaetano, 163
Sambuca di Sicilia, 28, 122, 139, 196
San Antonio de los Baños, 77
Sanatorio. See Cooperative medicine
El Sanatorio del Centro Español, 199
San Biaggio, 88, 124
San Carlos Club, 176
Sánchez, F. S., 207
Sánchez, Manuel, 74
Sánchez, Mario, 307
Sánchez, Serafín, 74
Sánchez-Haya cigar factory, 66, 178
Sanfeliz, José Ramón, 112, 186
San Pedro, Vincenzo, 274
Santa Fe, Argentina, 32
Santiago de las Vegas, 77
Santo Stefano Quisquina, 9, 16, 17, 18, 20, 84, 86, 87, 89, 123, 146, 165, 174, 201; and the church, 23; crops in, 18; economy of, 18, 21, 22, 23; and emigration, 31–32, 33, 35, 36, 37; and *fasci*, 24, 25, 26–27, 28, 30; population of, 21; records of, 21, 35–36; and socialists, 29, 30; social structure of, 22
Scaglione, Alex, 101, 137, 248, 263
Scaglione, Josephine, 186
Scaglione, Pietro, 148
Scaglione family, 186
Scheleman, Arthur, 279
Schipa, Tito, 183
Sciacca, 20
"Scrub, the," 57, 59, 306
Scurti, Sebastiano Cammareri, 30, 40
Second Seminole War, 44
Seidenberg Cigar Co., 105
Seminole Heights (Tampa), 51, 292
Settecasi, Francesco Pupello, 266
Seventh Avenue (Ybor City), 5, 245–46, 255
Sezione del Partito Socialista, 29
Sicilians: arrival in Ybor City, 34, 82; birth-rates, 20–21; migration strategies, 27–28, 30–32, 268; old-world culture, 20, 23, 35; proverbs, 175; religion, 23, 213, 216, 220, 221, 222; socialism, 26, 29–30, 37, 144, 197
La Sicilia Rossa, 174
Sicily, 167, 197, 212, 220, 221, 222; and anticlericalism, 23; and the Catholic church, 23; and *comuni*, 21; economy of, 22; and emigration, 31, 35–36; and *fasci*, 24–28, 30, 31; population of, 20–21; and taxes, 22
Sidello Cigar Factory, 267
Sigma Iota, 289
Simon, Jules, 107
Siracusa, 88
Sisters of St. Joseph, 212, 213
Socialists, 129, 143; Anglo images of, 240; and *fasci*, 26; and groups, 144–45, 147, 151, 170; ideologies of, 44, 149–50; in Italy, 26, 27, 28, 29–30, 144, 172; and labor organizations, 112, 113, 119; newspapers of, 165–67, 174; and Panepinto, 26–29, 30, 143; and politics, 146–48, 170; and race relations, 152–53; and World War I, 154–56, 172; in Ybor City, 144, 146, 151–52, 170
Socialist party, 123, 129, 146, 151, 152, 166, 167, 169, 170
Socialist Study Circle, 166
La Sociedad de Libre Pensadores de Martí-Maceo, 186–87
La Sociedad de Torcedores de Tampa. *See* La Resistencia
La Società Italia, 191, 309
La Società Italiana di Mutuo Soccorso Italia. *See* L'Unione Italiana

La Società Santo Stefano Quisquina, 191
La Società Sicilia, 191
Sonnino, Sidney (Baron), 20
Sons of Italy, 308, 309
South Florida Railroad Co., 47
Spain, 70–71
Spaniards, 70–75; and anarchists, 71, 80, 94, 112, 113, 151, 159, 171, 212, 220, 240; arrival of, in Ybor City, 74–75, 177–78, 235, 268, 272, 273; and the Catholic church, 70, 211, 217–19, 221; in the cigar industry, 177, 178, 260–62, 264–65, 266, 289; in the cigar unions, 177; economic patterns of, 260, 262, 264–66, 268–69, 270–71, 281–82, 284; and education, 286–92; and emigration, 71, 72–75; marriage patterns of, 75, 253–56, 268; and mutual aid societies, 175–84, 248–49, 305; and newspapers, 287; old-world origins, 70–71; and politics, 301, 312–13; and radical groups, 171; settlement patterns of, 235–36, 238–39, 269, 298, 300; and socialists, 240; social/racial relations of, 178, 180, 184, 189, 195, 196, 233, 240–41; and sports, 247–53; and theater, 182–83
Spanish-American War, 91, 106, 113, 164
Spicola, Carlo, 82
Spicola, Guy, 305
Sports, 187, 190, 194, 196, 247–53
Spoto, Filippo, 136
Spoto, Giuseppina, 16
Spoto, Louis, 273
Spoto, Philip, 33
Spoto family, 255; and community, 319; and education, 288
Stassi, Isidro, 282–83, 285
Strikes: of 1887, 111–12, 136; of 1887–1894, 114; of 1899, 115–16; of 1901, 110, 111, 117–18, 137, 138; of 1910, 119–22, 124–25, 138–39, 185, 267; of 1916, 110; of 1920, 127–28, 133, 160, 182, 185, 266, 267–68, 276; of 1921, 130; of 1931, 130–32, 133
Stough, Rev. Richard, 257
Suarez, Manuel ("El Gallego"), 281
Suburb Beautiful (Tampa), 51
Sulphur Springs, Fla., 182, 239
Summerlin, Jake, 44
Suoto, Fermín, 74
Syndicalists, 151

Tagliarini, Domenica, 167
Tagliarini, Francesca Adamo, 36
Tampa: Afro-Americans in, 43, 57–58; and antifascism, 162–64, 298–99; and boosterism, 54–55; climate of, 13; and cooperative medicine, 197–205; and decline of cigar industry, 289, 290, 291, 300, 301; early history of, 44–45; ethnic groups in, after World War II, 198–300; ethnic revival in, 307–15; geography of, 10, 56; image of, 54, 130; and immigration, 9–10; industrialization of, 298; and mutual aid societies, 175–210; neighborhoods in, 51; and organized crime, 54, 280–86, 301–3; and politics, 51–52, 58–59, 146–48, 301–7; and race relations, 10, 57, 58, 152–53, 186; records of, 13; and the red scare, 154–60; and the Spanish-American War, 45, 49, 50–51
Tampa Bay Hotel, 47
Tampa Board of Trade, 65, 136
Tampa Chamber of Commerce, 52
Tampa Citizen, 158
Tampa Daily Times, 52–53, 176, 283
Tampa Electric Co. (TECO), 51, 61
Tampa Gas Co., 61
Tampa Guardian, 65, 66
Tampa Heights, 51
Tampa Journal, 112, 176, 234
Tampa Morning Tribune, 52, 115, 181, 192, 193, 199, 254, 267, 268, 274, 275, 279, 281, 301, 302
Tampa Police Department, 282–85
Tampa Sunland Tribune, 47
Tampa Tarpons, 250–51
Tampa Times, 52
Tampa Tribune, 179, 301
Tampa Wholesale Produce Market, 277
Ten Years War, 72, 73
Termini Imerese, 20, 88
Terrano, Angie, 222
Theater, 182–83
Thernstrom, Stephan, 236
Thistlewaite, Frank, 21
Thompson, E. P., 8, 12
Tierra y Libertad (Barcelona), 102
Tilly, Louis, 84
Tison, Marshall, 307
Tobacco Workers International Union (TWIU), 131
Tourism, 130
La Traducción, 162, 165, 250
Traina, Giuseppe, 85
La Tramontana (Barcelona), 77
Trapani, 88
Tresca, Carlo, 126
Tribuna, 102, 103
La Tribuna del Pueblo, 80
Tuberculosis, 177, 197, 200, 205, 209
Tyrrell, Rev. William, 212, 213, 214

La Unión, 187
L'Unione Agricola, 29
L'Unione Italiana (Italian Club), 188–97, 207, 216, 247, 248–52, 298, 300, 304–5, 308, 309
La Unión Martí-Maceo, 153, 185–88
Unità, 308
University of Florida, 289
University of Havana, 199
Urban League (of Tampa), 187
Urban renewal, 4, 304–7
Urso, Frank, 241
U.S. Department of Justice, 129, 139
U.S. Immigration Commission, 75, 105

Vaccaro, Cirio, 283
Vaccaro, Frank, 15, 123
Vaccaro, Giovanni, 40, 122, 123, 127, 129, 146, 147, 148, 159, 162, 208
Vacirca, Vincenzo, 149, 163
Valdes, Armando, 307
Valdespino, Ramón, 173
Valdez, Eddie, 306–7
Valdez Insurance Co., 307
Valenti, Giuseppe, 277
Valenti, J. C., 277, 278
Valenti, Joe, 33
Valles, Manuel, 179
Vasta, Achille, 213
Vecoli, Rudolph, 7, 8, 123, 137, 300, 309
V-E Day, 299
Los Vengadores de Maceo, 186
Verbenas, 4
Verro, Bernardino, 11, 40
Vicari, Stefano, 276
Viscusi, Lou, 251
A le Vittime di Satti (Panepinto), 25
Vittore, Pasquale, 195
V. M. Ybor and Co., 65, 66, 69
V. M. Ybor School, 287
La Voce della Colonia (1911), 166
La Voce della Colonia (1929), 167
La Voce dello Schiavo, 145
La Voce dello Schiavo, 165
Volstead Act, 284
La Voz del Esclavo, 174
Vuelta Abajo region, 73, 100, 134

Wall, Charlie, 53, 54, 283, 286
Wall, John P., 53
Wall, Joseph B., 57
Ward, David, 236
Warner, Sam Bass, 236
Watergate, 304
Weight Strike of 1899, 115, 116
Weinstein, James, 146, 174

West Tampa, 43, 55, 97, 98, 120, 157; churches in, 225; and the cigar industry, 67, 97; creation of, 67–68; economy of, 268, 276, 292, 308; ethnic groups in, 191, 241, 287, 292, 308; migration to, 223; and politics, 123, 148, 303; postwar, 300; and radicals, 144, 146, 154
White Municipal party, 53, 58, 147, 148
White Primary, 147–48
Wiebe, Robert, 49
Williams, Ramón, 76
Wilson, Woodrow, 154
Witt, Eli, 128, 129
Wolf, Eric, 22
Wolff Mission School, 227
Wood, James, 118, 138
Works Progress Administration (WPA), 183, 303
World War I, 50, 51, 52, 127, 128, 145, 152, 154–56, 172, 180, 193, 265, 286, 298
World War II, 4, 13, 180, 236, 298–300

Yancy, William, 311
Yans-MacLaughlin, Virginia, 7, 109
El Yara, 79
Ybor City, 3, 4, 5, 6, 9, 10–14, 17, 37, 55; Afro-Cubans in, 78; and antifascism, 162–64, 298; boundaries of, 234–39; and the cigar industry, 67–69, 99–103, 107, 108, 110–13, 135, 260–73; and cooperative medicine, 197–205, 309; and crime, 280–86, 301–3; Cubans in, 66, 73, 76–78, 80–81, 111–13, 130, 137; and decline of the cigar industry, 289, 290, 291, 300, 301; and education, 251–52, 286–91; ethnic economic patterns in, 260–92; and ethnic revival, 307–14; and ethnic variation, 244–45; founding of, 5, 63–67, 176–77; health conditions in, 176–77; housing in, 66, 234–39, 270–71, 299–300, 306; intermarriage in, 253–56; Italians in, 82, 83, 85–88, 91, 104–18, 122–25, 130–38, 155, 162–64, 173; labor relations in, 11, 111–22, 124, 125, 127–28, 130–33, 136–39, 160; and mutual aid societies, 175–210; neighborhoods in, 233–39; and politics, 53, 58, 147, 148, 283–86, 311–12; and the press, 164–68, 172; and prohibition, 240, 284–86; race relations in, 56–59, 153; and radicalism, 10–11, 12, 80–81, 144, 146, 151–52, 154, 170, 172; recreation in, 240–41; and the red scare, 157–60; and religion, 210–32, 305–6; Seventh Avenue, 5, 245–46, 255; social relations in, 232–58; Spaniards in, 74–75, 111–14, 115–16, 151, 159, 171; and

Ybor City (*continued*)
  sports, 247–53, 310; and urban renewal, 4, 304–7; and World War I, 50, 51, 52, 127, 128, 145, 152, 154–56, 172
Ybor City Land Co., 61, 234–35
Ybor City Rotary Club, 309
Yellow fever, 177, 197, 211, 225
Yglesias, José, 111, 131, 143, 168, 183, 185

Y.M.C.A. War Council, 154
Young, J. L., 303

Zabot, 196
Zarzuela, 4, 182, 183
Zingarelli, Italo, 29
Zola, Emile, 102
Zucchi, John, 86

www.ingramcontent.com/pod-product-compliance
Lightning Source LLC
Chambersburg PA
CBHW020217170426
43201CB00007B/243